Interestingly Enough…

THE LIFE OF

TOM KENEALLY

Interestingly Enough ...

THE LIFE OF TOM KENEALLY

Stephany Evans Steggall

NERO

Published by Nero,
an imprint of Schwartz Publishing Pty Ltd
37–39 Langridge Street
Collingwood VIC 3066 Australia
enquiries@blackincbooks.com
www.nerobooks.com

National Library of Australia Cataloguing-in-Publication entry:

Steggall, Stephany Evans, author.
Interestingly enough: the life of Tom Keneally / Stephany Evans Steggall.
9781863957588 (hardback)
9781925203448 (ebook)
Keneally, Thomas, 1935–
Authors, Australian—20th century—Biography. Australian.
A823.3

The author acknowledges with gratitude the assistance provided in the writing of this book by the Hazel Rowley Fellowship 2013.

Cover design by Nada Backovic
Cover photograph by Richard Saker
Text design and typesetting by Tristan Main

Printed in Australia by McPherson's Printing Group.

FSC MIX Paper from responsible sources FSC® C001695 www.fsc.org

For Helen Neill, sister and travel companion,
and for Terry O'Neill, friend and adviser.

This copy for
Professor Robert Folkenflik
Thank you for your
interest in, and
assistance with, the
book.

Stephany Evans Steggall
May 2016

Contents

1

The Arrival of Thomas Keneally

This might have been a different story – although it is unlikely that the story of a Father Thomas Michael Keneally would ever have been told, except in eulogy or obituary. The everyday scenes in the life of a popular parish priest are not often reconstructed. If he had become an activist cleric on a wider world stage, or a white-collar writer directing the spotlight on the social injustices of the day, then there may have been a book about Father Keneally.

Keneally had been destined for some unremarkable parish as the hero priest of his boyhood imaginings, but the would-be cleric had a severe crisis of doubt shortly before his ordination. In the days before he left St Patrick's College, Manly, on Sydney's northern shoreline, the students in a lecture room could hear Keneally above them, treading the wooden boards of his solitary chamber. His unheard monologue, about doubts and guilt and shame and failure, took him to the office of the rector, the Right Reverend Monsignor James Madden.

Madden was expecting him. There had been notes from a Dr Kyneur about Keneally's 'psychological sufferings'. His patient, Kyneur concluded, should postpone ordination as a priest.[1] Keneally told Madden that he had decided to leave and not proceed to a priestly life beyond the closed community at Manly. 'I'm not sure that I am worthy of being a priest,' Keneally confessed. 'I am driven by doubts, so I must leave.'

Mick Keneally, as he was known at the Manly seminary, had shown evidence in recent times of being unbalanced. For instance, he had drawn attention to some cracked cups in the refectory, insisting they were unclean vessels. He could not ignore them, he said, and risk being responsible for someone's illness. Madden and Bill Voght, the bursar known as Blinky Bill, had laughed it off, but then came the visits to the doctor, the sick leave and so on. Nervous breakdowns at Manly were not unheard of.

'I am not in a fit state for holy ordination,' Keneally wrote in his petition to the Vatican about reverting to the lay state. 'I will never in the future be able to undertake the onerous duties of the priesthood.'[2]

The young man who had commenced seminary life in 1953 at the age of seventeen, endorsed by references that spoke of outstanding character and very good abilities on the literary side, left Madden's office empty-handed.[3] Madden had dismissed him, blankly refusing his request for a reference.

No one marked Keneally's leaving. He was just not there any more, in the refectory or in the chapel. His room was empty.

A slight, bespectacled figure in black made his way alone out of the main building, which he later described as 'the cavernous symbol of his unhappiness'. Keneally had walked down Darley Road to the Manly ferry terminal many times, but never without permission. On this day of departure he was in too much turmoil to appreciate his freedom. The ferry berthed at Circular Quay, on the other side of Sydney Harbour, even before he was aware it had left the Manly wharf.

The last leg of Keneally's journey was by train to Homebush, in Sydney's western suburbs. From there it was a short walk home. Home meant facing down failure, hearing trains instead of bells day and night, listening to secular music and television instead of observing strict silence each evening, sharing a room instead of occupying a single cubicle, and seeing suburbia instead of the sea.

Keneally was broken and broke. An old friend, a fruiterer who had a stall at the Flemington Markets, gave him £50 to help out. There wasn't much work to be had when all he could lay claim to was a degree in Sacred Theology.[4] Keneally avoided teaching for as long as he could, not ready to face a crowd and reluctant to return to a Catholic environment. He taught, however, for three years or so at Waverley College, a Catholic boarding school for boys near Bondi Beach.

Keneally started jotting down story ideas on paper torn from school exercise pads and examination booklets. He had been a scribbler since schooldays, and there was a poetry society at the seminary to which 'MK' had contributed verse. The college magazine, *Manly*, had published an article written by Keneally with the title 'The Unique Colonial'.[5] The biographical piece was about Charles de Foucauld, a nineteenth-century French maverick priest who had returned to the Catholic fold at about the same age that Keneally would leave it. The Frenchman had responded to a so-called 'delayed vocation'.[6]

Keneally the writer of fiction started his new life as 'Bernard Coyle'. A story about a defecting priest at the recognisable 'Peninsula College' was accepted by *The Bulletin*. The bigger story goes that Coyle's yarn, 'The Sky Burning Up Above the Man', was based on the true story of Father John Jenkins, a Manly old boy, who married a girl in his parish.[7] Keneally's transformation from failed priest to successful writer began at this point. Authorship would be his 'delayed vocation'.

In the holiday break of December 1962 to January 1963, he wrote *The Place at Whitton*, published under the name Thomas Keneally. The real place is St Patrick's College, Manly, and there are repeated references to men who want to be *worthy* priests; 'If they were sure they wouldn't be worthy, they'd leave this place.'[8] In *The Place at Whitton* Keneally questions with dark humour the doubts that drove him away from the fraternity at Manly.

The book heralded 'The Arrival of Thomas Keneally', announced by Max Harris in *Australian Book Review*.[9] With his first book, Keneally made his debut in another show, one performed before a fickle audience over an extended season. The popular, regularly revised script follows the fortunes of a famous writer, a witty, kind and compassionate man, a blatherskite, partygoer, bullshitter, boozer and outrageous flirt whose public face beams bonhomie. What follows in these pages does not always stick to that storyline, and it may not be the definitive, final script, but the drama – at times tragic, comic and melodramatic – is true to life. The opening scenes are about *Mick* Keneally – or Michael, to his mother – the grandson of Irish immigrants, sickly kid, eccentric teenager and priestly candidate, who preceded Thomas.

2

From Cove to Cove

Keneally's paternal grandfather, Timothy Thomas Keneally, was part of the Queenstown story, which began with the convict ships that left Irish shores for Australia. Queenstown (also called Cove or Cobh) was the principal port of departure. Timothy Keneally was not on board any of the Irish convict ships, nor was he among the desperate countrymen who fled the Famine. Besieged Ireland was held hostage then, as ship after ship took away captives of a different kind from the convicts.

Timothy's parents, Jeremiah and Anne (née McSweeney),[1] had married in St Finbarr's South Parish in Cork City in 1856. Early in their marriage they had lived in Glenlara, but they later moved to Gortnaglough, where all their children were born. They had barricaded their home against many threats but were defenceless against the reality of nine children without a future. In the 1901 Census of Ireland, Jeremiah was listed as an 'Emigration Agent', living in Newmarket, County Cork, north-west of Queenstown.[2] His daughter Nell (Ellen) made reference to this work in a letter to Timothy's oldest daughter, Molly, in 1934: 'Hanna [Anne] does well in the shipping business that my father [Jeremiah] held but there is a ban on immigration to United States for the past two years which makes it dull just now . . .'[3]

All the children – Ellen, Honora (Nora), Julia, John (Jack), James, Johannah, Maria, Timothy, Anne (Hanna) and Jeremiah Joseph (Jerry) –

were reprieved, with passages being booked by one of the shipping agents to be found in nearly every Irish town, and began new lives in Australia or the United States of America.[4] It is ironic that the Keneally family itself managed one such agency, arranging passages for emigrants. They would have had ample experience in the procedure.[5]

The birth of Timothy, in 1859, was registered in a baptismal record simply as 'T. Keneally, born of Jeremiah Keneally and Anne McSweeney', while his marriage certificate and obituary refer to him as 'Thomas'.[6] (To avoid confusion with the other Thomases, he will be called by his first name, Timothy, in this account.) In 1882 or 1883 he was among the noisy throng at Queenstown harbour with their bundles and baskets, waiting to board.[7]

Often only letters followed and returned. Jeremiah and Anne held the oblongs of paper as reverently as rosary beads and despatched their own missives longingly, like prayers. The contents of each treasured letter could be called to mind as readily as responses in Mass. In one letter to Timothy, dated 13 January 1892, Jeremiah prophesied mournfully: 'I fear an eternal decree that during my life I shall never again see you or any of my exiled children – which is painful to endure on your part and ours . . . I need not say our exiled children trouble us – nothing else – we have plenty of comforts of life, but what in comparison of the deprivation of those who are dearer to us than life.'[8]

At least three other children joined their older brother in Australia. Timothy sponsored the migration of two siblings: Jerry, aged thirteen, and Johannah, aged twenty. They arrived on the *Abergeldie*, which docked at Sydney on 23 December 1884.[9] Nora also migrated to Australia.[10] Ellen and Hanna ultimately returned to Ireland from the United States, and assisted with the shipping agency.[11]

Jeremiah and Anne were dead and buried in the Newmarket cemetery called Clonfert long before their great-grandson Tom came to pay his respects. He would read the inscription beneath a big brown cross not far from their grave: 'To the memory of the famine victims 1845–1847. An event has happened upon which it is difficult to speak and impossible to be silent.' When Keneally saw starving Ethiopians and Eritreans in the 1980s, he understood how the famished Irish peasants must have looked. Years of work would be invested in *The Great Shame*, about the multitude of Irish Troubles.

Timothy Keneally had chosen to leave the Troubles behind him. The passengers on the immigrant ships were leaving one of the world's largest natural harbours for another, Sydney Cove. Timothy's future wife also left for Australia from Queenstown, on the *Cardigan Castle* in 1883.[12] Kate was born at Broadford, in eastern County Clare.[13] She farewelled her parents, William and Annie; her sister Annie had gone ahead of her and opened a shop in Kempsey, in northern New South Wales. Annie Kenna (later Annie Draper) signed as a witness at Kate's wedding to Timothy Keneally on 12 August 1889.[14]

The many localities of County Galway include Lawrencetown, birthplace of Hugh Larkin (or Lorcan), an ancestor of Keneally's future wife, Judith Mary Martin. Hugh, a Ribbonman, was transported for life to Australia for his crime of protest, which was considered under law an 'outrage'.[15] Larkin left on the convict ship *Parmelia* in 1833. In Australia, in 1848, he married Mary Shields of Limerick, who had been convicted of theft and transported to Australia on the *Whitby* in 1839.

The northern county of Donegal is the ancestral home of John Coyle, Keneally's maternal great-grandfather. Donegal is rugged terrain, and the same might be said of John, who led a most adventurous life from the age of twelve, when he left Ireland.

Although most of these exiles would never return to their homeland, their author descendant has done so repeatedly, recording their stories as a kind of Gathering, the bringing together of a family of Irish descent. Mention is also made of Irish exports, for want of a better term, whose influence over the young Keneally was considerable.

Some were disciples of Edmund Rice, who opened his first school for poor boys in Waterford in 1802. From that beginning, the Christian Brothers left Ireland to open schools around the world, including St Patrick's Christian Brothers' College in Strathfield, in western Sydney. Keneally was a student there for several years.

Dublin is a sombre city, if outward appearances are anything to go by. 'What counts for the visitor is the Dublin we bring to Dublin in our heads,' Keneally wrote in *Now and In Time to Be*. Dublin is a pilgrim city, home to a literary conclave. Gerard Manley Hopkins, Keneally's Jesuit hero poet, was Professor of Classics at University College. His view of Dublin was mostly limited to a cold upper room in Newman House, where he marked hundreds of undergraduate papers. Keneally has stood in the room in which Hopkins worked, reflecting on the thankless life his muse endured. Hopkins had found Dublin to be 'a joyless place', but he was in a melancholic state by the end of his life, in the period of his 'Terrible Sonnets'. One of these, 'To Seem the Stranger', speaks for every exile. Hopkins longed for his home in England: 'I am in Ireland now . . . a lonely'. Hopkins was buried in the Jesuit gravesite at Glasnevin cemetery.

James Joyce is everywhere in Dublin, and Ireland. His classic story *A Portrait of the Artist as a Young Man* was in the cupboard at the back of the classroom at St Patrick's College, Strathfield, and Keneally read it avidly, recognising in the troubled life of Stephen Dedalus some of his own youthful questioning about conscience, vocation and Catholicism.

St Patrick's Seminary at Maynooth, in County Kildare, trained secular parish priests. The palatial establishment was the model for St Patrick's Higher Seminary, Manly. Maynooth, Keneally believed, 'set the tone by which the clergy in Ireland and the new world operated, and so it has a lot to answer for and a lot to be proud of'.[16] Thousands of priests left the seminary for duty all over the world, armed with the formidable Irish Catholicism under which banner men like Keneally would enlist. Such men often deserted, battle-scarred.

The Irish priest of yesteryear wielded power – terrible or awful power, some would assert. 'No king or emperor on this earth has the power of the priest,' one of the anointed tells Dedalus in *A Portrait of the Artist as a Young Man*. 'No angel or archangel in heaven, no saint, not even the Blessed Virgin herself, has the power of the priest of God . . .'

This reverent notion of power – the power to do good, and to be loved for doing good – was paramount in the thinking of impressionable Keneally when the time came for him to decide on his vocation. His emigrant grandfather Timothy and his countrymen respected the authority of the village priest with unquestioning obedience. Priests were the spokesmen for their flocks, holding out the hope of social justice to poverty-stricken communities. They could never exercise the same power to bring about social change as they could over the submissive penitent, but they were a force to be reckoned with. The faith of the Irish fathers came to Australia in the nineteenth century, clothed in the cassock and the homespun jacket.

3

Pudding Genes and Potato Faces

The two-storey shop in Rudder Street, Kempsey, stands on a hill overlooking what was once the mooring place on the Macleay River for coastal steamers. Tim and Kate Keneally bought the shop in 1901, moving from the Bridge Store down the hill. At that time they had seven youngsters to fill the living quarters above the shop: Mary (Molly), Maude, Francis, Ellen, John, Annie and Daniel. Another son, James, known as Taidy, followed, and the last was Edmund Thomas, born on 3 December 1907.

The youngest child, and the future father of Tom Keneally, was called Tommy or Harper, an abbreviated version of the Harp of Erin, the name of the family's first store. Previously, Timothy Keneally had worked for a storekeeper, recorded in local archives as Mr P. C. Hall, before taking over a pub at Jerseyville on the lower Macleay River when he married Kate Kenna in 1889.[1] Kate was five feet tall, doughty and durable. Her grandson Tom describes her as peasant practical. To his regret, he says jokingly, he inherited her 'pudding genes and potato face'.

Timothy took his bride to the Pelican Island Hotel at Jerseyville, where the wide upstairs verandah overlooked lush paddocks reminiscent of the Emerald Isle. Kate and Timothy were gregarious licensees, but Kate was the more competent when it came to business. The second shop in Kempsey bore Kate's name on a board between the two storeys, and she took control.

The Keneallys were a devout family, jostling and squeezing into a pew at the All Saints Catholic Church each Sunday. It was the one day of the week when peace reigned among the brothers and sisters, because Timothy demanded silence around the Sunday dinner table. He was given alternately to great melancholy and vivacity, mood shifts being endemic in the family. Timothy was a Sinn Feiner who refused to serve Orangemen or anyone else who spoke rashly on the Irish Question.

Gradually, the Irish brogue of father and mother was drowned out at home by the chorus and clamour of the family's less musical country town timbre. They didn't sound like their parents. Keneally describes the difference in *A River Town*, his fictional take on the place where his paternal grandparents staked a claim in the Australian way of life: 'It was if the sun had got inside the nose and throat and dried all the cords ... This is what it is to be an emigrant ...'[2] Kate Keneally never did learn to pronounce an *h*, and spoke of *T'ursday* and *t'roat* and *cat'edrals* till the day she died.

Her offspring were a generation removed from the Irish Troubles. Theirs was an Australian childhood in a river playground. They jumped from the bridge that spanned the Macleay and engaged in East versus Central Kempsey water fights. Their swimming prowess was a source of fearful pride and wonder to their water-shy parents. Another favourite place to play was the swamp behind the shop, which they shared with venomous brown, bandy-bandy, tiger and red-bellied black snakes. Tommy had a lifelong dread of snakes; his older son, always warned about the 'Joe Blakes' (or snakes) by his father, was not nervous of them but has said that one of *his* greatest fears is the funnel-web spider, also prevalent in the district. A recalcitrant horse, Pee Dee, a popular character in Keneally family folklore, also favoured the swamp.

Timothy and Kate kept the business going for twenty-six years as the family gradually dispersed. John (called Johnnie) went off to fight the Hun, much to his father's displeasure. His son should not have been fighting for the English when their troops were murdering Irish nationalists on the streets of Dublin. But fight Johnnie did, at Flanders, Amiens and the Somme. Kate read Johnnie's letters to Tommy, telling of 'full scale battles in which the bullets were so thick you could not understand how a fly, let alone a man, could live'. Johnnie survived the Great War, but his cousin Denis Cusack, eldest son of Timothy's sister Nora, was killed and buried in France.[3] Johnnie Keneally said in a letter dated 18 May 1919, shortly before his return: 'Fancy young Tom watching the papers for my name. Well Mum I hope he will be rewarded very shortly . . .'[4]

It was hard adjusting to the home front. Johnnie was implicated in a plot to blow up a granite obelisk erected at nearby Trial Bay Gaol in memory of the German internees who died there.[5] Keneally, who has always had an ear for a good story, heard the local yarns about the Germans at Trial Bay and later researched the history of the era. His short story 'In the Day of Anger', about a German farmer at 'Verdant Heads', interned at 'White Cape' prison, has never been published.[6]

In 1920 Johnnie left home for good and roamed further afield. Writing to his mother that he'd 'had enough of travelling to last me a lifetime', he planned to 'settle down in some quiet spot when this bit of a squabble is over'.[7] He never got as far as Ireland, as he had hoped to when 'out of the line' and on leave from France. He had declared in a letter to his brother Dan: 'I am going straight up to where the old shamrock grows . . .'[8]

Johnnie's oldest sister, Molly, remained single and opened a milliner's shop in Taree, south of Kempsey. She shared a home with her sister Annie, also resigned to spinsterhood, and their parents in the years before they died (Timothy in 1933 and Kate in 1938). Later, Molly opened another shop of feminine apparel in Belgrave Street, Kempsey.

Their youngest brother, Tommy, made his mark as a five-eighth in first-grade rugby league, but he too was destined to stand behind a counter. The sedate shop floor was at odds with the football ground, where he liked to 'come the knuckle', throwing the first punch and then standing back to watch the referee sort out the ensuing fight. Tommy played for the Taree Old Bar Rugby League Club, 'an awesome outfit in the bush in the 1930s, one that was not beyond stacking its team with famous visiting players from Sydney, offering them an introduction to the local girls and a skinful of beer'.[9]

He was unemployed during part of the Depression era, but life took a turn for the better when he met an attractive shop assistant at Barsby's called Elsie Margaret Coyle, 'the Belle of the Macleay'. She was a good 'catch' – a spirited woman, striking to look at with a mass of thick hair and a ready smile. Tommy had to sort out a few rivals who were 'eyeing off' Elsie at the football ground or loitering outside Barsby's at closing time. Barsby's was the emporium in downtown Kempsey where primly dressed assistants stood behind glass-fronted counters and wrote dockets that were despatched in brass canisters along hissing wires to the accounting office.

Elsie was the daughter of an engine driver, Michael Thomas Coyle (Mick), and his wife, Hilda Madge (née Holdsworth). At one stage Mick had worked in the stables at a property where he took a fancy to a girl at the big house whose name was Elsie. The daughter he called Elsie was not pleased about being her namesake; she told him that, in films, the girl called Elsie was usually a barmaid or a prostitute. Tommy was twenty-four and Elsie twenty-one when they married at All Saints, Kempsey, on 1 May 1935. (Tommy will be referred to as Tom from now on.)

Their older son, Thomas Michael Keneally, was born just five months later, in Coogee, Sydney, on 7 October 1935. His mother had specified the name to be Michael Thomas, but in the fluster of new fatherhood, Tom incorrectly registered the newborn as Thomas Michael. 'He is definitely to be called Michael,' Elsie insisted. 'It means, "He who is like unto God."' Keneally (as he will be called in this account) reckons that he kept 'Thomas' in reserve to use as a writer, disclaiming the potential of Michael as a hopeful choice of his mother's rather than a realised one. He was called Mick at school and at the seminary, and sometimes Mike or Michael.

He was a premature baby, but not so much as to allay the suspicion of relatives. His parents, Keneally assumes, made the trip to Sydney to conceal Elsie's advancing pregnancy, and to have the baby away from the disapproving eyes of Kempsey's small-town gossips. Mick Coyle would not have been happy about his daughter's premarital pregnancy. Women of Elsie's generation were generally tight-lipped about personal matters, so the son born too soon was only ever aware of his birth and earliest weeks being a sort of family secret.

'My father, although times were tough,' Keneally says, 'was determined to have a private hospital because there was talk of a mix-up of babies in public hospitals. God knows, he may have been better off with some other kid! But that's how I came to be delivered by a famous old patriarchal obstetrician called Dr John [Richard St John] Honner.'[10]

Dr Honner and Nurse Moran are listed on Keneally's birth certificate as 'witnesses' to the event at Boonara Private Hospital, Coogee. Tom and Elsie had been staying in a little flat in Nelson Bay Road (now Bronte Road), Bronte, but they returned to the north coast with their baby son. They did not go back to Kempsey, but shared a home with Molly and Annie for a while in Taree. Kate was still alive and part of the household. Tom resumed work as a shop assistant.

By the early 1940s, Tom, Elsie and son were living at 30 Sea Street, Kempsey, just below the Anglican Church at which the historian Manning Clark's father, Charles, was briefly a curate. From the bank of childhood memories, Keneally draws out a few he likes to smooth out like creased old notes. He recalls sitting down into a basin of boiling water as an unforgettable and very painful experience. Playing in Aunt Molly's shop, where he trailed sticky fingers along the racks of dresses, caused much adult consternation; inviting the whole school to attend his cousin Tricia's fifth birthday party caused even more. Family opinion is divided on that one: it may have been Tricia herself, daughter of Tom's brother Daniel, who was lavish with her invitations.

Keneally often played with his cousins Gwen and Margaret Bulley, the children of Joe and Hilda Bulley. Hilda was Elsie's oldest sister. He remembers playing on the front verandah of their West Kempsey home. 'We shared books, so I read *What Katy Did* and *Little Women*. They lived further up the street from my Coyle grandparents.' The Coyle grandparents lived at 100 River Street, where the verandah, the big back yard and the river just below the back fence comprised a place to return to in thought for years to come. There he listened to yarns about trains and opinions about politics.

Grandmother Coyle was of English descent, although one of her great-grandfathers was an Irish tailor called Phillip Burke. Grandfather Mick Coyle's father, John, born in County Donegal, had been sent as a child to live with an aunt in Boston, where he was bound as a factory apprentice at the age of thirteen. John ran away to New York. He took on a job carrying powder and ball to supply the cannons being used in the United States–Mexican War. He ran away again and made his way to the California gold diggings. Eventually, he followed the gold trail to Australia, but settled down to married life with Margaret Russell of Campbells River, near Bathurst.

Their son Mick was 'built like a boiler, short-tempered, whimsical and sentimental'.[11] One sadness of their life was the death of their child, Betty, killed by a speeding car. The drunken driver, the son of a wealthy landowner, was not charged. Keneally wrote a story about it, titled 'Death of an Innocent':

> Of my mother's nine brothers and sisters, only one failed to survive childhood. This was one called Sylvie. I always heard of her as 'your aunt Sylvie' and the idea of seven year old aunts amazed me by comparison with the worn creatures who also bore the name. The story of her death was often told and became not only a fact of history but also an article of faith. There was no family reunion at which the wraith of my child-aunt was not conjured up by a cautionary grandfather . . .[12]

Grandfather Coyle had a big influence on Elsie's boy, peddling Irish republicanism to him. Keneally reckons Mick Coyle's grasp of history was not great but he knew about the Famine and other Irish grievances. 'He had this Christian Brothers' version of Irish history which was all English bad, all Irish good; all landlords bad, all peasants good. A very uncomplicated view, but he wouldn't stand up for "God Save the Queen" in the cinema or any of that stuff. Now, I've had to grow out of that Mick Coyle attitude. He was a great bloke. Both my grandfathers were very strong Labor men.'

The Keneally and Coyle men were left-wing Catholics, influenced by public-spirited priests to think about social justice, impressed by leaders like Ben Chifley and Jack Lang. Keneally has an 'up the workers' mentality; he credits his mother with having an explicit sense of social justice, and his father with a more instinctive sense. Elsie and Tom were Labor people, like Stell and her brother Matt in *The Fear*, who were 'bred by old Finnie on a sense of the sacredness of work and protest . . . their God visited the sins of the vested interests only'.

Keneally inherited a strong sense of being both Irish and Catholic. From an early age he was aware of being separate from Anglo-Saxon Australians, not sharing their loyalty to England and the Empire and the Royal Family. Elsie, who attended the same convent school in Kempsey as her son, told him that, on Empire Day in her time, the convent kids marched to the showgrounds waving the Australian flag, while the state school kids marched under the Union Jack.

Keneally likens the general distrust of Catholics to that of Muslims in twenty-first-century Australia. 'But I was not conscious, growing up, of any anti-Protestant hostility. Our attitude to Protestants was one of pity. We called other people "non-Catholics", which implied a sort of failure on their part. It wasn't intellectual tolerance – that wasn't taught from the pulpit or the rostrum in the school – it was pity.'

Keneally's education started shakily. On his first day at St Philomena's Convent in Kempsey he became very sick. The doctor diagnosed diphtheria and the boy was confined to hospital for two months, often in an oxygen tent. The experience of nearly dying, of not being able to get breath, was terrifying. Keneally's strange experience while in a coma-like state is described in a book for children, *Ned Kelly and the City of Bees*. When he was at the Manly seminary, Keneally wrote a poem, 'Diptheria [sic]: the Crisis', which recalls 'the hell night of my life' and his mother's vigil beside 'little child dying'.[13]

His father had just taken a job as a postman in nearby Wauchope. Keneally made a fresh start there in the sacristy of the church. Keneally covered his slate with the letter 'I', giving the capital a special flourish. 'Do you want to try some other letters now?' asked the teacher, a young Irish nun. She taught her charges to sing a hymn which began 'Hail, glorious St Patrick, dear saint of our isle'. Keneally sang the words as he walked to school: 'On us thy dear children bestow a sweet smile / And now thou art high in the mansion above / On Erin's green valleys, look down in thy love.' Outside the cool sanctuary, the country was brown with drought or black from bushfires.

The dust and smoke triggered Keneally's asthma. Elsie was frantic about some of the asthmatic states that her son got into because there was no relief. He was too young for adrenaline to be administered. Asthma has stalked Keneally's life, causing him to panic in the worst episodes. Like another famous Australian writer, Patrick White, the boy Keneally took refuge in books. He and Elsie spent a lot of time together, talking, reading books and trying all the possible remedies for the disabling condition. For Elsie, it was baffling and humiliating: mothers – not infections, climate, grasses or dust mites – were usually blamed for children's illnesses in that era. 'You're being hysterical,' a doctor reprimanded her once.

This state of affairs puzzled father Tom, a wiry, tough man, who didn't want his son to be a mother's boy. Tom relied on whisky toddies for congestive illness, and methylated spirits or friar's balsam for abrasions and wounds. Tom did not approve of mollycoddling a sickly kid.

Keneally's father was a sportsman, an Aussie bloke who relished boxing and wrestling. He was also a very good raconteur, colouring his plentiful supply of stories about life in the Macleay Valley with earthy bush imagery. His older son, who wanted to be like him but so far was not in the race physically, could at least attribute any wit in his writing and his gift of the gab to his father. There was a streak of melancholy about Tom the father, too, which manifested itself in dissatisfaction with himself and with the state of the world. There were bouts of heavy depression. These, too, were traits which his son would share in adult life.

4

I Hope the Germans Do Shoot You!

The suburban train known as the Red Rattler came to a halt at Central Station, Sydney. Elsie Keneally stepped down onto the platform firmly holding the hand of her son Michael. It was a chilly night in October 1943, and Keneally should have been indoors. He would probably be wheezing by the time they got home from this unusual expedition, made to say goodbye to their husband and father, Tom, who was about to leave for service with the RAAF in the Middle East. Leading Aircraftman Edmund Thomas Keneally was off to do his bit after a short stint as a postal employee, and then lengthy military training at Deniliquin, in western New South Wales, with only occasional leave.

The milling crowd and the uneasy mix of nervously raised voices, forced laughter and unashamed crying was an all too familiar scene in 1940s Sydney. The palms of Keneally's hands were itching with love and anxiety for his father. Tom, small and sad, tugged at the heavy jacket where it rasped against his reddened neck. He felt altogether unhappy. Should he have applied to his commanding officer for compassionate leave because of Elsie's pregnancy? Perhaps his embarkation could have been postponed till after the birth of the baby for which they had waited so long.

Tom thought of his previous leave, when he had tried hard to occupy the last clumsy hours. He'd taken his son to the Vogue Picture Palace in Homebush to see a Western. It had been Keneally's first visit to the Vogue, and he always remembered watching a cowboy riding a big black horse across a table-top mountain, as large as life on the screen. When the horse reached the edge it went back on its haunches, rider intact, and slid down the escarpment.

Tom had been glad of that diversion. Idleness soon turned to melancholy in him. Tonight was misery. The bugle sounded and men started to board the train. 'Fall in, K battery!' Elsie, considerably taller than Tom in her hat and heels, hugged him tightly. Then he opened his arms to enclose his son. He trudged away, clutching in one hand a squat biscuit tin filled with small fruit cakes he called 'kill-me-deads'. The men were bawling out 'We'll Meet Again' as the train departed. 'It's as if they don't know that some of them won't come back,' said Elsie.

Keneally could not sit still in the train as it took him and his mother back home. An image of his lonely father striding away to board a different train made him restless. He was haunted by an incident when Tom had reprimanded him. 'I hope the Germans *do* shoot you!' the boy had shouted back. It was an outburst that he always remembers with shame.

Tom had enlisted in December 1942, and then the family had moved south to Sydney. Keneally wrote in *The Fear*:

> Our old home, my parents' and mine, had been no more than 400 miles northwards and not even in another state. Still our migration plunged me into shock. The heat was duller. The air was full of sweat. By night I choked with asthma. By day I haunted the yard, not believing that from it you couldn't sight a brown elbow of river, Guernseys cropping the emerald floodplain, the smoke-blue tangle of New England hills. My eyes constantly returned to a galvanised iron fence, and beyond it the brick butt-ends of shop residences.

The Sydney home was an upstairs flat at 7 Loftus Crescent, Homebush, where wartime restrictions prevailed. Keneally played with his toy soldiers and joined in war games with the neighbourhood kids, pretending to be Gene Autry and other heroes. They listened and watched for the troop trains bringing American soldiers up the Western Line to training camps, their hopeful faces uplifted to the soldiers, who flung coins and comics and gum from the windows and laughed as the kids scrabbled and fought in the dirt for this coveted largesse.

Civil defence men visited St Martha's Convent in Strathfield to teach the pupils, including Keneally, how to defy death from the sky. Keneally was armed with a white linen bag, worn on the hip, which contained a bisected tennis ball (for cupping over the ears during a bombing raid), a plug of gauze (to bite into, rather than the tongue), a safety-pinned roll of lint bandage, a whistle (to blow if trapped beneath rubble) and a tin of salve for burns.

The school air-raid shelter, a low-roofed cranny, was located as a matter of faith beneath the high altar of St Martha's Church. 'God would never permit the high altar to be hit,' the nuns reasoned. The space was accessed by a little door in the outer wall of the church. The roof was reinforced with steel to take the weight of the altar. To reassure the scared children, the nuns led them in singing the hymn 'Faith of Our Fathers'. 'I'm not going to come in here,' Keneally wheezed after the first practice, 'even if the Japs bomb this school.'

When Japanese reconnaissance planes threatened that possibility, Elsie appeared outside the church. She bore down on her son before he was towed into the shelter. 'I'm going to take Michael home,' she told the nuns. Mother and son were the only people all the way down Homebush Road as the air-raid siren shrilled, Elsie scanning the skies, and Keneally sailing happily beside her.

Out in the Indian Ocean, it sometimes happened that no boats could go to the rescue of ships about to be consigned forever to a place much darker and deeper than the air-raid shelter at St Martha's Church. Tom's ship, the SS *Temeraire*, was at risk from Japanese submarines. The men huddled in life jackets outside the radio shack, listening to distress calls coming in, but under order of radio silence. They were sure they would be the next target. In his diary Tom recorded a couple of warnings given about the danger that lurked below: on 13 November he noted a 'warning Sub. in locality of ship', and a week later he described 'a very nervy night after warning'.[1]

The torpedo did not come. Tom's ship reached its destination, Port Suez, the troops proceeded to Cairo by train and he began his duties among RAAF ground staff as a postal clerk. He reported on 4 December 1943:

'Mail in today and the work is definitely on now.' As his first Christmas away from home approached, he wrote: 'Mail arrived. 960 Bags, Worked like bloody horses to get some finished before Xmas. Had Xmas and Boxing Day off. Boxing Day Mass in the am; played football pm, Australia v. New Zealand.'

Tom sent home parcels, including a football for his son's ninth birthday with a letter enclosed:

> Darling Michael,
>
> Here is your football and hope you get some fun out of it. I know you will be a little bit disappointed that I could not get you one like you use at school but I am looking out for one for you but they are very hard to get. I hope you have a very happy birthday and that I will be home for your next one . . .

In another letter Tom told the boy, whom he sometimes referred to as Mickey or Mikey, about the 'chaps in the Middle East' who had trained monkeys to give the Hitler salute. 'You can imagine the fun we get out of it.'[2]

On leave, Tom was able to visit the Pyramids in Egypt and, later, sacred sites in Jerusalem and Bethlehem, but he never got as far as Ireland, where he had hoped to go, just like his brother Johnnie during the First World War. His concise accounts – written neatly in ink in a pocket-sized diary, and illustrated with little maps – show a keen interest in his surroundings and an eye for detail. Tom senior could write well. He included mention of brief but memorable encounters: 'Saw Churchill, Roosevelt and King Peter. We were in a truck [in Cairo] and we drove straight pass [sic] them.' That entry was dated 3 December 1943. On 15 April 1944 Tom reported that he had seen Queen Farida, 'quite close to car as she drove past. Quite a nice looking woman.'

He sent home Nazi memorabilia recognisable from the pictures showing in the Vogue Picture Palace. Keneally went to the Vogue on Saturday afternoons to watch Westerns; he was disconsolate if a romantic comedy or musical was to be shown. On one Saturday evening Elsie and Keneally dressed up and went to a show at the Vogue. There on the screen was the newsreel footage of German concentration camps liberated by the horrified Allies. Around Keneally and his mother in the suddenly darker theatre, women gasped with shock and disbelief.

It would be many years before the young Keneally became famous for his book about the death camps, *Schindler's Ark*. In the 1940s the boy was fighting a personal battle with asthma. During many days and nights he struggled for breath, wheezing and panting. He went out in the yard to play with other kids, but any contact with paspalum or privet, which was all through the suburbs, meant a sleepless night for Elsie. He picked up infections easily and survived regular bouts of pneumonia. He often woke to see the white and blue apparition of a nun beside his bed at the Little Company of Mary Hospital.

Keneally wrote about the sufferings of the asthmatic Daniel Jordan in *The Fear*. Another early indication of its prominence in his life can be seen in the short story 'In the Day of Anger'. The condition of Dr Erich Bucher, one of the internees, was described with understanding: he was 'biting at the air for breath, his back heaving, and his chest creaking tightly from congestion'. Keneally's Bucher was a man of dignity, as was the asthmatic school teacher McCreadie, the hostage in *The Chant of Jimmie Blacksmith*, but unlike Ernest Moriarty, the miserable schoolteacher in Patrick White's *Happy Valley*.[3]

White hated the weakness of asthma, and imposed his self-loathing on Moriarty. Some of those who knew White said he had 'a nervy kind of asthma. Little things set him off, like people not walking fast enough or walking too fast.'[4] Attacks were also triggered by unfavourable news about his books or by poor work in progress, but he was at the mercy of the weather and other triggers too. Keneally's family doctor, Buckley, explained in a reference when his patient was seventeen that he had suffered from bronchial asthma for most of his life, 'sometimes as frequently as every morning, often worse with approaching examinations and similar worries'.[5]

Elsie had become accustomed to the asthma attacks, and to keeping things going on the home front in general. She plied her son with books and the oft-repeated adage, 'A child with a book is never bored.' Keneally, like his character Bettany in *Bettany's Book*, had 'since childhood a capacity to be consumed by stories'. Elsie was company and comfort, their bond evident in the poem 'Diptheria [sic]: the Crisis'. Keneally, writing that poem as a lonely seminarian, was recalling the unstinting love of his mother. The poem also pointed to the deep desire he harboured to please his mother; until his success as a writer, he believed he was repeatedly letting her down. The first manifestation of 'failure' was the look of anxiety on Elsie's face when he appeared gasping for air.

He engaged in activities that might free him from the unmanly cosseting. He had no allergic reaction to boxing, provided the fight took place well away from paspalum. One such fight, in Keneally's recollection, took place on Parramatta Road and lasted for more than an hour. The grocers from Moran and Cato's and the butcher's men left their shops to watch and barrack. 'The ambition to "come the knuckle"', Keneally reflected years later, 'did reside, however ineffectually, in me, and my mother was not enthusiastic about it.'[6]

From an early age Keneally was determined to flaunt his maleness and compensate as best he could for his physical weakness. Yet he has a ready ability to relate to women; his liking for them – his pleasure in their presence and company – might perhaps be traced back to the influence of Elsie in childhood. He admits to an interest in women's clothing and jewellery but he is anything but effeminate. Father Tom, despite his 'ocker' image, was more of a dandy than his son would ever be, and pleased women with his ready compliments. Both father and son knew how to charm.

Into a household of ailing child, anxious mother and absent father, another boy came on 15 November 1943. When Elsie went into labour she called a taxi, but the driver had used up his petrol ration for the month and couldn't come. Elsie, accompanied by her older son and Aunt Annie, walked over a mile to get to the hospital for the birth of John Patrick, whom his older brother called Johnny. Keneally had one grievance: 'My sole jealousy attached to the fact that he received a special government ration of prunes, and I believed in his case the organs generally associated with the action of prunes were operating quite satisfactorily without federal intervention!'[7]

In Egypt, Tom wrote in his diary on 19 November 1943: 'Very impatient to get to Cairo to receive cable from Elsie regarding Baby.' It was there waiting for him with news of his second son's birth, and he was permitted to send one in reply. By the time another year had passed,

Tom was 'very homesick and full up of everything. Wanting badly to go home . . . very downhearted . . .' He was crossing off the months on the diary's calendar. On 20 April 1945 he wrote: 'Please God I will be out of this place this time next year.'[8]

His prayer was answered and Elsie received a letter from the RAAF Personnel Department telling her that he would arrive in Sydney 'about 4 November 1945'. The letter continued: 'You will be advised by telegram just as soon as we are in a position to give you further information, when it will be stated the time it will be possible to meet him here, but the notice will be necessarily short.'[9]

Elsie and the boys left early on the appointed day. They were herded into a huge hall, watching as the men arrived, laughing and talking, glad to be alive. The noise was deafening. 'The Ks are coming!' a jovial corporal told them at about four that afternoon, and at last the K families were taken out to meet a truck, from which their men jumped. There were lavish caresses and an unfamiliar pat on Michael's cheek. Tom reached out to hold his second son for the first time.

Tom's brother Dan and sister-in-law Nora received a postcard photo of him and his older son, taken soon after Tom's return, with this ironic message on the back:

> Not a very good [photo] of me but you would never imagine that I had two years and three months in the desert eating Raw Camel and Donkey, and only a quart of water to wash in and drinking purposes. Well that sounds bad, don't you think, but of course it is all lies; however I am mighty glad to be Home again and believe me Egypt and surrounding countries are not what they are supposed to be. Love, Tom.[10]

Relieved to have his father home, and with his conscience salved a little, Keneally repeated what he'd been told many times: the bullet had not been made that could fell Tom Keneally.

In Kempsey, before the family moved to Sydney, father Tom and a nephew, Pat Bolster, delighted in teasing the young militia men who made for the pubs after training at the showgrounds. Tom thought it was a great joke to get his son out on the verandah to shout, 'Choco!' This was short for 'chocolate soldier', meaning one who would melt in battle.

The chocos were looked down on as cowards who wouldn't face combat. These young men were later engaged on the Kokoda Trail, and when the truth about that conflict was made known, Tom said to Keneally, 'I'm ashamed I wound you up to do it.'

Keneally's own brush with military service came in 1957, when he was a seminarian. He received a letter from the Registrar of the Department of Labour and National Service with this advice:

> Following the introduction of revised arrangements for National Service, your liability to render service under the National Service Act 1951–1957 has been deferred. This means that, under these present arrangements, you are not required for service. You may, if you wish, volunteer to undertake NS training . . .[11]

Keneally did a stint in an artillery unit of the Commonwealth Military Forces in the 1960s but was discharged because of his asthma.

The story of his father's war is partly told in *The Fear*, Keneally's second book, and in *Homebush Boy: A Memoir*. Also of interest for this early stage of his life is *An Angel in Australia*, in which Keneally took a retrospective look at wartime Sydney. The setting and the situation are unmistakeable: 'St Margaret's Church' and the adjoining school, the close relationship between mother and son, the childhood illnesses, the boy who reports, as Keneally did, that 'My Daddy's in the Middle North', the school air-raid shelter and practice, the resident maiden aunt, and the homes in the 'Crescent'.

When Tom was absent, Elsie had the company of his sister, Auntie Annie, an eccentric but amusing companion, whose hopes of marrying Lou Goodwin (brother of Aub Goodwin, who married Annie's sister Nellie) were dashed when he was killed a week after arriving on the Western Front during the First World War. Years later, Keneally saw his journal. The last entry read: 'Going on patrol . . . a bit windy, but the older blokes said it's nothing to worry about.' One of Elsie's sisters, Marie, had also stayed with the family while working as a wartime welder at a light engineering works in nearby Burwood. The women had enjoyed many sessions in the little dining-kitchenette, making the best of things and indulging the two boys. Keneally remembered that Marie's sweetheart,

Lou Gurney, when on leave from his armoured tank division, would sometimes visit with his brother. 'I used to sweat on them turning up. They added a bit of colour in the week.'

After Tom's return, the cosy flat occasionally became the scene for arguments. In the confined quarters Keneally could not help but overhear. The idyll of the man of the house back in his rightful place did not last long. Like many a returning father, he was critical of the mother's method of raising the kids in his absence. According to Keneally: 'There were arguments in every house where there was a returning serviceman. There were other problems too: what the serviceman had been through etc. The hiatus that it imposed on them as regards a working career was often highly significant and often condemned men to a life of drudgery so that, while it is true that in the 1950s there was full employment, I don't think there was always fulfilment.

'My father was, I think, fulfilled in his work, although not when he was at the railway works for a while – I don't think he was happy there. Then he ran a store in Granville that belonged to a sister of his – my Aunt Nellie Keneally and her husband, Aub Goodwin – in Blaxcell Street, Granville . . . He didn't want to be in debt – he was a Depression boy – he never took a loan to start a business of his own which I think he should have done. My mother would have run it! She had, as so often happens, administrative talents.

'Then, after that store with the Goodwins, he worked at a store called Hodgsons at Petersham. He was great there – you meet people who loved him. They introduced late-night shopping on Thursday, which he abominated, and called "wog night". Being one of those old right-wing Labor guys . . . he didn't quite approve of immigration, but he used to say that the wogs would always wait to be served by him! Anyone who was unsure or nervous. A lot of people have told me that. It seems that the old man, again, had this natural liking for the battlers.'

Waltons took over Hodgsons in 1962, and it became known as Waltons' Summer Hill department store. Tom was a salesman in the 'soft lines' section, a dapper man in his starched, long-sleeved white shirt and dark tie and trousers. Tom regarded himself as a 'boofhead'; Keneally suspects that it must have been the nuns who convinced him that he was dumb. Tom had an inferiority complex about education all his life, as did Elsie.

The family slowly settled down to life in drab post-war Sydney, a city plagued by strikes and discomposed by the bewildered Europeans who sought refuge there from trauma and grief. Tom and his boys were getting to know each other. Tom was kind but quick-tempered, ready to take on people who offended him – and still all too quick to 'come the knuckle'. His absence for two and a half years, plus the time away training beforehand, undoubtedly affected Keneally. 'At first I felt odd with him, like many of the children of that era who greeted returning fathers,' he said in 2002. 'I sometimes think we could take a class action against the Commonwealth of Australia! All jokes aside, we were, in a small way, victims of the war.'[12]

The father did not have a comfortable relationship with his older son, although Keneally was quick to defend him as 'a fond old bugger – in his lights, very loving'. Tom was not always the sociable, blithe man known to his customers and acquaintances. At home he could be morose and melancholic, and his two boys were sensitive to his moods. Over the years Keneally worried, in the sensitive repentant way he has about past wrongs, that his reckless words as a child – 'I hope the Germans *do* shoot you!' – meant something more subconsciously. 'The utterance,' he wrote in 2013, 'seems to encapsulate everything painful and double-bladed and unresolved about fathers and sons.'[13]

The relationship improved in time, although in 2009, when asked by an interviewer to whom he would most like to say sorry, Keneally replied, 'My father, because we were mutually uncomprehending of each other.'[14]

5

The GMH Fanatic

'Oh, Sister! Look what's happened to his page!'

Necks craned in the classroom to see what Keneally had done. His ineptness with ink and his constantly runny nose resulted in a messy exercise book every time. There was nothing quite like the contempt of the girl who shared your desk 'telling Sister on you'.

Life at his little Dominican parish school, St Martha's in Strathfield, was not always pleasant. While other writers recall from their childhood the stigma of glaring poverty or the isolation of a loner or the torment of bullies, Keneally put up with sneers about snot. He says that Sister Felicitas, the teacher of Grade 2, Infants Section, 'later claimed me as one of her happier memories but for quite a time it wasn't a happy experience for me. It was stressful and it was combined with air raid practice, which terrified me.'

Elsie Keneally had ambitions for her boys which began with the Sisters at St Martha's. Keneally was not very promising material, but his mother, to her credit, never reproached him. 'I wanted to be the kid who gratified my mother by taking home the rubber-stamped stars for good work,' Keneally wrote in 2013. 'Failure bound me irrevocably to my mother by our shared dreams of validation. Because even then I noticed something peculiar and unrepayable – she never lost her fiercesome faith in me.'[1]

It was left to the younger boy, Johnny, to redeem the family name at St Martha's. Johnny was a bright boy with a photographic memory. Keneally was always amazed at how smart he was and realised with a pang how pleasing he must have been to the Sisters with his curly hair and neat habits. The brothers embarked on Sunday afternoon adventures, including visits to a Telecom training station where the deserted army huts intrigued Keneally. He told Johnny that this place had been a prisoner-of-war camp, and that all the German and Japanese prisoners of war would break out and grab the boys. Keneally also convinced his brother that prisoners were regularly hanged right there, in Homebush Road. The much younger brother believed all the tall stories. He was soft-hearted, crying in pity for the animals that, according to other yarns told by his older brother, were homeless, unloved and unfed. Keneally's precocious talent for telling stories began with those he told Johnny.

Away from school, Keneally roamed the streets with his mates, including some from the state primary school. There was the occasional stone-throwing or name-calling incident between Protestants and Catholics, typical of many places in mid-twentieth-century sectarian Australia. The boys next door had a communist father, who had a precarious job at the meatworks. The older boy, Jimmy Coy, had motor neurone disease, and the affliction was used to end the fight if he and his brother, Jacky, and Mick Keneally were coming off second-best. 'You'd better stop!' they'd yell to their adversaries. 'Jimmy is gonna die when he's thirteen!'

The pummelling would stop. 'Are you really gonna die?'

Back came the answer: 'Too right.' Hostilities would cease for the day, and the boys went back to the overhead bridge to count the rolling stock on long goods trains.

The teenager Keneally became the self-proclaimed 'Celestial' described in *Homebush Boy*, and wandered about with his friend, David Viney (Mangan in *Homebush Boy*). The name allowed them to pretend that they did not live in mundane suburbia, but in a more exalted place. Any hope his father might have harboured that the Christian Brothers would make a tough man of the boy were dashed somewhere during the transition from childhood to adolescence. Keneally was more concerned at this time with applying a sticky substance called Fix-a-Flex to hold his auburn, Beethoven-esque cowlick in place.

Viney disdained Fix-a-Flex, as his brown curls matched his languid manner. Another boy, Gerald Walsh (Larkin in *Homebush Boy*), was tolerated as a 'fringe' Celestial because of his agnostic stance, but he and Viney had one advantage over Keneally: they lived on the 'right' side of the Western Line – the southern, more attractive, more socially acceptable side of the tracks. Keneally longed to be on the other side, where the 'silvertails' lived.

The school he attended from the third grade, St Patrick's Christian Brothers' College, was on the right side. One of the teachers, Brother Crichton, a Great War veteran, was easily distracted in religion class by the casual question, 'Brother, who shot down the Red Baron?' Crichton had been a despatch rider for a Brigadier-General Brand. One day in 1918, on horseback riding from Amiens to Corbie with a message, Crichton saw a red plane flying very low in pursuit of a British plane. According to Crichton, Australian soldiers manned machine guns to bring down the famous pilot, Manfred von Richthofen, and later buried him.

'I know you all thought I shot him down,' Crichton said to Keneally years later. 'But it wasn't me personally. I was involved though.'[2]

The Brother's story always ended with a prayer: 'Join me now, boys, in praying for the soul of Baron von Richthofen and all the faithful departed.' For Catholic youth, it did not seem strange to be saying an Our Father and three Hail Marys for a dead German. Keneally had spent an afternoon in his sixth-year class saying the rosary for a Labor Caucus meeting. Viney had attended a Mass for the repose of the soul of another baron, the poet Byron, whose personality cult of the defiant, melancholy young man appealed to the Celestials. Keneally had sometimes, while reciting the rosary, remembered Talleyrand, the French bishop and statesman, who had impressed him in history classes.

Keneally discovered the modern poets when he borrowed a copy of the *Albatross Book of Modern Verse* from Brother McGlade. 'I was so excited by it that I wanted to change cells with it somehow,' he wrote in *As the Twig Is Bent*. 'It became dog-eared and I had to buy him a new copy for his little library. Then after I'd wrecked one edition of the *Albatross Book of Modern Verse* I wrecked an edition of Gerard Manley Hopkins on him.'

McGlade introduced Honours English students to a cupboard at the back of the classroom filled with modern books. 'Virginia Woolf presented herself and T. S. Eliot burst on us with the force of revelation,' Keneally recalled in the obituary he wrote for McGlade, 'and there was Gerard Manley Hopkins, both so theological and so sensual, as if to show you could be a Catholic and a wild poet too.'[3]

Keneally referred to Hopkins the poet priest with casual familiarity as 'GMH', and replaced the *Albatross Book of Modern Verse* with the Oxford University Press edition of Hopkins's works in the breast pocket of his blazer; a misshapen blazer, a loose tie and a crushed felt hat were all part of the so-called Celestial image. 'Thinks he's as flash as bloody paint!' Tom growled to Elsie.

As far as Elsie was concerned, it was better to see her son posing as an aesthete than to hear him scream asthmatically, as he did one night, 'If I had a gun I'd kill myself!' Keneally said there were times when he was reduced to a state of panic and thought he really was going to die. Releasing him from his tightened chest and blocked airways was Elsie's main mission in life.

Keneally explained, through his character McCreadie in *The Chant of Jimmie Blacksmith*, the procedure for the asthmatic that he had gradually mastered himself:

> 'The secret,' he grunted, 'is to get rid of the entire load of air before breathing in again. Most asthmatics take short, quick breaths, but that only makes things worse. A person must never panic, or think that each time he breathes out is the last.'

The stout-hearted GMH, who suffered throughout his life from a nervous disability, was dogged by a sense of failure such as his young devotee would experience. In time, GMH would attract his own cult following, and Keneally, who wrote on the flyleaf of his GMH book 'Michael K., Professor of Hopkinsian Idiosyncrasy', was in the vanguard. He studied the poet's use of sprung rhythm and read his poems – 'Pied Beauty', 'The Windhover', 'Felix Randal' – with a hopeful bardic intonation. The poet's mastery fed the schoolboy's ambition to write. More than fifty years later Keneally said that he 'fell in love, not physically, but spiritually, with a Jesuit poet called Gerard Manley Hopkins, who I thought expressed the sort of Christian I wanted to be.'[4]

This fascination with a dead poet was beyond father Tom's understanding. He was sometimes seen working in his vegetable garden, a solitary man as far removed from his son's daydreaming as Keneally was from the grandeur he craved. In retrospect, Keneally thought his father was mourning something he could not communicate.[5] A barrier of mutual embarrassment separated them. Tom was a wordsmith in his own right, once describing a neighbour disparagingly as 'a flobble-gutted, wombat-headed garper', and the neighbour's wife, with whom Elsie engaged in battles over laundry rights, as 'slow as a gin at a christening'. Their daughter was 'straight up and down like a yard of pump water'.

Tom had inherited his sense of imagery from his mother, Kate, with whom he had, as the youngest in a big family, spent as much time as his older son had with Elsie. In his own way he had been a 'mother's boy' too. Keneally savoured his father's sayings, especially the one about 'a fella about the one age of me', a phrase he had never heard said by anyone else.

Keneally, in his last years at school, frequented the church in a way that seemed abnormal to his father. The son went to Mass during the week as well as on Sunday at St Martha's Church, where Monsignor Power conducted the service in resonant Latin at a solemn pace; Tom preferred priests like Father Williams at St Dominic's, Flemington, who raced through the litany and released the congregation as quickly as was decently possible. Keneally promised himself that if he ever became a priest, he would not rattle through the words but would give them their full measure of meaning.

Keneally was at St Patrick's College for nine years, and his accounts of his time there have taken on a mythical quality. The Christian Brothers schools have had, in the past, a bad reputation for heavy-handedness and sometimes a cruelty that left emotional and physical scars. A classic example can be seen in Ron Blair's play *The Christian Brothers*, set in a 1950s schoolroom. One monologue – hectoring, threatening and reminiscing – is the recognisable voice of an overworked, under-appreciated Christian Brother, but it is at the extreme end of their conduct.

In the collective memory of Catholic boys, there is agreement that priests and Brothers varied greatly in age, outlook and teaching ability. The straps with which they 'beat it into them' have been described with Dickensian detail. The Prefect of Studies at Clongowes Wood College in *A Portrait of the Artist as a Young Man* was a demon with his 'pandybat', and delighted in flogging 'lazy idle little loafers'. The description of the unjust treatment of Stephen Dedalus at the prefect's hands is one of the most agonising in literature. Graham Greene's miserable character Pinkie Brown in *Brighton Rock* 'looked with loathing into the past – a cracked bell ringing, a child weeping under the cane'.

According to Keneally, mythologising about the strap was a favourite preoccupation of the younger boys at St Patrick's. 'Some Brothers were rumoured to practise giving it in the secrecy of their cells,' he wrote in *Homebush Boy*. 'Some – we believed – stiffened the thing, others made it more flexible. (We were not, of course, aware of any Freudian imagery in our legend-making.)'

Homebush Boy is a story about Keneally's world in one decisive year, 1952, when he decided to become a priest. As various players in the story have commented, some of Keneally's recollections are fanciful, others inaccurate. Paul Crittenden, a contemporary at St Patrick's, has described Keneally as telling the story in 'imaginative form'.[6] The book, while entertaining and humorous, shows Keneally in a mock-heroic role, as an 'out there' boy who is going places.

St Patrick's College existed to turn working-class boys into something better – to give them the chance to improve their lot in life. Keneally had visions of greatness beyond the usual choice of engineer or doctor: he aimed to become the pope or win the Nobel Prize for Literature. Such ambition was well-hidden in the unreliable chest of a quiet but enthusiastic student, yet not one who stood out for the right or wrong reasons, unlike his friend Viney, always in trouble for his unpunctuality and cool dismissal of the college's expectations. 'I had seen him take beatings and humiliations because of some inscrutable point of honour,' his Celestial companion observed.[7] There is no mention of Keneally himself taking a beating. Like Father Darragh in *An Angel in Australia* he was diligent and capable, and so 'did not need to be punished in the muscular way of the brothers' community with leather straps and fleas in the ear'.[8]

Keneally was just an agreeable, docile boy who became animated, Crittenden says, with his small group of like-minded friends, the Celestials. 'He was more vital, with a great sense of humour. He was already a storyteller in his imagination.' Keneally achieved some greatness by being placed first in the state of New South Wales in the 1951 end-of-year

English examination. Further recognition came when he won second prize in the annual Newman Society essay competition. His topic was the venerable GMH. Elsie was extremely proud, but Keneally, afraid she might embarrass him, did not want her to attend the presentation. In later life he was ashamed of his refusal to include Elsie.

The winning essay, by Leone Manning, was about a New Zealand poet, Eileen Duggan, who came from an Irish-Catholic family.[9] Very little Australian literature was finding its way into schools at that time, let alone any New Zealand writing, although McGlade had introduced poets like Kenneth Slessor. For his prize book, Keneally chose *Elizabethan Recusant Prose*, the writings of Elizabethans who refused to take their oath to the Queen and remained loyal to Rome. They were the sort of heroes favoured by the Celestial Keneally.

McGlade, called Dinny McGahan in *Homebush Boy*, encouraged Keneally's literary ambitions and his appreciation of classical music. Keneally and others were invited to after-school 'soirées', at which music by Mahler, Beethoven and Mozart was played, and books discussed in an adult manner. McGlade read and passed on books that some members of the Catholic clergy were uncomfortable with: *The Heart of the Matter* and *Brighton Rock*, both by Grahame Greene, came in for particular condemnation from the local pulpit as containing seductive arguments contrary to the Catholic faith.

The funniest book Keneally read before he left school was *The Loved One*, Evelyn Waugh's hilarious memento mori. Other favourites included detective novels such as *The Daughter of Time* by Josephine Tey, and historical novels by Walter Scott. Thomas Chatterton was considered noble; 'I was fascinated by the fact that he was so young,' Keneally says. 'I was pretty berserk at poetry.' Keneally was keen on Tennyson, too, singling out 'In Memoriam'. He had, he confesses, 'an obsession with death as a liberation. I was fascinated, in a morbid way, with young heroic death. Chatterton was one and John Keats another.'

The Celestials had a phase as poetasters. Some of their efforts decorated the flyleaves of textbooks, with the hope that, one day, the compositions would be included in their published *Early Poems*. Such were the dreams of boys trying to transcend their commonplace surroundings.

6

The Goodly Company

The group waiting and chattering on the platform at Strathfield railway station made an attractive tableau. Two sisters, Pamela and Margaret Davis, stood beside two other sisters, Mary and Ruth Rafferty. A couple of boys completed the scene: Mick Keneally and Patrick (Paddy) Downie.

Paddy Downie (Matt Tierney in *Homebush Boy*) was the first blind boy in Australia to attempt the Leaving Certificate in an 'ordinary' school. An albino, he had been blind from birth after his mother contracted rubella during the early stages of her pregnancy. Keneally, Paddy's study companion for the year at St Patrick's Christian Brothers College, readily included Paddy on weekend outings as well. On this particular Sunday afternoon the group, which Keneally calls 'The Goodly Company' in *Homebush Boy*, was going into town to listen to the soapbox orators in the Domain, a large open space across the road from St Mary's Cathedral. They squabbled over whose turn it was to guide Paddy onto the train, because Paddy's carer travelled for free. The others had to pay sixpence for the journey.

The attraction of the entertainment at the Domain was that it was free. Keneally's group liked to heckle John Wallace Campbell, a dedicated anti-Catholic spokesman who published a paper called *The Rock*. The group from Strathfield questioned him and called out objections to his diatribe. On one occasion Campbell's supporters chased Keneally and his friends out of the Domain. They probably made their way to the nearby art gallery, which they liked to visit.

Mary Rafferty (Rose Frawley in *Homebush Boy*) remembers that Mother Philomena at Santa Sabina once questioned her about the visits to the Domain. 'Have you been listening to the communists?' she asked. 'No!' replied Rafferty breezily. 'They are boring! We go to Campbell of *The Rock*!'

'We also liked to listen to Bernard Curran, a Dominican priest,' Rafferty remembers. 'He was ready to stand up to opposition in the crowd. He was witty and articulate.'[1] Rafferty makes it clear that Keneally's recollection, in *Homebush Boy*, of her father, James Rafferty, as an active 'industrial grouper' (one of an organised group opposed to the Labor Party's apparent support of communist-controlled unions) is inaccurate. James Rafferty may have talked about the local band of groupers who were determined to outwit Campbell's plans to 'raid convents and liberate young nuns', but he was not one of them.

The group of friends regularly attended Sunday-afternoon concerts given by the Sydney Symphony Orchestra at the Town Hall. Keneally also recalled going to the Mitchell Library in the city: 'That was a place enchanting to me and my friends. We used to drag Paddy Downie in there – the blind kid – and we'd just walk along the racks and pull something out. We wouldn't work systematically on anything. We didn't know how to.'

The Rafferty girls were like sisters to Keneally. He enjoyed going to their place at 36 Broughton Road, where the seven Rafferty siblings and their kindly parents made him feel at home. He yarned away to Mrs Rafferty, calling her 'Mrs R' and making casual reference to his mother as 'Elsie'. Mary Rafferty was blunt and inclined to tease Mick about his pretensions. Spotting the outline of the GMH book in his blazer pocket, she demanded: 'Haven't you finished reading that bloody book yet, Michael?' She thought he talked of things beyond the usual teenage talk. 'I could never understand where he was coming from!'

The Davis family's house at 62 Shortland Street, Strathfield, had a special charm because of the eldest girl, Pamela (Bernadette Curran in *Homebush Boy*), who enchanted Mick.[2] Keneally has told many interviewers about 'the ways I tried to woo her, how my heart would beat faster when I would see her, but my efforts were all in vain.'[3] Davis was 'a handy *belle dame sans merci*'.

Davis thinks Keneally used her in his writing in many ways. She has described Keneally as 'a nervy type – very bronchial. I can remember my parents trying to get him to sit down in the house. He paced up and down mostly.' As far as Davis was concerned, Michael was 'just part of the group. I liked him but had no particular feelings for him. There were other boys who attracted me more.' She was inclined to agree with his own assessment, in *Homebush Boy*, that he was 'a very strange little bugger'. Keneally says she thought he was an oaf, and 'she was right on the money'.

St Patrick's College had a strong sporting ethos, although Viney was contemptuous of his fellow Celestial's obsession with sport. 'No poet has ever worn shoulder-pads,' he told Keneally witheringly. Keneally has written humorously about Viney's reluctant participation in 'The Cyclical Supremacy of Australia in World Cricket'. When it came to field placements, Viney was placed at deep fine leg, beyond the reach of most balls hit by schoolboy batsmen, where he dreamt and ignored the action. Occasionally, a ball would come his way and he inevitably dropped the catch or missed the ball altogether. 'Bloody drongo,' growled his teammates.[4]

In his pre-adolescent years, Keneally used to play a cricket game he had devised: using an old *Cassell's Encyclopaedia*, he'd select a team of composers and a team of writers.

> I remember that Tolstoy went in at first wicket down for the writers. Thomas Hardy was always high in the batting order yet for one whole summer managed a batting average of only about 11 . . . Handel and Bach, despite their paunches and their progenitive urges, were the stars of the composers' line-up, and I remember that Borodin – though a Russian and low in the batting order – sometimes scored a century at eighth wicket down . . .[5]

Proper cricket was played at St Patrick's, but rugby league was the game on which the school's sporting reputation rested. After the mandatory recital of three Hail Marys for victory, the side took to the field. Keneally had an older cousin who remembered a Christian Brother coach who used to strap the half and dummy-half at the interval if they'd not been distributing the ball deftly enough.

Keneally coveted a position in the First XIII, and had once tried out for half-back and also five-eighth, the position his father had played. The trial was held on the school oval in front of a crowd of spectators, including father Tom and his cousin Pat. Much to Keneally's chagrin and his father's disappointment, McGlade told him that he would start him at five-eighth in the third team. Keneally declined the offer. 'Brother,' he lied, 'I think I'd better miss rugby this year. I've got the asthma coming back.' In McGlade's recollection, Keneally was not particularly capable at sport but was always ready to participate and to support the school.

Keneally called the matches of the school's home games for his sightless friend. Sometimes, after the footy was over, they would change into running clothes and do a few laps of the oval. Keneally, slightly ahead, rattled Nugget boot polish tins full of Braille type-pieces to assist Downie to stay on track. Downie showed his mettle at the last athletics meet in 1952, but Keneally was angry that the coach, Brother McMahon, would not permit him to run against boys his own age; he could compete only in the under-fourteen races. Downie won the 220 yards and came third in the 100 yards.

Apart from the risk to Downie as he took the turns, the coach may have wanted to minimise the spectator value that attached itself to the boy. In a short story called 'The Performing Blind Boy', Keneally speculated about the possible damage done to 'David Clift', blind from birth, by the attitude of those who wanted to see him perform 'a jumping through the hoop' routine. 'But he did race in a race like the one recounted ... And his friend rattling counters in tins was me, and I was doing it for all the wrong reasons – sentiment, for a start. And then because I wanted to look good in the eyes of the girls in the crowd ...'[6]

Keneally wondered later if he had contributed in some way to Downie's debasement. Yet others have spoken of Keneally's kindness and genuine desire to treat the blind boy as 'normal'. The Goodly Company and other schoolfriends contributed to this endeavour. They took turns on a tandem bike that enabled Downie to pedal away at the back while they steered from the front. 'We complained that, sitting in the back seat, he was inclined not to pedal as hard as he might,' recalled Paul

Crittenden. 'Pat smiled, but conceded nothing.'[7] Later, when Keneally was at the Manly seminary, Downie visited him; seminarians who saw them together remarked upon the way Keneally treated Downie, 'looking after him all day with such kindness'.[8]

Keneally's chance to perform came in the 'Nine-Stoners' football team, playing at the state championships in the last year of school. The team was trained by Brother Markwell, against whose unyielding back Keneally had broken his nose the previous season. 'I was told never tackle from behind,' Keneally recalled, 'but sure enough, I tried. And sure enough, when it happened, I heard a crunch as my nose went into the small of the Brother's back. He simply turned around and said, "I told you so!"'[9] While Viney regarded the oval as a wasted space, Keneally always had 'a fascination for well-tended green areas surrounded by seats'.[10]

The Christian Brothers also asked the boys if they had a calling to the priesthood. As Richard Connolly – an Australian composer and broadcaster, who later met Keneally in unusual circumstances – saw it, a Catholic boy couldn't aspire to anything better in those days. 'That's the way we saw the priesthood then,' he said.[11]

Keneally had his mind fixed on being a writer, or a composer, or an orator; perhaps all three. He was certain that he did not want to follow in the footsteps of the Brothers, spending his life correcting kids' bad behaviour and their endless homework. He had occasionally entertained the dream of becoming a priest, seeing himself as a moral hero nurturing the needy flock. He had also been influenced by his reading of GMH, the poet who wrote so impressively about the grandeur of God and adhered to what the youth understood later to be a sensual theology.

Early in Keneally's last year of school, priests appeared seeking candidates for the various orders or for secular priesthood. Father Kevin McGovern was the Vocations Director who visited St Patrick's. He was called Father Byrne in *Homebush Boy*, described by Keneally as 'thin and ageless . . . mystical, penitential and angular'.[12] In real life, McGovern was of medium height, with a solid build, a ruddy complexion and reddish hair. 'He was very earnest and dedicated,' explains Paul Crittenden. 'He would have been in his early to mid-thirties when he went around visiting schools in the 1950s.'[13]

Keneally went along to hear McGovern's spiel on the off-chance that he *might be called*. The priest listed the signs of a possible call, and Keneally responded to each in the affirmative: he went to Mass more than once a week; he faithfully took his turn as a Mass server, or altar boy; he engaged in spiritual debates rather than worldly discussions; he attended the confessional regularly; he prayed to the Blessed Mother fervently. Keneally exalted in the feeling of well-being after making a *good* confession, whether it be about reading Greene or yearning after one particular girl. He began to like the idea of himself as a confessor, invested with the power of the priest who donned a purple stole and absolved sinners of their guilt.

There was potential power in the sacraments, too. Keneally thought that earnest Father McGovern was 'wonderstruck with the doctrine of Transubstantiation, the transformation of the substance of the bread and wine into the body and blood of Christ by the word of the priest.'[14] Keneally was wonderstruck too: this was investing the priest with divine *authority*, a seriously Celestial authority.

'There is to be a vocations' day at the major seminary at Manly,' McGovern informed him in the early winter of 1952. 'A deacon will show you around the place and answer your questions. Would you like to go?'

Keneally caught the train to Wynyard Station and walked down to Circular Quay to board the Manly ferry. The waters of Sydney Harbour are often choppy, and the big green and yellow ferries plough and plunge across in all kinds of weather. The journey is one of the most popular ferry rides in the world, with the spectacle of the Sydney Harbour Bridge, the unchanging headlands and the unsurpassed beaches. Keneally became very familiar with the Manly ferry in the years ahead.

The neo-Gothic main building of St Patrick's Seminary stood on a sandstone headland behind high walls. Keneally and the other recruits were met by the deacons, students in cassocks who were by that stage approaching ordination. 'Even to someone as young as me,' Keneally wrote in *Homebush Boy*, 'there was something very appealing about their freshness, their new-minted quality. And every one of them a potential cardinal, a possible first antipodean Pope.'

The boys tried to imagine themselves in this august place; for many, it was too much to take in. They escaped down Darley Road to the ferry terminal and a milkshake at the wharf. The Paragon milk bar in the Boulevard, Strathfield, where the less ecclesiastically minded boys congregated and flirted with the girls from Santa Sabina, was highly appealing for Keneally at that point. Nevertheless, in August an anxious Keneally was back on the train to the city.

This time he went to St Mary's Cathedral, where the waiting room was filled with boys who were there to meet Cardinal Norman Gilroy, Monsignor Charles Dunne, Rector of St Columba's Minor Seminary, Springwood, and Monsignor James Madden, Rector of St Patrick's College, Manly. They questioned each boy about his priestly aspirations.

The cardinal commented favourably on Keneally's scholastic achievements and his current studies in Leaving Certificate Latin as well as Honours English and History. Father Frank Darragh in *An Angel in Australia* could be Keneally:

> . . . he suffered from no learning problems or laziness . . . he was competent alike at such contrasting puzzles as cricket and algebra. Nothing befell him, not even in adolescence, to drive him to rebellion, or make him seek a world other that the one he knew . . . he had been exactly the sort of unsullied, unworldly, yet not stupid young man the seminary sought . . .[15]

'Have you made a definite decision yet, my dear young man?' asked the Cardinal.

Keneally was naive and lacking in maturity, but made his decision to go in good faith. Brother McGlade argued in 2013 that it was no different to deciding to be a doctor or engineer. 'He [Keneally] was not pushed or persuaded. But it was our sacred duty in a Catholic school to give religious instruction; it was the reason for the school's existence. To us, the most important part of the day was the talk we gave about the faith at midday every day before lunch.'

Keneally imagined himself transformed by ordination, advancing to bishop, cardinal or pope, treated with respect and even reverence. In *The Place at Whitton*, the book that reveals so much about the boy who would be a priest, the character Stenner, who 'at sixteen opted for the priesthood', sounds similar to Keneally:

> The priest, arriving in some dusty village on Sunday morning, having ridden or motored any prodigious distance . . . was a person of heroism and authority with the priestly powers in his dusty body, an ear to hear sin, a hand to blot it out, a tongue to change mere bread and wine . . .[16]

The Irish priests, or at least the village clergy and their counterpart parish priests in Australia, as Keneally understood it, were still living according to a social justice system. They ate the same food as the congregation, they did not live in grand houses, they owned no land and they were the spokesmen for their people. They had considerable political power, too, because of the clergy's long association with the Labor Party. The Homebush boy wanted to be a good and wise man who worked for his flock as a social justice advocate, as well as a holy man of the cloth.

At a deeper level, in a way that he could not articulate at the time, Keneally was aware that the homes he saw around him were not always happy. It did not seem such a hard thing to renounce marriage and family life. Although Father Darragh in *An Angel in Australia* was 'attached to his parents by an intense love of the kind which pre-empted any questioning,' Keneally wrote, 'he had seen nothing in their marriage to attract him to the married state.'

> Marriage – both their faces said it at different times – was hard, and uncertain . . . real life, and dogged love, seemed noble yet squalid. The memory of physical love, of what people called sex, seemed to tease people with wistful memory rather than make them happy. The priesthood, with its arcane knowledge, the drama of the rites, rose above the doubt and the ordinariness of the moment. It had a vestment, an incantation, and a soothing code only its priests understood. Who would not want to become a priest, and consider it an honour?[17]

Keneally was 'a slow developer', taken by surprise when he was confronted with a clear mental image of a woman with ample breasts, and also aware of recurring thoughts of a dark-complexioned girl in a blue dress, especially when one of the Brothers mentioned 'the holy state of matrimony'. He did not know what to make of these imaginings but was unsettled by them. He could see that there was ambiguity in McGlade telling his class that women were not interested in sex and men must make allowances for that lack of interest, while at the same time introducing a story like *Cakes and Ale* by Somerset Maugham, in which the promiscuous Rosie contradicted everything McGlade was saying about women and sexuality.

In the Christmas season of 1952 Keneally had a job in the packing room at Pellegrini's, Devotional Object Dealers and Booksellers, in George Street, Sydney. One day the unpleasant supervisor took his new assistant and a typist from the office down to the basement to find some shipping crates. The reason for the typist's presence soon became clear, as the supervisor crudely fondled her. Keneally was mortified by what 'sex' appeared to be: shame, reluctance, bullying, force and fear. It did not seem such a hard side of life to deny.

Keneally's indecision was a worrying presence as he worked his way through the final weeks of school. He was busy collecting Downie from his home at 17 Shortland Avenue[18] and reading textbooks to him; going to Mass regularly; studying for the final examinations; playing sport; consorting with Viney and the other Celestials; attending McGlade's after-school gatherings; and visiting the Rafferty and Davis homes.

A major change was about to happen in the Rafferty home. Mrs Rafferty was a good-hearted soul who regularly visited St Lucy's School for the Blind, where she did odd jobs for the nuns. Her daughters, Mary and Ruth, were sometimes there too, running errands. Mary took one of the blind girls, Diana Morgan, to Santa Sabina in the same way that Keneally took Downie to St Patrick's. Mother Philomena at Santa Sabina asked Mary if she was interested in becoming a Sister, and she said yes, although her mother was not happy about it. Keneally could not imagine how his outspoken, energetic friend would tolerate the silence and obedience expected of a Dominican.

Keneally has outlined in some detail the steps that led to Pamela Davis's decision to join the Dominican order too, a decision prompted (in his *Homebush Boy* account) by the deathbed request of 'Mother Concordia'. Davis has denied that any of the events took place: 'This is all nonsense. None of it happened.' Davis does agree with the *Homebush Boy* scene in which her mother was giving out cups of tea, just as

Keneally described it:

> As Mrs Curran [Davis] gave us tea, I said to her, 'I don't know about becoming a priest. Mrs Curran, I wonder if all your beautiful daughters would wait till I find out.'
>
> Everyone laughed, Rose Frawley [Mary Rafferty] indulgently. 'What a drongo,' she said softly to her tea.
>
> Mrs Curran said, 'I think you'd better stay at home with us, Mick.'

Other details that Keneally wove into his story about Davis and Rafferty entering the Dominican novitiate together are also fictional, but it is true that in October 1952, when he turned seventeen, Keneally made it known to his friends and family that he would 'go'. Breaking the news to his parents was the hardest part. Elsie reacted in much the same way as Verissimo's mother does in *The Place at Whitton*:

> She began to cry helplessly. 'I've put up with old dresses and shoes, *and* with your father's temper, just to get you a proper education. Now all that grinding and skimping will go for nothing. I want you to do what you like. But I don't want to lose you. It'd be as if you died. Don't go away! Please don't!'

Elsie had taken some comfort from another mother who said that boys inevitably married and then often neglected their mothers. For a priest, his mother remained the female focus of his life and he would be a truly filial companion.

Elsie had already taken it upon herself to tell Tom that their older son was thinking of becoming a priest. He made gloomy remarks: 'Just because Mary has volunteered, it doesn't bloody well mean he has to.' Elsie had persisted in her efforts to bring him around to the possibility. Tom wanted to know: 'Why doesn't he go to university and get a degree first?' That alternative had occurred to his son, but Father McGovern had strongly counselled against it, knowing that many promising boys liked the secular institution too much and forgot about the seminary.

Verissimo's father in *The Place at Whitton* is working in the garden when his wife comes to tell him of their son's decision.

> 'What a bloody waste,' his father said. 'But those bastards have no right ... We do all the rearing and sweating and they just step in and take him away.' Mrs Verissimo said with great clarity, 'If we don't let him do what he wants, it's all been wasted. We gave him what we did so that he can do what he wants to do.' After a silent dinner and a drab tea, she told him that he would be able to go with their blessing. And after a year or so they became aware that their son was a child of election ...

In fact, Tom and Elsie did start to take some pride in the idea of their son the priest. When word of his 'call' got around, they received consolatory and congratulatory greetings. Father and son had a few good times together before Keneally left home. One day they played tennis at the school. Tom asked, 'Do you think I'll get a discount in bloody purgatory? For having a son a sky pilot?' A 'sky pilot', in Tom's lingo, was a minister of religion.

Keneally, in the weeks before his departure, sometimes joined his father in the garden and tried to engage him in conversation about music and poetry. 'Too bloody deep for me,' Tom responded. 'Give me Banjo Paterson any day.'

Keneally did well in his Leaving Certificate examinations, taking second-class honours in English and history, and four As in his other subjects: Latin, maths, physics and chemistry. He won a scholarship to university, which he did not accept. By February 1953, when he entered the seminary, the Goodly Company had dispersed.

7

This Closed Society

Mick Keneally was an impressive Mark Antony. He played the part after weeks of rehearsal for the production of *Julius Caesar* at Springwood seminary. The part allowed Keneally, always an aspiring thespian, to orate dramatically. He gripped the folds of his white toga while showing the citizens of Rome the wounds to Caesar's body, including that inflicted by Brutus's dagger, 'the most unkindest cut of all'. Brutus, he said repeatedly, claimed that Caesar was ambitious, 'and Brutus is an honourable man'.

There is no photograph of Keneally the eager actor (who was also the director of the play), but there is one of the solemn seminarian a few years later at a graduation ceremony. M. Keneally, S.T.B., stared at the camera, his hair tonsured, his eyes blank behind large glasses. He was in formal regalia: black cassock, white clerical collar and crimson sash. But the young man who had so eagerly anticipated the glamour of the caped soutane would never wear it.

The Mick Keneally who entered Springwood seminary was ambitious, but his zealous spirit was cut down by men and their methods in what he had once believed to be an honourable institution. This destructive process began at Springwood and intensified at Manly. The perpetrators may not have been murderers, nor should their methods be blamed for the downfall of all 'spoiled priests', but some were undoubtedly villains or traitors to the church. Their various stabs destroyed something at the core of Keneally, and of many other well-intentioned young men.

Mark Antony pointed to Caesar's clothing: 'You all do know this mantle: I remember / The first time ever Caesar put it on ...' Keneally remembered the first time he donned the cassock, a proud moment at the start of his new life. The cassock provided comforting warmth in the chilly corridors of St Columba's College, Springwood, in the Blue Mountains west of Sydney.

For the seminary training of secular clergy in New South Wales, there were two stages. Springwood was the minor seminary, where candidates studied languages and literature, and began their studies in philosophy. They then progressed to the major seminary, St Patrick's at Manly, for advanced philosophy and theology and other 'heavy' subjects.

At the start of the academic year in 1953, Keneally boarded a train at Central Station to make the journey to Springwood, watching from the window as the illusory blue of the distant mountains became grey-green when the train climbed higher. He was about to commence life as a seminarian in what he would term 'this closed society'.[1] He soon became familiar with the relentless daily timetable, which began as one of the students walked between the rows of iron bedsteads in the dormitory, ringing a large bell.

The young men shivered as they washed and dressed in the big unheated room and made their way to the cold chapel. Morning prayers and meditation were followed by Mass before the first meagre meal of the day. Classes were interspersed with periods of recreation; then there was study in the evening and lights out at 10pm. Religious practices, like the 'Examination of Conscience' before the midday meal, were strictly observed. An evening walk was permitted, before the *summum silentium*, or 'solemn silence', descended on the place, not to be broken until after breakfast the next day.

Keneally was acutely depressed during his first two weeks at Springwood. The devout young Catholic could not understand this heavy state of mind. 'I finally decided that it was a test – a Christian test – to see if I was really made for the place,' he admits. 'That was typical of a devout Catholic – to see all your miseries as a test from God.' He has likened his unquestioning religious devotion to that of his pious grandmother,

Kate Keneally, who wore various scapulars and recited endless prayers for the release of souls in purgatory. 'In 1953 I had a strong belief, like the Irish farm girl my grandmother once was,' Keneally reflects. 'I prayed fervently and could sense the presence of God and the saints and the Virgin Mary. I felt that they were hearing my prayers.' As time went on, though, he suffered more 'dark nights of the soul', when he felt abandoned by God.

Keneally enjoyed studying, especially philosophy. Father George Joiner, who taught the first-year class, was not particularly inspiring as he worked his way through the textbook. He was nicknamed 'Anyway, Anyway' because he repeatedly used that phrase. In Keneally's opinion, Father Con Keogh, the lecturer in second year, was the most cultivated of the teachers, but by midyear he was a sick man. Students observed him staring fixedly at a picture of St Jerome in the hallway. The more he looked at it, the more he saw in it. This compulsive, paranoid behaviour ended with a mental breakdown and his removal from Springwood.

Keneally did not have a good relationship with Monsignor Charles Dunne, the rector, a sour, unlikeable man who taught Latin and English. Keneally admitted that he probably presented as an annoying, immature kid, prone to neurotic behaviour. He recalled that Dunne took an interest in the production of *Julius Caesar*, although he refused the director's request to play 'God Save the Queen' before the curtain went up. Keneally wanted his play to have the recognised atmosphere of a professional theatre, and the anthem preceded most Australian events of any note at that time. Dunne did not see it that way and proposed instead that the audience sing a hymn to the Virgin Mary, 'Hail, Queen of Heaven'.

After the very successful play, when Dunne gave a full review for the benefit of the college, Keneally himself rated no mention at all, realising later that it was because he had 'too much vaunting ambition. They – authority – don't like that.'

Before being accepted as a seminarian, Keneally had filled out an 'Information Paper' for Dunne's approval. Dunne was informed that Keneally had been 'adopted' by the Archbishop of Sydney, that his parents hoped to be in a position to contribute to the £100 annual pension needed to keep their son at the seminary, and that there was no hereditary sickness or insanity in the family. There had probably never been a professional diagnosis, but some years later Keneally wrote that his father came from a family that was 'spectacularly manic', and that there was also 'a marked eccentricity combined with this extraordinary melancholy'.[2]

Keneally also had to provide his certificate of baptism from Mary Immaculate Parish, Waverley; his certificate of confirmation from the Strathfield Parish; and his parents' certificate of marriage from the Catholic Presbytery, West Kempsey. Keneally worried later that one reason for his parents' reluctance to approve his entry to the priesthood was perhaps that they were ashamed of the authorities seeing a 'discrepancy' in the dates between their wedding day and their first son's birth.

Dunne was also given a medical certificate from the family doctor, Dr Buckley, which read: 'Michael has suffered from bronchial asthma for the past fifteen years, sometimes as frequently as every morning, often worse with approaching examinations and similar worries. However he has not requested any medical attention in the past five years, so mild are the above asthma attacks.' In pencil below the typed report, Buckley added: 'Sit on him if he has any attacks!'[3]

To Keneally's parents, Dr Buckley privately voiced his concerns about how their highly strung son would cope with seminary life. His young patient was altogether too scrupulous, and showed compulsive or obsessive tendencies. 'Scruples' could be regarded as a disease, caught or aggravated in seminaries and convents where too much time was devoted to mystic rites and meditation. In his submission to the Pope some years later, as he sought permission to 'revert to the lay state', Keneally explained that by the end of his third year of theological studies at Manly, his 'naturally scrupulous disposition began to manifest itself to an ever greater degree'.[4]

Father Williams, the priest in charge at St Dominic's Church at Flemington, told Dunne that he could highly recommend Keneally as a candidate for the priesthood. 'He is quite bright mentally and has a very good moral character,' Williams wrote in the reference that went ahead of the aspirant to Springwood. 'I wish I had a few more like him to send along.'[5] Brother Garvey, the principal of St Patrick's College, Strathfield, assured Dunne that Keneally was a lad of outstanding character. 'It is with the fullest confidence that I recommend him in his intention to study for the priesthood.'[6]

Springwood was spartan, but no more so than many boarding schools of the era. Prefects prowled about with orders to report miscreants to the Dean of Discipline, or to the rector for serious breaches of rules. His presence, like that of a much-feared headmaster, was a contributing factor to Keneally's anxiety; he regarded Dunne as an emotional bully. When the rector was away in Sydney, a carnival atmosphere prevailed at Springwood.

Unlike the young men who left school life behind to go to university or enter the workforce, Keneally and the other seminarians lived an institutionalised existence well into adulthood. This was often a contributing factor to unhappiness or discontent, and a cause of stunted maturity. 'There was nothing in the program to make you grow up,' Keneally says now, sixty years later.

Edmund Campion, who began his seminarian studies at Springwood in 1954 after attending university, points to a lack of freedom that could break the spirit. 'You were expected to be totally absorbed in the community. You were there to be re-moulded into an obedient cleric. You were not encouraged to think outside the circle.'

Campion recalls that Keneally was a 'good boy' who observed the rules and showed no signs of rebellion, as some did. Keneally was obsessed with rules. When he was producing *Julius Caesar* he was aware of time constraints and the near impossibility of being ready for the allocated night. Cast and crew worked overtime to bring the play together, making scenery and costumes. They slipped out of study rooms to work on the sets, which caused the director acute anxiety. 'I was tormented by the knowledge that I was a party to their violating the rules. I felt the rules were there to be kept at all cost, and disobeying them was a grave sin. These sensible young men were risking punishment for me and my play.'

Peter Harrington, who attended St Patrick's at Strathfield before Springwood, recalls that Keneally was well recognised for his piety: 'He was a very intense and focused student who addressed all areas of seminary life with great seriousness ... In my case, I was a very average student, a compliant seminarian who balanced the rigors of seminary life with my great interest in and participation in a range of sporting activities that were made available to us.' Harrington got to know Keneally well, and one day he admonished him: 'You take the rules too seriously.'

Other students remember Keneally as a quiet boy, small in stature, who could become animated in company and whose strong imagination frequently asserted itself. Most have happy memories of the long-term friendships they forged, even though one of the rules was that students must not form 'particular friendships'. It was inevitable that some young men became infatuated with other boys at the college. Keneally found that his innocent friendships with other students were important in rousing him from his initial depression, but he did not notice anything untoward in their behaviour. 'I wasn't aware of any funny stuff,' he says, 'but I wouldn't have expected to see it. I was innocent of that kind of knowledge, about homosexuality.'

Later, at Manly, Keneally knew that there were 'romances' or special attachments between boys who had become men in the transition from the mountains to the seaside. Suddenly, those involved would be gone and nothing said. Terence O'Neill, who attended the Corpus Christi seminary at Werribee in Victoria, says that there were some students with whom he felt very uncomfortable. He believes sexuality was badly handled at the seminary: 'It was not adequately discussed, but rather repressed or ignored.'

According to Keneally, Dunne was not always silent on the subject of sexuality, but what he did say was harmful. 'People only marry for lust,' Dunne claimed. He did not believe that there could be love or affection. In his own thinking about the accusations of sexual abuse levelled at Catholic priests, Keneally has concluded that those abusive practices may well be linked to the secrecy on the subject of sexuality in the priests' training years. 'Not having normal relationships was emotionally stunting,' he reasons. 'The seminary was a good – or bad – breeding ground for paedophiles. Not that they [seminarians] would go there intending to become paedophiles.'

In *An Angel in Australia*, written in 2002, the character Father Darragh is confronted in the confessional by a Christian Brother who has abused a boy. The Brother confesses:

> 'I took a boy, one of our favourites, to a private place, and I touched him, and he touched me.' Darragh had no idea why a young man would harbour *that* desire and then act upon it. For it destroyed the core of his vocation; the shepherd became the wolf. 'This child was put

into your care by God . . . Do you think he will ever forget? Do you think you can ever restore his innocence?'

Mental health was another issue. Keneally has grappled with the manifestations of madness that he saw in students and staff. Why were such vulnerable men, including himself, so attracted to the priesthood, for which they were temperamentally unsuited? 'What comes first?' asks Keneally. 'Is it the psychological flaw that draws them there, or is it the institution that brings out the flaw?' In some of his writing he has examined the unmaking of troubled young men.

These questions of madness and morality were far from his mind as he adjusted to Springwood. He was only seventeen years old. He sometimes joined the bookbinding team, which made covers for missals, extending the life of cardboard-covered books with mock leather jackets. He liked gardening as the workers could talk and enjoy being out of doors, and joined in rugby league and running. Chris Geraghty recalls Keneally as an enthusiastic footballer who would trudge indoors after the game, covered in mud. Keneally tried boxing too, drawn to the sport after seeing many boxing movies as a boy.

'At Springwood I boxed with a bloke called Murphy,' he remembers. 'He'd knock me about, but I was never concussed. I wasn't any good. Boxing was perfect for a neurotic Christian like me. I regarded all the blows as a test to my endurance! I'd think, *This is doing me good*.'

Most students had as much fervour for football matches as they did for religion. Rugby league contests dominated Thursday mornings at Springwood, with the annual match against Manly a much-anticipated highlight. Usually, the Manly 'red' team prevailed over the Springwood 'blue' in a contest somewhat reminiscent of State of Origin matches in the secular sporting world. Other than the big day of footy, when for once the refectory provided a lavish meal, outsiders and special provender were tolerated on two Sundays each semester. Elsie, Tom and Johnny made the trip to have a few hours with their son and brother, but the contents of Elsie's picnic basket had to be eaten on the day as rules forbade the hoarding of food.

The seminary picnics were happy outings. Springwood is situated in a beautiful location from which, on a clear day, the Sydney Harbour

Bridge and city buildings are visible in the distance. Campion remembers Keneally quoting Wordsworth as he took in the surroundings. Outdoor orators around Springwood were not unusual: some boys regularly read aloud to the trees, perhaps in an effort to memorise passages from textbooks or to hone their public speaking skills.

The seminarians also took it in turns to read to the assembled priests and students, with pious works chosen at breakfast and secular at the evening meal. The reading at the midday meal consisted of the Roman martyrology for the day, read in Latin. Without the help of a microphone, the reader at the rostrum was often inaudible amid the clatter of plates and cutlery, but Keneally could always be heard. He had a carrying voice and an enthusiastic style. He recalls reading from a book by Canon Patrick Augustine Sheehan, an Irish author and political activist.

Mass was celebrated daily. 'I liked the liturgy,' Keneally reflects. 'I still do. You could be happy during the Mass. The rituals and the vestments were serious business which I liked.'

The scruples that dogged Keneally at Springwood intensified at Manly, but as he made the transition from one seminary to the other, he still had no doubt at all about his vocation. He had been called to be a priest.

8

The Place at Manly

The building at St Patrick's seminary was 'a grotesque stone bulk growing from the earth as emphatically as a cathedral ... this cavernous symbol of his unhappiness'.[1] This is how Keneally remembers the place after he had fled its long corridors and lonely spaces, but he agrees that an aura surrounded St Patrick's College. When Cardinal Gilroy addressed the students, he liked to remind them, in his distinctive voice, of 'the superb-a view from Man-ly College'.[2] Gilroy enjoyed his own superb views at the 'Cardinal's Palace', just across Darley Road from the college, where he also had an exquisite private chapel; acolytes from the seminary assisted at his worship.

Gilroy routinely interviewed the seminarians individually. Each one would enter his study, close the door, genuflect, take hold of His Eminence's cold, soft hand and kiss his episcopal ring. Once seated, the student was put through a series of standard questions about health, studies and spiritual progress. Rarely would one make a complaint or raise a difficulty, although the question of food quality and quantity hovered on everyone's lips.

'Why don't you mention the matter of food to the Cardinal?' asks Joan in *The Place at Whitton*.

'I've got friends who have threatened to do that,' Verissimo replies. 'But when you get into the immaculate cardinalatial room and approach the man himself down that long polished table, and see the distinguished hand with its gleaming ring come up like a signal letting a train through... well, it's hard to think of this tack we eat and the Cardinal both existing in the same universe.'

Blimey Ted, the bursar in *The Place at Whitton*, dares to tell the Cardinal, as 'a matter of conscience', that he cannot keep dishing up the food on offer at the college, and cannot make the dietary budget stretch far enough to make improvements. The response is: 'Do you know that I have interviewed every student at Whitton within the past few months, and not one of them has complained about the food, and not one of them has looked underfed...'

Ed Campion has pointed out: 'As in a prisoner of war camp, so in a Tridentine seminary: your mind was constantly on food. It was like that at Whitton too.'[3]

Campion starts his book *A Place in the City* with the chapter heading and first sentence, 'It wasn't much fun living in the same house as Cardinal Gilroy.' Nor was it much fun living in the same house as Monsignor James Cole Madden at Manly, although by all accounts he was a mild man who genuinely cared about 'his' boys. In *The Place at Whitton*, Dr Stenner is recognisable as Madden (whom his students called Jimmy), 'known for his paternalism towards all the men of Whitton ... He ran a peaceful community, where the rules were well kept, and a startling variety of young men subordinated themselves to the good of the whole. Nothing was more important to him than the priesthood, and under his roof priests were made.' Madden is also Dr Nolan in *Three Cheers for the Paraclete*, Keneally's second seminary novel; the author observes that 'in so many ways he and his house were kindred. His conversation had a dated air that proved contagious.'

Keneally remembers telling Madden about a discovery he had made in literature: 'I had just read a novel by a young Tasmanian, and I told Jimmy how remarkable it was that a young kid who had been to a Catholic school in Tasmania had had a novel published. I was bowled over by that. It was Christopher Koch and *The Boys in the Island*. The book was given to me by Eddie Campion, who was up on that sort of stuff. I told Madden about it: "They went to parties for all sorts of people including jockeys and they called them jags!" I lost him at "went to parties"!'[4]

At Manly, Dr (later Bishop) Thomas Muldoon, Professor of Dogmatic

Theology and Dean of the Pontifical Theological Faculty, stood out as large as his titles. Nicknamed 'the Bull' because of his roaring voice and bellicose manner, he becomes Dr Onions, Stenner's sidekick in *The Place at Whitton*, and the canon lawyer Dr Costello in *Three Cheers for the Paraclete*. Costello is 'a princely man' whose blithe methods for 'plumbing the Godhead' are the source of jokes among students. Muldoon, like Costello, was destined for high office. When Madden announced at breakfast that Muldoon had been appointed auxiliary bishop to Cardinal Gilroy, Keneally was present. He may well have whispered, as Maitland does in the fictional version: 'Three cheers for the Paraclete!' He is ironically suggesting that the Holy Spirit is supposed to choose wise men. Keneally saw at first hand Muldoon's self-aggrandisement, as the lordly 'vessel of election' beamed and strutted.

Keneally despised Muldoon and undoubtedly took pleasure in taking him down a peg or two. He sums Muldoon up as 'a drunk and an arrogant bastard'. Chris Geraghty remembers a day when Muldoon was talking to visitors in the college grounds: 'He was holding his cigarette high in the air, talking loudly and demanding attention. Suddenly he turned to a student, handed him the butt and said, "Here Mick. Take this out and get rid of it." Tom Keneally took the sacred relic and obediently disposed of it. But he did feel somehow compromised. This regal way of treating students offended Tom's Australian sense of egalitarianism.'[5]

In *Three Cheers for the Paraclete*, when Costello, the bishop-elect, is entertaining a circle of priests in the parlour and disparaging Gerard Manley Hopkins, he hands his half-smoked cigarette to Maitland. Costello says, 'Would you mind getting rid of this for me, James?' Maitland shakes his head. 'He could see in Costello's sovereign-looking cheeks the assumption that no one could refuse him anything so simple, decent and do-able as this.'

Many of the inmates of the 1950s and early 1960s have images so firmly impressed in their minds that they still dream of Manly. 'For years afterwards,' Campion wrote in *Rockchoppers: Growing Up Catholic in Australia*, 'I would have nightmares that I was back inside those walls. The Abbé de Sieyes, when asked what he had done during the glorious years of the French Revolution, replied simply, "I survived." That was my attitude to the seminary.'[6] Paul Crittenden always dreams of the main building that was the centre of his universe for several years. In Keneally's dreams, he knows that he has to leave: 'I have to escape. I am going to leave one night and I'm worried about packing up – I have always taken too much luggage!'

In his years at Manly Keneally was working his way through some heavy subject matter, including ethics, cosmology, canon law, and all sorts of theology: fundamental, dogmatic and moral. Keneally was admitted to the award of Bachelor of Sacred Theology (*Bene Probatus*) in 1957. The number of subjects each candidate had to study was daunting – eleven in 1957. Keneally's marks were consistently high, particularly in sacred scripture and ecclesiastical history, and his thesis was based on the works of the early church fathers, including Tertullian. Patrology, the study of the writings of those men, was one of his favourite subjects. He did not do so well in Greek or Hebrew, and his results in 1959 were noticeably lower.[7]

To reach the goal of ordination, Keneally had to advance to various levels, which began with a ceremony at the end of his first year of theology. He applied to the Right Reverend Monsignor James Madden on 14 September 1956:

> Dear Monsignor,
>
> I, Thomas Michael Keneally, as a student of the first year of theology, destined for the service of the Archdiocese of Sydney, humbly request to be promoted to the First Tonsure and the Minor Orders. I make this request of my own free will, convinced that I have a divine vocation and determined to persevere with divine help in my efforts to obtain to the Priesthood.
>
> Yours obediently, T. M. Keneally.[8]

Tonsure at Manly meant the cutting of a lock of hair from the crown of the head. The ritual was accompanied by admission to the Minor Orders of doorkeeper and lector, and a year later to those of exorcist and acolyte. At the end of the third year, Keneally applied for Major Orders: subdeacon and deacon. The ultimate honour of priesthood would be conferred in the middle of the fourth year of theology.

Like Springwood, Manly permitted a literary and debating club, which Keneally enjoyed because he loved public speaking. Crittenden remembers that Keneally won the oratory competition, which was usually judged by Muldoon: 'Keneally won at least twice. He was a revelation to me. A lot of what was said by others was correct and rather dull and didactic. Tom spoke with a passion, in a rich voice. It was quite impressive. I can remember the two topics that he spoke about: one was a sort of paean of praise for the Middle Ages. It was a kind of troubadour performance. It was perhaps an exaggerated picture of the period but a great performance. The other one was when he spoke about the race to the South Pole, the great race between Robert Scott and Roald Amundsen.'

There was also the 6.45 Club, which focused on cultural aspirations; Keneally read a paper on modern literature at its inaugural meeting. Predicting the future of modern fiction, the young man who would be at its forefront in Australia, almost within the next decade, became expansive:

> All is set for a change in fiction. There are those who say it will be given a new vitality, a new freshness from the introduction of a new, vivid, infinitely penetrating, infinitely fresh character, namely God. And it will tell of human goodness and not of human evil only. But good or bad men, good or evil actions, the presence of this active, real character will give them all a meaning. That is something new.

Keneally went on to examine Graham Greene's book *The Heart of the Matter*. Greene, he said, was obsessed with Catholicism and sordidness:

> . . . and because of the second he is certainly a danger for young people. But it wasn't the sordidness that made people like this book. It was God who stole the show because he gave Scobie's suicide an intense meaning such as few other suicides in literature have. And this book is but a hint of what can be done with a new type of fiction which could and should come, which would be accepted.
>
> Now this new fiction would deal with men and women like those of the old, but they and their actions would be judged and regulated by the entry of a new, virile, intensely alive, intensely penetrating character, namely God . . . Simply it will tell of men and women and their actions but whether it tells of good men or evil men, good actions or

> evil actions, it will do so in the light of the love of the ever-fresh, ever-new, ever scintillating personality, God.

In many Keneally books to come, the central character would not be God but what Campion calls 'members of the God squad'.[9]

Keneally also wrote some tentative poetry at Manly, including 'Diptheria [sic]: The Crisis', already mentioned. Another poem was 'Ten to Six', written in 1957:

These are your people, God.
Their lives: straight as a knife,
And clean in Your sight.
Their hearts, plump with your love,
Shrug off the night
While the sea is still a black plain.
My Farmer, swift with your hoe!
Swing it and show
Gleam of their fruit in the day.
Hidden earth they.
Seeded and moist.[10]

The young priests who went out into the world from Manly shared Keneally's idealism. They certainly weren't all bad, and many did a lot of good. Keneally was not among them, but he writes about their shared training experience in his 'seminary novels'. His descriptions of 'the place' are familiar to all 'Manlians': the magnificent Cerretti Chapel, the upstairs and downstairs rooms of the old building, and even the pigsties, where the first murder in *The Place at Whitton* presumably occurred.

The murderer is on the loose on dark, stormy nights, prowling about a big, ugly building: classic whodunnit stuff. The absurdities and depravities of the book, including a suspected *mauvais prêtre* (evil priest), are bolstered by a humorous poke at some of Manly's prohibitions and pretensions. Verissimo has regular visits from 'Joan of Arc', laughable in a place that banned women but in which many longed for a feminine presence. From Keneally, who loves women's apparel, comes the line, in Verissimo's voice: 'Don't you ever get sick of the same clothes?'

In both seminary books, Keneally gives prominence to students who are sick. Verissimo has visions and is close to a nervous collapse. He tries to explain his state of mind to Dr Onions: 'Your mind begins to shuttle round and round in the one compulsive circle; Whitton suddenly becomes a prison. There are no distractions to slow down the mind or draw it off its track. There's too much silence; the night is too long; prayer is a torment . . .'

Verissimo has a mild case of insanity, lightened by the farce of what is happening around him. Maurice Hurst in *Three Cheers for the Paraclete* is a more seriously ill victim of the system – his repeated assertions that 'I find it hard sometimes not to run wild at table' are not really comic. Hurst is 'a nervous student perpetually brought down with boils, viruses and impetigo, [who] wrestled angels in his sleep and snuffled at the job'. His confessor, Costello, hears his distressed outpouring about his extreme scruples:

> He [Hurst] explained how he had begun by feeling liable, in God's terrible eye, for all the corner-cutting, jay-walking, bus-hanging and variously endangered species of that city. He had once pulled the emergency chain on a ferry because children were running around the decks. Not that he thought of their lungs bursting fathoms down in the bay. But he was convinced that *he* was liable with unlimited liability. Under God.

Keneally worked his own experiences into those of the sick men. As he neared the end of his time at Manly, he showed indications of a mental breakdown. Even during holiday time at home, he felt compelled to draw the local council's attention to some cracks in the pavement. It was his duty to prevent an accident, or so he believed. When talking about his experience more than sixty years later, the hurt of it all is still evident:

'As the abuse stories show, there was no social justice there, and there was no social justice when blokes got sick, whether physically or mentally. They were let go and the church paid for nothing. When I was going crazy they sent me to a psychiatrist. I paid the bills. They sent me to a bloke who was more under the counter than they thought. He gave me a little book on self-damage to help if you felt that the will had to be supreme over everything. That's what we were told – the will, with the help of grace, is supreme over everything. That's what the child abusers were told ...

'They [the authorities] did have a sense of intervention when men had deteriorated beyond the pale; they'd seen it all before. Hurst was partly based on me. I've got this obsessive streak. It's helped me be a novelist. Your greatest weaknesses are also your greatest strengths. Your greatest virtues are also your greatest vices. I became obsessed that some of the crockery was cracked. I knew that bacteria thrived in crockery and I felt I had to go and see about it. It was a sign of how sick I was – I went and saw the rector, and told him there were cracks. He thought it was pretty funny.

'I do feel a lot of scruples. I don't carry my sins lightly. I tend to spend a lot of time suppressing memories of meannesses and viciousnesses in my past – they recur in idle hours. The old scruples will rush in as they did in those days.'

St Patrick's was a cold sanctuary in more ways than one. The damp, unheated main building was a breeding ground for tuberculosis, as Keneally recalled in 2002: 'The government required all citizens to have annual chest X-rays, but, because of the unhealthy nature of the building, had sought the rector's approval to check the seminarians biannually. The rector, a monsignor, refused. His concern was not that we might be overexposed to roentgens but that every time the X-ray trailer, with its crew of young nurses visited the seminary there would be an increase in the number of seminarians departing for "the world".'[11]

Madden himself was not a robust man, and every winter he had a severe cold or bronchitis. Yet, Keneally continues, 'when two of my friends contracted TB and needed lung surgery, the rector and the archdiocesan authorities took no responsibility. My friends' parents bore all the medical expenses, including those for long recuperations in a sanatorium. The young men were welcome to return if they recovered, but they received no gesture of sympathy, no gift, no visits from the staff of the seminary.'[12]

Keneally wanted, like Hurst, to be at all costs an ordained priest. Like Verissimo, he had 'coveted' that day of being 'priested' for all those years. He had to reach the point of accepting, as Hurst did, that to be a priest was not everything. Maitland urged Hurst to reconsider his vocation. 'I think we're two good lads ruined by the poisonous old idea that willpower will get you anything,' he suggested to Hurst.

Maitland tells Nolan, in language that Keneally's father would have gleefully used, that he has nothing but contempt for the House of Studies: 'It depressed the tripes out of me as a student and gives me the gorblimeys as an adult.' Maitland is resigned to the probability that his fate will be 'some parish accustomed to rugged fund-raising clergy who trained the youth organisation football team to a grand-final pitch and held boxing evenings'.

Keneally was not destined to share that fate.

9

Jesus and His Mates

Keneally still believed, as he had written in a letter to his bishop, Gilroy, on 18 November 1958, that he had a calling from God:

> I, the undersigned, Thomas Keneally, in presenting to the Bishop my petition for the reception of subdeaconship and deaconship, as the time for the sacred ordination is near at hand, having carefully considered the matter before God, do upon my oath testify in the first place that I am urged by no sort of compulsion or force or fear in receiving the aforesaid sacred orders, but I do spontaneously desire and of my own full and free will wish to receive the same, because I know and feel that I am truly called by God.
>
> I acknowledge that I know fully all the burdens and other consequences which flow from the said sacred orders, and these I freely wish and propose to assume; and with the grace of God I resolve to keep them faithfully during my whole life. I declare especially that I am clearly aware of what the law of celibacy entails; and I firmly resolve with the help of God to fulfil that law willingly and to keep it in its entirety until the end.
>
> Finally, I sincerely promise that I shall always, according to the sacred canons, obey most exactly all the precepts of my Superiors, and whatever the discipline of the Church requires, being prepared to give

an example of virtue either in work or in word, in such wise that I may desire to be rewarded by God for the assumption of so great an office.

This I promise, this I vow, this I swear so help me God and these sacred Gospels which I touch with my hand.

Thomas Keneally[1]

Keneally became a subdeacon in November 1958, one of the smiling group photographed in their albs and lacy surplices outside the chapel. Keneally left the seminary later that day and was not present the following morning, when his group became deacons. His absence was much talked about before the students left for the Christmas holidays; it had been noticed the previous evening and a tremor of concern had passed around, but by then the college was in silence. His fellow subdeacons assumed that Keneally was ill or had suffered an attack of 'nerves'.

The latter conjecture was close to the mark: Keneally had felt unable to make a further commitment. The title of subdeacon was more readily dispensable, but becoming a deacon was to enter a Major Order, a more formal obligation on the way to the priesthood. While his friends enjoyed their new status as deacons, he retreated. His plan was to take leave. In his papal petition in 1961, Keneally explained that it was 'with apostolic indult' that he was 'subsequently ordained to holy Diaconate'.[2] An apostolic indult was a formal permission from the Pope to do something that was outside the standard provisions of canon law.[3] In Keneally's case, it must have been a concession about the period of time permitted between his ordination to the diaconate and then to the priesthood. It is probable, then, that Keneally was ordained a deacon at some time between March and July 1959.

At this point, the church did help out, finding a suitable occupation for the unhappy deacon-elect. Interestingly enough (as Keneally is fond of saying), Bishop James Carroll contacted him with papers concerning 'the Movement', which Carroll wanted documented. A strained relationship existed between the Melbourne and Sydney branches of the Catholic Church in their support of B. A. Santamaria's organisation, which had been established under general church backing in Melbourne against communist power in the trade unions.

The Melbourne line (led by Archbishop Daniel Mannix and Santamaria) was to push on with more social and political reform under church direction; the Sydney line (led by Gilroy and Carroll) was that the communist-linked crisis in Australian politics was largely over and the church should step back. Carroll was a political operator with strong connections to the Australian Labor Party (ALP), especially in New South Wales. In 1954 the ALP had split: members of the Movement were expelled and went on to form the Democratic Labor Party (DLP).

Carroll was the man in Sydney who opposed Santamaria on behalf of the hierarchy, which had decided that the church should not continue supporting a political machine like the Movement. It is probable that Carroll needed the services of a young man known for his skills as a researcher and writer to formalise all that had happened, perhaps in a detailed submission. Keneally's name was put forward, perhaps also with the hope that the work would help him recover his health and wellbeing. He would be accommodated in Bowral, an attractive town about 120 kilometres south-west of Sydney.[4]

He says: 'I forget who it was took me down to Bowral to a guesthouse of some fashion, à la 1959, saying it was his favourite boarding house. It could have been the fruit wholesaler who gave me money when I left the seminary or someone surnamed David, for he certainly came into it somewhere, as a Maronite Lebanese Catholic. I started working on documentation about the Movement and wrote a draft in longhand, which I gave to the man I remember as David. But the project did not proceed. As readily as a ruined priest will take guilt, I don't believe the cessation of the project was my fault; something happened to negate it. I was interested in the project because I believed in the cause.'

Keneally believed in the Movement's anti-communist focus, and he also believed in the way it was driven by social justice issues, but he was not aware of an agenda in the work he was asked to do. 'I was aware that the Sydney archdiocese was not as wrapped up in the Movement as Melbourne, but that it was their anti-communism which united them. Like Campion, I was a believer but the scales fell from my eyes, and though that residual Catholicism–communist tension remained with me, I was never a DLP man. That was rather characteristic of the Sydney archdiocese. As great a taste as I had for extremism, and an appetite for the relief offered by subjecting yourself to a great orthodoxy that did the thinking for you, I was reaching a frame of mind in which Catholic issues meant less and less to me, other than that the church itself was venal.'[5]

Keneally returned to Manly, where only he could settle the dispute in his mind about ordination. Instead of being among the beaming, newly ordained priests at St Mary's Cathedral on 18 July 1959, the group he had been with for several years, Keneally had started consulting a doctor not far away in the city. On 13 July Dr Frederick Kyneur wrote to Madden:

> Dear Father Madden,
>
> I saw Michael Keneally. I am able to give him definite help for his psychological sufferings. It will take time. I suggest his ordination may be best postponed for twelve months. Regardless, I will continue to help him.
>
> Yours sincerely,
>
> F. J. Kyneur

Keneally went back to see Dr Kyneur two weeks later, and Madden was duly informed:

> Dear Doctor Madden,
>
> I have seen Mr Keneally this afternoon. He has got hope about his whole condition. He is tired out; and I agree a rest in the country would be excellent. I suggest two months. I will see him after his return.

When his patient made the return visit on 23 September 1959, Dr Kyneur issued him with a 'Continuation Certificate', which read: 'This is to state that Thomas Keneally has seen me today. He is still suffering from nervous exhaustion and is not fit to resume his training for a further three months.'[6]

Kyneur was 'subversive' in his approach to Keneally, or so the patient described the doctor's probing. 'He questioned the role of the will,' Keneally says. 'He did not see the will, as we had been taught, as omnipotent.' Kyneur gave Keneally a tract about progressing by resignation rather than by forcing the will to the point of exhaustion. Although Keneally remembers Kyneur as one of the most sensible men he had ever met, he was unable to achieve that level of complete resignation. This was an issue that he confronted later with alcohol. Willpower, as Maitland tells Hurst in *Three Cheers for the Paraclete*, will not prevail over everything. Hurst's doctor agrees. 'He doesn't like the way we're trained. He thinks it's anti-human,' Hurst reports. 'He says that we are taught that the will can conquer anything and that we wear ourselves out by trying not to – in my case – maim people.'

Keneally did not have any desire to maim people, but he had worn himself out. He had tried to express some of his doubts to his 'spiritual director' at Manly, as he recalls: 'Mark Hall, the spiritual director, was a dear old bloke but hopeless at the profounder questions. But he was a bloke you could go to without being judged and a bloke you could easily talk to. I went to him. You had to go to your spiritual director who was a priest. I didn't ever really define my problems to him except in terms of "Father, I might be feeling doubts." To which he said, "Just wait it out. It will all come back. Act as if you have faith and faith will be given you."

'In *The Verdict*, a favourite film of mine, Paul Newman plays the part of an Irish lawyer in Boston. He says if you have problems with faith, act as if you have faith and faith will be given to you. This was a convenient aphorism which was commonly offered. Basically, Hall's response was the same. It was a relief to operate on a fairly easy level! Although my confessor told me that my doubts were a direct temptation from Satan. I forget who it was. It could have been Bishop Muldoon.'

Keneally's crisis of confidence had little to do with discovering that certain priests were odd or capable of cruelty. The Keneallys' family doctor had warned Elsie that 'Michael has idealised the Church. It's going to be a great shock to him when he finds out that priests are human.' And it did not take Keneally long to do so. 'A week in the seminary taught me that much,' he wrote. 'The crisis came from my realisation that, behind the compelling mystery of Catholicism, with its foundation in the message of "Caritas Christi" (words engraved on a stone wall at St Patrick's), lay a cold and largely self-interested corporate institution.'[7]

As his disenchantment with Manly intensified, Keneally dared in small ways to defy the sterility of it all. In a seminar conducted by Monsignor Veech, Keneally made casual reference to 'Jesus and His mates'. Veech, who could not countenance such irreverence, spat out, 'Jesus didn't have *mates*.' He thought that Keneally was a strange man and Keneally thought the same about him.

Chris Geraghty recalls an occasion when Veech was critiquing a 'practice' sermon that Keneally gave. Veech commented favourably on the young man's delivery but was cruel in his personal comment. 'You are not physically prepossessing as a public figure in the pulpit,' he told Keneally.

For a while Keneally exchanged one community of men for another by becoming a builder's labourer. He travelled out to Hay by train in the spring of 1959. It would be hard to think of any greater distance, both in miles and imagination, than that between a big old Gothic building on Sydney's North Shore and a corrugated-iron hut out on the Hay plains in south-western New South Wales. This was the area that A. B. Paterson wrote about in 'Hay and Hell and Booligal':

And people have an awful down
Upon the district and the town.
In fact the saying far and wide
Along the Riverina side
Is 'Hay and Hell and Booligal' . . .

Keneally's uncle Lou Gurney had been an ally since wartime days, when he'd visited the house in Loftus Crescent to court Elsie's younger sister, Marie. After the war Lou took on work as a building contractor, and when his nephew needed to get right away from Sydney, Lou offered him work.

After the psychological rigours of a place where you could seemingly never do anything right, Keneally had now entered a very different camp of men who were good-humoured and tolerant, if bemused by this young stranger who had exchanged his cassock for work clothes. 'The blokes I worked with were very earthy,' Keneally recalls. 'Every second word was a swear word. They tried to suppress it but it would come out. They got used to me and found I was a harmless unworldly sod.'

The men were pulling down old soldier-settler houses built after the First World War. Keneally wielded a pinch bar to pull up the floorboards and stack them. He recalls: 'They were very poignant places because you'd find newspapers from the 1920s and '30s when they [the soldier-settler farmers] went broke . . . The other workers got on with more sophisticated stuff. I'd pull the nails out of the corrugated iron and stack the sheets of iron. That would keep you busy! If the men were working on a new house I did all the nail punching and puttying – I did stuff like that rather than fine work, but it was not all charity. I was handy to have around. There was a house Lou was building north of Hay, and the bloke he built it for had taken his hay in and had no one to load it, so he used me and a couple of his other workers. It cut my hands to ribbons. Only sissies wore gloves.'

Back in town at the end of the day, the men all headed for the nearest pub. 'I began my association with drink, which has been an ambiguous one,' Keneally admits. 'Another new experience then – I didn't get drunk but got merry! I still had the seminarian conscience. To get drunk was a mortal sin!' In response to a pre-ordination questionnaire, Keneally's parish priest's answer to the question 'Is he fond of comforts, of much wine or liquors, and profane amusements?' had been: 'No! He is most abstemious.'[8]

The character Buchanan in *The Place at Whitton* has a fear of cold and of thirst:

> His thirst craved far richer satisfaction than water and tea and hinted at profound fires on some level of his soul rather than a mere dryness in the chest ... Buchanan had sworn that no matter what the loneliness, no matter what had to be escaped, he would never look for an opiate in a bottle. To belong to the jaded ranks of the international fraternity of escapist drinkers would be death for him. But his basic fear was that some all-knowing enemy would discover these two frailties, and use them to decompose his soul ...

Reading that sixty years later, Keneally laughs. 'There speaks a future problem drinker!' Alcoholism would be a lifetime concern, but perhaps at this stage the 'real' Keneally was also starting to emerge in a different environment. This was the man who loved to talk and be part of a convivial crowd; the man with a marvellous sense of humour, who could mix easily with all sorts of company. 'I found I liked pluralist society,' he said in 2002. 'I got a taste for pluralist Australia.'[9]

Occasionally, Keneally boarded a train and travelled home. This meant confronting his future again, but he could not discuss it with Tom and Elsie. The familiar sense of failing them returned as he grappled with his anxieties: 'When I first left the seminary I told them it was a passing problem. You couldn't say I'm tormented; they [the church] have no charity. We know now that was the way the institutional church dealt with its problems. But to say it then would have been the height of heresy. I'd just talk about the work at Hay. Men were supposed to be boiler proof in those days. They certainly never admitted they had doubts or problems . . . I think my father was depressed after the war but he would have lacked the vocabulary to say it. That generation never said anything like that.'

After a light brush with 'the world' in remote Hay, Keneally had begun to see things in a different light. He identified himself as a 'late developer'; in those last months at Manly his sexuality was 'kicking in'. He was never tempted by other men in the seminary. 'I had absolutely no sexual encounter,' he says. 'I think that was true of a lot of the blokes. They were so concentrated on suppressing their heterosexuality that they didn't see any adequate remedy.' In the scraps of early stories and ideas for stories that have survived, there is one that Keneally started writing in red biro:

> At sixteen, very devout and pinker than a baby, he had been all sorts of heretics. He had believed in predestination. He had been a Manichean, hating the flesh, which for him meant marriage, horrific familiarity with some woman – the same bed, the same table, the same toilet. To such a boy, the priesthood suggested itself as the highest form of beauty and refuge. As he grew older he was amazed to find that people regarded celibacy as an exotic, crippling superfluity . . .[10]

Keneally in his early twenties was shy and awkward around girls. He was, according to that questionnaire sent to his parish priest at Homebush, 'most proper and respectful' with persons of the opposite sex.[11] Keneally recoiled when one of his female friends from schooldays tried to kiss him on the cheek. He had begun to question whether his increasingly irrepressible desire for women was a sin. Sexuality was not the overt issue for his decision to leave the priesthood. 'But sexuality is always there,' he later reasoned, '[and] the more assiduously repressed, the more likely to cause psychic mayhem. Obviously, this sexual pressure had something to do with what I thought of – and still half think of – as a failure to measure up.'[12]

One day he had what he described as a feeling that there was someone out there who was part of him. 'I could feel her presence but I could not visualise her,' he recalled years later. 'But she was the other side of my soul, which is a very shoddy image, and there was an impulse in me to find that person. Actually my sexuality was so suppressed that I imagined us walking on the beach together. I didn't imagine any more intimate connection.'[13]

Somewhere along the way, Keneally's vision of the heroic priest had faded: he knew he was not ready or willing to be saying the Mass or advising anxious young matrons about birth control. Nevertheless, he returned to Manly at the beginning of March 1960, and prepared for ordination on 16 July.

It was rather like a bride preparing for a wedding: there was a venue to book for the ordination breakfast, invitations to print, vestments to design and purchase, holy pictures to order (which gave details of the first Mass, to be distributed as a memento to those in attendance), and a personal sacred chalice to consider. Elsie and Tom arranged the venue and caterers in Ashfield, invitations were sent out and two ladies who owned the local milk bar in Homebush gave him an expensive chalice. Each ordinand had to practise 'dry' or 'blank' Masses, going through the motions of 'saying Mass' at the small altars behind the main one in the chapel.

Classes continued in the lead-up to 16 July. Keneally had resumed fourth-year theology, having fallen behind during his absence the previous year, yet he was becoming more and more anxious. He did not confide in anyone, but talked easily and naturally to friends such as Crittenden, then a curate at Mosman, who spoke to him near the chapel about everyday things. Peter Downie, another seminarian, saw Keneally at the annual Manly versus Springwood football match, watching the game and chatting to people.

Campion heard Keneally walking about in his room above a classroom. Geraghty noticed Keneally wandering up and down, reciting the breviary and performing as deacon at Sunday High Mass. By early July 1960, however, it was all falling apart. 'I couldn't move,' Keneally recalled.

'I couldn't go to mass, I couldn't get to the chapel, I couldn't study. Classic signs of a kind of crack-up.'[14] Friends 'outside', like Mary Rafferty, felt he was becoming more and more withdrawn.

The ordination ceremony was preceded by a retreat at Manly. The typical routine over six days included communal and private prayer, meditation, Mass, chanting as in an abbey or a monastery, and a series of spiritual talks by the chosen 'Retreat Master'. A rule of silence prevailed throughout. After one day of this, Keneally was finished, and he informed Madden that he could not proceed to ordination. He also asked Madden for a reference which might help him start life anew. Madden's response was chilly: 'The Church does not give references.'

The refusal affected Keneally deeply. 'Although I had willingly tried to satisfy the demands of the Church for six years, he was telling me that the institution owed me nothing,' Keneally would later record. 'It was up to me to remake myself with the few un-useful resources I had acquired (among them an ability to speak Medieval Latin). The rector's indifference to my future was not the "social justice" of which bishops spoke, and I left the meeting furious.'[15]

Keneally's departure went virtually unnoticed, but David Coffey, who was completing his doctoral studies at Manly in 1960, was on the ferry that Keneally boarded. Coffey was surprised to see the priest-elect there, knowing that he should have been on retreat. Nothing was offered in the way of explanation, and the two men talked of various things. It was only when Coffey returned to Manly later in the day that he heard the news: Keneally had left and he was not coming back.[16]

Twelve months later, on 31 August 1961, Keneally submitted a request to Pope John XXIII, who had given this advice to seminarians a few months earlier: 'We say to you, first of all: Walk worthily. These words outline for you the necessity of leading a worthy life, harboring high ideals and purposes, and preserving a spotless priestly character.'[17] Keneally would walk worthily, but not as a priest. His letter to the Pope was written in Latin; translated, it reads:

> Most Blessed Father,
>
> I, Thomas Keneally, who has signed below, a deacon of the Archdiocese of Sydney, having prostrated myself at the feet of Your Holiness,

> humbly petition that I might revert to the lay state, with the remission of all clerical obligations, specifically those pertaining to the recitation of the divine office and to the observance of celibacy.
>
> Having completed to the end of the third year a course of theological studies at St Patrick's Seminary, Archdiocese of Sydney, I was ready for ordination to holy Subdiaconate, which I received in the month of November 1958, and then with apostolic indult was subsequently ordained to holy Diaconate.
>
> After ordination to the Diaconate my naturally scrupulous disposition began to manifest itself to an ever greater degree, such that, as the time of my ordination to the priesthood approached, in the middle of my fourth year of theology, I began to fear that I would not be able to cope with the responsibilities of priestly life. Following expert medical advice I spent part of the 1959 scholastic year at home; however, still aspiring to the priesthood I resumed fourth year theology in the following year, 1960. To be frank, however, my scrupulousness has not been overcome and thus I am not in a fit state for holy ordination. With a full year now having elapsed, I have been made aware that I will never in the future be able to undertake the onerous duties of the priesthood. Therefore for the good of my soul I humbly implore Your Holiness that permission be granted for me to revert to the lay state.

Madden submitted a document supporting Keneally's request, the Sacred Congregation for the Propagation of the Faith acceded, and Cardinal Gilroy communicated the decision to Keneally. All of these documents were written in Latin. On 22 September 1961 Keneally signed a statement in English: 'I have read and understood the Rescript referred to above [in Gilroy's statement], and do this day freely accept the favours and dispensations contained therein.'[18]

10

Banal and Glorious Motives

Knowledge of Latin, the language of the Roman Catholic Church, was one of the positive things Keneally took away from the seminary. Understanding the origins of words and appreciating their history would be a valuable asset for him as a writer. In future there would be a lighter side, too. One day his daughter Margaret asked Keneally to translate some common rugby league phrases into Latin, including 'Don't spit the dummy', 'He's been doing it all day, ref' and 'Keep him onside, ref'.

When he walked away from Manly, though, Keneally could never have imagined such levity in his life. Nor could he have predicted how language would soon *become* his life. All he needed in 1960 was the silent language of protective loyalty, and Tom and Elsie spoke this eloquently. The way they welcomed him home without reproach was a source of wonder to Keneally, who attributed it to their working-class spirit of solidarity.

Keneally returned to the small back bedroom at Loftus Crescent which he shared with his younger brother, Johnny, who had begun studies in the School of Medicine at the University of Sydney. Keneally was lethargic, wanting to do nothing more than slot pieces into a jigsaw puzzle, which seemed somehow symbolic of his need to reconstruct his life. He was the semi-invalid of his asthmatic days again, lying about with a book or talking to Elsie. His childhood sense of failure returned, and his longing to make it up to his parents. Elsie worried about him, as she always had, fearing he might end up in a psychiatric institution.

Keneally's almost irresistible desire to flee the real world intensified. 'If it had not been for the sense of duty I had to my parents, I think I would have joined the merchant navy,' he now laughs. Tom and Elsie made no demands, nor did they deliver any ultimatums. Keneally felt he was in debt to them.

His work experience was limited. He once worked in the Christmas holiday period for Marchant's, a soft drink company, delivering orders to shops throughout Sydney. Keneally has good memories of that job. 'I remember one sweltering day just before Christmas we went to the Villawood Migrant Camp and delivered cases upon cases of soft drinks. The soft drink would occasionally explode in the back – you'd hear it go off like a rifle shot. The heat would shine down and set a bottle off and there'd only be eleven left in the box, so you had to make up the dozen from another box ...'

He also worked as a copy-editor's assistant for *The Catholic Weekly*. He liked the copy-editor, whose bawdy commentary would one day be matched by Keneally's own irreverent sense of fun. 'The bloke who did the copy-editing was also a ruined priest and a bit of a lost and lonely soul,' he says. 'But he had talent and wit and could have written a novel easily. I'm not saying that the system only produced victims; it produced quite viable human beings. This bloke was approaching middle age. We had great fun – he was a funny bloke! We'd read copy to each other and pick up the mistakes.' It is probable that this was Ken Scully, who published poetry in *The Catholic Weekly* and elsewhere using the name of John Dawes.[1]

Keneally applied half-heartedly for a couple of jobs and accepted an offer of work as a clerk in the Sydney office of the Department of Territories, processing orders for such things as Tilley lamps that were required in Papua New Guinea. 'I had to check the invoices against other documents,' Keneally says. 'Someone from New Guinea would send down orders for three dozen mallets or something – we'd process the orders ... It was very banal work in an office down near Circular Quay, around about Harrington Street or Gloucester Street – I went in to work on the train. It was a nine-to-five job . . . I didn't mind it, but the wages weren't good.'

Keneally has almost willed himself to forget that unhappy time. He was depressed and demoralised, unable to talk about his misery. The undemanding work was all that he could cope with, but it only reinforced his sense of failure. 'I got to know the other fellows, and we'd go to the pub together after work for a drink,' he says. 'Our supervisor was a particular kind of disappointed man – there are men like him who reek of disappointment. His task was almost as menial as ours. Young [John F.] Kennedy was coming into prominence and was campaigning – it was a very exciting time politically, even though I was out of it all.'

Keneally's drinking with the other men was an attempt to get into the world, although by his reckoning it wasn't 'boozing'. 'I hadn't become a boozer then. In those days the pub was where the world was, the world of men and the mutual reinforcement with men pretending to be strong men. That was always the venue in that period of Australian history – it was where you went to pretend to each other that everything was fine, that mateship was a golden virtue, that misogyny was reinforced with profane jokes.'

One of Keneally's companions in that era was Paddy Downie, who had started university studies in social work. Keneally had a genuine care for the disabled, perhaps as a result of observing Downie's problems. His article 'Short Change for the Deaf', which described their problems in education and society, was published in *The Australian* in 1969.[2] He also attempted a novel about a blind boy: 'Michael detested his circus animal status and rebelled against the expectations of authorities'. Keneally labelled the manuscript 'Rough draft of an abortive novel about blindness'.[3]

Downie lived at home and was a regular in the bar at the Horse and Jockey Hotel on Parramatta Road, Homebush. Sometimes, if he'd had too much to drink, he would telephone Keneally and ask a favour: 'Would you mind walking back home with me, Mick? I've had a few schooners too many and the old lady will get into me!' Keneally's presence prevented the tirade.

Keneally also took Downie to the movies and to orchestral concerts. The free concerts at the Town Hall were very influential in forming

Keneally's musical taste. 'Being in the seminary caused me to miss out on the birth of rock,' he notes, 'and I've never caught up with that. Even people I admire, like Peter Garrett, I can't read their rock. It just sounds like noise to me! I know every dreary old fart says that, but it did from an early age, because I was not there when the language of rock was laid down. I suppose the Beatles were just starting to emerge, like me!'

Keneally did a lot of solitary walking, especially on Sundays, when he pretended he was going to a different Mass to the one attended by his parents. He was a sick man, deeply ashamed of his deception and mortified by his emotional immaturity. 'I just walked the streets – I didn't go to Mass,' he says. 'Here was a man in his twenties who couldn't tell his parents that he was in a deep hole and he had no more faith. I thought it [the Catholic faith] was all ... not just smoke and mirrors, but pernicious smoke and mirrors. Or smoke and mirrors run by pernicious people. It's a bit unfair. I had a lot of regard for some of my classmates.'

Keneally's father was depressed after the war, but it was not an era in which one might confide something that could be construed as weakness or whingeing. Tom senior's horizons had been briefly broadened by his wartime adventures in faraway places, but he had returned to a narrow, mundane life in which there was never enough money, and he had no prospects of improving his lot. Like his son, he probably felt he was a failure. He didn't know how to talk about it. Neither did Keneally know how to explain what was happening. He assured Elsie that the depletion in his spirits was a passing illness, while desperately hoping that it would prove to be so.

He left the clerical job and started teaching at Waverley College, a Christian Brothers School in Sydney's eastern suburbs. Keneally had been there earlier in 1960, when one of the teachers, Steve Frangos, had asked him to talk to his class about Christian Doctrine. 'Ask Mr Keneally any questions you like,' Frangos had said. 'He is up to date with the answers.' The boys included Moy Hitchen, who recalls that this was an unusual privilege: 'Typically, only a priest running a retreat would take questions on religious matters. I thought he must be very clever. I remember Mr Keneally as a rather scrawny young man, with thinning wispy dark hair, a bit self-effacing at first, but obviously confident in answering our questions.'

Keneally the teacher travelled on the public bus with the boys. He wore a shirt and tie and a tweed jacket and carried a brown leather case. After school, the boys would see him standing at the bus stop on Bronte Road, reading a book. According to the school scuttlebutt, he read three books a day.

'I was trying to avoid teaching,' Keneally said, 'but they recognised my Bachelor of Theology degree and gave me a job . . . This was a period when a good teacher kept the class absolutely still. You could bore them shitless as long as they didn't talk. The criticism old teachers would make – "I couldn't settle your class down" – was a severe criticism to me. I had problems with the discipline. I have problems now! These little kids [his grandchildren] run rings around me! Some Waverley students I met later said, "You made History interesting." At one stage I did some work with Grade 4 children in the primary school, but generally it was first, second and third years of high school – junior high – History and English, big classes, probably forty boys.'

Paul de Launay was one of the students for whom Keneally made history interesting. 'To this day I still find the subject interesting,' he reflects. 'Tom was our only lay teacher . . . kindly and humane. I don't recall him using the strap.' Keneally presented another student, Warren Turner, with a book for some work Turner had completed in history. Turner kept the book for many years.

Hitchen remembers Keneally's lectures about the Earl of Montrose: 'To this day, fifty years later, I have no idea why he chose this, what relevance it had for a class of fifteen-year-old Australians, or where it fitted in the history curriculum. But, without a textbook, he spent days lecturing us on Mary Queen of Scots, Lord Darnley, the Earl of Montrose, and all the convoluted politics and conflicts that swirled around them. He did it well! He told a gripping story with great detail and much relish. He captured the drama, intrigue, treachery and violence, culminating with Mary's beheading at her cousin Elizabeth's behest . . . It was certainly the most absorbing history topic I ever covered in secondary school, and has stayed with me as a great yarn – and a demonstration of one man's passion for history.'

Bill Guest thinks the boys were seeing the Tom Keneally of the future. He has one personal memory that endeared his teacher to him. When he was fifteen, Guest was called from class to the headmaster's office to be told that his mother had died. The college staff and students were sympathetic, but only Keneally sent the boy a note of compassionate condolence.

Another student, Paul Dellit, saw Keneally as tentative and occasionally reflective, finding it difficult to maintain class discipline: 'I do not recall him as a happy person – he seemed preoccupied when he would walk on the outskirts of the playground when not teaching, frowning, never smiling. He seemed like a decent man to me, unlike some of the other teachers who were less inclined to engage with students, except on their prescribed terms. If you asked Mr Keneally a question he would consider his answer and, it seemed to me, not talk down to the students.'

Keneally could get angry. Some boys thought he had a fiery temper; others thought his occasional explosions of anger were put on for effect: 'By heavens, sonny, I'll . . .' His threats were usually idle, and they knew it.

The headmaster was Brother Michael O'Connor, an eccentric Irishman nicknamed 'Mad Mick'. Keneally thought he was 'strap-mad': if a boy was sent to him O'Connor wouldn't bother to ask questions. He pulled out his strap and whacked the culprit hard and repeatedly, then sent him back to class. One of Keneally's unpublished stories, 'Spoil the Child', about the flogging of a schoolboy, was written after he had watched O'Connor's method with distaste.[4]

O'Connor interrogated his newest staff member a couple of times. The first time was when Keneally went away with another teacher, Malcolm Dickson, on a trip to the coast south of Sydney. 'Mick quizzed me when we got back about what went on between us,' Keneally says. 'He obviously was worried about homosexuality . . . I didn't get why he was so interested in our trip. I mean, can anyone be as naive as that these days? I didn't know that I was being suspected of homosexuality!'

Desperate to belong, Keneally made other friendships among the teachers at Waverley. Peter Watson had written a textbook on economics, which greatly impressed Keneally and stoked his literary ambitions. Watson, in charge of public speaking and debating competitions, enlisted Keneally to adjudicate debates on Friday nights. His other extracurricular contribution was coaching the 12A and 13D rugby union sides. The weaker teams had no illusions about their lowly status, but Keneally was keen to motivate them. He wore his old St Patrick's College jersey and turned up for every practice session. In a match against Cranbrook, Moy Hitchen took a pass and set off down the field, with his coach running down the sideline and shouting, 'Run, Hitchen, run like hell!'

Another teacher, Greg Parnham, said that the Mick Keneally he knew in 1963 was vastly different to the extrovert known worldwide as Tom Keneally fifty years later. 'As a schoolteacher, he was not comfortable,' Parnham says. 'As a young man, he did not have any confidence in himself or in his position in life. He feared that no woman would ever love him and that he would never get married. He was most uncomfortable with life.'

Keneally became friendly with Parnham, envying his social confidence. Parnham also played football for the Sydney Roosters club, and Keneally watched his matches with Parnham's family. Afterwards, he often went back to their home in Bondi Junction to talk about the game.

Parnham was a former Marist Brother, as was another friendly teacher, Peter Lawler, who was studying law part-time. 'They all, in their way, wanted to get out,' Keneally says. 'They still had the faith, and I nominally still had the faith ... There were glimmers of others escaping their past. Even with someone as positive as Greg Parnham or Peter Lawler, there was the sense that they were continuing in a Catholic institution in a lesser role than they had held before. The Brothers couldn't help looking upon themselves as the elite – I'm sure Mad Mick did – but the vocations were beginning to dwindle. Waverley was a big school with dynamic rugby teams and this Christian Brothers culture that was good at exams. My job was to coach the boys towards those exams at a junior high school level.'

According to Lawler, Keneally was rather uncertain and withdrawn, almost shy. While Lawler had enjoyed a lively time at Sydney University prior to Waverley, at a time when the student body included such nonconformists as Germaine Greer, Clive James, Les Murray and Richard Walsh, Keneally was still emerging into the 'real' world. Lawler says the younger members of staff knew their place in the pecking order and were often obliged to listen to tirades by the older teachers, not daring to offer a contrary opinion.

One of the older men harangued his fellow diners at lunchtime about the dubious benefits of television, then still relatively new in Australia.

The violence was dreadful and damaging, he declared, and too much 'on the box' was bound to have a bad influence on the young. Other senior teachers made dire predictions. Lawler noticed that Keneally was scribbling on a serviette. 'You were being very conscientious, Mick! What were you writing?' he asked. Keneally laughed and showed him a poem, 'When 7.30 Comes at Night', a spoof of what the television critic had been declaiming. Lawler kept the poem:

When 7.30 comes at night
And television sets are bright,
With many a gruesome adult show,
Where men's blood does in buckets flow,
Where Al Capone shoots Mack the Knife,
And Cheyenne gambles with his life,
Our parents say: 'It's time to go!
You'd never understand this show.
Besides, the violence will sow seeds
Of future naughty deeds.
And so, I fear, it's bed for you!
You're much too young to teleview
This show
So low
And interesting!'
And so we find ourselves in bed
Thinking of stories we have read,
The gentle stories children love:
How Jack climbed high up, up above
And brought the giant down to the ground
And caused an earthquake all around
And roofs fell in on people's heads
And chandeliers fell on the beds
And all the baddies thus were squashed
Like flies in summertime
And how Jack pulled a big steel sword
And slashed the giant's jug'lar chord [sic]
And blood fell down like waterfalls

And absolutely soaked the walls.
These tales will do us well enough
For television is too rough!
So we're told.
So we're sent to read a story
Lest we grow up wild and gory.
Programmes that our parents see
Tell how wild we boys can be,
Show what trouble we could cause
Breaking other people's locks,
Opening other people's doors,
Eating other people's stores;
Eating Baby Bear's warm gruel,
Breaking Baby Bear's new stool;
Goldie, clumsy as a mule!
Oughtn't there to be a rule
Against such girls as Goldie.
Poor underprivileged Goldilocks
Running, as the forest rocks
To the tread of three wild bears . . .[5]

Keneally was often thinking of possible storylines. After preparing lessons and marking homework at night, he sometimes stayed at his desk. When his asthma was bad and he was haunted by the past, he found it difficult to sleep. He confided in friends Shirley and Kevin Yates that he felt 'as if I'm in a long tunnel and I can't see the light at the end of the tunnel'. When he was wakeful, he wrote. A few snippets and snatches of dialogue, scribbled on scrap paper, have survived as reminders of his earliest attempts at fiction writing.

The seminary debacle occupied his thoughts so much that he finally did write about it. 'The Sky Burning Up Above the Man', with its ironic humour and unexpected characters, would have appealed to many readers, most of whom had no idea about the background to the story. Keneally managed, within the restrictions of 3000 words or so, to explain the attitude of local people to the students at the seminary he called 'Peninsula College', as well as describing the appearance, shortcomings and rituals of the place. There are some secondary characters who add a fun element to the yarn, as they do in all Keneally's stories, like an old monsignor who complains that some of the 'young fellas' had put fruit saline in his chamber pot. 'Yes, fruit saline,' he says. 'When my bladder woke me in the dead of night I thought I had galloping effervescence.'

The asthmatic Maurie is 'a man who had become a priest in search of approval, and might become a demon for the same silly reason'. All around Maurie and his friend Dan, the pervasive heat matches the feverish state of Maurie's mind and his manic physical activity. Dan reasons that Maurie is worn out: 'You find it hard to do any work. Your earlier years have exhausted you.' Maurie has to confront the consequences, as Keneally had, of leaving: 'People will love to see you fall. You set yourself such a high standard . . .'

'The Sky Burning Up Above the Man' was submitted to *The Bulletin*, and Desmond O'Grady, its literary editor in 1962, therefore has the distinction of being the first editor to accept and publish Keneally's work. 'I like this story very much,' O'Grady wrote, 'but it is somewhat let down by the conclusion. Do you think you could change it so [it] gives a specified working out of a theme which runs right through the story?'[6] Keneally obliged. Years later many readers would question the apparently double ending to *The Daughters of Mars*.

'I still remember the phrase in the story "the Cardinal knelt in lapidary prayer"', O'Grady said fifty years after 'The Sky Burning Up Above the Man' was published. In it, Keneally describes the cardinal (based on Gilroy) in some detail: 'This man was princely. He never betrayed himself into scratching the back of his head, blowing his nose heartily, wringing his hands, or spilling food on his clothes.' Then Keneally added his own mischievous idea: 'A literary friend of Dan's, speaking once of this statuesque impeccability, promised to write a novel beginning, "The bishop's arse was itchy."'

Whether or not Gilroy, who preferred the *Sydney Morning Herald*, ever read the story is not known; however, the clergy who had gathered in Sydney for a conference on the day the story was published – Saturday, 23 June 1962 – would have relished the cheeky suggestion and the perceptive comments packed into it. Newsstands close to St Mary's Cathedral sold that week's issue of *The Bulletin* in record time.[7]

On the following Monday, Keneally walked out the front door at Loftus Crescent, went down the stairs and crossed the road to join the throng at Homebush Station. He still had to face his classes at Waverley despite the excitement of publication. He could see people buying *The Bulletin* at a nearby newsstand. Once on the train, he watched others boarding at each station and imagined them reading his story. 'This was a miraculous feeling to me,' he later explained. 'It gave me a sense of a possible escape from what I saw as the ignominy of my position.'[8]

Keneally used a pseudonym, Bernard Coyle, in his phase of writing short stories. This shielded his identity, he thought, although he 'blew his cover' by telling friends about the publication. He feared the reaction of O'Connor, who might not have approved of his junior teacher going public with such a thinly veiled exposé of seminary life at Manly. O'Connor did question him intensely about the publication, defending the church against the author's attack.

By this time Keneally was studying law part-time; the course was run by the Law Society of New South Wales and completed largely by correspondence. He wanted to become a barrister, a career option he had contemplated when finishing high school. Keneally was not attracted to criminal law but to industrial legislation. He was fascinated by the case of *Grant v. Australian Knitting Mills*, in which the appellant claimed damages on the basis that he had contracted dermatitis from underwear manufactured by the respondent. Grant's claim was that an excessive amount of sulphites had been left negligently in the garments during the manufacturing process. The 1936 case attracted a lot of attention, partly because of its unusual nature but also because it was a landmark damages case in Australian legal history. Keneally was also interested in groundbreaking confrontations such as the Harvester case of 1907, which paved the way for the institution of a basic wage allowance for Australian workers, and in political decisions such as the Curtin government's legislation to ratify the Statute of Westminster in 1942.

Keneally never finished his legal studies, but he did go on to prosecute cases against the Catholic Church throughout his literary career. His early writing undoubtedly portrays his struggle to advance from indoctrination to individuality. 'He had to get all that out of his system,' suggests Ed Campion, 'before his imagination could blossom. If he had stayed there and become Father Keneally, I doubt whether his creativity would have expanded as magnificently as it has done.'

Gaining recognition for his skill with the written word enhanced Keneally. 'I loved that phenomenon of being published and, I've got to say quite frankly, of being praised,' he later admitted. 'Writers never say these things. They never say, "I wrote it because I wanted to be praised." But it's one of the chief motivations . . . It's like the priesthood – a combination of banal and glorious motives.'[9]

Keneally has written a few other short stories during his writing career, including 'Blackberries', about a schoolteacher, Austin North, and his infatuation with a student.[10] Most of his early unpublished stories are about places and events familiar to him. These include 'Death of an Innocent' and 'In the Day of Anger', which have been mentioned already. Another story, with the title 'Partners', is about an abortive fishing expedition at Clyde Heads, recognisable as Keneally's favourite Crescent Head, with 'a splendid beach, a broad sickle of it five miles long with the wilderness of scrub and green mountain behind'. When he returned to Crescent Head for holidays, Keneally fished from the beach. If the bream or whiting or flathead were biting, he says, 'you could make your living off this beach with a hand-line'.

In the May school holidays, when the fish were on the move north for the winter, Keneally could almost believe in such an idyllic lifestyle. He was not content at Waverley. He contemplated taking an 'easier' job and writing part-time. He applied unsuccessfully for a job as a copywriter-clerk and another at the Egg Board.[11]

On 1 February 1964 a second story of Keneally's, 'What's God Doing This Week?', was published in *The Bulletin*.[12] It is a curious title for a curious tale, which can best be described as a projection of what Australia might have been like under a communist regime. Life would have been brutal, by the reckoning of this story, full of the fear and deception that Australians in the 1960s associated with Russia and China. Keneally wrote drafts on the back of Waverley examination papers – on which, ironically, questions such as 'What is meant by the term "basic wage"?' and 'What is a Federal system of government?' were printed.

The boys at Waverley College were a long way away from the denunciations, the informers and the squalid poverty of Keneally's imagined world. In that world, only those who precariously held sway in the 'Executive Council' live well. For one of its worthies, who wants to resign, there is a beach far up the coast, 'where the weather was always temperate and the bream crowded in the fishing holes'. Party Hall – presumably Parliament House in Canberra, with 'its flock of silver lakes around its flanks, trembling in the wind' – is the place where the Executive Council hatches plots and despatches the expendable. 'There was no God,' Keneally writes. 'Matter evolving was God. And the highest form of matter evolving was the Party . . .' The false 'God' is redeeming, re-educating or exterminating men who had been the 'best' communists.

The story appeared at the height of the Cold War, and communism was a big topic. As a child at Homebush, Keneally knew a man next door called Coy, who was a communist. Coy became 'Comrade Lenin' in Keneally's second book, *The Fear*, published in 1965, eighteen months after 'What's God Doing This Week?'. His second published short story anticipated his second book, in much the same way as his first had presaged *The Place at Whitton*. 'The Sky Burning Up Above the Man' is an incipient novel.

11

A Roman Catholic Writer

The summer holidays beckoned Keneally. He shrugged off his jacket and loosened his collar. The tie could stay in the drawer until the 1963 school year at Waverley began. He piled the schoolbooks on shelves already laden with legal and medical textbooks, novels and journals. His desk wasn't large, but big enough for an exercise pad and a biro, all that he needed for the book he was about to begin.

Keneally could write anywhere: sitting in the garden, standing at a chest of drawers – even, a few years later, at the dining table with a baby crawling over his feet and the telephone ringing. His bedroom at Loftus Crescent, Homebush, wasn't quiet, but the rattle of trains and the blast of horns were familiar background noises. In summer the window was open to allow the occasional flicker of fresh air. Keneally's thoughts in December 1962 were heading in an easterly direction, to a chapel thirty kilometres away where sea breezes blew.

Keneally could recall the Cardinal Cerretti Chapel at St Patrick's Seminary exactly, and he began his story: 'Really the chapel was cold, chaste and barn-like in a good old monasterial way. Only the electric lights and the hum of the electric organ limbering up for a motet, gave you the clue that this was not a late medieval sanctuary ...' The neo-Gothic chapel was the perfect place to start a murder mystery.

Did he write a draft of *The Place at Whitton* while still at Manly?

'Keneally was writing his first satire before he left the seminary, his friends believe,' critic Gloria Moore declared in 1994. She claimed that when Keneally left the seminary, 'Muldoon arranged for Richard Connolly, who had studied at Propaganda Fide in Rome and was then with the ABC in Sydney, to read Keneally's first novel. (Connolly advised Keneally to leave writing and take an arts degree.)'[1]

Richard Connolly does not recall Muldoon arranging any such thing. 'There was no mention of a novel or a manuscript,' he claims; Muldoon had chosen him to advise Keneally because he had studied at Springwood and at Manly, and he had left the seminary shortly before ordination. Connolly would not have been working as a producer in the ABC if he had not previously completed a BA degree at Sydney University. He had done this largely on the advice of Brian Doyle, a Catholic intellectual and associate editor of *The Catholic Weekly*, who had pointed out that it would be helpful for Connolly to rid himself of the 'spoiled priest' tag and 'laicise' himself.

Connolly told Keneally the same thing. They talked for about an hour, during which Keneally kept reaching for his briefcase. 'I've written this novel,' he ventured. Connolly kept urging the university idea. He later regretted his disregard for the contents of the briefcase, feeling he should have humoured the hopeful author. A few years afterwards, Keith Adam, a presenter on ABC Radio, invited Connolly to 'come and meet this new author Keneally, who's written a novel about a murder in a Catholic seminary'. The embarrassed Connolly said he was too busy.

He did come face to face with Keneally at a literary festival in Queensland a little time later. Connolly was with a group, including Keneally's hero, Christopher Koch. 'I'm ashamed to meet you,' Connolly said to Keneally, who replied genially, 'I thought you were very nice.'

Keneally does not recall the 'manuscript in the briefcase'. Perhaps he had something he had written at Manly, although he has no memory of anything that would have rated the description 'novel'. He had written 'novels' at high school, in the tradition of Walter Scott or James Fenimore Cooper, and had once even attempted a Western. The most extensive effort was based on the life of one of his favourite poets, Thomas Chatterton. Fellow students at Manly remembered fragments of a thriller short story; they also recalled 'Mick' Keneally's twin ambitions:

to be published in both the *Saturday Evening Post* and the *New Yorker*.[2]

'I don't remember [writing] anything substantial till *The Place at Whitton*,' Keneally himself says, 'and I don't have any memory of starting that while still at Manly. Whatever it was I wanted to show Richard Connolly would have been very raw. Perhaps in my shame of being unemployed and uncertain I wanted to shake something in front of him to impress him, or perhaps I may have just mentioned that I wanted to write. Memory and subsequent events can trip us up.'

Keneally added that he revised his opinion of Muldoon after being reminded of his kindness in introducing him to a suitable adviser. In an article, 'The Humanist Priest', published in 1969, Keneally did not mention Muldoon's help. When he left the seminary, he explained, he had no clothes other than black, no money, no training, no job. 'In the latter matter, I approached His Lordship Bishop Muldoon and was referred to the local Commonwealth Employment Agency and the employment columns of Wednesday's *Sydney Morning Herald*.'[3]

When Keneally had written the first chapter of his novel, he gave it to Shirley Yates, whose maiden name was O'Leary. The Keneally and O'Leary families were friends from shared times at Kempsey and Crescent Head. Yates had previously typed out one of his short stories for him, and he asked her to do the same now. After he read the chapter aloud to Shirley and her husband, Kevin, they asked, 'What happens next?'

'I haven't written it yet!' Keneally replied.

The chapters arrived one by one, with the Yates waiting for the next instalment. Keneally liked visiting them at Epping, and especially enjoyed the time he spent with their two young daughters, Dene and Kerin, to whom he read stories and gave books (among them *The Adventures of Blinky Bill* and *The Magic Pudding*). In time Yates would produce the typescripts of the first two Keneally books. He inscribed *The Place at Whitton* to 'Shirley Yates and her family, whose encouragement was ¾ of this book. From the author.'

Keneally gave a handwritten draft of *The Place at Whitton* to Greg Parnham, his friend at Waverley College. Parnham agreed to read it, and Keneally awaited his appraisal keenly. 'Well, to be honest, Mick,' Parnham told him doubtfully, 'I had great difficulty deciphering your writing and many of those big words you used were a bit much for my simple brain. But go for it, Mick. If you don't take it to a publisher you will never get it published.'[4] Keneally had the manuscript ready by Easter 1963.

Around this time, Keneally's parents noticed a change in their son: he seemed happier, more talkative and more ready to engage with the outside world. The transformation that occurred with *The Place at Whitton* was his 'deckchair after the Titanic', Keanelly later said, and he intended to cling to 'this floating deckchair and hope it takes me to good places. I think if that book hadn't been published I might have become a psychiatric patient or a drunk or a homeless person in time . . .'[5]

In time, he became – temporarily, at least – a person adrift, but it was always the next book, the next project to be finished, that rescued him. Writing became his 'way of escape', a phrase coined by Graham Greene, for whom writing was 'a form of therapy; sometimes I wonder how all those who do not write, compose or paint can manage to escape the madness, the melancholia, the panic fear which is inherent in the human situation'.[6]

Keneally sent the manuscript to Cassell & Co. in London because he thought it was the publishing house most likely to accept it. Acknowledgement came in an aerogram dated 15 July 1963, promising to give the manuscript serious consideration.[7]

Then came the first letter of acceptance for a Keneally manuscript, dated 10 September 1963, informing him that Cassell would like to publish *The Place at Whitton*. The following terms were offered: an advance of £150, with half payable on signature and half on publication, a royalty on home sales of 10 per cent of the British published price on the first 3500 copies, 12.5 per cent on the next 4000 copies and 15 per cent on all copies sold thereafter. The same scale was offered on the Australian published price for sales in or to Australia. For all other export sales, Cassell offered 10 per cent of the price received.

Cassell questioned Keneally's wish to use the same nom de plume, Bernard Coyle, which he had used for the stories published in *The Bulletin*. The publisher had a preference for publishing the book under Keneally's real name and launching him as a writer. Cassell contended that 'it is much more satisfactory for you to be established as a writer under your real name as once you get known under a pen name it is very difficult to undo it and may well cause confusion at a later stage'.[8] Keneally feared repercussions from the novel, as he did with the first *Bulletin* story, but he accepted the publisher's preference and Cassell undertook to publish *The Place at Whitton*, by Thomas Keneally, in June 1964.[9]

Writing in 1966, Max Harris dubbed Keneally 'a Roman Catholic writer whose gothic sensibility and demonic obsessions set his writings apart from the Australian tradition of social reportage in fiction. He writes novels using both the imagery and thematic concerns of the poet. His is the new voice, if not quite the sort of voice we had expected to hear.'[10] Keneally did not want the tag 'Roman Catholic writer', but Harris's praise of his first books was a tremendous fillip. 'The important thing about *The Place at Whitton*,' Harris wrote, 'is not the story, nor even the hit-and-miss principles of characterisation. The important thing is the way Thomas Keneally writes. He manages, as few writers do, to combine intellect and high imagination in a completely satisfying synthesis.'[11]

Harris was impressed by the compelling way in which the author depicted a community of priests. So effective was the result that readers would feel 'convinced that Thomas Keneally is, or has been, in the priesthood . . .' Harris was closer to the mark than Noel Buckley, a reviewer for *The Bulletin*: 'Despite his Irish name, Keneally, a schoolmaster who lives at Homebush, doesn't seem to know much about priests, their beliefs or behaviour, and as they are characterised as speaking in the same idiom as all the other characters, be they policemen, book-sellers or taxi-drivers, one suspects he has never met one.'[12]

The 1971 edition of *The Place at Whitton*, published in the United States of America, describes the book as 'A tale of malevolence in a modern monastery'. Under that alliterative heading, the back-cover blurb included this endorsement: 'Great strength and exciting originality.' The quote was attributed to one Sidney Herald – presumably an esteemed Australian reviewer!

Forty years later, Keneally rejected his first book as 'a genuine catastrophe of technique', an enterprise to which he took with 'great gusto and heroic cackhandedness, and the essential though ill-informed confidence of the young'. It was a rather improbable yarn with 'fairly passable pastiches of the last person I had read. Here was Patrick White, over there Graham Greene; here Wallace Stevens, over there an inadvisably lush rework of Dylan Thomas.'[13] He relied on the *deus ex machina*, the convenient event that tied everything up.

Keneally had also been influenced by the mystery novelist Josephine Tey – and in particular by her book *The Daughter of Time*, first published in 1951, which was regarded in its day as one of the best examples of detective fiction. Graham Greene's presence is obvious in *The Place at Whitton*. One of his short stories is called 'The Hint of an Explanation', in which a man by the name of Blacker, who hates Catholics, bribes and threatens a child, David, to steal a wafer for him when serving Mass. 'I want to see what God tastes like,' Blacker informs the child. When retelling the story as an older man, by which time he is a priest, David says that Satan or the Devil had tried to corrupt him and use him as a weapon against the church.

In Keneally's book, a young witch called Agnes, expelled from a convent, is a sort of Blacker. She is also similar to Rosaleen Norton, the 'Witch of Kings Cross', who was a notoriety in Sydney about the time Keneally was writing.[14] Agnes conducted 'Black Masses', defiling the Host upon a stone table in her apartment. Notably, at the end of *The Place at Whitton* the murderer remembers the saying 'Between the stirrup and the ground, / Mercy was asked and mercy found'. This is also the last thought of Greene's Pinkie Brown in *Brighton Rock*.

For some years Keneally shared his literary mentor's incorrect label as a 'Catholic writer'. Greene became a Catholic in 1926, which meant, he noted, that 'all my books, except for one, were written as a Catholic – no-one noticed the faith to which I belonged before the publication of *Brighton Rock*. Many times since *Brighton Rock* I have been forced to declare myself not a Catholic writer but a writer who happens to be a Catholic . . .'[15] In 2002 Keneally explained that he was 'a haunted young writer when I was writing those early books. I did have a kind of a theological seriousness still about me – I was still a priest, I was still in a strange way writing about good and evil, redemption, alienation and darkness . . .'[16]

Thea Astley, one of the first Australian writers with whom Keneally became friendly, once told him that every writer should be a Catholic, at least for two or three years. Keneally believed Astley was influenced by her ex-Catholic neuroses, which were helpful in giving her books a mythical dimension and in explaining her characters. The same might be said of much of his own writing.

According to Keneally, Christian mythology, and the more manic form of it in Catholicism, was a great trigger to the imagination. 'It gave you a sense of great forces batting their heads against each other and it provided you with that same Christian context that people got from studying the New Testament in Hebrew and Greek at places like Oxford and Cambridge. I would not compare St Patrick's seminary to Oxford or Cambridge, but there were students who had studied there, and the journey between the two would not have been great in certain disciplines.

'Catholicism so permeated the culture I knew at that stage. It gave you interesting insights into permutations of self-blame, nuances of feeling, and it made you neurotic. There was one exercise we did about midday [at the seminary] called the examination of conscience – you'd sit down in silence in the chapel and examine the state of your conscience. Of course it was self-accusatory and narcissistic as it built you up into a great offender. God was up there and you had the capacity to offend him. It's also extremely neurotic, this inward turning and encouragement of neurotic scruples and compulsions.'

What of the reaction at Manly to Keneally's work of 'fiction'? Although Keneally was taking satirical aim at some of the practices and practitioners, there was nothing that slurred anyone in particular. Stenner (the rector) and Onions (the vice-rector) are in fact quite likeable characters. Stenner is 'a gentleman', while Onions is 'intelligent, strong, handsome, forceful'. Just the same, Crittenden and others teaching at Manly when *The Place at Whitton* was published agree that Madden would have been puzzled and hurt. 'He was friendly and genuinely concerned for students, but completely a servant of an insensitive institutional church,' Crittenden says. Peter Harrington said to Keneally: 'Well, now that you've got that out of your system, you can get on with your life.' Like others, he expected that Keneally would get on with being a Catholic, too.

Keneally maintained his friendship with many of the seminarians, both those who continued in the priesthood and those who did not. In 1996, when Father Ted Kennedy was celebrating twenty-five years of work at Redfern, his homily at the anniversary Mass made reference to groups excluded from the public life of the church. Campion recalled

Kennedy's address: 'One group comprised "all the clerical and religious dropouts", those who had the foresight "to see the storm clouds forming and the thick fog rolling in. It was you who had the imagination to suggest ways of coping with the coming storm and were willing to pledge your young lives to act accordingly with courage. And when you were made to drop out, the clericalists desperately tried to cover over the holes, to pretend that you never existed in the first place . . ." Kennedy included Keneally in the list he read out in St Vincent's Church, Redfern.'[17] The church could not pretend that Keneally had never existed: his writing about the institution, which began in earnest with *The Place at Whitton*, ensured that he would remain a thorn in its side.

By the end of *The Place at Whitton* the reader is taken back, yet again, to Crescent Head, the scene of violent endings and estrangement in this book and in the next one, *The Fear*. The violence is strangely at odds with a place where Keneally knew only happiness – Pontifex in *The Place at Whitton* calls it 'the landscape of his soul'. At the coastal village called Prospect in that novel, the schoolteacher Pete Dawes fishes contentedly: 'There was a touch of heroism about being alone on twelve misty miles of beach with the weather down and the sea up. Behind the noise of surf and wind, you could sing, recite *Jabberwocky*, deliver "This day is called the feast of Crispian" far more extravagantly and boomingly, though the wind washed your words away . . .'[18]

Perhaps Keneally was returning to childhood, to a place where he once scared his cousins with ghost stories when it was pitch-black. In seminary holidays he sometimes stayed with an uncle, Dan Keneally, and his family in Killick Lane, Crescent Head. He was also a regular holiday visitor at the O'Learys' home. Keneally has always had a fondness for melodrama, and the sinister, hovering presence of the Trial Bay Gaol may have pushed his imagination in that direction. Crescent Head was also the only place beyond Sydney whose landscape he knew well enough to describe convincingly.

Keneally had taken one of the first handwritten copies of *The Place at Whitton* with him when he visited Crescent Head in May 1963. He showed it proudly to his cousin, Rosie Cady, and her husband, Peter. They were astonished at the critical acclaim the book received later. John McLaren, *Overland*'s reviewer, wrote that *The Place at Whitton* had 'probably attracted as lavish praise as any Australian first novel since the war. It is first of all a fast-moving and gripping murder mystery … its distinctive quality is its metaphysical concern, which makes it unique among Australian novels.'[19] This was the 'honeymoon' era for Keneally as far as reviews were concerned. They would not all be so congratulatory; indeed, he would bristle at some of the more damning ones. He even, on occasion, 'called some reviewers on', to use Tom senior's phrase for picking a fight.

Meanwhile, in the afterglow of critical approval, Keneally had already written his next book. *The Fear* was another autobiographical novel, and coincided with a tumultuous time in Keneally's life.

12

The Fear

Not long before he left Waverley College, Keneally entered the classroom carrying a large volume of foolscap sheets, bound in paper covers. He walked to the teacher's desk and faced the students. 'I have something to tell you, boys,' he said. 'This manuscript has been accepted by a publisher, and the book will be published soon. It might be considered controversial by some people, and I am concerned that it may lead to negative publicity for the school if I stay. I have talked it over with Brother O'Connor and I have decided to resign.'

Keneally's dramatic announcement stayed in that class's collective memory. No teacher had ever done anything like this before. 'I advise you not to read the book,' Keneally said to another class. 'You are too young.' Of course, most of them borrowed *The Place at Whitton* from local libraries as soon as it was available. A couple of students who followed Keneally up Birrell Street one day noticed a jauntier walk. 'He left the seminary and now he writes books,' one whispered to the other.

O'Connor, unlike Madden, was prepared to provide a reference:

> This is to certify that for upwards of three and a half years I have known Mr T.M. Keneally as a member of our Teaching Staff. During this period Mr Keneally has given us excellent and conscientious service. He has been most obliging; and, not content with performing

> his duties diligently in the classroom, he has voluntarily undertaken extra-curricular activities – cricket and football coaching, public speaking contests and any other duties dictated by his good judgment after his regular school hours. I have the utmost confidence in recommending Mr Keneally to any employer seeking efficient and conscientious service.[1]

Keneally was offered a part-time job through his friendship with Mick Whelan, who came from the sort of Irish working-class family that Keneally knew and liked. 'One day when I was teaching English at Waverley,' Keneally recalls, 'a bloke turned up at the door. I went out and saw him. It was Mick Whelan, and he said, "I want you to teach me English. I want to do the HSC and have a political career." . . . I started teaching him Shakespeare but it was hopeless, because in every line he'd make double entendres or hilarious homonyms for what Shakespeare was saying, so just to get through a scene was an ordeal. This was on Friday nights at his place after work. Mick and I became friends but he never got the HSC. He became ultimately a trade union consultant, and he would travel all over the world speaking to unions.'

Whelan introduced Keneally to an AMP insurance company supervisor, Vince Punch, from Ashfield: 'This is a good bloke but he's an old DLP candidate!' The Democratic Labor Party was the Catholic and anti-communist breakaway from the Australian Labor Party. Punch employed Keneally as an insurance collector and took him around the area he was to canvas, the inner-city suburbs of Newtown and Enmore. In that era, working-class people, including Keneally's parents, used to buy insurance by the month or week (a modest amount of one or two shillings) and the job entailed visiting their homes to collect the money. That was the work of two days, and then the employee was supposed to spend the rest of the week selling more insurance policies. Keneally, though, used the hours away from his beat to write another novel. 'I'm afraid I was rather unscrupulous about this . . . I was writing a second book. It was going to be an account of World War II from a child's perspective of growing up in Homebush. The novel everyone writes about their childhood . . .'

That novel was *The Fear*. Like James Joyce's *A Portrait of the Artist as a Young Man*, it was largely autobiographical. In both novels squalor and deprivation are the lot of children observing a bigger, darker grown-up world. Old-fashioned Catholicism may have pervaded their lives at home and at school, but inquisitive youngsters like Danny Jordan (*The Fear*) and Stephen Dedalus (*A Portrait of the Artist as a Young Man*) are attracted beyond their boundaries by danger, violence and their own disturbed emotions.

Jordan is a refugee in Sydney during the Second World War, removed from the Macleay Valley – the Mid North Coast area around Crescent Head – because of the threat of Japanese invasion. He and his parents, Stell and Brian, live next door to Leonard Mantle, a communist bully, drunken wife-beater and no-hoper who is known as Comrade Lenin. The Comrade takes an immediate set against Jordan, with his 'skinful of all sorts of dogmatics and lies'. The Comrade's attack comes after Jordan baptises Joseph, one of the Comrade's sons, because that unfortunate boy is expected to die soon from a muscle-wasting disease. Chapter Four of *The Fear* describes the ceremony in comic detail: a serious business in the midst of squabbles and obscenities. Jordan is satisfied that he has 'done the work of the Lord that day'. Nan Hutton, who read the manuscript for Cassell, said in her report: 'I laughed myself silly over Danny baptising Joseph Stalin Mantle.'[2]

A communist by the name of Coy really did live next door to Keneally's family in Homebush, and Keneally really had baptised an older boy who was crippled by motor neurone disease. 'The nuns said if you found a child dying [outside the faith] you could do that,' he says. 'I also used to fight him – he was the only kid a year older than me whom I could beat, so my Christianity was purely doctrinal! When I made my first confession, anxious to please, I said in my loud voice, "I hit Jimmy Coy, I was disobedient to my mother" – all the usual things. A seven-year-old making up a catalogue of sins. This young priest, who was quite gentle, said, "Boys do hit each other." I didn't want my crime minimised so I said, "Jimmy Coy is a cripple!" Don't try to undermine my sin, you bugger!'

In *The Fear*, Daniel is determined that Father Peters must not underestimate the magnitude of his sins. The First Confession described in Chapter Ten compares creditably with the experiences of Stephen Dedalus. The evocation of a Catholic childhood is the strength of the book, but Keneally also manages to convey well the half-real, half-imagined world of children's games.

He started writing *The Fear* immediately after hearing that his first book had been accepted for publication. He excitedly told Greg Parnham and his family all about it during a post-football gathering. Parnham's mother, Eileen, had asked about the writing and many hours later the would-be author was still talking about 'the next book'. Mick Keneally, they all agreed, had really come out of his shell.

Keneally met with Desmond Flower, chairman of Cassell, when the Englishman was visiting Australia, probably to discuss his company's plans to expand to Melbourne. Flower was interested to know about Keneally's next book and asked him to send a report on its progress.[3]

The Fear, with the working title *No Need of Spoils*, arrived in London in July 1964. Keneally had the cheek to ask Flower for a large advance. Flower was shocked by the amount: £1800. It was out of the question. If Keneally wanted that much he should try elsewhere. Flower offered to return the manuscript.[4]

The manuscript was returned to Australia, although not to the author. Cassell was about to expand its business and had plans to publish authors locally, with Robert Sessions as its first Australian editor. In 2013 Sessions recalled how he was given 'a grimy office above a warehouse in Queen Street in Melbourne (circa 1964) and told to "get on and publish some books". I was lucky enough to find a dusty manuscript by Thomas Keneally that had lain in the corner, unrecognised, for many months (it was *The Fear*, published in 1964).'[5]

Sessions later told Keneally that he had little to do with *The Fear*, except for the title.[6] Having read the manuscript and Nan Hutton's report, Sessions wrote to Flower in London. 'Desmond and his son Nicholas, who had been appointed to watch over the fledgling Melbourne operation, encouraged me to make it, *No Need of Spoils*, one of the first titles on the new "Australian" list.' In the end, Keneally settled for a modest advance.

A couple of years after its publication, Keneally was anxious to disown *The Fear*. 'I wanted to show the development of a boy towards adolescence, but I lost track of the theme,' he told an interviewer in 1967. 'I kept putting in things that shouldn't have been there, in the mistaken belief that that was how to hold the reader's interest.'[7] Nan Hutton's observations were particularly perceptive: 'I don't for a moment think that this is the best the author can do, but I would be quite happy to predict at least three or four more getting progressively better. And even if – as does unhappily happen – something should go wrong and he doesn't get any better, he is still as vivid and original and readable as half a dozen others put together.'[8]

The book is useful, giving insights to Keneally's life in Sydney during the absence of his father, and making observations about a war-restricted city, but its implausible ending at Crescent Head (called the Cape) was unexpected and unnecessary. 'I like to think I might have spotted its [*The Fear*'s] "broken back" if I had been editing it,' Sessions told the author in 1968.[9] A later version of the book was given the title *By the Line*, and the Crescent Head section was cut out.

In 1967 Keneally agreed to write a fable version of *The Fear* for the F.W. Cheshire series 'Authors and Artists for Young Australians'. Barbara Buick, children's book editor at Cheshire, was pleased: 'How good that you have the feeling that stories for the young merit the best a writer's imagination can bring.'[10] Nevertheless, she declined the manuscript, revealing that 'my Melbourne colleagues were concerned with the possible competitiveness of the superb continental picture fables for children, especially those from Czechoslovakia . . .'[11]

Out on the streets, Keneally discovered that selling insurance was not without its adventures. He had bought his first car, a Vauxhall Victor: 'It was not a sure-fire starter. You know, you had to argue with it and have a discourse with it before it would start. I parked it outside a woman's terrace house in Newtown, a woman to whom I was to return part of her payments because she had abandoned the policy and I was to give her one pound, ten back – thirty shillings. I was at the door giving her the money and she was very twitchy. From the back of the house a door slammed and in the hallway appeared this huge man with a bloated face – engorged with rage. He saw me giving his wife thirty bob, which was around about the price of certain services in those days. He came raging at me! I had to run and jump a wrought iron fence with spikes on the top. I cleared the fence and got into my car, but I was already despairing because I knew it wouldn't start. So I was going to be beaten up by this fellow. I turned the key – and it started. I was out of there!'[12]

In the hours outside of writing, studying law and collecting insurance, Keneally gradually extended his social life. Some of his friends, former seminarians or Brothers, were starting to meet women, but some only had each other, which bothered Keneally. He wanted to escape the fate of what he referred to as the second circle of former seminarians.

In the years before Springwood and Manly he was fairly confident around girls – mainly his cousins and the Rafferty girls. During the seminary years, his only contact with women was after Mass with his parents present, but he was uncomfortable, not knowing what to say, and conscious of his clerical image. In the post-seminary years things were not much better because he felt such a failure. He once took Wendy O'Leary, Shirley Yates's sister, out to dinner at a Chinese restaurant in Sydney.

Dawes, the 'harmless schoolie' introduced in the last chapters of *The Place at Whitton*, may well have been describing Keneally's own first uncertain attempts to woo a girl. Pontifex, the murderer, understands Dawes's need. 'Can't you see how lonely he is?' he asks Collette, the girl with whom Dawes is fishing. 'I can tell them. I can tell the lonely ones. Dear Lord, I'm a specialist in loneliness. Your mate down there is a beaut as far as loneliness goes.'

Keneally's loneliness was about to end. Having a book published had done wonders for his self-esteem. A new man started to emerge – or perhaps just one who had repressed his ebullient nature for many years. Keneally's darker side still sometimes got the better of him, but he was cheerful and chatty when he visited Elsie in the Lewisham hospital after she'd had a major operation. During his childhood, Keneally himself had been a regular patient at this hospital, run by the Little Company of Mary.

Elsie told him about a nurse to whom she had given a copy of *The Place at Whitton*. 'I remember being quite disturbed by it,' the nurse, Judy Martin, said later, 'because I was reading at night. But Elsie also gave me the manuscript of *The Fear*, which I thought was glorious.'[13] As Martin was nursing his mother, Keneally told Shirley Yates, 'I suppose I'll have to meet her.' Their meeting would lead to marriage.

Martin's ancestry has been partly traced by Keneally in *The Great Shame*: in the preface he reproduces a petition from Esther Larkin, of Laurencetown, Galway, begging for permission to travel with her two sons to New South Wales to be reunited with her husband and their father, Hugh Larkin, a Ribbonman transported for life. The petition was refused and Larkin eventually married Mary Shields, another Irish convict, in Goulburn.

Her story is also told in *The Great Shame*. Larkin and Shields's eldest son, Thomas, and his wife Harriet (née Jones) had a large family, the youngest of whom was Judy's mother, Eva. Keneally also wrote the script for a musical play, *Transport*, which tells the story of Mary Shields, Judy's great-grandmother, and the other women on the transport ship *Whitby*. The show opened at the Irish Repertory Theatre in New York on 6 February 2014.

Keneally could not ask Judy's father for permission to marry his daughter; Arthur Martin had died of cancer before they met. But he did ask Shirley Yates for advice about buying an engagement ring.

'Spend more than you can afford,' Yates advised.

'What?' demanded Keneally.

'She'll always look back and remember,' Yates insisted. Yates was also thinking of the poverty endured by most writers, and imagined that an expensive ring might yield a stay of penury for a little while if it ever had to be pawned!

Keneally went to confession on the eve of the wedding, which was to be celebrated with a nuptial Mass at eleven on the morning of 21 August 1965. Prenuptial confession was the usual procedure for a Catholic bride and groom. 'You had to go – it was not difficult,' Keneally recalls. 'Actually, it was a bloke who'd been in the minor seminary – a parish priest who'd been up in Springwood – Father George Meredith. I confessed to the normal things engaged people do and he was very lenient. We were married in the chapel at St Patrick's Christian Brothers College. There was an inward turmoil in us both about it all.'[14] The wedding breakfast was held in the same reception rooms booked a few years previously for Keneally's ordination breakfast: 'Jonroe', in Ashfield, which at the time was *the* venue for 'westies' – those who lived in the western suburbs.

During the year before his engagement and wedding, Keneally had endured another dark night of the soul, although he could find no reason for it. 'I was, for the first time, admitted to St John of God Hospital, Richmond, a psychiatric hospital. There was a bloke in there I'd been to school with. He was older by about two years, a big, robust, freckled Aussie kid who'd played in the First XV, and that was magic to me at school. He had studied in the Franciscan seminary and gone bonkers like me, except he was worse. All the time I was there he was profoundly sedated, and occasionally he'd have a little rave.'

Keneally had finished *The Fear*, but he felt drained and uncertain. 'Novels are very psychologically testing ... I think it was the post-seminary thing that was on me all the time; I had time alone then with the book and the doubts and it all came to a head. A day came when I couldn't operate – I just couldn't move. As far as I remember, it was very much drugs that got me through. I can remember above all the St John of God Brothers coming around and giving out tablets and so on. I think I was there about a month, in a ward. After a while I was able to read. There was a lot of just sitting there unconsciously. No shock treatment, but some of them there did have it.'

The institution was at Richmond, north-west of Sydney, and Keneally describes it in *Three Cheers for the Paraclete*, when 'Father Egan' is admitted to a psychiatric hospital:

> Sixty years past, the house had belonged to a pastoralist, had begun its life as one family's stone bungalow, with tower. It had suited the departed sheep king's swank; and it suited the present dwellers, all suffering classically named diseases, that Jason striving should hold up the balustrade, that lumpy girls labelled Hebe and Nike should stand in the stained-glass windows, or Apollo and Daphne languish asexually above the main door. The humble brothers of a Hospitaller order passed with bed-pans and white mixture ...[15]

Keneally has said that no specific diagnosis was made, and he gradually emerged from the depressed state in a pattern that would become all too familiar. 'It should have bothered Judy that she was marrying someone with a mental problem,' he says, 'but I think she understood the precarious ledge on which that background could lean. When I get the guilts about how mad I was, as I often do, and how obsessed I was about writing, I feel very bad.'

As Keneally began married life in suburbia, he started another novel, this time about a Catholic couple whose marriage was vastly, unimaginably different to his own – and destined to end very badly. 'Did you read the dedication in *Bring Larks and Heroes*?' he asked a journalist. She nodded and Keneally smiled at his wife. The dedication reads: 'to Judith who nursed this poor herd of chapters to pasture.'[16]

13

Individuality of Style

Whenever Keneally pushed open the heavy door of the Mitchell Library, in Macquarie Street, Sydney, he anticipated a voyage of discovery. Its main reading room is a huge stateroom, with book-panelled walls, high, handsome ceilings and workmanlike reading tables. Here Keneally could delve into documents about early Australia. He wanted to understand the 'sly antiquity of the place', as his next main character, Phelim Halloran, describes it.

In 1965 he was at the Mitchell Library to read the journal of a soldier-writer who had set out on his own voyage of discovery: Watkin Tench, an officer in the Marine Corps, who sailed with the First Fleet to Botany Bay. Tench was a keen explorer, and recorded his observations of the new land in a journal: *A Complete Account of the Settlement at Port Jackson* was published after his return to England.

Keneally was particularly impressed by two passages in Tench's journal: one about two Aborigines who were brought out of the bush, with the best Rousseauian hope of turning them into eighteenth-century gentlemen, and the other about a convict woman who was sentenced to be hanged. 'She tells them they can't hang her because she's with child,' Keneally explained to an interviewer in 1967. 'They empanel a jury of convict women to examine her, then the chairwoman says "Your Honour she's as pregnant as I am" and they hang her the same afternoon.

Tench doesn't tell the story with any squirming; he tells it as an interesting yarn. When I read these two passages I thought, whacko, I'll write a novel about the true motivation of the eighteenth century gentleman!'[1]

Keneally had been 'feeling his way' towards his next novel, initially considering the portrayal of a political mystic, perhaps a Père Joseph or Joan of Arc in modern dress, but, having been 'blasted for improbability' over *The Fear*, changed tack. He told Patricia Rolfe, a journalist at *The Bulletin*, that he might try a Gothic picture of the convict system. 'The central figures will be an Irish marine and a convict woman, who decline to go through a marriage service because there is only a Protestant clergyman in the colony.'[2]

The Irish marine is Phelim Halloran and his Irish servant girl is Ann Rush. Corporal Halloran claims convict Ann as 'my secret bride, my bride in Christ' under the dispensation offered by a small treatise written by Dean Hannon, *De Vera Amoris Disciplina*. 'The book that Halloran read did exist,' Keneally says. 'I probably read it in the seminary.' It contains a law stating that 'two people, moved by mutual affection to contemplate the holy state, yet so placed that they will not, with reasonable certainty, find within a month a priest before whom to exchange their vows ... are permitted to administer the sacrament to each other by giving the normal marriage pledges. They are then as truly married as if they had spoken their promises before the Holy Father himself in the Basilica of St Peter.'

Keneally was attracted to dilemmas of conscience and questions of moral correctness. Halloran is a casuist, and once was a priest in training at Wexford, presumably with Hannon as one of his teachers. He confesses to Ann that Hannon's teaching has left him rather in pieces as a lover: 'Love is a fusing of the mind and will to God, said the Dean, all other loves are good only in so far as they flow from this love ... Of course, there is some sort of dull but steady affection between spouses, aimed at the dull and steady begetting of children ...' This, or a version of it, was what Keneally had been led to believe as a teenager and seminarian. The relationship he built between Halloran and Ann, no doubt influenced by his own newly wedded state, is meant to transcend the warped views of Catholic dogmatists.

Keneally started married life in a white timber bungalow at 5 Hibble

Street, West Ryde, not far from Homebush. Long hours went into producing something to justify a $4000 Commonwealth Literary Study Grant, which he received from the Commonwealth Literary Fund (CLF). Typically, using taxpayers' money bothered Keneally's conscience. He could not just churn this book as he had the earlier ones. He would write seven drafts of *Bring Larks and Heroes* over eleven months before he was satisfied.

When the first draft, with the working title *Old Enemy Road*, was complete, Keneally wrote to A. L. Moore, secretary of the CLF:

> What has emerged is definitely a work of the imagination, a novel and not a documentary, a novel with, I think, a chance of being a good one, but chaotic and uneven as yet ... I realise that, however bashfully and reluctantly, some indication of the plot should be given. The central character, from inside whose mind all the other characters are seen, is a melancholy and witty Corporal of Marines called Halloran who is stationed in a penal colony in the South Seas. He himself has light thrown on him, firstly, by his dedication to a transport lady who works in a grotesque colonial household, and secondly, by his being scandalised at *the System*. He is not emotionally scandalised. He is not appalled by what he sees, as we would be. He is morally scandalised and trapped into a treason for which he and his transport lady die. It is a case of *the System* expelling these two rather raw innocents, of a rotten body killing off its two healthy cells. I'm afraid Halloran's a bit mystical, like some of Randolph Stow's characters, but this was not in imitation, as, to my shame, I got around to reading *Tourmaline*, for the first time last week ...
>
> In telling the story, I've tried to avoid incidents and social features which have been covered in the strictly historical novels which deal with early Australia. Halloran dominates, and it is a novel about him, and an historical novel only in so far as he needs an authentic background against which to function ...[3]

When asked why he chose anonymity of place, Keneally explained that he was not a historian. 'I didn't want to have to stand on my documentation,' he told journalist Gavin Souter in 1967. 'I think this is why Patrick White fictionalised Voss. He had a vision of Voss. If he had called him Leichhardt, he would have had people saying that Leichhardt had four stallions and seven geldings, not eight stallions and three geldings.' Keneally did not want his readers to carry too many preconceived ideas about penal Australia to the book. 'Phillip, Collins, Tench, convict, First Fleet: these words are all too evocative. I wanted to break free from them.'[4]

In his contribution to *In The Making*, Keneally told Craig McGregor that Patrick White was a strong influence on him as he wrote *Bring Larks and Heroes*, and that he had 'swallowed the Nolan and Drysdale interpretation of Australia wholly'. He also acknowledged that his reading of Ernest Hemingway, Dylan Thomas and Vernon Watkins was evident in the book. At that early stage of his writing life, Keneally was a self-conscious writer who often worked images into a draft later. He looked back at these first books and saw their language as eccentric: 'I felt you couldn't just say he left the room; he had to leave the room in a manner that sliced his soul open like a saveloy.'

Alec Bolton, who read *Bring Larks and Heroes* for the publisher Angus & Robertson, appreciated the overall impact of the language:

> I can't remember many books that gave me the feeling of slipping into a past time, with so little of the usual period apparatus to help me along. I don't want to sound hysterical with praise, but you would think Keneally had been reincarnated to write this novel, having in a past life been both flogged and hanged. The book electrified me at all its big scenes, but really is full of memorable passages.
>
> I will never forget the phrase (it was only an aside) describing the old man 'clawing up the breakneck face of his 86th European winter'; or Halloran addressing his imagined child in the womb; or the arrival of the messenger with a single pebble, having, as you casually learn, dropped the other on the way. And all the time you have the strange sense of other-worldliness hanging over the book, as if the drama is in not entirely human terms. In a way I suppose the characters are a bit like people in a miracle play. I didn't fully understand the symbolic dimensions of it all, to tell you the truth. I felt that as the novel becomes more prophetic in tone, the dialogue takes on the quality of Biblical utterance.[5]

The final typescript was submitted to the CLF on 16 December 1966, two months after the arrival of the Keneallys' first child, Margaret Ann, who was born on 13 October 1966 at the Mater Hospital in North Sydney. Keneally was enchanted by his daughter, but had difficulty in getting the typing job done. 'I therefore apologise that the typescript is typed on two different sizes of paper and in two different type faces,' he wrote to Moore. 'However, I am confident you will find it satisfies the requirements.'[6]

The book's title, *Bring Larks and Heroes*, has a poetic ring; it comes from a poem Halloran writes.[7] The colony's Governor, who would determine the fate of Halloran, reads the verse, but 'the pages looked threatened in his big hands. What he saw was the debris of minor inspirations, much crossing and blotting. Two verses seemed to be written whole, although a great number of rhyming words had been written down beside them and scratched out. "Larks and heroes," he said, "smiles of our shy granddaughters. Not my kind of souvenir." He rolled the papers in his palms and put them in the fire.'

In 1970, addressing senior students in an ABC broadcast, Keneally said that Halloran has 'a superstitious belief that if he keeps his moral code, he will somehow find his way back home, to a place where, ultimately, the smiles of his shy granddaughters will bring larks and heroes to his hedge.'[8] It was the desire of the Irish exiles to find their way back home – most did not.

The original handwritten composition was written in a lined exercise book. The page is covered in jottings, like the ones that the Governor treated with contempt, with lists of rhyming words and a few deleted lines. Keneally had also put down a few sums, an indication that his family responsibilities were never far from his mind.[9] 'The idea [for the poem] came from the subconscious desire to surround the Australian hedge with heroes and singing birds,' Keneally explained in 2013. 'Look at the monetary calculations! Characteristic of my attitude towards writing: poetry and money!'

For a while Keneally taught part-time at Holy Cross College, a school for boys near his home. At that stage it seemed a good idea for a writer to keep a part of himself in the real working world. That is what he told journalist Neil Jillett, although Keneally also needed to supplement his income; *The Fear* had not netted a basic wage.[10]

Having finished *Bring Larks and Heroes*, he immediately started work on his next book, which he delivered to his publisher before its predecessor went on sale. The author-entrepreneur estimated that if he wrote and published one book per year, the royalties from these, combined with occasional commissioned work such as reviewing, would be sufficient for him and his family. He saw himself simply as a working man writing a book, or possibly two books, with another one just ahead and a fourth around the corner. He often talked of keeping public service hours, with a break for lunch and weekends free. Theoretically, it could be done, but the pressure Keneally heaped on himself put him on a collision course with his publishers and agents, and meant that his output was inconsistent in quality and acceptability.

Keneally was off to a good financial start with *Bring Larks and Heroes*. James Moad, chairman of Cassell Australia, wrote to tell him that he would be paid an advance on royalties of $2000 for *Old Enemy Road* [*Bring Larks and Heroes*], but considerable negotiation preceded this agreement, as it would with future books.[11] Keneally drove a hard bargain, while publishers protested and sometimes refused to pay the suggested amounts. Moad told the author that Cassell would not consider the advance suggested by Keneally and was certain that no other publisher would agree to it. Moad pointed to the option clause in the contract for *The Fear*: 'The Publishers shall have the first option of publishing the Licensor's next full-length work suitable for publication in book form on terms to be mutually agreed, such terms to be *fair* and *reasonable* . . .'

Moad contended that Keneally's proposal was not 'fair and reasonable'. Firstly, he had not had time to consider the new work and secondly, because sales of *The Fear* were not as good as he had hoped for, the suggested advance was not an economic proposition. He reminded Keneally that if the book became a bestseller, he would reap the reward he was looking for and then possibly be in a position to look at full-time writing. Moad pointed out that few writers of novels alone were in such a happy position. He offered a $500 advance.

Keneally said that he recognised 'a certain indebtedness to Cassell', but persevered until Moad finally agreed to the $2000 advance with this warning: 'When you submitted *The Place at Whitton* we decided to publish feeling that some day you could be recognised in Australia as one of our foremost fiction authors. This thought remained with us with your second novel, *The Fear*, and this is why we wish to publish your new manuscript, despite the fact that the aforementioned two novels have not shown the return desired…'[12]

Bring Larks and Heroes was entered into the competition for the Miles Franklin Award for Literature, a prestigious prize of $1000 for the winning Australian novelist. A press release on 2 April 1968 informed readers of the judges' decision: 'Fifteen novels were submitted "for the novel of the year which is of the highest literary merit and which must present Australian life in any of its phases." In the judges' opinion only five of these novels had sufficient quality to be seriously considered and of those the most outstanding was *Bring Larks and Heroes* by Thomas Keneally.'

The judges agreed that 'individuality of style and conception make this a novel unlike any other. The writing has freshness and flexibility; humour and joy balance the starkness and cruelty of action and setting. The symbolism of good and evil, the conflicts of conscience, have evocative echoes as the story moves like a ritual to its inevitable climax.'[13]

David Halliwell, reviewing for *The Spectator* in England, did not appreciate the book's 'individuality of style' and pronounced it 'unreadable'. He wrote:

> This novel, first published in Australia, comes to us with a fanfare from its native critics: Thomas Keneally has been hailed as 'Australia's most individual stylist since Patrick White.' A stylist he most certainly is. He is all style. Perhaps this is wise of him since his material seems to consist of little but platitudes. A platitude is a platitude is a platitude until it's been tricked up to become a profundity. Mr Keneally applies his style to every obvious idea and commonplace event in sight until they become almost incomprehensible. Almost, because if you want to play detective you can still discern the dreary old bones. The style itself is awkward, disjointed and lacking in rhythms. Mr Keneally beats up a phrase until it dies of dislocation. This is why the book is so tiresome to read.[14]

In Australia, the opinion of literary contemporaries such as George Johnston and Charmian Clift counted for much. Johnston did not have any objection to Keneally's style. He thought Keneally was a better novelist than either Randolph Stow or Patrick White, both of whom had 'an over-obsession with what we loosely define as "style"'.[15] Johnston and Clift fought to be the first to read *Bring Larks and Heroes* and they were both very impressed.

Half an hour after reading the book, Johnston wrote to its author, describing himself as 'quite overwhelmed'. Keneally was thrilled by the letter. Johnston said:

> As another writer my admiration, and indeed my envy, is quite complete. It is a beautiful piece of work which more than deserves the praise it has been given: I sincerely hope it gets the success among readers it equally merits. Aside from the fact that it is the best Australian novel I have ever read – and I do feel that it restates us and Australian writing as Melville with *Moby Dick* restated America and American writing – it will always count with me among the finest of any books I have ever read. I consider it a beautifully contained and flawless work which certainly sings for me. I wish to God I could have written it.
>
> You are enviable indeed to possess such brilliance and artistry so young, and I know you will go on from strength to strength. My very sincere good wishes will go with you. I deeply admire your compassion. Keep writing. You are greatly needed here – and thank you for a great novel.

In a handwritten postscript, Johnston added: 'All this sounds so pompous. I just mean "Good on you, sport!" G.'[16]

Johnston said that Clift intended to write separately, and she did, succinctly: 'I wish you a hundred shy grand-daughters, hedges bursting with larks, and as many heroes as you can sing. I am ravished. Oh sir, we've all been waiting a long time for you. With admiration, Charmian Clift.'[17]

Keneally was starstruck by Johnston and Clift, whose expatriate life in Greece seemed impossibly romantic. Johnston was a good conversationalist with an infectious laugh and a charismatic presence, a forerunner of Keneally on the literary scene. Johnston described Keneally, who had become a close friend, as 'a witty and dancing conversationalist . . . gay, bubbling, unaffected and endlessly curious.'[18]

Patrick White, by contrast, did not like the younger man Keneally. Possibly he was jealous of his success, or annoyed that *Bring Larks and Heroes* was compared favourably with his own work. White wrote to a friend, James Stern: '[I] should like to write about *Larks and Heroes*, but I am prejudiced by all the publicity from this rather revolting little bog-Irish almost priest married to a renegade nun. His book is powerful, but the scenes flicker on and off, and the novelette keeps taking over, and I couldn't count the number of times somebody kicks someone in the crutch – or spikes – and the girl even punches the hero in that place to show her affection. What Australia doesn't do to the Irish Catholics!'[19]

White was notoriously scathing about other writers, and had a reputation for breaking friendships, including that with Thea Astley. Keneally met White on a couple of occasions. 'Sometimes when he took a dislike to people it was in the middle of dinner,' he recalls. 'I was never invited to dinner – those occasions were full of stellar artistic people. I never gave him any reason to dislike me, other than my forwardness in being above my station . . . he was a nasty human being, no question; the only problem being he was a genius!'

In an earlier, more moderate letter to Geoffrey Dutton, White commented: 'I suspect a lot of this [critical enthusiasm] is because he [Keneally] is a decent little bloke who will appear at seminars, PEN functions, and gatherings of Australian writers, instead of a cold, peculiar monster who won't pander to them, and who tells them about their present-day brutalities. As that is what I feel I must continue doing, I suppose I shall continue sinking lower in their estimation.'[20]

Keneally's next book, *Three Cheers for the Paraclete*, became a source of renewed contention with his publisher, Cassell. Keneally had already made overtures to other publishers with *Bring Larks and Heroes*, including Angus & Robertson. Jacqueline Kent explained that move in her biography of Beatrice Davis. John Abernethy, who had been put in charge of local publishing there after he left *The Bulletin*, 'very much wanted him [Keneally] for A&R, [and] brought the new manuscript into the office for everyone to read and make editorial suggestions.'[21] Alec Bolton finished his reader's report by saying: 'It is exciting to think we might get this book and this exceptionally good writer. The novel will take a while to earn its advance, I feel, but the money is well spent ... I can only say that there is no recent A&R novel of which I would expect to sell more.'

Keneally had also approached John Curtain at F.W. Cheshire in Melbourne. Curtain made 'an informal approach' on the strength of Keneally's intimation, at a University of New England seminar in January 1966, that he might reconsider his 'present arrangement'. Curtain wrote: 'We now have the overseas contacts, as well as our local retail outlets, to develop a world market for our "stable" and we are breaking our necks to have someone with your ability and potential. However there are ethics in this game which we willingly subscribe to, and any moves must be made by the author ...'

Then Curtain wrote more cautiously: 'We only publish a few works [of fiction] each year. This is because many of the major novelists publish with English firms, and we do as well as we can. However Cassells is a specialist fiction house, and (Andrew Fabinyi would sack me on the spot if he read this, so please, not a word to anyone) I think that if your present situation is reasonably satisfactory, you are on a fairly good thing already. Please accept this as a very personal, off the cuff sort of comment ...'

Keneally sent the final manuscript to Curtain, who responded: 'It is really magnificent. I am sure that Cheshires' would be very happy to publish it if it were offered them ... it has your magnificent prose with its evocation of atmosphere, with, I feel, a new power of real character portrayal and handling of plot ...'[22]

Despite this enthusiasm, Keneally took Curtain's advice and stayed with Cassell, where he was ethically bound for the present and where he was looked after well. He mentioned *Three Cheers for the Paraclete* to Robert Sessions, who had been thrilled at the chance he was given to work on *Bring Larks and Heroes*. 'It was a real step up from anything I had read by Tom before,' he says, 'and I wallowed in his imagery and the historical detail. There was little editing to do, I recall. I remember to this day the image of a trail of ants, scurrying inside from an impending storm, "having carried in the sunlight on their backs"'.

At the time, Sessions' response to the prospect of *Three Cheers for the Paraclete* was encouraging: 'I was most interested to read your letter of

July 6th and to know that you are so far advanced with another novel. Of course we want the opportunity of reading your new work, and when you have finished THREE CHEERS FOR THE PARACLETE please do not hesitate to send it down to us . . .'[23] Keneally sent the manuscript in early September 1967 and Sessions started reading at once: 'I am well into it and am finding it to be powerful stuff. I am also enjoying it hugely . . . I hope you will bear with us for a while now whilst we give this new novel the consideration it demands.'[24]

By the time James Moad wrote to Keneally to say that Cassell wanted to publish *Three Cheers for the Paraclete*, Keneally was moving towards Angus & Robertson, where he was establishing a good relationship with John Abernethy.

Moad was understandably annoyed about this because a contract had been sent within the three months specified between receiving the manuscript and making an offer. The only way that a book could be successfully published was with mutual confidence, he told Keneally, and 'if the association breaks down, neither side benefits'. Moad stressed that Cassell had made an investment in Keneally, but by the end of February 1968 the relationship was severed.[25]

Keneally accepted Angus & Robertson's offer to publish *Three Cheers for the Paraclete*, which came as a shock to Sessions. He had put a lot of time into the manuscript, seeking the opinions of other readers and making detailed suggestions for revisions in what he called his 'treatise' on *Paraclete*. He and Keneally had reached the stage, he thought, that they could discuss the work frankly, 'in the best tradition of author/editor relationships'.

Keneally had expressed his anxiety that aspects of *Bring Larks and Heroes* had not been worked through fully, which Sessions took to mean that he was not satisfied with the final editing. 'I believe we prepared and produced it to look, feel and become a best seller,' Sessions wrote. 'You tell me that you will "implement my suggestions" [for *Paraclete*] and at the same time mention the possibility of "another stable". My loyalties are to Cassell naturally enough and it sticks a little to think of a job half done to be completed under a different association. I had necessarily become very involved in *Paraclete*, and not being able to see that involvement through to its logical end is a very great disappointment.'[26]

Rumours about Keneally changing publishers would follow him for his entire writing career. Sessions and Moad both agreed that a literary agent would have prevented or at least mitigated misunderstandings. Keneally asked George Johnston about his agent, and Johnston wrote on Keneally's behalf to David Higham Associates in London, which had acted as his overseas agent for many years. Nothing came of this inquiry, although Bruce Hunter from the agency wrote to Keneally expressing an interest in representing him.[27]

Soon after *The Place at Whitton* was published, Keneally had received a letter from Jacqueline Reynolds, director of the International Literary Management Agency, London, asking him to consider allowing it to represent his interests.[28] She contacted Keneally again when *Bring Larks and Heroes* was about to be published, by which time she was working with Curtis Brown, a well-established agency in London: 'I am, as you know, a great admirer of your work and it would give me immense pleasure to handle it for you. I appreciate that if you have just come to a satisfactory arrangement with a publisher, you may not feel that this is the right moment to take on an agent . . . but I do hope that you will bear in mind my enthusiasm for your writing should you feel at some point that our help could be valuable . . .'[29]

Enter Peter Grose, a journalist who had been appointed as *The Australian*'s first London correspondent. After a few years he was ready to make a career change. He heard that Curtis Brown wanted to open an office in Australia, and was asked whether he would be interested in working for the company there. 'I went to meet Spencer Curtis Brown,' Grose recalls, 'at the Savoy! He told me I'd recognise him instantly because he was "tall, bald and dull"! I did three months with Curtis Brown being taught how to be an agent, then I was on my way.'

As Grose remembered it, Curtis Brown began operating from an office on the verandah of a flat that he rented in Warung Street, McMahons Point: 'It was part of a mad old house called Il Nido, with a ton of character, and a drunken and eccentric landlady, Mrs Matthews, who would occasionally set fire to it and then douse the flames with water, which flooded into our bedroom. We always knew when Mrs Matthews fell asleep with a fag in her hand.' The new business operated precariously there from January to July 1968, after which it had a basement office at 186 Liverpool Street in the city. At some stage, Abernethy, with whom Grose had made contact, said to him: 'I don't often say this, but I think Tom should have an agent.' Abernethy arranged for the author and the agent to meet. On 21 January 1970 Reynolds wrote to Keneally from London, saying she was pleased to have heard from Grose that Keneally would be represented by Curtis Brown.[30]

Negotiating publishers, agents, reviewers and readers went with the 'business of writing' that Keneally was building. Sometimes mistakes, and even enemies, were made. The publication of *Three Cheers for the Paraclete* had one reviewer enthusing that Keneally 'writes like an angel', for instance, while Keneally was exchanging verbal blows with another because of that reviewer's 'massive misconceptions' about the novel.

14

I Stand by the Book

Graham Greene was one reader who appreciated Keneally. He read *Three Cheers for the Paraclete* with pleasure. 'I found it very funny indeed,' he said, 'the rather awful comedy inherent in a priest's life, especially a post-conciliar priest's life.'[1] Keneally and Greene met for the first time in 1970. 'I enjoyed meeting you during my brief visit to Sydney,' Greene wrote afterwards. 'I do hope you and your wife will look me up when you come to London in September.'[2] A second meeting did not occur, but Keneally cannot remember the reason. 'We may have talked in Sydney about *The Heart of the Matter*, which raised so many questions of Catholic theology,' he says, 'and he would have read *Three Cheers for the Paraclete*. We would have had much in common!'

James Maitland, the main character in *Three Cheers for the Paraclete*, is a young cleric, 'a rare one', according to Costello, the canon lawyer in the story. Maitland is 'a man of good faith protesting where he sees need of it'. So was Keneally. As he wrote *Three Cheers for the Paraclete*, hopes were fading that Vatican II would bring major lasting changes. Some Catholics wanted to make their faith into something more liberal, and were trying to push the limits of Vatican II. Keneally was in contact with 'trendy young blokes' he had known in the seminary, who were conducting 'family eucharists' and speaking at anti-Vietnam rallies.

He knew Roger Pryke, a chaplain at the University of Sydney, whose 2009 obituary in the *Sydney Morning Herald* was headed 'Chaplain Championed New Kind of Catholic'. Ed Campion, who wrote the obituary, said that Pryke had directed students to 'the new thinking then energising the Catholic world'.[3] Pryke's way was to combine the old dream of social justice with theology. 'They were suddenly extremely politically activated and were getting a heady thrill from shocking their bishops,' Keneally wrote in *As the Twig is Bent*. 'They were getting the excitement of doing things priests had never done before and were coming to terms with their celibacy in ways that didn't take literal account of the canon law. I can remember being on a committee of protest about the Pill.'

The protest committee was about the papal encyclical *Humanae Vitae*, which made clear the Catholic Church's opposition to birth control by artificial means. Keneally recalls: 'There was much anger about the fact that in the late twentieth century women were not being given the choice about the number of kids they had. If she was sexually active, a woman should have as many as she could. The rhythm method was tried by conscientious Catholics – not only was that terribly artificial, but it was also inexact! Society was filled with little rhythm-conceived Catholics!

'We were very shocked when the gynaecologist, who was very smooth with a lot of charm and who delivered the girls, came out as a spokesman for the church upholding *Humanae Vitae*. He must have known of the problems that women had. I was aware of friends of ours who had suffered post-natal depression, and they were in a terrible state. There were others who had hypoglycaemia and so on. He was asking women to line up again for things that shortened their lives.'

Keneally went to see Pryke before he began writing *Three Cheers for the Paraclete* to talk through some of the issues he intended raising in the book. After Pryke read the finished book, he wrote to Keneally: 'You get the spirit and musty ethos of Manly and the clerical club very very well even with incidents that must appear bizarre though I know what many of such like have happened [sic].'[4]

In those days the church was a living question for Keneally. 'I still wanted – and I think this was true of a lot of ruined tykes – to extract a show of humanity from this obdurate parent under whom we had grown up,' he told author Candida Baker in 1986. 'We wanted them to say, "Yes, we've been hard on vulnerable humanity and therefore we are going to operate in a new way." But of course that was not to be, and probably never could be.'[5]

Three Cheers for the Paraclete is about a radical young priest in conflict with his superiors and Keneally seems to be ticking off grievances through the book. By the end, Maitland knows he does not belong in the House of Studies. He reflects that 'it's a sad life for a priest if all he knows is that the old-style religion won't wash, but doesn't know yet what will. If I'm visibly that way I'd be better off out of this place.' Yet he stays on. 'I'm an institutional being,' he says. 'My one hope is to wait for my institution to re-establish contact with the ... living truth again.' He admits that he has nothing to set up against his colleagues' dogmas, and he does not even resent them effectively. 'I can be angry, I have been. But it doesn't last.'

Keneally was angry with the church. Perhaps he wondered as he wrote the book what it might have been like if he had stayed within its confines, but at the time of leaving his mental state had made that impossible. Men like Ed Campion (on whom the character of Maitland was loosely based) stayed on, in the hope that the institution would reconnect with the 'living truth', but even if it did not, they would interpret their priesthood individually.

A reviewer for *Time* magazine pointed out it was likely that, sooner or later, 'conflicting views [in the Catholic Church] would be explored in fiction; it is only strange that the first credible and moving novelistic exposition of the crisis of faith among clergy and laity that followed Vatican II should come out of Australia.'[6] The book had come to Keneally easily after the hard labour of *Bring Larks and Heroes*. It all seemed a sort of revelation of what he knew about 'the iron realities of a priesthood which three out of four men did not believe in'. The book is a composite of characters and situations he had experienced, and in it he manages to articulate, with biting wit, some kind of a protest against the inhumanity and self-deception he had witnessed.

Keneally received a Commonwealth Literary Fund Fellowship, worth $6000, following the publication of *Bring Larks and Heroes*, and then won the Miles Franklin Award again, this time for *Three Cheers for the Paraclete*. He also received an encouraging letter from Manning

Clark, whom he much admired and to whom he had sent a copy of the book. 'What I specially liked about the work was the daring you had displayed – or rather the courage to probe to the very bottom of belief in 1968,' Clark wrote. 'I am not going in for all the trite remarks about your gifts to create people, your gifts as a comic writer, and your gift to keep a story moving. What really matters to me is the heart of the person who is directing all these characters, and what I like most of all is what that heart tells the author to say.'[7]

Despite such recognition, Keneally reacted angrily to reviews. Brian Kiernan's review in the *Australian* may have damned the book with faint praise, but he commented fairly that it was 'highly relevant to Catholicism today', and that it confirmed Keneally's 'significant development' as a writer, 'in maturity, control and craftsmanship'. Kiernan's tone could perhaps be interpreted as patronising, but not more so than that of many other reviewers.[8]

Keneally responded in a personal letter to Kiernan, admitting later that he was breaking a fundamental rule: 'Never answer a reviewer.'[9] He wrote:

> I do not presume that an attempt to correct your massive misconceptions about this novel would be met with any enlarging of your undergraduate perceptions . . . one despairs of the moral arrogance of a young man who can fling about terms such as 'spiritual vacuum'. It may have taken you three seconds to conceive the phrase; it took me seven months to examine the sources of the book and decide them valid . . . In fact, the book is open-ended – it is an examination of a spiritual desert brought about by the fossilisation of dogma and observance. Maitland is actually *meant* to be spiritually vacant – the questions remaining being (a) is spiritual vacuum a fit theme to attempt? (b) is it well delineated in the novel? Since you fail to perceive (a), you can hardly have answered (b) . . .

Keneally ended the diatribe by saying: 'Let me tell you though. I stand by the book.'[10] That sounded like Maitland telling His Grace that he believed his book, *The Meanings of God*, was a valid book. 'Even a good book.'

Kiernan replied immediately:

> I was upset to read that my review had proved such a disappointment to you. Apart from the title ['Great Expectations – Not Quite Realised'], which you would know I wasn't responsible for, I thought it read as a favourable review . . . your objection is primarily to the phrase 'a spiritual vacuum that seems as much the author's as the hero's'. This was not intended as a personal comment on yourself, which I agree would have been most impertinent . . .[11]

Mollified, Keneally wrote back saying that the critic had done 'the very thing calculated to pull up dead a rampaging author – i.e. shown humility and some graciousness'. Kiernan had offered to make a public apology, which Keneally declined. In the long letter, he continued his defence of *Three Cheers for the Paraclete*, as if trying to convince himself. Then he deprecated *Bring Larks and Heroes* – unexpectedly, given his various public statements stating unequivocally that it was a good book. He wrote to Kiernan:

> I believe that it [*Three Cheers for the Paraclete*] is more genuinely and honestly a novel than BLAH ever was . . . Halloran hanged in Nov '66, the bastard, but his shade plagues me still. *Paraclete* is a good book in its own right, and – that Irish yob! BLAH isn't even a novel. It's a prose work, grotesquely overestimated. If you wish to esteem anything, why not a novel, a work of *irony*? . . . I hope, if ever you're professor of Australian lit., if you *have* to make them read anything, make it *Paraclete*. It's for real. It's the stage innumerable men of good faith are at.[12]

To which Kiernan replied:

> *Paraclete* seems to be arousing a lot of interest down here [Melbourne] – for the issues it raises as well as for its intrinsic virtues. As you would know, Melbourne is strong on liberal Catholics and those, and outsiders, I've spoken to welcomed its insights. As an outsider who takes a not unsympathetic interest in issues like the recent encyclical, I found the novel provided an imaginative insight.[13]

Kiernan said many years later that he was upset by Keneally's personal letter because he had naively assumed that the distinction made by New Criticism between the reader's sense of an authorial presence in the text and the actual author would be familiar to him. 'It wasn't,' he says. 'Later, academically trained critics similarly gave offence when they declared, often to their faces, that authors were dead.' In the revisionist ways of authors in the public eye over a long time, Keneally would see later that *Bring Larks and Heroes* is the book that has endured, and even been granted classic status. Kiernan included it in courses he was teaching. He also gave the book a place in his 1971 canon of Australian novels in *Images of Society and Nature*. Kiernan's opinion that *Paraclete* provided imaginative insight has also stood the test of time.

Keneally's outburst to Kiernan was a knee-jerk reaction by a man who, at this stage of his life, was ever ready to 'come the knuckle' when angry or offended. George Johnston in 1968 described Keneally as a very natural man gulping natural air 'in the sometimes rarefied air of the world of creative arts, with its high-strung temperaments and sensitivities and prickly conceits'.[14] Keneally could rightly be numbered among those with high-strung temperaments and sensitivities, but he had nothing to worry about with Johnston, a committed admirer of his work, who read *Paraclete* in one sitting. 'I got totally caught up and simply couldn't put it down,' he wrote to the author. 'As a protestant – indeed as a lapsed Presbyterian! – I found the Catholic as well as the human dilemmas profoundly interesting and moving. Characterisation I thought superb. The setting – and indeed the whole novel – has a wonderfully compelling ring of truth.'[15]

To survive the cut and thrust of literary criticism, Keneally had to learn not to overreact, nor to pen a hasty retort. Even his first published story, 'The Sky Burning Up Above the Man', had its detractors. In the issues of *The Bulletin* that followed the story's publication, the 'Letters' page included a few negative responses from readers who were stung by the 'anti-Catholic' imputation. One reader had been buying the magazine and recommending it to others because it gave the Catholic point of view a fair hearing, 'but that story was a mistake . . . I am not a narrow-minded Catholic by any means, but this does disappoint me. I am sure it will lose some of your new sales.'[16]

Michael Wilding's comments in *Southerly* about *Three Cheers for the Paraclete* were more damaging than Kiernan's. Wilding pointed to many deficiencies, as he saw them: too much plot, a 'volume of incident', changes of plan, careless shifts of consciousness, dead language, and irresolution in the conclusion. Wilding permitted 'the generous richness' of Keneally's writing, but it was a richness that always ran the risk of sloppiness. 'He writes in bold hit-or-miss emotive strokes . . . Keneally is writing too fast to revise, too fast to listen to the contemporary world. This is the destructive trap for the full-time professional writer in Australia.'[17]

Keneally responded to Wilding's criticism of *Three Cheers for the Paraclete* – without mentioning his name or that of any other critic – in a defiant article, 'The Novelist's Poison', published in *The Australian Author* in October 1969. Wilding told Kiernan that he thought the article 'seemed to be replying quite closely to my *Southerly* piece'.[18] When he wrote that article, Keneally was awaiting, with some trepidation, the publication of his fifth book, *The Survivor*, so he was getting in first. He was anticipating harsh criticism.[19]

Thirty years into his career, when asked what kept him awake at night, Keneally replied: 'Fear of critics.'[20] He could complain that people were at liberty to say nasty things in the public press about writers, and the writers had no redress, but it could equally be said that he was saying nasty things about the Catholic Church with impunity. Earlier in his career, Keneally had said that he was not concerned about the effect his writing might have on Irish-Australian Catholics. 'I write about them, not for them,' he said defiantly.[21] *Paraclete* maligned the church more openly, and the words he put into the mouths of his characters were offensive to some: 'You think of the Church as Christ's young bride already come into the fullness of her beauty. I think of her as a scruffy old eyesore with half her tats drawn who's whored around too much with politicians.'

The media 'got hold' of Keneally as a ready spokesman and 'authority' on all that was wrong with the Catholic Church. His views were shared by some of his contemporaries; some old friends laughed at this outspoken critic whom they had known to be a shy and uncertain man, while others looked on having expected some sort of outburst.

In 1968 Peter Harrington wrote to Keneally:

> Congratulations on your latest book. Four to your credit is indeed a great achievement in such a short space of time and its reception promises great things for the fortune; sorry, Mick, I meant the future. I have read *Three Cheers* . . . with great interest and naturally it contains a lot of familiar people and places. I did enjoy reading it, Mick, and to me, aware of many of the problems it portrays found it very challenging . . . I realise, Mick, that in writing a book like this, you are endeavouring to penetrate and understand so much of what went and what is going on in the life of the Church and its Priests here in Sydney. I believe that your writing will make a great contribution to our country and to the Church in time.[22]

Pat Connor also wrote, telling 'Michael' that he had preached three times at St Mary's Cathedral on the afternoon of 20 October 1968:

> As I paced up and down the corridor that leads from the sacristy into the transept (which reminded me irresistibly of the tunnel one walked through at the boxing stadium at Brisbane before entering the ring) I kept thinking of Maitland doing his stuff from the same pulpit . . . Just for the hell of it, I asked Eric Burton, before he went out to say mass, whether he had read your latest novel. He launched into a tirade against you, the gist of which was that you were a 'spoiled priest'. What stuck in his craw, it seemed, was that when Phelim [Halloran in *Bring Larks and Heroes*] was waiting to be hanged all he worried about was whether he would foul himself – 'no thoughts about our Lady' . . . I did enjoy the Paraclete – and found it, in your deathless phrase, 'quite unputdownable'.[23]

Many years after receiving that letter, Keneally said that Connor was 'the best priest we ever met'. Connor was a radical priest, whom he met at the Catholic Church in Epping. 'He was a pacifist, anti-Vietnam and anti-apartheid,' Keneally said when he heard of Connor's death in 2015. 'We played tennis together and formed a lasting friendship.'

People like Burton, who regarded Keneally angrily as 'a spoiled priest', and Paddy Downie's mother did not appreciate Keneally in the role of vengeful critic. Vena O'Leary, long-term family friend and mother of Shirley and

Wendy, accused him of being too proud and did not want to know him for quite a long time. Ed Campion, remembering 'The Young Keneally' for an article of that name in the *International Catholic News*, knew that there were people, 'driven by some curious loyalty, who refuse to read a Keneally novel and who counsel that he is "certainly a danger for young people"'. The possibility of his being a danger to young people was a reference to what Keneally had seen in Greene's *The Heart of the Matter* when he'd spoken about it at the Manly 6.45 Club thirteen years previously.[24] Tom and Elsie, supportive as ever, closed ranks, confronting for the first time just how deeply the seminary years had embittered their older son.

'There was an element of vengeance in what I was saying,' Keneally admits. 'A part of me was shocked and embarrassed by some of the things I was saying! It got to the stage that I was embarrassed to approach them [family members and friends]. People thought I considered myself grand, and that was said. But it was embarrassment.'

Keneally's article 'The Humanist Priest' directed readers to 'the petrified structure of the Church'. He described priests known to him who operated in an 'underground parish', working for people privately, on a human level, often on terms contrary to canon law. Many voiceless junior clergy, he declared, despaired of the anti-human moral code they learnt in the seminary and yearned to serve usefully. 'In the meantime, the Australian community receives back a constant stream of émigrés from religious orders, convents, seminaries. Many of them are in bad psychiatric health, others are unqualified for anything other than the shadow world they are leaving. Nothing is done for them.'

In 1965, when Keneally had been at a bar at the Western Suburbs Leagues Club with Peter Lawler and Greg Parnham, a Catholic assistant headmaster had said scathingly in their hearing: 'That's what a seminary's for – weeding out.' Keneally had lunged at him, shouting, 'Yes, but people aren't stalks of bloody paspalum!' Only the press of people around them prevented the angry ex-seminarian from landing a punch.

He took a lighter approach in 'Keneally on Critics: Have a Chocolate-Coated Funnel-Web', published in *The National Times* in 1972. In it the author singled out David Halliwell, who had been so critical of *Bring Larks and Heroes*. 'I considered writing a letter: "Dear Mr Halliwell, I feel it my duty to tell you that your wife has run off with a Rugby League second-rower from Huddersfield. She sends her assurances that she was not swayed by brute good looks, but by the heady intellectual stimulation the new liaison offered."'

Brian Kiernan and Carl Harrison Ford, he wrote, were 'two members of the "trying to please their old professors" school. The characteristics of this school are dull style, a capacity to spot a nit at 40 paces and a belief that they are somehow patrons of Australian letters. There is a streak of puritanism in this group too. They disapprove of rapid composition on the part of novelists . . .'[25]

Kiernan believes that the author's open letter to him and Harrison Ford 'clearly indicates that Keneally resented academic critics opining whether he was eligible for inclusion in their national literary pantheon or condemning him for falling short by their standards. His was a fair comment.'

Keneally was receiving good reviews in the United States of America, with Martin Levin saying in 'The Ordeal of Father Maitland': 'Mr Keneally, an Australian, and very much his own man, is by way of being a poet. His novel about a doubting priest is rich in unexpected visions and sudden epiphanies . . . According to his publisher, Mr Keneally studied for the priesthood but did not take orders. Nonetheless, he did not completely relinquish the sphere of divinity. He writes like an angel.'[26]

'In my vanity when I was young,' Keneally admits, 'I wanted all reviews to be good. This was a stupidity that pursued me into middle life. [Australian playwright] David Williamson and I have discussed the fact that we both have that sensitivity and we behaved stupidly towards people in the past. We're not the only writers like that, mind you, and we didn't extend to horsewhips.'

Williamson once wrote a rather sad and disillusioned letter to his critics, among them some of Australia's best-known playwrights. A copy has been kept in Keneally's papers at the National Library. It read, in part:

> Dear Playwrights, I wondered, in my dream, why all of you could be so collectively ungenerous, when generosity of the human spirit seemed to be so highly prized by you all. I thought that the one good thing was that I now know how you *do* feel about my work and I won't embarrass any of you by behaving as if I am your artistic equal. Then I said fuck the lot of you and woke up . . .[27]

As a reviewer himself, Keneally always tried to find the good in a book. 'I realised I was playing with people's lives,' he says. 'I wanted reviewers to be more careful on an industrial level because they did have a bearing on how many copies were sold, especially in those days. I don't think that's as true anymore. I did think that some reviewers were too cavalier in marshalling their arguments against a book that has taken a long time to write. Now I believe that's the nature of the game and you'll never change it. Something that took you three years will be condemned in 600 words by a bloke who took an hour and a half to write the thing. Those are the terms of trade, whereas I was foolishly trying to change those terms. In trying to change them, I turned reviewers against me, as probably did David Williamson.'

15

Why Not Write the Great Australian Drama?

In December 1968 Keneally's garage-cum-office in Hibble Street, Ryde, was abandoned in favour of a room at the University of New England, Armidale. The family relocated to a weatherboard house at 7 Catherine Street in the small inland city north-west of Kempsey, a 'university town on the tableland to the wheat, sheep and cattle towns on the inland plains'.[1] Their new home was in a pleasant location, with a market garden and orchard nearby, and horses grazing in the paddocks.

Keneally was ready for a change from writing nonstop, juggling family demands and media requests. He now had a second daughter, Jane Rebecca, born on 12 November 1967 at the Mater Hospital. Keneally was making a reasonable living but the pressure to produce an annual novel was starting to tell. It was like an experimental crop, he thought, as anything could go wrong. He wanted the security that a regular job offered – at least for a while. 'It was very attractive to have a steady income for a change instead of waiting for royalty cheques,' he told the university's student newspaper in 1969. 'And you know, royalty cheque waiting *does* tend to startle bank managers!'[2]

He was appointed as a lecturer in drama, working for the Department of University Extension, in a building which 'faced a park full of thick British trees secreting deep cool beneath their heads of foliage'.[3] It may seem strange that Keneally, a novelist, should be lecturing in drama, but he had by now written two plays, both of which had been performed in Sydney, and he was keen to write more. The first was *Halloran's Little Boat*, based on incidents from his work in progress at the time, *Bring Larks and Heroes*. The University of New South Wales Drama Foundation, in association with the Elizabethan Theatre Trust, produced *Halloran's Little Boat* at the Jane Street Theatre. The first performance, by the Old Tote Theatre Company, was on 15 November 1966.

Because *Halloran's Little Boat* was Keneally's first attempt at writing a play, he needed, as the critic Geoffrey Hutton pointed out, the Jane Street Theatre's 'workshop atmosphere, its economy productions and its emphasis on criticism, including self-criticism'. Hutton also compared the adjustment from novelist to playwright to that of a painter becoming a sculptor: 'In the novel he is working on a flat surface, he can show his subject in the widest range of tones, filling in his background and exploring the most diverse effects of light and colour. On the stage he works in the round, cutting out his characters with a cold chisel. They must appear solid and they must support themselves.'[4]

Few writers have succeeded in moving smoothly from one medium to the other, but the play went on to have a successful season at the Perth Festival. There, it was performed by St Martin's Theatre Company, which repeated the production in Melbourne at its home theatre in St Martins Lane, South Yarra. *Halloran's Little Boat* was also the first Australian play produced by the Independent Theatre in Sydney.[5]

Rehearsals for Keneally's second play began on 15 January 1968, and they were, according to its producer, John Clark, one continuous and quite radical workshop of the script.[6] The play, *Childermas*, was commissioned by the Australian Committee of Responsibility for Children of Vietnam, and began as a group project on the Piscator–Brecht pattern. The original synopsis was an interpretation of the Nativity story in which the Three Kings made their journey through a decimated Asia to a burnt-out manger. Keneally took over responsibility for the script, but the general opinion was that the finished product still showed evidence of the dictum that 'a camel is a horse put together by a committee'.

Keneally interpreted the committee's vision by equating the plight of modern children in war-torn parts of the world with the biblical 'slaughter of the innocents'. The word *Childermas* refers to the Feast of the Holy Innocents. Many people queried, after seeing the play, what it was all about. Ric Throssell, who produced it with the Canberra Repertory Society in 1969, explained that *Childermas* was not abstract drama:

> You need no magic spectacles. But it does call for a rather different kind of audience involvement. This is not the 'well-made play' with three neatly constructed acts, tightly contrived plot and a convenient unity of style. You do not expect a tidy exposition, an orderly development of theme, scene by scene, until all is explained and nicely packed away at the final curtain.
>
> It is as if Thomas Keneally is asking, 'Wait a while. Hang on. Let me finish.' So that the whole play is exposed, impression upon impression, idea by idea, before the audience is invited to reach its conclusions. Even then questions may remain unanswered, perhaps simply because there is no answer. But the theme remains like a torch in the darkness: the eternal search of men for an ideal; for faith; for peace. This is the symbol of Holy Child and the Song of the Innocents. An ideal, debased by Authority in the name of War and Order, but in the end unquenchable.[7]

The play opened at the Old Tote Theatre, Sydney, in February 1968 and was also performed under Throssell's direction at the Playhouse, Canberra Theatre Centre, in October 1969. It had a brief season at Her Majesty's Theatre, Brisbane, and in the town hall at Armidale, where the audience was, generally speaking, perplexed. They saw a revised version of the play, with a new text issued through the Department of University Extension early in 1970. By then, Keneally was about to leave the university.

In early 1969, however, he had started well in his new role. The campus was already familiar to him because of regular visits he'd made since 1966 to participate in residential programs for adults organised by the Department of University Extension. The first one in which he was involved was the 'Australian Literature in Education' seminar, run by Derek Whitelock; the other speakers included Andrew Fabinyi, John Curtain, Max Harris, Russel Ward and Judith Wright. The 1967 program attracted an impressive line-up of tutors, including Keneally, Wright, Thea Astley, Charmian Clift and Ivan Southall. The time spent at Armidale was a pleasant interlude for the writers: they taught, exchanged ideas and established friendships.

In June 1967 Campbell Howard, assistant director in the Department of University Extension, approached Keneally about giving a series of Commonwealth Literary Fund lectures in September.[8] Keneally agreed, and his audiences and the Extension Department staff members were impressed. Frank Bitmead, a lecturer at the Lismore branch, asked Keneally to return in May 1968 to conduct a School for Writers to mark the first Australian Library Week. So it was that Keneally flew north again with several talks prepared: 'Why Not Write the Great Australian Novel?', 'Why Not Write Immortal Prose?', 'Why Not Sell a Million Copies?' and 'Why Not Write the Great Australian Drama?'.[9]

At that point in his literary life, Keneally wanted to write the Great Australian Drama. 'If I could afford not to go on writing novels I would try to write a good play,' he told Craig McGregor. 'Try and try and try. Theatre has a chance of living . . . Theatre has a great potential audience – it is far more involving than television. You can make it into the twentieth century Mass.'[10]

Before starting full-time at UNE, Keneally had to fulfil the requirements of the second CLF fellowship he had won, which included submitting to the CLF the manuscript he was working on after *Three Cheers for the Paraclete*. Until that was done, he could not receive the final payment, nor could he be engaged in full-time work. He had also received notification of his winning the Miles Franklin Award. It was early April 1968 and the family was at Crescent Head, so they sent him a telegram: 'Three cheers for Daddy and Miles Franklin. Margaret and Jane'.[11] After a diversion in Antarctica, which will be discussed in the next chapter, Keneally arrived in the more temperate climate of Armidale by the end of the year.

Keneally enthusiastically began work in January 1969, directing the tenth annual drama school's varied program. Plays for detailed study and performance included *The Trojan Women* (Euripides), *Ring Around the Moon* (Jean Anouilh) and *The Tempest* (Shakespeare). The school was followed by a seminar series, 'Australian Writing in a World Context', which was tutored by Keneally, Thea Astley and Gwen Kelly. The idea was to trace the strengths and weaknesses of the novel, but the highlight for participants occurred when the tutors talked about their own work.

Keneally felt strongly that although it was not possible to teach someone to write, it was important for the would-be writer to have feedback. 'If this sort of teaching [lecturing and tutoring at UNE] has taught me anything,' he had told *The Age* in 1967, 'it's that a young writer usually needs someone to look over his shoulder and tell him where he's going wrong. The writer mightn't agree, but at least the process makes him aware of weaknesses in his work. I wrote two novels before I developed any sound sense of self-criticism; before I properly understood how a novel should be shaped.'[12]

He had particular ideas about the problems faced by dramatists, too, having blasted theatre critics in one of his CLF lectures. He believed that drama critics were intolerant and indifferent to the 'native growth' of Australian plays: 'Although there are some critics who adopt a mature attitude to Australian play writing, these are in the minority. Irresponsible criticism compounds the difficulties of having an Australian play produced. Theatre management knows that local critics will not attack a play that has won acclaim overseas.'[13]

In the first half of 1969, Keneally met with drama groups throughout the district, including the coastal towns of Byron Bay and Coffs Harbour. He organised school drama weekends and a visit by his friend Alexander Hay, senior tutor at the drama school, who had a big influence on Keneally. During the May and August/September vacations, Keneally conducted several seminars for research students in the English department.

A playwrights' retreat took place at the university in August for fifteen novice dramatists of promise to 'square up to the potential of a typewriter and an uncluttered fortnight, to read scripts and to hear words spoken'. Keneally organised the tutor, Harold Lander. The most important individual achievement, according to John Ryan, who has chronicled 'Thomas Keneally in Armidale', was by Michael Parer, 'a former priest and film-maker ... who had a manuscript on "how and why I left the priesthood" ... issued in 1971 as the uneven *Dreamer by Day*.'[14]

For Keneally himself, 1969 was a punishing year, and no easier than the one that preceded it. Alongside his university work, he was occupied with revisions of one novel and the writing of a second, and another play. This imposing schedule, as well as health problems, would force Keneally to take sick leave from the university and, later, leave without pay.

16

The Survivor

Keneally loved telling and hearing stories. 'Novels grew,' he wrote in 1969, 'from tales half-heard and ill-digested that lodge nonetheless in the imagination and demand to be creatively dealt with.'[1] One evening, towards the end of 1966, he was yarning to Alexander Hay, who told him about dining with Apsley Cherry-Garrard, a survivor of the British Antarctic Expedition of 1910–1913, led by Robert Falcon Scott. Cherry-Garrard had talked on and on about his part in the catastrophe in which Scott died. The survivor was obsessed by feelings of guilt.

A year went by after the talk with Hay, and Keneally occasionally mulled over a novel about an aged Antarctic survivor obsessed with something that had happened more than forty years previously. Keneally knew about obsessions and the imperative to be rid of them. In the novel he would exorcise the explorer's demons. He began an intensive reading of all the best-known books and journals about Antarctica. One of his characters observes in *The Survivor*: 'They say nothing of the gulf between man and man.' Another character complains: 'They make expeditions sound like masonic lodges on ice.'

Keneally wrote to every agency he could think of that had interests in Antarctica. Phillip Law, then the vice-president of the Victoria Institute of Colleges, in Melbourne, replied:

> I was most interested in your friend's talk with Cherry-Garrard. I had heard years earlier of a similar talk that a friend of mine had with him and it was apparent then that he was obsessed with certain facts relating to the Scott tragedy ... I am no longer with the Antarctic Division ... There is no chance of your going South with an Australian expedition. A few years ago you could have easily persuaded the Americans to take you but they have clamped down pretty heavily on visitors lately ...[2]

Keneally visited Captain Morton Moyes, who had gone to Antarctica twice with Douglas Mawson and once with Ernest Shackleton. The walls of Moyes's cottage were papered with photographs of Antarctic scenes, and the old man talked readily about personality problems in the explorers' camps. Keneally also met David Burke, a Sydney journalist who had survived more recent expeditions; he had written about his experiences in the novel *Monday at McMurdo*, in which a VIP party, including a US congressman, encounters difficulties in Antarctica. Keneally also corresponded with Charles Blackman, a friendly attaché at the US Embassy in Canberra, but Blackman, like Law, was not optimistic that Keneally could go to Antarctica: the Navy had cut down on taking visitors there.

In his home office at Hibble Street, Ryde, Keneally started to write about the 'pure and terrible' continent, his eyes turning often to a large map of the region hanging on the wall. Two-year-old Margaret, who sometimes visited her father while he worked, became familiar with the geographic mass of Antarctica. That was in the summer of 1968–69, and the author's hand, damp with perspiration, stuck to the page as he wrote about a frozen wilderness.

The new book was provisionally called *On Ice*, but Keneally was finding it difficult to pull together his ideas about guilt (of the Scottish Calvinist kind), obsessions and cannibalism. He began to think that he should have persevered with his original idea of using the CLF money to write a novel about Harry 'Breaker' Morant, the Australian balladeer who was court-martialled during the Boer War.

On a humid day that had started early in the hectic household, Keneally was feeling harassed and depressed. He had been rewriting parts of the Antarctica novel for weeks, but the central character was still wrong and his motivation wasn't correct. Then the phone rang. It was the US Embassy giving him details of an appointment with the then ambassador, William Crook. The desk was immediately, happily abandoned.

Keneally met Crook and his wife in Canberra on 23 October 1968. Crook's wife, Eleanor, charmed Keneally: 'She's a doll!'[3] After talking to Crook, Keneally wrote to Zelman Cowan, then the vice-chancellor of UNE, asking if he could postpone his start there until later in November. 'By all means go to the Antarctic,' Cowan replied. 'We shall look forward to seeing you before long.'[4]

On 11 November 1968, a rainy day, Keneally was on the tarmac at Fairbairn airport in Canberra, waiting to board a plane bound for Norfolk Island and Christchurch, en route to the South Pole. Among the small party there was one other Australian, Sir John Overall, Planning Commissioner for Canberra, who had been the commander of a special commando group during the Second World War. The junior member of the group was twelve-year-old William Crook, son of the US ambassador, who would become the youngest person ever to reach the South Pole. Keneally's brief included covering his activities.

The plane landed on the sea ice at McMurdo Sound. The passengers lined up near the rear hatch, stepping back involuntarily when the door opened and a blinding glare hit them. It was achingly cold, and Keneally's head felt heavy and congested. Standing there under a pale-blue sky that reminded him of New South Wales's Riverina district, he wondered about the 'Antarctica hysteria' that had led men like Scott on, day after day, in appalling conditions. And for what? A geographical spot of only mathematical interest, reached at huge cost. As Keneally looked at the endless white space, such explorations seemed futile; seeing the huts where Scott and Shackleton had sheltered and flying over the Beardmore Glacier left him bemused.

When the group went by plane to the South Pole from McMurdo Sound, Keneally suffered severe nausea and giddiness from the altitude. Wearing glasses was an added impediment because the moisture from his breath froze on the inside of the lenses. The group stayed at the McMurdo Sound base and in an underground facility at the South Pole, getting to know each other well. Individual weaknesses and stretched relations would be more apparent for those who lived together for extended periods. This, like the amazing location, was something Keneally wanted to explore.

'I had never known it could be so massive a place,' he wrote in his account of the trip, 'that the light could be so bright and burning, that the ice could be so all-pervasive. I felt reassured about the novel. This was certainly a continent on which obsession could be built.'[5]

Keneally was back in his hot office after three memorable weeks and keen to rewrite parts of his novel. Then he began work full-time in Armidale. One of the reasons he'd accepted the position was his interest in enclosed groups, evident in the seminary novels and *Bring Larks and Heroes*. He could now observe the mores of a university community and incorporate these in the book. Longstanding Armidale residents have pointed to *Death of an Old Goat*, by Robert Barnard, as the novel that was a more overt send-up of the local university and its staff.[6] *On Ice* (published as *The Survivor*) would be Keneally's campus novel, a popular genre of the time, with predictable characters such as the vice-chancellor, a philandering professor and a resident poet. But Keneally would have two communities in his novel: Antarctica and academia. He had always been drawn to the unspoken tensions in an all-male society and wanted to test his belief that there could not be pleasant fraternity on those arduous polar expeditions. There were bound to be secrets and betrayals among men who lived together too long.

On Ice places Alec Ramsey, the survivor of an old-style Antarctic expedition, in a provincial red-brick university, where he is the director of extension courses. Through a series of flashbacks, the reader is taken to Antarctica, where the leader of the expedition, Stephen Leeming, died. Ramsey is consumed by guilt about Leeming's death, to the point that he is close to a nervous breakdown. The focal points are the petty campus scandals and rivalries, and Ramsey's manic preoccupations.

John Abernethy at Angus & Robertson was uncertain about the book: 'The truth is that it's had us a bit baffled – more baffled, in my case, than any novel I can recall ... what you've done is quite publishable as it stands – compelling scene by scene ... And yet none of us except our first reader was entirely satisfied with the way Ramsey's story is worked out.' The anonymous first reader applauded characters who 'fairly crackled with life and human crankiness and variability. They are at once characters and personalities.' That reader identified a third story behind what was happening in the present at the university and in the past at Antarctica: 'the conflict between pure morality and the human compromise that most people have to make to live comfortably with themselves and other culpable, weak mortals'.

Having studied Abernethy's detailed report and questions, Keneally responded with notes of his own, but noted: 'My answers raise their own problems. I think the book is beyond redemption.'[7] By January 1969, with so many other commitments, he had tired completely of the Antarctic story and looked on it as something pretentious and inconsequential, even though he was still enthralled by Antarctica itself.

For years afterwards he dreamt of that trip with the Americans: the menace and the beauty of Antarctica were like no other place on earth. In a book written about twenty years later, *The Place Where Souls Are Born*, he wrote: 'I still dream of McMurdo Sound icebound, of the sea lions sunning like slugs amongst the upheaved ice slabs along the shore, of the fuming volcano Erebus rearing behind one's back, of the Royal Society Range across the Sound, with the midnight sun five degrees above their summits and shining down the glittering length of glaciers.'

Keneally returned to the Ross Ice Shelf in 2003, his main mission being to return a portion of a hardtack biscuit that he had taken from Scott's hut as a souvenir on the previous visit. The biscuit was in a can of Huntley and Palmers biscuits, the sort of hardtack that soldiers in the First World War ate in the trenches. Keneally's souvenir, near ossified by Antarctica's perpetual freeze, had been displayed at his home in a glass case.

For that second trip, Keneally had a berth on an icebreaker, the *Kapitan Khlebnikov*, which offered 'The Great Explorers: Ernest Shackleton and Robert Falcon Scott Voyage to the Ross Sea'. As it turned out, Keneally left the New Zealand port of embarkation without his guilty biscuit, but it was finally returned by Nigel Watson, head of operations at the New Zealand Antarctic Heritage Trust. Keneally was relieved that he did not have to sneak it back; Watson wrote reassuringly: 'I am pleased to advise the biscuit arrived safely . . .'[8]

Keneally persevered with *On Ice* because he had to fulfil the conditions of a second CLF fellowship, won after *Three Cheers for the Paraclete*. *The Survivor* was written almost entirely in highly charged dialogue, like a play, with two stage settings and, as Nancy Keesing put it in her review, 'many entries and exits'. Given Keneally's interest in drama at the time, it is likely that the analogy is based in fact. But the novel did not work for Keesing, who wrote: '*He* [Keneally] can see his people and *he* can remember their roles and relationships … So many characters (some with obliquely offered official and/or nicknames) were presented and, before they were properly established in terms of the novel, were whisked away. The stage can afford this. The novel cannot.'[9]

Michael Wilding told Brian Kiernan that he had begun reading the 'new Keneally' with some trepidation. 'So far, oddly, I'm enjoying *The Survivor* – much better written, much less verbally careless than the *Paraclete* for the first 50 pages …'[10] Wilding thought that '[t]he comedy of the environment is deftly handled … The exploration of Ramsey's guilts and fears coheres admirably with the campus setting.'[11] Kiernan, undaunted by his earlier brush with Keneally, disagreed and went on the attack as soon as the book was out: 'Apart from the final scenes in Antarctica and a few successful attempts at comedy, I found the novel confusing and the writing frequently laboured … The writing lacks the narrative confidence of the author's earlier novels and is unexpectedly pedestrian …'[12]

This was one of the worst reviews yet of a Keneally book, but it was not totally unexpected. The author had never been really satisfied that he had 'nailed' it in *The Survivor*. He felt, as he had with *Bring Larks and Heroes*, that the motivation of his central character had not been sufficiently proven. One review in particular angered him. Writing in *The Age*, Judah Waten summed up his opinion by saying: '*The Survivor* is certain to generate controversy. I do not think it represents any advance on the author's previous work. It may not be as good. Much of the character drawing becomes painfully apparent: the dialogue is portentous in manner and stilted. Thomas Keneally is a talented man; one expects and looks for something more in his fifth novel. All too frequently it was difficult to fathom just what he thought he was getting at …'[13]

Keneally objected to Waten's criticism that descriptions in the book of 'the acts of hetero and homosexual intercourse were rather commonplace and conventional and therefore distasteful. The lack of art and style in these paltry copulations is particularly brought into evidence by their clashing with the high level of writing in some other parts of the novel.' Keneally annotated that part of the review: 'Simply not true. I hope Waten has read the damned book.' He wrote a letter to the editor of *The Age*, protesting:

> I have scrupulously avoided description of 'the acts of hetero and homosexual intercourse', not for any reason of virtue so much as for the fact that there comes a point where such acts are no longer validly of artistic interest . . . The two chapters in which some mild sexual by-play occurs are direct mockeries of similar scenes in modern novels and are deliberately and fairly obviously meant as a joke. I can understand a writer of Mr Waten's stodgy literal-mindedness missing the point. But being a man of exactitude, he could be expected to know what actually happens in the book.[14]

He regretted the outburst later, especially as Waten, as Kiernan had, declared an immediate truce.

Keneally had entertained thoughts of an Antarctic trilogy. One book would be about a genuinely neurotic explorer, like Scott, and the other would be a humorous one about a modern American sailor in Antarctica. That plan never eventuated, but he did write another book about a doomed polar expedition, *A Victim of the Aurora* (1977). Back in 1969 he hoped that Abernethy's expectations about Viking Press in New York doing a good job on *The Survivor* would prove correct; Abernethy had written to say: 'I'm delighted that they've assigned Cork Smith your regular editor from now on. He's one of their best editors and a terrific bloke . . .'[15]

Again, Keneally was reviewed more favourably in the United States. *Kirkus Reviews*, for example, claimed that the book retained a firm hold on the reader and 'there's no denying its fierce and fateful power'.[16] William Crook, to whom Keneally dedicated the book, wrote to say that he liked the book. He had read a review in the *New York Times* claiming that Keneally wrote like an angel – 'Except I know you aren't.'[17]

Many reviewers (and readers) in Australia did not 'get' Keneally. Sales in Australia were slow, prompting Abernethy to advise Keneally that Angus & Robertson was obliged to remainder the unsold 2800 copies.[18] Penguin Books published *The Survivor* in 1970, and reprinted it in

1971, because the book had shared the 1970 Captain Cook Bicentenary Award in the novel section with Barry Oakley's *Let's Hear It for Prendergast*. Abernethy was jubilant, writing to Keneally that 'it was good to see the Australian reviewers of *Survivor* given such a belt across the mouth'.[19] The ABC's drama department then produced a television version of *The Survivor* in November 1971.

Some of the characters in *The Survivor* resembled known identities, and this gave offence in a small community. In an author's note at the front of the book, Keneally asserts that 'no don, living or dead, has a counterpart among the provincial academics who appear in this book'. Some readers thought otherwise, recognising, for example, a parody of a previous vice-chancellor in the comic 'Chimpy'. Keneally had once been guest speaker at a Rotary Club function, and early in the book he satirically describes all the rituals and characters at a club dinner.

John Ryan, an academic at UNE, was sure that Keneally was having a go at his university colleagues, 'yet it would be wrong to suggest that the book is a *roman-à-clef*, since its purpose is much more than this . . . it might just as fairly be said that *The Survivor* is the first to deal with the problems of the university, its staff, and its philosophies and cultural pretensions on the current Australian scene. This basic artistic purpose should not be lost amidst the social comedy, sly gibes at persons and disciplines, or the very clear description of the campus, the colleges, buildings and social aspects of the Northern Tableland, the Liverpool Plains and the coastal area to the east.'[20]

Keneally was still pursuing his interest in drama. He had accepted an offer from the Adelaide Arts Festival Committee to write a play for the 1970 festival, which would be under the direction of Sir Robert Helpmann. The fee for an accepted play was $1000. Keneally had his doubts about the play, a fable, fearing that it might be rejected as indecent. The play was about a homosexual society of eight people who lived in couples on top of four skyscrapers. 'They look on heterosexuality as an unnatural vice, but they're all burdened by Original Sin, and are trying to become extinct,' he said. 'Then there are two young liberals who hold heretical views and doubt the validity of the system . . .'[21]

Keneally has described *Upstairs: An Apocalyptic Melodrama in Five Acts* as 'a bad pudding of a play', but he wrote to the committee: 'I shall be a happy man if the Adelaide elders pass the play on the grounds both of decency and talent. There is nothing in the play to make a gentleman blush – other than the theme itself. And I must tell you – because lying authors are always punished by some very level-headed god – that it is a good play and even better than good . . .'

It was rejected by the committee. Unfortunately, the first pages of the letter from Rosemary Sweetapple on the committee's behalf are missing; however, on the third page she wrote: 'The Festival in the past refused *The One Day of the Year* and Patrick White, so I guess you are in good company, and they have not the best of records for discernment.'[22] In Keneally's recollection, the play was not rejected on grounds of impropriety. 'They just couldn't see it being staged,' he says. 'Every emerging writer, as I was then, got asked to do everything; give their opinion on everything. A novelist and aspiring playwright was asked to submit a play. They were right to reject it.'

The play was workshopped by the University of Adelaide Theatre Guild in 1969 before being shelved.[23] The script was sent to Penguin Books for consideration, and a request for it was made by Ron Blair of the ABC's Radio Drama unit, but neither the publisher nor the broadcaster went ahead.[24]

Keneally had planned to visit England in April 1970 to take part in a British Drama League Course in London. In his application to the British Council's Visitor Programme he said that the purpose of the visit was 'to receive tuition of the kind that will improve my ability to lecture and tutor in drama, to manage residential schools and organise and take part in drama festivals in this region . . . I would like further to be able to visit the London theatres and increase my rather limited grasp of its demands on the playwright.' He was awarded travel grants by the Myer and Potter foundations, with the option of spending a term in the drama departments at Bristol or Manchester University.[25] But Keneally was groping his way through another 'dark night of the soul' and it proved impossible for him to proceed.

The trip to Antarctica the previous year had provided the sort of escape he craved from time to time. The huge, uninhabited space, remote and forbidding, was far away from the increasingly burdensome demands of the real world. He took recreational leave from the university in October 1969, and then leave without pay. He returned to UNE in January 1970 to direct the eleventh annual drama school, and to participate in the residential school entitled 'The Poet in the Global Village'. By then he had moved back to Sydney's north-western suburbs, notifying correspondents of a change of address to 40 Chester Street, Epping.

Keneally began regular visits to Dr Joseph Brassil, a Catholic psychiatrist in Ryde, and tendered his resignation to the university in May 1970. Kevin Long, the academic registrar at UNE, replied: 'Although no date is mentioned we have assumed your resignation will take effect as from the date of your letter. We regret that you have found it necessary to terminate your appointment.'[26]

17

A Literary Juggler

In Epping, Keneally was close to family and friends again. Margaret, his older daughter, was enrolled at the North Epping Kindergarten at the start of 1970. She would be four years old that year, and her sister Jane three. A Labrador dog named Lindy had joined the family. Keneally had happy childhood memories of Nippy, a black cocker spaniel brought down to Homebush on the train from Kempsey as a pet for him and Johnny. Keneally and the girls took Lindy for walks, getting to know the neighbours, who included Alan and Margaret Smith.

The Smiths knew Thea Astley, who lived nearby in Dorset Street with her husband, Jack Gregson, and their son, Ed. Keneally was nominated as Ed's sponsor when he was confirmed in the Catholic Church. Ed was very fond of Keneally, and always entertained by his endless jokes and anecdotes, his black humour and his skill as a mimic. The morose side of Keneally's personality was never seen at these social occasions. He was good company and enjoyed informal neighbourhood gatherings, as he recalls: 'Jack [Gregson] was pleasant and whimsical, very verbal. Visiting their place was just an endless wordplay. Not a smart alec wordplay. Thea and I had a similar background. She had a compulsive disorder. She occasionally said to me that when she was driving along and there were headlights on the other side, she sometimes felt drawn into them and had to resist them. An academic who later worked with her at Macquarie

University said she'd turn up at work some mornings and say, "I'm sure I ran over someone on the way here." She obviously hadn't but she had this terrible guilt thing. I think, to be even-handed, while it was made worse by the Catholic emphasis on guilt in the old days, she could have come from an evangelical family and still carried an equal load.'

The friendship cooled when Astley said something to which Keneally took exception: 'We didn't have a fight but she said something that I considered hugely insensitive ... She could be insensitive. In those days – by your mid-twenties – you should be making your own world but we tended to stay clear of each other. We met at festivals and exchanged greetings. We were not alienated. If it were now we would have remained firm friends. We are responsible, but naturally if you get into a relationship you have to mature at a rate of knots and that happens to people, even to people who are sane and have fulfilling careers too! In my relationship with Thea I was in a heavy learning curve.'

Astley, according to her biographer Karen Lamb, had the idea that she was an expert in human relationships. She would have spoken to Keneally as if he were still an inadequate seminarian, incapable of really understanding a woman's perspective. Like White, she had a habit of breaking friendships and falling out with people over slights, real or imagined.[1]

Once, at a book club meeting in the home of a friend of Astley's, the group did not know that the writer herself was present; she had told her friend that she did not want to be identified. The group discussed one of Astley's books and were harsh in their criticism. She sat in the corner and listened, then introduced herself at the end of the meeting. Margaret Smith told Keneally about how embarrassed everyone was. 'I was humiliated,' she said.

He laughed. 'That's Thea! She would enjoy scarifying herself!'

Years later, Keneally's daughter Margaret wrote an admiring article about Astley, who knew her as a child in Epping. Margaret referred to Astley as 'the doyenne of Australian literature'. Astley told her that 'writing is a disease – you don't just do it to pay the bills. You do it because you're addicted.' By the time Margaret published the article, in 1993, Astley had published twelve novels.[2] Margaret knew all about the addictive nature of writing, having watched her father at work on book after book. She had ambitions of becoming a novelist herself.

Recognition and attention came too quickly for Keneally. Fame was hard for him to cope with, especially since he needed time to write, time for his family and time to sort out the mental health issues that dogged him. Interviewers would not have seen, below the welcoming, cheerful persona, a man with serious problems. He was too obliging and generous with his time. After a few months of constant interruptions, Keneally rented office space near the Epping railway station and left home for work each day like his neighbours did. However, the arrangement did not prove successful. He missed his familiar environment, and even some of the distractions.

Without the regular income that the university position had provided, Keneally was struggling to make ends meet. Recognition had brought awards, but not all of them were monetary. The Australian Arts Award, for example, given by the Grenfell Henry Lawson Festival of Arts to the Australian considered to have made the most outstanding contribution in the arts over the past year, was a bronze statuette. Keneally won it in 1968. A journalist pointed out: 'As seems appropriate to anything bearing Lawson's name the award carries no cash. We imagine that Keneally, conditioned by early years in a seminary and later ones at a typewriter, is relatively indifferent to money, except insofar as it buys him freedom to write . . .'[3]

Not so. 'People think I earn more than the Prime Minister,' Keneally complained. 'This is not true. We don't live at the swimming pool level, but since *Bring Larks and Heroes* my family can live off my writing.'[4] The challenge to produce a book a year remained, as did the worry that he might not be able to repeat the previous performance. While finishing his sixth book, Keneally took on other commissions, including the script for a film production, *John Eyre*. He received $1000 for five weeks' work, starting in March 1970.[5]

Keneally also wrote book reviews, but he was always uneasy. His experience as the reviewed, rather than the reviewer, had for the most part been unpleasant, at least in his home country. He stopped most review work when he could afford to do so because of what he called 'an irrational fear of ever having to say something derogatory about the work of fellow Australians and because the various Australia literary critiques inevitably encourage a system of repaid favours'.[6] Sometimes a review could cause embarrassment for the reviewer. Keneally wrote a careful review of *Lincoln: A Novel*, by Gore Vidal, a book he thought was wooden. The editor at *The New Republic*, the journal in which it was published, gave the review the instantly condemning heading 'Bore Vidal'.[7]

Some reviewers in Australia did not like, or did not understand, the next Keneally novel, *A Dutiful Daughter*. Alec Bolton at Angus & Robertson had warned that *A Dutiful Daughter* would be new territory for readers; he wanted a blurb that would provide 'a sort of map that can help them to find their way in it by stating the theme and its implications'.[8] Keneally had expressed concern that the blurb might upset his parents. 'I can see that you might feel a bit uneasy about the personal effect of the first sentences,' Bolton went on, 'but don't you think that if your parents were troubled by the blurb, they would be no less troubled by the book itself?' The inoffensive blurb reads:

> *A Dutiful Daughter* explores the ambivalent relationship between children and their parents by means of a fable charged with poetry, compassion, and shocking comedy. Only one thing about it is certain – it is an act of exceptional and provocative imagination, an authentic specimen of the new fiction which is not content merely to reproduce realities, but insists on making them up.

The story is about the abnormal lives of Barbara and Damian Glover, whose parents have metamorphosed into bovine centaurs under the care of Barbara, who reflects: 'What I am getting at is how, in the end, parents, for all their preaching and threats, turn out to be children.'[9] With its intimations of hypnotism, interbreeding and incest, the book was seen to be, at best, disquieting and moving; at worst, it was 'as silly as it was nasty'.[10] The Americans seemed more comfortable with *A Dutiful Daughter*, having digested James Purdy's parent–child fable, *Malcolm*, and having become familiar with more expressionist styles. One *New York Times* reviewer revelled in the complex fable and in the author's 'diabolical ingenuity'.[11] *A Dutiful Daughter* was a choice of the Book of the Month Club in the United States.

Keneally delighted in a review published in the *New York Times Book Review*:

> For solid performance every time out, the best of these Catholic novelists is also the youngest, Thomas Keneally. He has built up his vision of a world 'between-gods', with patience and growing economy, through six novels ... The last [*A Dutiful Daughter*] is best; it puts the Cheiron myth to better use than Updike had, takes Joan of Arc's witchcraft more seriously than either Shakespeare or Shaw did, and details nightmare in daylight realistic style without any reliance on Kafka. It is an extraordinary book in every way.[12]

'I don't know if the term *Catholic* novelist is justified,' Keneally declared, 'but I'm willing to rattle my rosary beads with the best of them for the sake of a review like that.'[13] He admitted later that *A Dutiful Daughter* was written by 'a very black young man, whom I barely remember ... looking back to my alienated younger self I think the cattle business is a fair representation of what adolescents and particularly girls would like to do to their parents. To turn them into beasts of the field!'[14]

John Abernethy encouraged Keneally to live overseas for twelve months or so, something the writer was keen to do. 'In those days we considered Australia as so limited,' he recalls. 'I wanted to see the northern world and, as I say in *The Daughters of Mars*, cross from the colonised world to the world of the owners of culture. I didn't quite know where to go but I knew I'd be on my way. It was an era that the young now would find hard to relate to, but back then you couldn't be a writer unless you'd been and visited the wellsprings.'

Keneally planned visits to the centres of the literary world, London and New York. Among those young Australians who went before him were the feminist Germaine Greer, the art critic Robert Hughes, the satirist Barry Humphries and the writer and broadcaster Clive James. Keneally was also keen to see Morris West, whose name, in 1970, was 'in large letters in the West End [London], outside the theatre where his play *The Heretic* was being performed'. Later, when the Keneally family lived in Avalon, Sydney, Keneally and West would meet and enjoy long discussions.[15]

On 15 September 1970 the Keneally family boarded a plane bound for New York. Corlies ('Cork') Smith at Viking Press courted the Australian author graciously and made a big impression on Keneally. 'These men,

Cork Smith, Tom Ginsburg and Chauncy Truack were Cheever-esque, Updike-esque Yale/Harvard kind of gents! Such polished guys, such worldly ways. Meeting them was life-changing; it blew out your map of the potential universe! I had seen some of their influence on John Abernethy, with his glamorous manners, like Maxwell Perkins. America at that stage was still hugely fancied in terms of sophistication and novelty and the things we had been bred by the movies to think of as magical. I went to the football with Cork Smith on that visit. He took me, the footy yobbo, to see the Jets play at Shea Stadium. That was American footy, gridiron. I've got a certain time for it, but it's not up there with rugby league!'

David Carter, in a critical 2013 article titled '*Traduit de l'américain*: Tom Keneally and the Mechanics of an International Career', explained that 'Keneally joined a small group of Australian writers at the time – a group including Patrick White, Jon Cleary, and Morris West – who had an American publisher willing to invest in them as "list authors" over successive titles'. Carter also noted that Smith and others contributed editorial advice in their own right.[16]

Keneally, on that first visit, discussed with his editors a work in progress about 'Henry', a schizophrenic, and said that he would be sending a draft from England. He had also been busy researching another story that would become a bestseller: *The Chant of Jimmie Blacksmith*.

After New York, the family went to London, where they lived at 5 The Grange, Wimbledon. The Grange was postcard England, a thoroughfare of big brick houses with two storeys, gable windowed attics and chimney stacks. The high street was close by for shopping, and Margaret and Jane could visit 'the man in the sweet shop' who let them pay by putting money in a piggy bank, which he would jiggle as if it were alive. The girls liked the nearby common, too, where they looked for Wombles, watched people ice-skating and rode Shetland ponies. For Margaret, another set of memories from Wimbledon and other homes 'revolved around story time. As bossy toddlers, my sister and I decreed this would be at 4pm every day and would yell, "Story time, Daddy!" at the appointed hour.'

The Keneallys became friendly with barrister Anthony Evans and his wife, Caroline, who lived across the road at number 22 and had two daughters of similar age to Margaret and Jane. Evans took Keneally to rugby test matches in Wales.[17] Keneally was visible to his neighbours across the road as he worked at his writing table in the downstairs living room. They were impressed by his diligent daily routine, but Evans says it seemed incongruous that the author of *Blood Red, Sister Rose*, graphically written, was his calm and well-mannered neighbour.

'On one occasion,' Evans recalls, 'Tom drove into Kensington and parked his car some distance from the address he was visiting. After his meeting he could not remember where he had parked it. He could not find it and the search continued into the next day. We ascribed this possibly to a writer's unworldly concern for practical things, but maybe it was just a good lunch!'

Wimbledon was the home base, but the family was in tourist mode. *The Bulletin* had commissioned Keneally to write a series of articles about his travels, starting with 'Keneally in New York'. The second, 'Keneally in Ireland', includes his first impressions of the place he had wanted to visit for so long, like his father before him and many other Australians of Irish descent. He found on this sentimental journey that Ireland was as he suspected it might be: a land of 'sad vacancies', abandoned land.

He did not go to Maynooth on the first visit. 'I am a campanophobe (fearer of bells),' he explained. 'I heard the Angelus pealing on the radio in Dublin, and although objectively speaking it makes a more aesthetically pleasing time-signal than the pips, it reminded me of the campanomania of a priest – well may he rest – under whom I'd studied in Australia.' He was referring to Charlie Dunne, the rector at the Springwood seminary, who was obsessed by how the bells should be rung, and consequently caused stress for those serving Mass. If they did not manage the perfect ring, he became enraged. Keneally met a number of clerics in Ireland and featured one in his next article, 'Keneally in County Galway'. The final piece he penned in Ireland was 'Keneally and the Girls of Ireland', which was followed by 'Keneally Meets a Welshman'.

John Abernethy enjoyed the stories. 'Is it possible that you might take a rest from the novel and do a factual book about the emerald isle?' he wrote. 'You really are a damn good reporter, and would do it well.'[18]

Abernethy had shown some enthusiasm for a manuscript called *Four Days of the Life of Jesus: Ha-nosri*, but he was not keen on a schizophrenic character, Henry, who was part of the Ha-nosri story.[19] 'When I suggested that you take Ha-nosri out and develop him and Henry into their own books,' he wrote in May 1971, 'I was trying, God help me, to save you from yourself: I was convinced that by putting them together you were up to what I regard as the old Keneally trick of shuffling up two or more not quite realised or reconciled themes and putting them across with something like legerdemain. I wonder now if I was wrong, and what Cork and others would think if they saw Henry and Ha-nosri together.'[20]

Cork Smith had already written to Keneally, saying that he wasn't impressed by the story about Henry:

> You've asked me for my frank opinion of your new novel, so with some trepidation I shall give it to you in unvarnished form. I think your theme is a perfectly valid one, but I do not feel that you have pulled it off. On the one hand, I honestly do not think that what you do with your theme is all that interesting; I shall even say that there were times when I was in fact bored.
>
> Secondly, it seems to me that what you are getting at is at times quite obscure, hence I'm afraid rather annoying. You are dealing with a schizophrenic and the novel is seen basically through his eyes. Okay, that's fine, but I as *reader* felt frustrated in that although Henry progressively loses his grasp on what is real and what is not, so too did I . . . I would like to have *some* objective fix on reality. This may sound odd coming from one who accepted the *donné* in *A Dutiful Daughter* hook, line, and sinker, nevertheless there it is.[21]

Smith did not suggest revising the manuscript, yet he was 'enormously intrigued' about another novel his Australian author was working on. The two works that preceded it, *A Dutiful Daughter* and Henry/Ha-nosri, were indicative of the darkness in Keneally's life, while the latest one was about a tormented man. It was the work, some would say, of another tormented man, but it marked a turning point in Keneally's writing life. Fred Schepisi, who directed a film based on this book, said that Keneally had written this novel during 'a very black period of his life'.[22]

Elizabeth Riddell, hailing the return of the 'literary juggler' to Australia in October 1971, wrote that the book had no official title yet, but might be called *Jimmie Blacksmith*.[23] Agent Peter Grose knew from the day he started reading it that this was a terrific book, but he was about to return to London. After drawing up the contract with Angus & Robertson, he passed responsibility to Tim Curnow, his replacement as managing director of the Curtis Brown Literary Agency in Sydney.

In 1970 Horwitz had reprinted Frank Clune's book *Jimmy Governor*, the true story of a mass murderer, which Keneally had first heard about as a child. Clune's book provided the background details about an apparently responsible, educated half-caste Aborigine called Jimmy Governor, who had turned psychopathic killer. Governor began his rampage at Breelong, near Gilgandra in north-western New South Wales, on the night of 20 July 1900, instigating one of the biggest manhunts in Australian history.

'I didn't agree with Clune's book, but I was sparked by it,' Keneally said in 1993. 'There was a pattern there that Clune wasn't concentrating on – he was concentrating on police and pursuit aspects only.' Keneally had a fondness for metaphors for the present which he saw in past events:

> When I was writing *Jimmie Blacksmith* our troops were in Vietnam – there was a lot of debate about that. At the time of the Blacksmith murders – the Governor brothers' murders in real life – we were in the Boer War; there was a lot of emotion about that. And there was a surge of nationalism which the New South Wales Crimes Act of 1900 was instituted to prevent: it says that whoever promotes the idea that there will come a time when the Monarch is not the sovereign of Australia is guilty of high treason.
>
> Basically, without being whimsical, there are parallels between Australia in the late 1960s and Australia in 1900 – a sense that the question hasn't gone very far in that time, in those sixty years, and a sense that these events were extremely dramatic . . .[24]

Keneally was finding it easier to have more control over books that had a form already laid down by past events. He enjoyed the hours of research, but as a novelist, he believed, he did not have to be as meticulous about the details as a historian. Jimmy Governor became Jimmie Blacksmith, whose story sums up everything that had happened between black and white people in Australia. Jimmie is to be seen as avenging all the injustices against his race, rather than as a vengeful madman. His brother Joe is an accomplice.

'The Governors were a focus for the connection white had made with black in Australia,' Keneally commented during the film's shooting. 'Their act puts curious light on the happenings of those times. Jimmy Governor's terrible hatchet fell on the Mawbey family within a few days of the ratification of the Australian Constitution, a document that failed to mention or give the franchise to Aborigines, partly because of the belief then official that the race would soon be blessedly extinct.'[25]

As a boy in Kempsey, Keneally had glimpsed the humpies at the Aboriginal Greenhill camp from the front seat of a council sanitary truck driven by his Uncle Joe Bulley; the situation of a white man collecting the black man's waste puzzled him. He watched the outcasts sidle past his grandparents' home in River Street. His mother had a sympathetic attitude to them, but some men in town saw the blacks' camp as little more than a brothel. In 1974 Keneally wrote in the *Sydney Morning Herald*:

> Aborigines from the blacks' camp three miles north of the town used to trail down the street, making for the commercial centre, the shops brimming with goods they couldn't buy, the pubs in which they couldn't drink. There was even a theatre called 'the blacks' pitchers'. It showed ancient films. Perhaps we pitied black children more because they couldn't see the latest Errol Flynn than because of the appalling shanty town they lived in, the sores on their arms and mouths, the white features that showed up in their faces . . .[26]

Keneally based the details of the Verona camp that features in his story on childhood memories and his conversations with a few Aborigines. He had met a few young Aboriginal activists at events around Sydney and listened to them talk. One was Gary Foley, who established the controversial Aboriginal Tent Embassy in Canberra in 1972. Keneally also met the activist Charles Perkins. 'I'd read about these Freedom Riders led by Charlie Perkins. He travelled with various white radicals like Jim Spigelman. They'd go from town to town, up the coast and into Walgett. They were like the American Freedom Riders, demanding integration, in cinemas, swimming pools and in other ways. Their progress through the countryside was very interesting – this was before the constitutional amendment of 1967. I saw Faith Bandler promoting the successful referendum that allowed the Commonwealth to legislate and produce uniformity throughout Australia.'

After the book was published, he dreaded speaking to another Aborigine for fear that he had got the story wrong. However, *The Chant of Jimmie Blacksmith* raised consciousness about the Indigenous population in Australia at a time when Aboriginal issues were in the news, nationally and internationally.

In the late 1970s Keneally visited Redfern, where Father Ted Kennedy was helping many Aborigines. Keneally wanted to know about their living conditions and he stayed around the parish for some time, observing the priest and his flock from early in the morning till late at night. 'I was pleased to find a good priest,' Keneally said, 'one who showed up the lack of compassion in others.' The presbytery was used as a shelter for some of the Aborigines, and Kennedy slept wherever he could find a space. Keneally told the priest that he found the situation depressing, to which Kennedy replied, 'I don't get depressed. I get angry.'

Cork Smith declared that he was delighted with the new novel, and sent a telegram: 'Hats shoes and gloves off to JB. We love it.'[27] Abernethy thought the book was the best that Keneally had written, and penned an effusive letter to the author:

> Scene after scene in it will haunt me for a long time: the first night of the axes, the visit to the sacred place outside Taree, the death of Mort, everything that happens after Jimmie is wounded in the river, the beautifully understated ending, your inspired handling of the federal background, and the eerie suspense you create by switching the viewpoint to Dowie, the hangman and McCreadie as you do ... Your entry into the full blood and the half-caste minds is nothing short of stunning, at any rate to an old city rat like me, and I can't help wondering how you did it. My hat is off ...[28]

Abernethy entrusted Douglas Stewart to look after the novel. Keneally had benefited from Stewart's editorial input on previous books and had once dined at his home – the night before Jane was born. It was an impressive gathering of poets, with A. D. Hope and Kenneth Slessor also present. 'You meet people when you are young,' Keneally says now, 'and it doesn't resonate as it does when you are older. You wish you could go back. I should have been taking notes all evening! If Stewart had Judith Wright there as well, what a quartet!'[29] Keneally devoted a considerable section of his book *Australians: Flappers to Vietnam* (2014) to Slessor, 'a companionable and genial fellow'.

A death in Keneally's family was linked indirectly to *The Chant of Jimmie Blacksmith*. In 1975 the Gilgandra hospital almoner contacted Tom Keneally senior about a John Keneally who had recently died there; were they brothers? This John was Tom senior's older brother, Johnnie, who had left the family after he and his father, Timothy, had parted on bad terms. Johnnie had told the hospital staff that all his family were either dead or untraceable, but after his death nurses had found a newspaper review of *The Chant of Jimmie Blacksmith* in his wallet. He was buried in Gilgandra cemetery, not far from the graves of the family murdered by Jimmy Governor – and a world away from the countless graves of those he had seen killed in France nearly sixty years before.

International reviewers of *The Chant of Jimmie Blacksmith* compared the Aborigines to the Red Indians, and concluded that this was a story that should trouble the Australian national conscience: it was 'nonfiction fiction', an apt description for many Keneally titles to come. His mastery of the historical novel, already seen in *Bring Larks and Heroes*, was confirmed with this new book, which won the *Sydney Morning Herald*'s literary award, announced in October 1972 to mark International Book Year, an event organised by UNESCO. According to the report in the *Sydney Morning Herald*, the judging panel had difficulty arriving at a verdict and the final decision was not unanimous.[30] Keneally was glad of the money: 'Everyone thinks I'm knee-deep in royalties, but the truth is I just make a very ordinary living and the *Herald* prize was a massive help.'[31]

The decision of the judges was endorsed when the book was shortlisted for the prestigious Booker Prize for Fiction in England. Keneally did not win, but he was informed that he had just been awarded another Commonwealth Literary Fund grant, this time for $4000.[32] The money was badly needed, as always. When the family was living in England, Keneally appealed to his publishers in Sydney and New York for financial help. Abernethy told him then that he would receive a $400 advance on the $2500 due on signature for the 'untitled agreement'. Smith at

Viking promised to check the money situation, 'which I am sure is manageable either in the form of an open advance for a new novel or as an early payment on the paperback money'.[33]

When he first returned to Australia, Keneally rented a house for $40 a week at 13 Beta Road, Lane Cove, a suburb north-west of the city centre. On the strength of the latest book's promising future, the family started looking for a house to buy. On 10 May 1972, as the sale of Keneally's Armidale property was being finalised, he signed a contract for a house at 14 Chisholm Avenue, Avalon, on Sydney's far north coast. This timber home was more isolated than previous homes, up the hill from the beachside village, accessed by a steep driveway. Beyond the encroaching bush, the house looked out to headlands and the South Pacific Ocean in the distance. When they reached school age, the girls were enrolled at the Avalon Infants School.

With a mortgage and a young family, Keneally had to maintain a steady income, and he appealed for government help. At the end of 1972 Gough Whitlam was elected prime minister – the first leader of the Labor Party to win office for more than two decades – and his government was promising much for Australian cultural interests. Keneally wrote him a long letter:

> As part of the raw material for the burgeoning Australian Literature industry, which employs dozens if not hundreds of academics for secure lifetimes, I – like other writers – work under conditions of pressure and insecurity such as no academic will ever experience. Like others I cannot afford to write an unpublishable novel in a given year. Like others I have stringent targets in terms of time and output that must be met if next year's income is to be secure. Like others I must grub about on the fringes of TV script work, I must review, lecture and perform dozens of other ultimately self-destructive, ultimately wasteful chores. At the moment, I (probably like others) am writing an ABC television script out of pure economic need, knowing that there is little chance of its being produced in a way that will do my name any good, knowing above all that there is a novel waiting to be written.
>
> I confess I write to you at a time when my *success d'estime* doesn't seem likely to produce much income in the second half of 1973. It

> might be most helpful to tell you that my gross incomes for the past three years are $14,000, $11,000, $10,000, certainly not incomes to complain of, though these last two incomes were achieved by my acceptance of unsuitable work (TV script writing etc.), by sometimes frantic scrabbling (I have on file a letter sent off in desperation offering to write *Homicide* scripts for Crawford) that does little for my real work and which I will find hard to maintain for a lifetime . . .
>
> Could I therefore, for myself and the handful of others who are considered to have made some contribution to our literature, suggest a scheme by which a proven author's earnings are supplemented and the uncreative insecurity of his situation be relieved? Such a writer, I suggest, could have his income supplemented to a professional level if it does not in any year reach that level . . . The benefit is that if he chose to work exclusively in his specialty, his income would be guaranteed . . .
>
> I nominate professorial salary not out of any paranoid jealousy of dons but because the most obvious gulf in the whole literary business is that between the academics who work on us and us ourselves. In the last edition of *Meanjin*, Dr Brian Kiernan published a full article of my work. As you know promotion for academics is largely based on this sort of material and I believe the man is already a senior lecturer. I do not resent this: I do however resent that such permanence and security of profession and living is set up for him and his family and not for me and mine.
>
> The flat, simple, unadorned, almost statistically certain fact is that I have already contributed more to what we might call Australia's self-awareness than most literary academics are in a position to do in a lifetime . . .[34]

In his reply Whitlam said that he had referred Keneally's letter to the chairman of the Australia Council for the Arts, who shared Whitlam's concern that many creative people had difficulty in earning an adequate income. 'I have recently announced the establishment of a new Australia Council for the Arts,' Whitlam went on, 'an important part of which will be a Literature Board whose function will be to consider the needs of writers in Australia. I will see that your suggestions are put to it for consideration.'[35]

Whitlam was about to make life a lot easier for Australian writers by fulfilling his election promise to introduce public lending rights (PLR). He declared that his government would encourage 'a whole new climate in the arts.'[36] Keneally attended the celebratory function at the Sydney Opera House, on 4 March 1975, at which Whitlam announced that he had authorised the first payments of PLR. Under Whitlam's administration, a Literature Board replaced the Commonwealth Literary Fund, with generous funding available for writers. In February 1974 Michael Costigan, director of the Literature Board, wrote to tell Keneally that the board was recommending to the prime minister that the author be paid a guaranteed income (fixed at $6000 per annum) for three years from 1 January 1974.[37]

In the course of this three-year allowance, *Gossip from the Forest* was accepted by the publishers Harcourt Brace Jovanovich (HBJ) in the United States, and Keneally was paid a $10,000 advance, plus $7500 for the book accepted with it, *The Terrible Island of Mus* (then referred to as *MUS*). With this, Keneally judged that he was 'doing okay' and had 'scruples' about using taxpayers' money. He was perhaps the only recipient in the history of the Literature Board to send back the balance owing on a grant. 'It was an act of naivety on my part to send the money back. They were amazed!'

'His act of abnegation is almost unique in Australian history,' Ed Campion wrote in 1987, 'and is still spoken of with wonder by other Australian writers.' Keneally, Campion continued, was one of the many triumphs of the Literature Board's supportive policies. According to the figures he quoted, some $19 million was granted to 2000 Australian writers between 1973 and 1987.[38]

Keneally was still obsessed with a small number of vocal critics, and was even known to amuse himself by devising exotic forms of homicide to be practised on them, like offering them chocolate-coated funnel-web spiders or bacilli-soaked postcards. 'He should worry,' observed journalist Margaret Jones wryly. 'If Keneally was listed on the stock exchange, you would call him a steady-growth stock. He will even, himself, tentatively use the word "boom" to describe his present financial situation, in a country where most creative writers must take other jobs or starve . . .'[39] Patrick White had also complained that, in his earlier years as a novelist in Australia, the local critics had 'ganged up against him.' Leonie Kramer, who regarded Keneally as 'very fluent and very productive,' rejected White's claims of shabby treatment: 'I believe he has had a better run than any other.'[40]

18

Don't Go Back, You Silly Bastard!

The more you write, Keneally reflected, the more you learn about your own personality. As a writer, you are obliged to undress in public, but just how much you expose depends on how discreetly the unrobing is performed. *An Awful Rose* – his play that opened at the Jane Street Theatre on 1 June 1972 – was a startling revelation. The blurb for the play described it as 'a gentle, honest, very funny and very touching account of the problems confronting a young priest in his chosen life – problems usually not talked about. Keneally brings them to the surface in a direct compassionate way.'

This was the Henry story, dismissed by his editors, reworked for the stage. Margaret Jones, reviewing the production for the *Sydney Morning Herald*, reckoned that *An Awful Rose* 'provided Sydney audiences with the best theatrical guessing game of recent years'. One of her friends asked plaintively, 'But what does it *mean*?' The friend was bemused by bleeding hosts, bloodstained altar linen and the mysterious appearance of stigmata on the person of an atheist priest, and by the awful rose itself, 'a vaguely floral object suspended above the stage which might (or might not) represent the cerebral cortex'.[1]

Father Lawrence Henry, a chaplain and teacher in an institute for the blind, has reached the point where he no longer believes in God or the church or his vocation. Henry's mother has been overprotective, his father a stranger. They have two sons, one a priest and the other a doctor, a source of considerable paternal pride. Henry loves his father, who is dying, but he cannot find the words to tell him; nor can he tell him that he wants to leave the priesthood. The dialogue between priest and friend, father and son reveals a playwright still at odds with his past.

Keneally had never been able to discuss religion in any meaningful way with his father, but in the play the progressive honesty between the two Henrys shows the relationship he wanted to have with Tom senior. Keneally, so quick with words, was inarticulate when it came to his father. Conversation rarely moved beyond the superficial; like Henry and his father, they spoke to each other with 'a tender flinching gruffness'.

The play was insensitive to Keneally's parents, who were shaken by it. 'In so far as it hurt them, I do regret it,' Keneally says, 'but there was a truth there. I think they feared I was writing about them. It was a very dark play written in a very dark period.'

The work was recognised by some as intensely personal; others found it demanding, witty or obscure. Public flagellation was distasteful to some. Patrick White wrote to a friend: 'Keneally's play *An Awful Rose* is said to be very good. We shall see if it transfers from Jane Street; I am not going to suffer any more Catholic conflicts on the Jane Street seats in the Jane Street draughts. The mixture sounds very familiar; anguished priest, rationalist mistress, blood on the altar cloths, priest loses mistress, leaves Church, taking with him the bloody cloths . . .'[2] The play did transfer, from Jane Street to the Parade Theatre on Anzac Parade, Kensington. Twelve months after its season at Jane Street, it opened at The Hole in the Wall Theatre in Leederville, Perth, where it was billed as a religious comedy.

Forty years later, Keneally describes himself as 'a shithouse playwright'. His biggest success as a playwright, he reckons, was reflected glory. 'At the Parade Theatre there was a double bill, and the other part of the bill was *Don's Party* by a very talented playwright called David Williamson, and that play has entered the vernacular. *An Awful Rose* was a sort of passable novel, whereas *Don's Party* was a real play! I used to overwrite plays.'

Williamson sat next to Keneally on the opening night of the two plays at the Jane Street Theatre. 'I promptly started to tell him how to rewrite it!' Williamson said in 2014. 'Shift this . . . do that. Most writers tend not to like this on opening nights! Tom sat there and took it all . . . "Thank you for your thoughts," he said. I wouldn't have blamed Tom if he had sat there stony-faced [during my play] and said what a shithouse play it was, but his infectious cackle rang out over the theatre and ignited the audience, turned it into a great success . . . Afterwards he spotted me across the foyer and called, "Good one, Davo!"'[3]

One handbill suggested that Keneally's play was about 'who mucks us up – ourselves or other people'. In other words, it was about victimhood: blaming others and institutions for personality defects and emotional problems. Keneally could see that he had been playing the role of victim, a modern product of medieval religious practices and obsessions, and that he had wallowed in this self-inflicted victimhood, blaming the indoctrination of Irish Catholicism at a young age and seminary failings at an older age for his problems.

Yet he had not quite put his preoccupation with the victim as hero behind him. After *The Chant of Jimmie Blacksmith* was on its way, he went back to the literary curiosity of Ha-nosri. The book was going to follow the last days in the life of Jesus, who would not be crucified but who elected himself to be the super-eminent victim, a voluntary blood sacrifice to put an end to blood sacrifices for all time. It was all very strange: Keneally's Christ would be taken prisoner by the Romans, have a haemorrhage and die from natural causes. The book died of natural causes too – it was put aside to be reworked when its creator had time for it, but other projects intervened. The manuscript is kept in the National Library, with this annotation: 'Failed Novel on Life of Christ: *Ha-nosri. From a History of the Last Four Days of the Life of Jesus: Ha nosri*.'[4]

Keneally had another book on the go as 1972 ended. This one was about astronauts, based loosely on the Apollo 1 disaster of 1967. Cork Smith was not impressed. At first he said that he thought the main characters were unsympathetic.[5] He revised that opinion, saying that he had oversimplified, but commented that 'the pieces don't fit together . . . *potentially* the most interesting character is the astronaut himself. Much has been written here in America about what's happened to all those guys who have been to the moon . . . The one common denominator seems to be that *something* happened to all of them while they were out there in space. And something happened to your astronaut. But he is a shadow in your novel . . . he doesn't engage the reader.'

Smith went on: 'How about (and you've heard this before) putting the novel on the back of the stove while you plow ahead with Joan of Arc? Which, by the way, I am more than eager to read any part of you feel like sending along (there is a great sentence). Viking, as I think I've said, would be happy to give you a contract on the basis of a partial script. Keneally, you see, is a writer that matters.'[6]

Simon King, an editor at Collins in London, also dismissed the astronaut novel. He said that he could not find 'a trace of the entertainment value that glued me to Jimmie Blacksmith's pages . . . there just isn't enough story to grasp hold of, not a sufficiently interesting human relationship to follow through'. King also encouraged the writer to move ahead with Joan of Arc.[7]

Keneally was fascinated by Joan of Arc and had already worked her into *The Place at Whitton* and *A Dutiful Daughter*. Before his research was well underway, however, Keneally had another idea, this time for children. He was finding parenthood a positive experience. The two girls were the uncritical component of his life, wanting just to be listened to and loved, and to be taken to the park or beach or zoo. They were good company and brought out the best in Keneally. Observing them and enjoying them led to his first foray into writing for a young audience.

Little Ben is dedicated to 'Margaret and Jane who first listened to it'. Ben is a clock whose father is a pendulum clock and his mother a dainty eight-day clock with a silvery voice. Ben's 'little springs are loose. His tick and tock are sometimes too fast and sometimes too slow. His voice is so small . . .' Ben is taken to a doctor who is 'a fine old grandfather clock'. Ben has to take toughening oil and do loud-ticking and deep-bonging exercises. In the end he is taken to London to be the clock in the city's highest tower, becoming 'Big Ben'. Keneally painted a couple of illustrations to go with the story.[8]

He sent the manuscript of *Little Ben* to Jackie Reynolds at Curtis Brown in London. 'I am enchanted by the story of "Little Ben" and only hope that that strange breed, children's book editors, will agree with me,' Reynolds replied. 'A&R have an excellent reputation, even over here for their juvenile list, so I am going to show the story first to Barbara Ker

Wilson, and I will let you know at once when I have her reaction. I hope that "Debra the Zebra" will follow!'[9]

The venture did not go any further, but Keneally was often grateful that his children provided the intrusion and abrasion that could deliver him from the obsessional tendencies of a writer. He had prayed himself into madness in the seminary, and there was now a danger that he would write himself into another state of paranoia. He often got depressed about the work in progress, especially when he was working more and more but seeing less for his labours. Writing was a lonely occupation, always with the risk of rejection at the end. There were rewards, though, when a satisfactory draft was finished and he felt affection for the story, or knowing that readers had reported a close connection with characters. Then the second draft was easier. Essential fuel to the discipline was the belief that the book was important, that it *had* to be written. Keneally really had that belief.

He decided to make a break from Angus & Robertson and take his future work to Collins. This had been in his mind for a while. Grose wrote to him while he was still in England, wanting to know what was going on. He had heard that his author was 'flirting with other publishers, leaning towards Collins and looking backwards at A&R.'[10]

John Abernethy, Keneally's friend and mentor at Angus & Robertson, had worn himself out making quick trips to 'Kill City' – his name for New York – and he died suddenly in December 1972. Keneally paid him this tribute: 'John Abernethy had tremendous respect for anyone who could write. When you're not sure of yourself, this is a great morale booster. He was endlessly patient about reading a manuscript at any stage you wanted to show it to him. I'm a fairly messy writer; it's more in control of me, than me of it. At the end I have something that's full of technical problems. John was very good at dealing with them.'[11]

Abernethy had been very attentive to Keneally, seeming to understand that the author was emotionally needy and wanted to be more than just a name on the publishing list. The editor sometimes became the nursemaid. The author, anxious about all sorts of issues to do with his book, had a solitary objective – prompt publication – that only the publisher, beset with the urgent demands of a host of other authors, could meet. Angus & Robertson editors were as good as any others in the world, but the problem for authors, as Keneally saw it, was that the firm failed when it came to marketing its books. He was always worried about the proper marketing of his books, which had a lot to do with his industrial attitude to writing: promotion was all-important.

'Authors are rather like footballers,' Keneally claims. 'They move around, perhaps because their team has lost direction, or they want to follow a particular coach, or they have been insulted – or, quite frequently, it's avarice!' He was reassured by Grose's assertion that Collins had some of the best book salesmen in Australia; their publicity and promotion were outstanding. 'Phillip Ziegler [an editor at Collins in London] has always liked your work,' Grose wrote. 'We've talked about it often enough and I think he would serve you well.'[12]

One reviewer wrote that 1972 was 'Keneally's Year'; in terms of recognition, with *The Chant of Jimmie Blacksmith* and *An Awful Rose*, as well as the monetary windfall, so it was.[13] Derryn Hinch, writing for the *National Times* from New York, observed that Keneally was 'breaking the US book barrier'. Hinch had interviewed an unnamed spokesman at Viking Press, who told him that Keneally had never sold as well as he should in the United States, but there were signs of a growing new readership. 'He sells very well over the long run.'[14]

Then came the break with Angus & Robertson, the death of John Abernethy and the caution with which his new editor at Collins was approaching the Joan of Arc story. On top of this, there was instability in Keneally's marriage: 'Our early marriage was characterised by my mental illness – it didn't have to do with sexuality; it did have to do with the past. Then quickly – due to fertility and desire – we became parents. We were not prepared for the changed conditions . . . it's sad to think how blighted our early marriage was by mental illness – it became the major issue of the marriage. I look back on my emotional immaturity in this matter not kindly. I am aware of my capacity to exacerbate things, just by having arguments . . . It led to a minor separation.

'When I went off I had the same mentality as at the seminary – rightly or wrongly, I had to get out. I felt things did reach extremities where there was no reasoning with each other left. A great love for each other, but life just seemed impossible, and since I couldn't take the children, I had to leave them behind.'

An opportunity to make a seemingly legitimate move came when *The Chant of Jimmie Blacksmith* won the Royal Society of Literature Prize, which was to be presented to the author at a function in London at the end of June 1973. He would also be inducted as a Fellow of the Royal Society of Literature, a considerable honour – but his acceptance was questionable, given Keneally's republican stance. 'I shouldn't have done it,' he admitted. 'I had to pretend to have a crisis of conscience!'[15]

At first, unable to see how he could afford the trip, Keneally asked his brother Johnny to accept the prize on his behalf. On 11 October 1969 Johnny had married Jane Josephine Hall, whom he had met at St Vincent's Hospital, Sydney, where she was a senior nurse and he was a junior resident doctor. By 1973 they were living in Liverpool, England, where Johnny was gaining more experience as a paediatric anaesthetist at the Alder Hey Children's Hospital.

Then Keneally appealed to Jean Battersby, executive officer of the Australia Council for the Arts, who talked to Geoffrey Blainey about providing Keneally with some living expenses for the trip to London. Blainey agreed that Keneally could be paid $600 from the council's International Fund.[16]

An agreement was also made with Qantas, which provided Keneally's airfare on certain conditions: 'At ceremonies to be held in London to mark the Royal Society of Literature Award for your novel *The Chant of Jimmie Blacksmith* and your election as a fellow of the Royal Society of Literature, you will mention QANTAS favourably during your acceptance speech. In addition, you will write for Q publications one substantial analytical article of 1500/2000 words and three shorter travel articles . . . In return for the publicity and the articles Q will provide you with one $758 Sydney/London/Sydney "excursion fare" ticket.'[17]

By the time Keneally reached London he was emotionally and physically drained, consumed by guilt at deserting his family and already in two minds about staying on in London after receiving the award. He rented a room in an attractive row house at 9 Cheyne Place, Chelsea, a short distance from what became his favourite riverside pub, the Eight Bells and Kings Head.

He was also close to 27 Smith Street, the home of the expatriate Australian Carmen Callil, founder of the publishing company Virago Press.

Keneally had met Callil in Sydney before she moved to London. When she told him the name of her new venture, Keneally laughed. She was not offended. 'Tom, you're supposed to laugh! That's the point!' He found her to be 'awesomely assertive' in an era when men were still adjusting to the idea of forceful, 'liberated' women. Callil was also a publicist for the London firm Quartet Books, which published *Bring Larks and Heroes* in 1973, and she gave a party for Keneally.

Callil was an extrovert, gregarious and charming. She has said that the era when she first had association with Keneally – at the end of the 1960s and into the early 1970s – was 'an absolutely wonderful period, parties every night . . . I was a party girl, and everybody used to whizz in and out of the office – in Smith Street, Chelsea, above the synagogue . . . in the seventies everybody was in love all the time . . .' Callil's flat, with its bright red tiles and lime-green paint was a happy, bohemian place full of paintings and cats.[18]

Callil wrote to Keneally soon after he arrived in London: 'I'm literally just around the corner from you – how did you manage to get a flat so near London's Australian Mafia?'[19] The 'Australian mafia' included the very sociable Don Bennetts and Anton Bowler. Keneally also made friends with Peter Smalley, a novelist, and his wife, Clytie, a couple whom he likened to Chip Rolley and Anne Summers, a well-known creative partnership in Australia. Callil has recalled going to a pub opposite her house, where she and her friends, including Keneally, used to gather, drinking with James Cameron, a prominent English journalist.

One indication of Keneally's newfound freedom was the zest with which he tried out all the best bannisters in London, such as one at the museum. However, he cracked a rib sliding down the bannister at Callil's house; it had a little ferrule that stuck out and caught him in the ribs.

The other occupants of Keneally's 'digs' were a source of endless amusement to him. The basement was occupied by Maggie, a tiny octogenarian Irishwoman, very devout. She insisted on feeding everyone who came into the house, and hauling their bags up the stairs as penance 'for the holy souls' in purgatory. Two upper floors of the house were occupied by its owner, Mrs Edome Broughton-Adderley, an avid collector of royal memorabilia, who casually wore old expensive gowns. Keneally was convinced that she was Evelyn Waugh's model for the crazily elegant

Mrs Stitch in the book *Scoop*. Mrs Broughton-Adderley lived with an orthopaedic surgeon, George Lloyd-Roberts. In the new resident's eyes, they were a handsome and classy couple, but the passing acquaintance had repercussions a few years later.

Above them lived an American journalist in his sixties and Lolita, his French wife, who was about twenty. At the top of the house a computer lady from Brigham, Texas, was in residence. Keneally's room on the ground floor was decorated with four large and hideous oil paintings, heavy green brocade curtains and faded green wallpaper. There was a bed in one corner, a vast high-backed sofa in the middle of the room and a portable typewriter on the floor.

Keneally at the time was working on 'an odd book about an Amazonian mystic'.[20] He had brought the first draft of the book, tentatively titled *Jehanne*, to London. His new editor, Simon King at Collins, had written before the author left Sydney to say he was pleased to hear that Sir William Collins, chairman of the publishing firm, was keen to publish *Jehanne* and that he had read the 100 pages Keneally had sent for appraisal: 'No, I do not have doubts about your ability to write the novel and neither is there any doubt in my mind but that you could do successfully. But yes, I did have *some* doubts about *aspects* of what I had read so far and I *do* believe they could be put right without any trouble.'[21]

It bothered Keneally that King was not quite in sympathy with what he was doing. The writer had toyed with making a novel out of a strange connection he had discovered: that Joan of Arc had been captured in the same French forest where the 1918 armistice was formed. Marshal Foch, a signatory to the armistice, was the author of a book about Joan and had a similar personality to hers, being addicted to the power of the will. Keneally could definitely write about that subject. He settled for making two books – one about Joan and one about the peace treaty. King could be forgiven for his uncertainty and reluctance to say too much until he had read the whole typescript.

'Simon King was a charming man,' the author recalls. 'Editors then would take you to these improbable London clubs. I remember his successor, Philip Ziegler, who was a very good biographer. As we were going up the stairs of the Travellers Club he showed me the brass railings that had been put in to enable the French diplomat Talleyrand to haul himself to the upper level. I pointed to a portrait of William the Fourth and I said, "He's a rather overlooked subject. Have you ever thought of writing a biography on him?" And Ziegler said, blinking his eyes rapidly, "I have, actually. I have already done so!"' Keneally was also invited to lunch with Sir William Collins in his flat above the office at 14 St James's Place.

Keneally settled down to give *Jehanne* his whole attention. It would be a very long book by his standards – a sort of psychological history. He had read a lot about his heroine, including Vita Sackville-West's *Saint Joan of Arc* (1936) when he was at the seminary. Having been accused in the past of not writing competently about women, he felt some pressure. He likened Joan of Arc to Germaine Greer: 'She had the incredible rudeness of the revolutionary, didn't apologise for her perceptions, and could give the same castrating replies to questions.' Keneally thought Joan was freakish but feminine. 'And because she was feminine, a male society punished her for participating in what belonged to it – politics and war.'[22] Keneally believed he was writing a feminist novel, in keeping with the times.

His neighbours never ceased to charm him. Don Bennetts and Althea Lockwood, who lived a couple of doors further along the street, had a Brazilian monkey called Hash. Whenever he escaped he would run along the rooftops, interfering with the television aerials of Royal Hospital Road. Keneally had hired a colour television set, and Hash took a liking to his host's favourite Westerns. Hash also took a liking to women on the set and 'fell in love' with them, and with some of the women who attended Althea's frequent parties. Keneally said that he fell in love with them too. At that stage, it looked as though his marriage was at an end, and he had some casual relationships with other women.

Keneally met the literary agent Tessa Sayle, who would work hard on his behalf for years. 'There was not intimacy with Tessa, but we had a profound friendship, such as I have had with a number of women in my life,' he says. 'Those were the sort of friendships that depended on not being sexual. I think such friendships are entirely possible. Tessa's was one of the most intense friendships I have ever had. I met her at a publishers' party during that time in London.'

Sayle asked him if he would like her to represent him in England. Keneally had been represented by Curtis Brown in Australia and England, but he was not satisfied with the London office's efforts, especially when negotiating foreign translation editions. In August 1972 Keneally had been approached by John Cushman Associates in New York, an affiliate of Curtis Brown, London, but he hesitated. He chose Sayle, who also arranged for the US agent Georges Borchardt to look after Keneally's interests there. Sayle had originally joined Hope Leresche & Steele; later, she ran the agency at 11 Jubilee Place, London, in her own name. She excelled at negotiating foreign editions of her authors' work.

Sayle had an Austrian title and was known as Countess Maria Theresa von Stockert before she married an Australian, Murray Sayle, a journalist. Keneally was amused by Sayle's weakness for Australians. He agreed with the general 'Pommie' view that Australians could be outrageous, with no sense of propriety about what should be left unsaid. He was used to the bewildered accusation: 'You're likely to say anything! It's delightful! We never know what you'll say next!'

Keneally's freedom from domestic responsibilities allowed him to mix more and to see some of the vibrant parts of London. There were some days that he referred to as 'dreadful expatriate days', but they were not all bad. On one occasion he was drowning his sorrows with a Scottish novelist and an Australian doctor when a couple of balloonists arrived. They suggested that the three go with them on a practice run in their hot-air balloon over the Cotswolds, an invitation which was immediately accepted.

Keneally chose to write *Jehanne* as a kind of film script, a decision prompted in part by his reading the published film script of *X, Y and Zee* by Edna O'Brien. It seemed to him that the script did not differ in texture or immediacy from her novel *Zee and Company*. The technique would be a practical way of dealing with the multiplicity of characters in *Jehanne*. The language was contemporary without being colloquial, which saved having to know and use archaic terms. When an official asked at her first trial about the kind of French her 'voices' spoke in, Joan snapped back: 'A damn sight better than yours.' Keneally's Joan was a feisty woman.

Keneally occasionally had working sessions with Simon King, who was finally won over by the novel once its author had settled on the one subject. King wrote a glowing report to William Collins after he had read the first hundred pages or so, having been particularly impressed by

Keneally's account of the assassination of Jean, Duke of Burgundy: 'This little section, just twenty-one pages, is I think one of the most brilliant pieces of literary re-creation I've ever read . . . Keneally has people behave just exactly, one feels, as they could have behaved . . . He shows people being stubborn, sulky, hot headed, angry and jealous, worried, sick, jittery, selfish, and these attributes clash at some particular moment to produce history in the form of a decision, a death, a deformed personality.'[23]

Keneally was much encouraged by King's enthusiasm, especially when he wrote about the final typescript: 'Never have I worked on such a remarkable novel! The novel works – this is how it all was, vivid and almost touchable on every page . . . a landmark in the development of the historical novel.'[24]

The novel was called *Blood Red, Sister Rose*. 'I'm still pleased that Tom allowed me to give the book the title it has rather than *Blood Red Sister Rose*,' King wrote in 2015. 'The use of the comma there allows the title to be read as Joan's voices talking to her. Otherwise it seemed to me to be too much of a bland statement. That was probably the only editorial change I proposed for the entire wonderful book. So do be careful about that comma. I treasure it.'

After *Blood Red, Sister Rose* Keneally turned his attention to other work. The ABC was waiting on his revision of a commissioned film script titled *Essington*.[25] It was a dreary tale of madness, murder and suicide in the middle of the nineteenth century, one of the first films to confront the negative impact of European occupation on Australia's Indigenous population. Keneally won Best Script at the 1976 Logie Awards for *Essington*.

He also began work on an autobiography. He started with his parents' families, only to discover that he did not really know much about them. He was also unsure about how to tackle the material, thinking that the old factual blow-by-blow approach was of no interest. Having now visited France, he toyed with the idea of starting with his Uncle Johnnie, motivated by thoughts about the war in which the black sheep of the family had fought.

Johnnie had survived the war but not the homecoming, and Keneally was constantly wondering about his own homecoming. He missed the girls acutely, but was aware that even though he had escaped, he was in denial about his marital problems. His departure had caused considerable conflict with his parents, who could not understand why their son would desert the family.

Keneally's parents had moved to a unit at 46 Kerr Parade, Auburn, a couple of suburbs further west from Homebush. Elsie was enjoying a part-time job as a saleswoman at Winn's department store, which had a branch in Auburn. She was like Auntie Annie, who had stayed with the family during Tom's absence in the Second World War. Annie was so eccentric that she was almost unemployable by the time she was ready to retire, but Elsie was finding a new lease of life in paid employment at nearly sixty.

Keneally's father retired soon after he reached the age of sixty-five in 1972 and he and Elsie planned to visit Johnny and Jane and their two boys, Ben and Tim, in early 1974. Johnny was working at the Children's Hospital, Great Ormond Street, London, and Keneally saw his brother occasionally. Johnny and Jane were amused at Keneally's T-shirts, on which were printed slogans such as 'It's Time' (the Labor Party's slogan for the 1972 election) and 'Check My Libido' (a promotional line from the film *Libido*, released in March 1973). The writer stood out beside the conservatively dressed doctor.

Keneally was unselfconscious in his choice of clothing, but constrained in conversation with his family: 'I was inhibited by my situation, but they knew what was going on . . . I couldn't really talk to them about it, yet I could moan to other people! I was conditioned to believe that it was my fault. I also had a kind of agnostic shame that lasted a long time. I mean, my system of family and friends knew how I had spoken out against the church and I felt inhibited in front of them because Johnny was still a good practising Catholic. We got better as we got older at talking about it.'

In November 1973 Keneally went to the renowned Headingley ground at Leeds to see Australia play England in a rugby match. On a savagely cold day, watching the players fight on iron-hard earth, he stood among 30,000 Yorkshiremen in cloth caps who screamed at the visiting team, 'Gi' home, you convict trash!' Australia won 14–6.

It was time for Keneally to go home too, although he was tempted to heed the advice of expatriate Clive James, who stood on a chair in

Bertorelli's restaurant and shouted, 'Don't go back, you silly bastard!'[26] This six months' escape had been a sort of 'growing up' time for Keneally, who was spreading his wings and discovering a world he should have gone to see years before. His life, of course, would have been much different without the cloistered seminary years and the faltering start on a new career, but he may still have had problems within a marriage.

One day Keneally received a postcard from one of his daughters, with this message written in pencil: 'Dear Daddy, I hope that you come back soon.'[27] He packed up his belongings in the Chelsea house and reluctantly said goodbye to the other residents. Before leaving London, though, and for some reason now forgotten, he stayed briefly at a place called 'The Mansions' in Clapham, where the landlady, Mrs Pamela Hardyment, worked for a publisher and was known to Tessa Sayle. There were other single men living there, and the landlady used to get them together for tea, knowing most of them were sad or lonely.

Mrs Hardyment was another one of those characters who endeared themselves to Keneally. One night she started talking casually over tea about a wealthy American in the publishing industry: 'If he thinks I'm going to sleep with him and his wife again, he's got another thing coming!' In her flat she had a selection of belts. 'I use them on different lovers,' she told her bemused lodgers. Keneally said to himself, 'And the English think Australians are outrageous!' A few years later, Hardyment replied to a letter from Keneally: 'Dear Love ... glad of a letter from my lodger. They all keep in touch!'[28]

Keneally was home in Sydney for Christmas, bearing gifts, but he did not stay at Avalon. He rented a flat at 4/10 Reed Street, Cremorne, an inner-northern suburb, about thirty kilometres from Avalon. The children had been the main factor in his return; if not for them, he may have stayed in London. He saw them regularly, but it was far from satisfactory because he felt as though he was playing at being a parent for two or three hours each week. The girls, Margaret (seven) and Jane (six), had been enrolled at the local public school in Avalon and were to return there after the Christmas holidays. Talking about the situation many years later, Keneally says: 'This period is very painful to discuss. I would like to go back, as so many would, and renegotiate those years. I still carried emotional immaturity from my childhood ...'

The family was reunited in March 1974. In the May holidays they went on a camping trip to the Warrumbungle National Park, in north-western New South Wales. In times to come, when tensions resurfaced, Keneally and his friend Iain Finlay went 'walkabout', travelling into western New South Wales, staying in country pubs, playing billiards and the new Pac-Man arcade game, and drinking beer. The mateship and some distance from the domestic scene helped. Keneally's frequent absences in the years ahead also provided space and time away from differences that were hard to resolve.

19

The Count and the Accusers

The Avalon house, as one interviewer observed, had 'a site perfect for a medieval castle', approached by a 'twin-hairpinned precipice of a drive intended to repel invaders'.[1] Bushwalking with the girls and jogging most days between the Palm Beach sand dunes and Barrenjoey Lighthouse, Keneally was hoping that there would not be a repeat of the particularly bad attack of asthma he had suffered in March 1974. He was feeling fit as the first anniversary of his return from England approached. *Blood Red, Sister Rose* was launched in Sydney, and Jane's seventh birthday on 12 November 1974 was celebrated with a party. The darkness had receded, for the present.

Sixteen children and eighteen adults had come to the birthday party. It was a 'scorcher' of a day, with a haze over the bush and the sea glittering in the distance. This familiar scene was a long way from France, but Keneally on most days in November was still mentally in Europe, revising his next book, *Gossip from the Forest*, about the signing of the 1918 armistice in a railway carriage in the forest of Compiègne. He wrote at a card table in the bedroom, with discarded manuscripts strewn on the carpet.

Keneally had the audience laughing at a festival of arts when he declared: 'I began life as a priest and then learned that God was dead. I left the priesthood to become a novelist and now I'm told the novel is dead!'[2] He told Rudi Krausmann that one of the reasons he believed this was because society was so fragmented that it was impossible to write about it in the sure forms used by eighteenth- and nineteenth-century novelists:

> There is too much pluralism, there is too much moral ambiguity and so on for people to write with certainty and the novelist is so alienated from society that he disappears up his own fundament. In a more superficial way I imagined that it was dead in the terms that other art forms, the movie and so on, had supplanted it. I think it just develops . . . I have written some conventional novels for the purposes of making a living and also because they're easier than the soul-destroying novels . . . The conventional novel is dead in the sense that it doesn't serve a purpose except as a preparatory movie script or as a preparatory television script.[3]

The novels written in this uncertain era are evidence that Keneally was writing with a stage or film set in mind.[4] A critic assessing his work to date would probably say that all his characters are presented with some great moral choice or have destiny imposed on them. In *Gossip from the Forest* it is Matthias Erzberger, the German delegate who was ultimately punished by German society for participating in the armistice, even though he did so against his will. Erzberger could not avoid that destiny, and the book explores the gamut of his feelings about this unwanted but historic role.

Keneally thought he could afford to go his own way, which was not an option for a historian. 'You must read until you're full up with the subject and want to start writing, whereas an historian has to read and read and take notes, and you know, at the end of the process comes the book. A novelist can start writing out of the fullness of the material he's been reading earlier than an historian can.'[5]

When he was in England, Keneally had accepted an offer to write the script for a film documentary on the last three days of the First World War. After he started researching he decided that he had the makings of at least one novel, and the documentary was forgotten. He spent many hours in the Imperial War Museum in London and read extensively, including *Foch: The Man of Orleans* by B. H. Liddell Hart, as well as books about Marshal Foch's deputy, General Weygand. Keneally also visited Compiègne in France, where he accessed the files of a French nationalist organisation called Les Amis de l'Armistice. The British Museum provided many works on military history, and the State Library in Sydney, surprisingly, yielded an extraordinary amount of useful material, including Erzberger's memoirs.

When Philip Ziegler at Collins first saw *Gossip from the Forest*, he was doubtful that the subject was suitable for a novel. 'I still think that you have set yourself a very stiff problem in selecting it,' he wrote, 'nevertheless I am certain you have brought it off triumphantly . . . a masterpiece of concentrated analysis. All the delegates are marvellously alive. This *must* have been how they thought, talked and looked. I made myself extremely unpopular with my family by continuing to read the typescript when I should have been entertaining them in other ways, and I defy anyone of intelligence and with a feeling for literature not to react in the same way.'[6]

Keneally began to entertain doubts about the book. He wrote to Ziegler: 'I myself, after revising it, believe that your first reaction to the MS is a correct one. Admittedly, the difficulty is that people believe they will get historical melodrama from the book, for the setting, the moment, the people support that supposition. I am fairly confident that most readers can/will see that they are getting something else.'

He had a contract and he needed the money: 'The planning of my modest economy has been justifiably based on that contract.'[7] Keneally's 'modest economy' was in difficulties as 1974 ended. In October the Bank of New South Wales at Avalon Beach informed him that his account was overdrawn; the manager at the Ashfield branch reminded him that some time had elapsed since he had paid into his loan account: 'Monthly repayments of $200 on your loan account are transferred from this account and the debt has therefore been increasing . . .'[8]

Keneally had trouble keeping his finances in order. He was in strife with the chief accountant at Collins in Glasgow for not submitting his tax exemption application forms, and the Department of Inland Revenue was always seeking more information. Keneally had to repeatedly explain to the inspector of foreign dividends that he had been a professional writer since 1966. Later, when the financial pressure eased, he kept a closer watch on his earnings.

Keneally was disheartened by a letter from Ziegler on 2 December 1974, in which the editor was also having second thoughts about *Gossip from the Forest*. Was the book a good novel or a masterly non-novel? Similar questions would be asked about *Schindler's Ark* further down the track, although not by Ziegler, who always assumed that it was non-fiction. Ziegler suggested that Collins transfer the contract for *Gossip from the Forest* to another book which he knew Keneally was working on; he believed this book's failure would harm the author's reputation.

Keneally was seriously anxious. He had to push his work more and was hopeful that an effective agent working on his behalf in the United States as well as in England would advance his work. He telephoned Tessa Sayle to inform her that Viking Press, which had published all his previous books in the United States, had rejected *Gossip from the Forest*. Alan Williams, a reader from Viking, explained: 'All in all, we feel that as much as we wanted to like it and as intriguing as your central situation is historically and dramatically, we don't think the book comes across with enough point or sufficient impact ... The really uncomfortable question we were left with was what purpose?'[9] They concluded that they would not be helping their long-term relationship with Keneally by going ahead.

The situation with potential publishers was complex. Keneally had also sent the manuscript of his next book, *The Terrible Island of Mus* (sometimes referred to as *Mus Means Fly* or simply *MUS*), to Sayle to assess and place. Viking was interested in that story, but Sayle had determined to 'sell' the author and his two new titles as a 'package deal', which was Ziegler's preference. Ziegler thought that Knopf was probably the liveliest publisher in New York then and he wanted to see Keneally on its list.[10]

Keneally then tried Simon & Schuster. Sayle said he had gone to them 'off his own bat', but this was not quite accurate. During a stay in New York he had made arrangements with Peter Kemeny, a new local literary agent, to market *Gossip from the Forest* and *MUS*. Kemeny met Nan Talese, then a senior editor at Simon & Schuster, who agreed that *MUS* needed extensive revision. 'I told her I am sure you can do a bang-up job,' Kemeny advised Keneally, 'primarily injesting [sic] real suspense, terror, and isolation in those pages, whereas now you just announce them, without evoking them for the reader. That is what you need to make it a Real Page-Turner, as the paperback types put it. She and others love *Gossip from the Forest*, as I do.'[11]

Kemeny also approached Knopf on Keneally's behalf. It had all but agreed to accept *Gossip from the Forest*, but reneged, thinking that 'it would be diabolically difficult to sell'.[12]

This was a very messy period in Keneally's desperate and sometimes ill-judged negotiating. While he had employed Kemeny, Sayle had opened negotiations with Georges Borchardt in New York. She asked him if he would assume the role as Keneally's American agent, which he agreed to do. 'I am so glad you will be handling Tom Keneally yourself,' Sayle wrote to Borchardt in March 1975. 'He is a brilliant writer and definitely deserves the best attention ... I am pleased that Tom is now safely in your hands.'[13]

Kemeny, understandably, was angry at being cut out, but he wrote a polite letter to Keneally saying that he did not blame him. Kemeny wanted some compensation from Keneally, mostly because of 'the sheer embarrassment'. Kemeny had proudly told others – publishers, clients and movie agents – that he was Keneally's new agent. 'Since you are a good and honest and fair man, what do you think is fair compensation, when the time comes?' he asked. He agreed to wait until Keneally had received his first advance from an American publisher.[14]

Meanwhile, Talese was very keen about *Gossip from the Forest*. Forty years later she could recall how badly she wanted that book: 'I think it's a brilliant book – a beautiful book, but I couldn't get it!' Talese's readers were enthusiastic, although two thought the book was not readily accessible.[15] Simon & Schuster told Keneally that it was interested only in *Gossip from the Forest*, not *The Terrible Island of Mus*, and it was prepared to offer a relatively low advance offer of $4000 to $5000.

Borchardt was also impressed with *Gossip from the Forest* and went to work, talking again to Talese but making no further progress. Talese wrote to Keneally: 'I do wish we could have offered to publish both *MUS* and *Gossip* because I know that is what you wanted, but *Gossip* is so brilliant and though *MUS* can succeed with work on your part it can never measure up to *Gossip from the Forest*.'[16] Talese assured Keneally that Borchardt was an 'absolutely first rate agent and a man of taste – he will do what is right for you'. Borchardt had great faith in Keneally's talent: 'Our agency always took on writers not because I thought they would produce best-selling books, but because I wanted others to read what I had liked, and because I feel it is our vocation to help writers attain their goals and get recognition. When I got *Waiting for Godot* published here, I had no idea Beckett would eventually win the Nobel Prize . . .'

Borchardt approached Tom Guinzburg again at Viking and Tony Godwin at HBJ. Borchardt wrote to Keneally on 2 April 1975 to tell him that he had worked out terms with HBJ for *Gossip*. Godwin, Borchardt assured the author, was 'a first rate editor'. Keneally was annoyed with his previous Viking editor, Guinzburg, who had suggested a complete revision of *Gossip*. 'Does he really have any conception of what it takes in time and less ponderable quantities to rewrite a book and turn what is basically a good story into an excellent one?' he wrote to Borchardt.[17] Then came the good news that HBJ would take *MUS* as well.

The critics generally applauded *Gossip from the Forest* with many superlatives; one enthusiast rated the book alongside Solzhenitsyn's *August 1914*.[18] George Steiner, in the *New Yorker*, was not so kind: 'Mr Keneally's presentation is as stylized as a Balinese dance-drama . . . *Gossip from the Forest* has a damaging knowingness. Behind the pointillist technique rumble great portents of foresight and allegorical finality. There is a tactical coyness even to the title. In short: an interesting failure, quite like the parleys at Compiègne so many (or was it so few?) Novembers ago.'[19]

Paul Fussell, writing for the *New York Times Book Review*, questioned 'the arch chapter titles and campy puns and use of stage dialogue', but conceded that readers would become sympathetic to Erzberger and that it was absorbing fiction: history boosted by 'sympathy acting on deep knowledge'.[20]

Keneally had become accustomed to more positive responses in the United States. In Australia, D. R. Burns, writing for *Nation Review*, was impressed 'by Keneally's possession of that other power of the master novelist – his sense of hard, tricky, intricate, unyielding fact. Tinder to flint, his intellect sparks in confronting it.'[21] Two familiar critics also came out on Keneally's side: Brian Kiernan thought the author was 'at the top of his form', while Neil Jillett ended his review by saying that 'if we took the pride in our writers that we take in our sportsmen, Thomas Keneally would be a national hero'.[22]

Morris Lurie, reviewing for the *National Times*, wrote that the book was:

> . . . *really* well written. Splendidly written … Mr Keneally writes as well as anyone in Australia, and good Australian writers are a rare commodity and I think they should be lauded and applauded at every opportunity and I want to laude and applaud Mr Keneally, except … Well, I can't see that his novel is *about anything*. No, that's not quite fair. It's about something all right. It's about the armistice signed in a railway carriage in Compiegne in November, 1918 … So what else is new? Where is 'history as seen under the floodlight of an artist's imagination' as promised in the blurb? What Mr Keneally does is re-create that meeting in atmosphere and detail and yes, you do feel you are there, but that doesn't seem to me to be enough. I want insights. I want interpretations. I want new slants …'[23]

The only vengeance to be had on critics, Keneally was slowly learning, was to not go away. He still resented the unfavourable comments, but comforted himself by underlining comments in the better ones. Kiernan had observed other writers who were sensitive to adverse criticism: 'It's an occupational hazard, perfectly understandable (even critics can suffer from it), but it responds positively to praise.'

Gossip from the Forest was confronted with a damages claim. In the first edition, published by Collins in England, Keneally used the real names of all the delegates, including Count Albert von Oberndorff (called Count Alfred Maiberling in subsequent editions). There had been indications in the documents Keneally read that the count had behaved in an unstable manner. In the fictional version, he is depicted as outspoken, irrepressible and frequently inebriated. Oberndorff's offended family, particularly his son, Count Charles von Oberndorff, put pressure on Collins and Keneally to pay compensation for the 'libel' and to suppress the first edition.

According to Keneally, the count's letters were full of baroque insults. The concluding sentence of one letter was typical of the rest: 'This vile injury can only be assuaged by the immediate transfer of £6,000 sterling to my bank account.' An English lawyer used to handling similar situations made a deal with the count: in return for a letter from Keneally to the *Times Literary Supplement*, expressing regret for pain caused to the Oberndorff family, the count would drop his charges.

Keneally wrote the letter, which was published in the *Times Literary Supplement* on 23 January 1976:

> I would be grateful if you would allow me to state through your columns that the character of Count von Oberndorff, as portrayed in my book, is fictionalised. The characters of Erzberger, Foch, Weygand and others are extensively researched, but because of the lack of easily accessible research material concerning Oberndorff, I wrote the book knowing little more about him than the most general outline of his career and that he was very distressed by the events of Compiègne, November 1918 – as any sane man would have been. Anyone reading the book would, I believe, realise that it does not claim to be historically exact in every regard, but it is the truth that by creating fiction about men from the past a writer can cause pain to living relatives. Therefore I wish to apologise sincerely to the living relatives of Count von Oberndorff for any pain *Gossip from the Forest* caused them.[24]

Oberndorff responded:

> Dear Mr Keneally,
>
> I have in front of me your letter to the Editor of 23rd January, *The Times Literary Supplement*. Its contents are, to me as the only son of Alfred, Count von Oberndorff, whose character you have filthily assassinated and memory clumsily disgraced in your novel, *Gossip from the Forest*, as well as to my six children, completely unsatisfactory.[25]

Ziegler was mortified. He reassured the count that hardcover stocks would be destroyed and that the count's name would be altered in future editions, which would also include a rider stating that the book was entirely fictional. While he was reassuring the Oberndorffs that Keneally was 'a thoroughly nice man and genuinely very ashamed of himself', he was angry. Sayle was also on the receiving end of Ziegler's displeasure: 'It is entirely Tom's fault that we had to scrap a lot of copies of *Gossip*, and I think it is pretty decent of us not to have asked for some compensation.'

This letter made Sayle 'apoplectic with rage'; she had understood from Keneally that he did not know about the 'scrapping' of *Gossip*. Ziegler wrote to Keneally:

> Of course we withdrew what was left of the edition of *Gossip from the Forest* (in fact only just under 100 copies). We could not possibly continue to sell something which cast such horrifying aspersions on poor Count Oberndorff's father, and Oberndorff is anything but content with the present situation, since he has demanded large sums of money which we have not paid him. If I detect a note of grievance in your letter I take it slightly amiss. We have been put to considerable expense and untold trouble as a result of your manipulation of history, and I have lost one of my oldest friends (she cut me dead at a party last week) . . .[26]

Ziegler's friend was a granddaughter of the count, and she continued to 'cut' him for about three years. Then she finally approached Ziegler at a party, saying, 'This feud has been going on long enough,' and the friendship was restored. Keneally was astonished at what he termed 'the vulnerability of relatives', and surprised that the *Almanach de Gotha* (the directory of Europe's royalty and higher nobility) could wield such power.

He was extra-cautious in the author's note of his next book, eventually called *Season in Purgatory*: 'This mere narrative derives from real events that occurred off the Dalmatian coast in 1943 and 1944. However, the characters – with the exception of Tito himself – are entirely fictional and are not meant to refer, either as regards appearance, behaviour or career, to any officer, doctor or partisan who occupied that place or period.'

That statement, strictly speaking, was untrue, but the real problem with the book was that another Australian author, Bill Strutton, had already written a similar story, *Island of Terrible Friends*. Simon King at Collins had apparently not heard of it and cheerfully agreed to see what Keneally had written: 'I would like to see your account of your landlady's demon lover's experiences as a doctor to the Yugoslav partisans. How could anyone not wish to see such a book and what a pity that you propose to spoil it by making it straightforward.'[27]

Trouble started when the *Nation Review* published an article by D. Jenkyn (a pseudonym of George Munster) under the heading 'Purgatory is Booked Out'.[28] Jenkyn claimed to have received an anonymous letter which said that 'a group of academics in one of our literature departments' had spotted a series of parallels between the two books. Jenkyn had tried to contact this group of 'textual critics', but they would not identify themselves. Jenkyn picked out all the parallels himself and put them together in his article, along with a photograph of Keneally captioned 'Honest Tom: a detail'.

Keneally responded to Jenkyn with a derisive rebuttal, headlined 'In Reply to D. Jenkyn'.[29] Keneally was quick to identify the literature department at Sydney University, where his nemeses, the academics, enjoyed 'good wages, tenure, superannuation and septennial overseas idleness for spotting affinities between books'.

Keneally had heard the stories that he wove into *Season in Purgatory* while staying in the fascinating house in Chelsea. Edome Carson-Frith (the name he mistakenly gave instead of Edome Broughton-Adderley) was one informant. 'There are similarities between my book and Strutton's simply because we both fed at the same source,' he noted. The matter did not rest there, as the journal *Quadrant* entered the fray with an eight-page anonymously compiled 'Quadrant Report', titled 'Thomas Keneally and the Strutton Connection'.[30] The reporter/s had found Strutton living in Surrey and given him a copy of Keneally's book to read.

The 'report' itemised all the similarities in the books and included Keneally's article from *Nation Review*, as well as comments from Strutton. Strutton had told George Lloyd-Roberts that Keneally was 'quoting actual dialogue he says he got from you, and which you well remember'. Keneally had not done that, although he did say that he had told Lloyd-Roberts before he left London in December 1973 that he would like to write about the Yugoslav experiences; 'I don't know if he was pleased or not.' Lloyd-Roberts denied this.

The seemingly damning evidence was that Lloyd-Roberts also denied that he and Mrs Broughton-Adderley had ever talked to Keneally about the wartime events. In fact, Keneally had not said in so many words that he had *talked* to Lloyd-Roberts, only that he had come across the material through living in the same house as the doctor. 'Edome Carson-Smith

[Broughton-Adderley] was also an informant,' Keneally stated. 'She told me all about Mrs Zon and said that the scintillating Yugoslav still visited George [Lloyd-Roberts] . . . In that house I had been hearing about George's operations on the partisans for some time before Strutton was mentioned, and then about October 1973 I was given a copy by Edome.' In another interview Keneally said that he'd got most of the information in London, 'from the man to whom it had all happened'.[31]

When Keneally had first realised that Strutton had beaten him to a good story, he approached Ziegler, who saw no objection to Keneally writing on the same subject. Ziegler was delighted with *The Terrible Island of Mus*.[32] He later observed, though, that 'the line between being inspired by something and plagiarising it is a fine one, but I think Tom probably stepped a little far over it on this occasion'.

The saga should have then died a natural death, with *Quadrant* jubilant that it had scored against Keneally. But it continued because Strutton decided to take legal action. Keneally feared that Ziegler would be finished with him, as he had affronted an important person in London society, Lloyd-Roberts, but Ziegler took his author's side and sent a telegram to Ian Morton, Strutton's lawyer: 'Totally unmoved by Keneally affair. Tom's talent is for transmuting lead to gold and this always annoys lead manufacturers.' To Keneally, he said: 'Of course there is a lot in common between your book and Strutton's – why on earth shouldn't there be? Please do not let all this nonsense worry you or put you off the most important task – which is writing the next book.'[33]

Sayle was also reassuring: 'I have had a word with Philip Ziegler and he agrees with me that Bill Strutton does not have one little toe to stand on, but these things can become very nasty and time consuming . . . Philip feels, as I do, that you have done nothing which is actionable according to the laws of copyright . . . There sure are some turds in this world who seem to have nothing better to do than make trouble. Don't let it get you down . . .'[34]

Keneally thought that a charge of plagiarism was the worst accusation that any writer could have levelled against him. 'It shouldn't be assumed that writers have a lawyer's knowledge of copyright,' he says. 'When I read Strutton's book I relied on a statement [in the author's note] that it was a true story. I did sincerely think that it was in the public domain. I didn't need to nick material.' Keneally was not knowingly culpable, but he had certainly been discredited.

His legal advisers negotiated a settlement but did not concede that the use of Strutton's book as a reference constituted an infringement of copyright:

> The plaintiff in a copyright action must demonstrate that the defendant copied a *substantial* part of the plaintiff's work in which copyright exists. Even if we concede – which we do not – that Mr Keneally copied part of Mr Strutton's original plot, characters and situation, it must be shown that the matter taken was a substantial part of the plaintiff's work.
>
> Mr Keneally is entitled to make use of historical facts and common stories about the islands during the war years. Mr Strutton's work purports to be a true story. Those aspects of plot, character and incident which Mr Strutton claims to have created are only a minor and insubstantial part of his work, and only a minor and insubstantial part of those aspects (if any) are contained in Mr Keneally's book.

The dispute did not go to court, but Keneally was obliged to pay Strutton's legal costs and 10 per cent of all income (net income after tax and payments of agents' commission) received in royalties from the sale of his book, and to acknowledge, in reprints and new editions, Strutton's book as a source of material.[35]

Keneally brooded on the *Quadrant* exposé, and when at a literary event he met one of the editors of *Quadrant* who had approved the copy, he complained that the journal had tried to destroy him. There seemed little doubt that *Quadrant* had it in for him, resenting his anti-Catholic accusations and his political preferences, and – in his mind – seeking to expose flaws in his character. Keneally's spikiness, his readiness to speak out and give an unguarded opinion, and his resentment of academics had fuelled a dislike of him that intensified through the 1970s.

Not long after the Strutton affair, and presumably unrelated, Keneally received death threats. The most serious was made via the crime roundsman at the *Sun* newspaper in Sydney, who was told that an attempt would be made on Keneally's life that day. The girls were immediately removed from the Avalon home and taken to a secure place. After a couple of anxious days the family relaxed, but other threats were made, usually in the form of anonymous letters. They scared Keneally. Some were responses to his republican views; others were the typical work of deviants who targeted people in the public eye. The threats were possibly also related to a plan of Keneally's to write about Juanita Nielsen, the publisher and urban conservationist who had mysteriously disappeared in Kings Cross.

Curiously, Keneally had contemplated using a pen name for *Season in Purgatory*, but his publishers had insisted he use his own name. At one stage the title had been *David Pelham's Yugoslav Education*; the book ended up being an education for its author. Tony Godwin at HBJ had insisted on titling it *Season in Purgatory*. 'If you let me call it that,' he promised, 'I can sell it in Topeka.'[36] (Topeka was the byword for a hard market in America.) Godwin, who shared Keneally's affliction of asthma, died of a heart attack while alone in his New York apartment in 1976. The title he had chosen was very apt for Keneally.

20

A Literary Bikie

Margaret and Jane were playing with their friends in the woods, where squirrels scampered up and down the tall, thin trees. Some racoons were ripping open a package and scattering the contents. The children, delighted with this windfall, picked up the papers and included them in their games, crumpling them under rocks and pushing them into the hollows of trees. Some drew pictures on the back of the sheets, which had typed writing on one side.

One of the children noticed a familiar name on a page and ran to tell Keneally, sitting inside near the fire in the cold dusk, that something belonging to him was now scattered over the woods. The children were told to find as many pages as they could and take them back to the rightful owner, Margaret and Jane's father. Before the dark and snow set in, he had every sheet.

It was December 1975 and the postman had left the package on the Keneallys' front doorstep. The racoons' heist was the original manuscript of *Season in Purgatory* and thirty-two pages of recommended changes from Tony Godwin. The early treatment by a few furry critters of the book was matched, Keneally later thought, by the critics' destructive relish and heedless disregard for the reputation he had worked hard to establish.

The woods where his daughters played were near New Milford, Connecticut. Keneally, driven by ambition, curiosity and the belief that New

York was the 'new Rome', wanted the experience of being there, or at least nearby. New Milford was rustic and charming, just a few hours' bus ride to New York. Keneally had briefly toyed with an offer from the University of Western Australia to teach in its English department, however, despite the lucrative salary, he knew from the Armidale experience that full-time lecturing would leave him little time for writing. Besides that, as he wrote to the university, 'the geographic and family problems involved in my coming to Perth are not easily solvable'.[1]

When Keneally left Sydney on 18 July 1975 he had plans to write a book on a small town in South Dakota which had a Native American village on its fringe. 'I hope also to complete my present book and take part in an American-Canadian lecture tour,' he told the *Sydney Morning Herald*.[2] The book about the town in South Dakota was not written, but a writing fellowship from the Association for Commonwealth Language and Literature Studies (ACLALS) foundation funded most of the touring expenses for Keneally, its first writing fellow. There was also assistance from a Modern Languages Association (MLA) fellowship. One topic about which Keneally spoke on the tour was 'The Problems and Rewards of Being a Novelist'.[3]

For the peripatetic Keneally, one of the rewards of the move was the opportunity to visit many new places. He and the family started their North American adventure in Vancouver, buying a van and camping along the way while visiting many places, including pre-Columbian indigenous sites, the Grand Canyon, Mesa Verde and other attractions in the mountains. Keneally always had 'a thing' about mountains. He sometimes led the family on a merry dance, such as the time he took them through a Montreal blizzard, insisting that they look at seventeenth-century buildings. Everyone had frostbite.

The family moved into a rented house at 4 Haviland Road, New Milford, which was reminiscent of their Avalon home with its steep steps and rocky, tree-enclosed location. They saw elk in the forest and the children raced their sleds down the steep hill. They could walk to the long and lovely Candlewood Lake, which iced over in the winter. Later, the Keneallys moved to a smaller house at 36 Candlewood Springs, beside the lake, a delightful place to be in the northern spring of 1976. Joe Keneally, one of grandfather Timothy's nephews, lived in Westport, Connecticut.

The girls attended the public Hill & Plain School in New Milford. Keneally delighted the children there by providing a play for them to use. The leaflet described '*How Vanilla Ice Cream Became Vanilla Riley* as told to Jane and Margaret Keneally by their father'. Keneally knew of a well-known writer living at nearby Roxbury, William Styron, but he hesitated to contact him. Whether it was shyness, a sense of inferiority or fear of refusal, he was not sure. At the time, Styron was probably writing *Sophie's Choice*, a book mentioned in Keneally's *Schindler's Ark*.

'We used to hang around a lot with a very accomplished English teacher, and professional piano player – John Schell,' Keneally remembers. 'He was a good friend, very literary, very funny, a survivor. He taught at the Kent School – one of those John Irving style schools – in a very beautiful village.' Schell was one of the many would-be writers who tentatively asked Keneally to 'cast an eye' over an unpublished story. In Schell's case, the story and the writing were impressive – in the tradition of *Moby-Dick*, by Keneally's reckoning – but Schell did not pursue publication.

In the summer of 1976 Keneally packed the van and set out with the family on a Southern trip to visit various Civil War battle sites. The findings from this trip would inspire him to write a big historical novel, *Confederates*. Before that book was sent to his editors, he travelled even further south in his imagination, back to Antarctica. He had always been disappointed with *The Survivor*; now he planned a more 'commercial' book, a sophisticated murder mystery.

Keneally attended a conference in California, and while there took the family to visit the parents of June Richardson, a close friend from Avalon.[4] They lived in a big retirement complex, Leisure World, in Laguna Hills, Orange County. Keneally was amazed at what he saw there and thought there was a novel in it, which he never wrote, but back in New Milford he wrote *The New British South Polar Expedition*. It begins in a Californian rest home in Laguna Hills – south of Los Angeles – where an old polar explorer/artist, Anthony Piers, is reminiscing about his part in an Antarctic expedition led by Sir Eugene Stewart in the years before the First World War. Anthony Piers is like one of 'the decaying plutocrats' whom Keneally observed at Leisure World.

Piers is in confessional mode, recalling all the players in an expedition overshadowed by the murder of one of Stewart's party. The book is about the polar world, but it is also an exploration of relationships. On homosexuality: 'Do they *really* couple and split apart for the same reasons as men and women? ... You have to understand that in those days the attitude to homosexuality was one of breathless abomination ... I was a child of my age and suffered from all its frantic prejudices ... closet queens ...'

Adultery is queried too. Stewart asks Piers: 'The younger man, the older woman. I think of the husband though ... Tell me ... The lovers ... do they mention the husband? Do you perhaps tend to mock him?' Piers replies: 'Most women ... would consider the sort of thing you mention to be the worst infidelity ...' Piers recalls Lady Anthea Hurley: 'When you remember such women you know that even now, in a Laguna Hills nursing home for decaying plutocrats, you are still in love with them.' She tells Piers, when he begs her to marry him: 'Marriage isn't a matter of desire. It's a matter of placid companionability ... You can fall in love again, but I am Oscar's last love.' Piers reflects: 'Admittedly I was always easily infatuated ...'

Keneally was at a reflective point of his life. Seeing the elderly at Leisure World confirmed a view that he would always hold: he would never go into an old community where the talk was inevitably of death and dying. He, too, was easily infatuated with other women.

The Laguna Hills visit came soon after Keneally had celebrated his fortieth birthday. He said to Pete McCarthy, who had interviewed him for a radio program in Armidale: '... you find out that your talent is limited, and that the more books you write, the more you learn about the limits of your talent and the limits of your personality; and that's dangerous knowledge to have. It can be an extremely destructive thing to a writer to have doubts about his talent and doubts about his capacity to produce in middle age or in old age ...'

'Did you really get a surprise,' McCarthy asked, 'to find there's life and love and passion on the other side of the bloody wall?'[5]

No, Keneally did not get a surprise, and this book about Piers gave him scope to think about the different dimensions of love. There is a reference to a man turning forty in *Season in Purgatory*. The surgeon Ellis confesses: 'I was all right till I turned forty. I even thought I was a clever fellow. Then the day I turned ... you see, I'd been carrying that date round with me since childhood as the date when everything starts ending. Well, suddenly I didn't know how to face growing old with the one woman and becoming more and more detached and wealthy. The old problem of dying before you've lived . . .'

This sounds like the standard midlife crisis, but Keneally feared that same problem. He wanted to write the big international bestseller – soon – before time ran out. He had done a lot of living, making up for time lost in his youth, always devising new plans and hurrying off to the next scene of action, but he did not have quite the ego of the younger writer he had been. As his fortieth birthday approached, Nan Talese told him: 'We all feel, and I most strongly, that your greater recognition and indeed financial future is going to come from you writing on your own terms, and extending your extraordinary talent, rather than from setting out to write a "commercial" novel.'[6]

Keneally had enjoyed writing his commercial story, although he thought it was 'a flawed novel'. The book, published as *A Victim of the Aurora*, was dismissed by some of its readers as 'an airport read', but Borchardt had high hopes when it arrived on his desk for assessment. He sent the manuscript to HBJ, and Keneally suggested that Borchardt should ask for a $10,000 advance, the same as for *Gossip from the Forest*. HBJ, however, was only prepared to offer $8500.

Publishers had trouble keeping up with Keneally, who was usually a couple of novels ahead of them, and the two previous titles HBJ had accepted had yet to prove viable. Ziegler also found the author's impulsive manner and sometimes unrealistic expectations hard to deal with, but Collins was still Keneally's English publisher. Tessa Sayle said to Keneally, 'just between ourselves', that other publishers – Cape and Faber & Faber – were making overtures. Bob Woodings of Faber & Faber had told Sayle that, in his opinion, Collins was not doing Keneally justice in England: 'I am not telling you all this to make you feel restive about Collins, but merely to let you know that many a publisher here is casting covetous eyes in your direction.'[7]

Keneally was impatient with revisions, always wanting to get on with the next topic, to wangle the next advance to fill the household coffers. He once described himself as 'a literary butterfly' or 'a literary bikie driving up every alley in a lifelong discovery of new material'.[8] He was impetuous, his eyes roving constantly for a potential story. In the United States he considered a book about the San Francisco earthquake and fires of 1906, a subject of interest dating from a distant Saturday afternoon at the Vogue theatre, Homebush, where he saw a film, *San Francisco*, about the disaster. Perhaps there might also be a sequel to Mark Twain's classics, *Tom Sawyer* and *Huckleberry Finn*.

'The People of Hannibal: A Treatment' was sent to HBJ for consideration. The idea was to trace events from about Tom Sawyer's twentieth year, in 1855, to his full involvement in the Civil War. It is a wonderfully fanciful tale, with Keneally pulling together a lot of unusual historical incidents from his research trip in the Southern states and tying them into a big yarn about Sawyer, who is by turns a journalist, riverboat pilot and soldier, with various romantic attachments along the way. He and Huck part company over the right and wrong of the slavery question. Huck joins the Confederate army and Tom joins the Federal army.[9] The manuscript was rejected.

Writing about legendary people was another challenge. Keneally's first commissioned book, *Moses the Lawgiver*, had to be completed within eight weeks to coincide with a BBC six-episode series about Moses screened in mid-1975, using a script written by Anthony Burgess. Keneally put his own interpretation on some of the miracles of the biblical narrative; his reconstruction is very dramatic, with horrible punishments, murder, rape, human sacrifice – some of which were present in the original – culminating at the 'Sea of Reeds'. The book, against all expectations, did not turn into much money for Keneally.

More satisfying was Granada Television's adaptation of *Gossip from the Forest*, scripted by Brian Gibson and scheduled for the sixtieth anniversary of the armistice. It was shown in Australia, too, as part of Stuart Wagstaff's World Playhouse series. Donald McDonald, then head of the Sydney Theatre Company, approached Keneally with a proposal for a stage adaptation, which was produced and then performed at the Sydney Opera House in May 1983. The play was published in a playtext series edited by Wayne Harrison.[10] Keneally also negotiated unsuccessfully with Peter Luke, one of the directors of the Dublin Gate Theatre, to write a play version of *Gossip from the Forest*.

There was always something on the go. There was some talk of Keneally writing a book about the Australian tennis star Evonne Goolagong Cawley, but it did not eventuate. A major project about the white man's experience of Australia, starting with a kind of 'ship of fools' leaving Cork in 1800, had been abandoned. Keneally was in his Günter Grass phase then, impressed by the German writer's Danzig trilogy. There was a manuscript well underway called *A Deal in Aged Whiskey*. Perhaps there would be a series of historical novels next – or something totally different.

21

Close to the Intention of the Book

Keneally, in his 'flight from the past', had never gone back to look at the house in Lane Cove he had rented after returning from his first trip to England. The place did hold two positive associations, however, and those were visits from John Abernethy and Fred Schepisi.

Schepisi had a similar background to Keneally, as he had entered the Marist Brothers' training establishment at Macedon, Victoria, where Peter Lawler and Greg Parnham, Keneally's friends at Waverley College, had also trained. Schepisi did not complete the course but wrote about the experience in a film script, which he handed to Keneally to read. Keneally was rather taken aback by his first encounter with this amply built man with a Sicilian name and blond hair. Schepisi had won many prizes for television commercials and industrial documentaries. He had a studio in Melbourne called The Film House, and he had recently tried to buy the film rights to *Slaughterhouse 5* from Kurt Vonnegut. 'I told Kurt I wasn't known,' Schepisi had said, 'and all I could offer him was that I wouldn't bugger it up on him.'

Schepisi did not get far with Vonnegut but also had his own script, which Keneally dutifully read. At that time there were many 'ruined' Catholics trying to make sense of their bad experiences, Keneally himself among them, but Schepisi succeeded where others had not in portraying a pubescent boy's torment amid the tedium of daily routines. 'It's good,' Keneally assured Schepisi. 'Now get on with it!'[1] The film, called *The Devil's Playground*, was written, produced and directed by Schepisi.

The boy in the lead role could have been a young Keneally, kind-hearted and friendly, but increasingly miserable and introspective at the institution. One of the Brothers is a zealot and some of the boys become fanatics, involved in a 'Purification Club' which insists on flagellation to drive away sexual desires. Keneally enthusiastically played the part of the Franciscan Father Marshall, the retreat priest, and was quite natural preparing the Host in solitude on his knees and delivering a sermon as he grasped the lectern. Schepisi reckoned Keneally had the kind of mischievous twinkle which was right for that priest.

The Devil's Playground, shown at the Sydney Film Festival in June 1976, was the only Australian film that year to win acceptance at the Cannes Film Festival. Before that, Schepisi had directed a segment of what he called a 'portmanteau' film of four parts, *Libido* (1973), in which the Producers and Directors Guild of Australia showcased the talents of promising Australian writers, directors and actors. The writers – Keneally, Craig McGregor, Hal Porter and David Williamson – fashioned 'original and fascinating characters from the Australian way of life in situations which were a far cry from the now cliché outback settings.'[2] The film was shot in and around Melbourne, with premieres at that city's Rapallo Cinema, and later the Gala Cinema, in Sydney.

Keneally's script was entitled 'The Priest'; the other segments were 'The Husband,' 'The Child' and 'The Family Man.' Father Burn, the main character in 'The Priest,' was played by the actor Arthur Dignam, and easily recognisable as a composite priest from Keneally's store of 'spoiled' priests. Burn wants to marry a nun, Sister Caroline (Robyn Nevin), but she will not go ahead without a special dispensation from the church, although Burn (like O'Halloran before him in *Bring Larks and Heroes*) insists that 'we could consecrate it ourselves'; Burn has had a nervous breakdown and is determined to leave the church with or without Caroline, who urges him to wait till he is strong again.

'I've tried to ignore the fact,' Burn reflects, 'that people grow out of each other, but it happens – the church, the state, husband and wife.' Although short, 'The Priest' is very revealing of Keneally in that era.

Schepisi had read the proofs of *The Chant of Jimmie Blacksmith*, and he read the book again and again when it was published. He was attracted by its wealth of visual images, and it seemed to him that Keneally had written the book with a film in mind. There were a number of images that Schepisi could imagine translated onto the screen, particularly the fugitive boys walking on the railway lines and on the post-and-rail fences so they left no tracks.

Schepisi wanted to make the book into a film, which was a big proposition given the uncertain state of Australia's slowly emerging film industry in the 1970s. Keneally had been told by every agent with whom he'd had contact not to sell film rights to a prospective Australian producer, because the risks of it ending in limbo were too great. Even though Schepisi 'kept badgering Keneally', he had not made enough to convince Keneally that he could deliver. 'He thought he would make really big money for this movie,' Schepisi says, 'but certainly not from me!'

Keneally was dubious about the book-to-film arrangements when it applied to some of his own books. When Borchardt told him about an offer for *The Place at Whitton*, he replied: 'As for Whitton, I'd prefer not to option it. I don't respect the book and want to get away from my image as a professional *mauvais pretre*.'[3] Keneally had been at the home of film producer Pat Lovell in Avalon, and wondered at her saying that she had got the money together to buy Joan Lindsay's *Picnic at Hanging Rock*. Where would the money come from to actually make the film, and how would distribution be achieved? Lovell's film became one of the Australian industry's early success stories.

If a film was to be made, then Keneally wanted to have a good financial return, and overseas options seemed more likely to deliver. He had an offer from Peter Clifton, then a Sydney expatriate, who approached him on behalf of Columbia Pictures in the United States. 'You'll get a Harry Belafonte Jimmie Blacksmith,' Schepisi predicted. Allan Scott and Chris Bryant, scriptwriters in England who were working on a film called *Don't Look Now*, offered an option on *The Chant of Jimmie Blacksmith* and were confident they could raise the money to convert it to a full contract. In Scott's opinion, 'the project needs an established "star" director in order to have a real chance of being made into a successful film.'[4]

'Only an Australian should be allowed to make this one,' muttered Schepisi. At last the film rights went to him. Keneally was asked if he would like to write the script, but he declined. He was satisfied that Schepisi's script was close to the intention of the book, which was hardly surprising, given the number of times Schepisi had read it. Keneally believed the director knew more about the book's meaning and intention than he did himself.

Keneally found the whole business of filmmaking a mystery, with the multitude of people on set, so many lenses to capture various nuances, and the endless activity. A few years earlier, when ABC TV had produced *The Survivor* as a mini-series, Keneally had watched some of the shooting of scenes at Frenchs Forest, a northern Sydney suburb, taking Margaret and Jane with him. He had enjoyed the communal aspect of so many people working together, all focused on one particular scene.

Keneally had a small part to play in *The Chant of Jimmie Blacksmith*, as a lecherous shearer's cook. When Schepisi first told him about the role he was pleased, but on the day of shooting he was nervous. The author Di Morrissey, then living in Wiltshire, wrote to her friend Keneally after seeing the film: 'You old ham you, see you got yourself a role where you get to cuddle a pretty girl!'[5]

In Schepisi's adaptation, the white people are portrayed sympathetically. 'My screenplay basically holds the integrity of the novel,' he said in 1978. 'But I guess I have tended to de-villainise the whites. I believe they were mostly acting out of ignorance. They hadn't the exposure to civil rights or ethnic understanding. But please, understand that in de-villainising them, I am in no way excusing them.'[6]

Schepisi had to portray the violence inherent in the story as savage, yet not too explicitly. 'We haven't been coy and we haven't been brutal,' he noted. Even so, it was harrowing for some of the cast. 'The intensity of the murder sequence knocked us all about. There were the added pressures of a schedule to keep, of drama to maintain, and we had actresses leaving the set and bursting into tears. There was general depression and a marked increase in beverage consumption all round.'[7]

The Chant of Jimmie Blacksmith premiered simultaneously in Armidale, Melbourne and Sydney on 21 June 1978. Schepisi was worried that audiences would see just a black/white confrontation. He was more interested in the underdog, in irrational acts, than he was in the old black-versus-white scenario. Robert Drewe, who interviewed Schepisi for *The Bulletin*, said it was to Schepisi's credit that he kept the novel's historical ironies and complexities intact in his 'thrice-removed Governor story'.[8]

Audiences were confronted by some graphic violence, but if they experienced discomfort, it was often because the film also confronted them with the possibility of their racism. One of Schepisi's acquaintances in Melbourne, a psychiatrist, let the director know in no uncertain terms that he didn't appreciate having his racism put so baldly before him. When Schepisi returned to his home to celebrate after the Melbourne premiere of the film, there was a large banner displayed at his home: 'Fred Schepisi, you are a cunt!'

The violence was too much for Keneally on the first viewing. 'He was unaware of the absolute power of some of the images he had written,' Schepisi reflects. 'On screen they assumed for him a frightening power and a dangerous power. He calmed down on that later; it was just the initial shock. He just had no idea how [the book] would translate. I did the violence as anti-violent violence, so that it's not exactly a blood ballet. It looks like the real thing – you think you see an awful lot, which was very hard to do.'

On a lighter note, Keneally was concerned when he first saw the film that the graffiti on a large outcrop of rocks, seen during the Blacksmith brothers' flight, looked too new. As he wrote in a short story, 'Going to the Fair', 'graffiti on a great boulder looked as if they had been painted there half an hour before filming, without being aged or weathered'.[9] It was Keneally's idea, though, to have a slogan written on the boulder: 'Fuck Federation!'

The film was shown to the Independent Television (ITV) censors in the United Kingdom, but it came back stamped 'Not fit for showing'. Finally, in 1979, ITV paid £90,000 for *The Chant of Jimmie Blacksmith*. 'The greatest praise I could have got from anyone,' Schepisi told Robert Drewe, 'was when Alexander Walker [the English film critic] said that the movie could not have been made anywhere else in the world, that it was a definitive Australian film, completely characteristic of our culture.'

Keneally was involved in writing a very different film script in the early 1980s. This was *Silver City*, directed by Sophia Turkiewicz and produced by Joan Long. When Turkiewicz became frustrated in her attempts to write the screenplay, which concerned post-war migrants in Australia, Keneally was asked to accept the role as co-writer. The script was eventually completed and the film won the Sydney Critics' Circle Award for Best Feature Film of 1984.[10]

22

Quite a Job

Contrary to the opinion of some critics, Keneally had not returned from America with 'his tail between his legs'. The fact that he was back in Sydney after barely a year's absence led his detractors to believe that he had tried to make it in the big league overseas and failed. To the contrary, he had enjoyed a good year, making contacts across the United States and collecting material for his next round of books. He had had various opportunities over the years to move overseas permanently, but there were his ageing parents to consider and the realisation that he would be no better off overseas.

'I really don't think that England and America are more congenial places to write, not by any means,' he told an interviewer in 1977. 'In the fifties and sixties Australian writers went overseas because they said Australia was a philistine country and there was something about its atmosphere which was entirely hostile to creation. If that was true then I just don't believe that it is any more. America is no more exciting – in fact it's less exciting because you are separated from your origins, from your roots.'[1]

Nevertheless, one of the manuscripts that Keneally worked on back at Avalon was all-American: *Confederates*, about the Civil War from the Southerners' point of view. This was the first novel for which Keneally used a dictating machine to initially record the story. The manuscript was then typed up from the tapes.

In 1983 Keneally described *Confederates*, half-seriously, as 'the last act of folly of my youth . . . I thought that Southerners with all their warts were very interesting. They were like Australians and they had a strong oral tradition. And they had an informality that didn't exist up in, if you'll pardon my saying so, up in Yankeedom. I wanted to write something about the rural proletariat, the rural poor in the South during the Civil War.'[2]

Much to Borchardt's annoyance, Keneally wrote to HBJ about the new book without consultation. 'We had thought of switching you to another publisher [due to the internal upheavals of that company],' the agent said to his author, 'but since you had written to Tom Stewart that we would be sending him CONFEDERATES you really forced our hand . . . From now on it would be best if you did not write to Harcourt about your plans beyond Confederates.'[3] Thomas Stewart, a senior editor at HBJ in New York, was positive: 'I've read Confederates and think it's quite a job. I'm terribly impressed by your research, and I think you've, for the most part, chosen well what to tell and how to tell it . . .'[4]

Ziegler in London had also seen the manuscript and wrote an encouraging letter: 'I am immensely pleased with Confederates . . . I thought it a superb story and a vivid and very moving evocation of one of the most brutal of wars. Provided the Americans do not get all uptight about the idea of an Australian writing their history for them, it should have a tremendous success in the States. I thought it far better than Gore Vidal's much acclaimed *Burr* . . .'[5]

Reviewers like Stephen Vaughan in England cautiously approved the latest Keneally: 'As an Australian writing about events so thronged with ghosts, altars and portents for our time but also so fervently and proprietorially American, Kenneally [sic] is treading on holy ground. Dangerous ground, too, with such forerunners as Crane, Faulkner, Bierce, Sandburg, but he avoids the pitfalls of pastiche in this noble book.'[6]

Despite Stewart's initial enthusiasm, HBJ decided against *Confederates*. 'I know you felt that *Confederates* has the best chance of all your novels in the US . . . Our problem, frankly, was the trail of red ink left by *Gossip*, *Season*, and *Victim* . . . Tom, it wasn't easy for anyone here to decide not to make an offer for *Confederates*. We've enjoyed and been proud of being your publisher . . .'[7]

Borchardt knew that Keneally was disappointed with the sales of his work in the United States, but he also knew that it was the usual fate of emerging literary writers. He has pointed out that other young novelists in the 1970s, such as Ian McEwan and Tom Coraghessan Boyle, also struggled for recognition. 'We have been representing Ian and Tom [Boyle] starting with their first books, both collections of stories, neither of which sold many copies,' Borchardt said in 2014. 'Gradually they became more and more successful, and we still represent them today. Loyalty of course benefits both author and agent. We see to it that all older books by our authors remain available, and keep an eye on details that might escape others.'

Borchardt sent the *Confederates* manuscript to Harper & Row, where editor Harvey Ginsberg read and rejected it. Simon & Schuster, Coward & Morrow and Doubleday all turned it down. Finally, Borchardt tried Harper & Row again, armed this time with a proof copy from Collins. Ginsberg – 'please call me Harvey' – then sent a contract to Keneally, swayed perhaps by the advice from Ziegler that the book had been entered in the Booker Prize.

'Keneally's best novel yet,' said the *Kirkus* reviewer, 'ripest fruit of an imagination that has been grinding on for years in an effort to energise history within its fiction – sometimes head-on, sometimes obliquely, but never with quite full success. Success has come … A grave and breathtaking book, a model historical novel by a writer growing even better.'[8] Otto Scott, however, in a review with the headline 'The Civil War as Seen by a Kangaroo', was as derisive as that title suggests: 'Keneally's work is, from the first page, one of blatant vulgarity.' Scott railed against the sexual depravities, profanities, excessive blood, stenches and death in the book, as well as its 'historical pretentiousness'.[9]

Confederates was shortlisted for the Booker Prize, but it did not win. Tessa Sayle was not impressed by the judges' choice, *Offshore* by Penelope Fitzgerald. 'As you say you will win the bloody prize one day but it was just infuriating to have it go to someone who simply is not in the same league.'[10] Most pundits had expected V. S. Naipaul to win with *A Bend in the River*.

In a letter to Keneally, Ziegler told him that he had also managed to slip another of Keneally's new books, *Passenger*, onto the Booker list, 'by nobbling one of the judges and getting him to request it . . .'[11] *Passenger* (originally titled *Boy-oh*) was finished and published before *Confederates.* It is about the relationship between a foetus and his mother, and is regarded by some as perhaps the strangest Keneally book yet. In the first drafts he did not divide the story into chapters, which gave it a mad, headlong pace.

Thomas Stewart told Borchardt that it was 'weird stuff, but magic, I think.'[12] However, he resisted Keneally's attempt to negotiate a bigger advance beyond $8500:

> We very much want to be Keneally's publisher – for this book and for the books to come. We believe that his work is important. We also have fun reading it and publishing it; there's nothing dutifully grudging about the way we've been approaching his books. Nor has there been, so far, much that's remunerative . . . There is no question, from what we have seen, that Keneally is gradually, gradually becoming better known to American readers as a novelist who can be counted upon to deliver a well-written, well worth buying and reading book . . . there's an audience out there, growing slowly, and the groundwork is being set for a book that will break out and sell like crazy . . . he continues to write superb, wonderful books. But we do not, in all honesty and despite our tremendous admiration and enthusiasm about the new novel, believe that this is the breakthrough . . . I'm mad about the book, so is Alan Kahn, so is Kathy Robbins . . . the book is a winning, improbable, brilliant piece of work that we will do our damnedest to sell.[13]

Passenger has added interest in the various ways the author incorporated details from his recent experiences. The Irish mother Sal has had a very restrictive education under the tutelage of nuns. She makes an appointment at the Great Ormond Street Children's Hospital, and she is writing a book about a crowd of political prisoners on board a convict ship, *Minerva*, in Cork Harbour, 1799, about to be transported to Australia. Sal and her Australian husband, Brian, live in a house in Royal Hospital Road owned by Clytie Heatherton-Meadows with her 'beloved', George, an orthopaedic specialist. Keneally was having his own fun, perhaps, with Clytie and George, taking some vengeance on their real-life counterparts from the *Season in Purgatory* calamity. Clytie is 'a bottled-in-bond British eccentric' who has a wardrobe of 1940s clothes, and keeps a Brazilian monkey called Ran Singh. The monkey falls in love with lady visitors and likes to watch Western movies and the chorus girls in *The Black and White Minstrel Show*. The comical account of Brian's unexpected problems after having a vasectomy was taken directly from a story told to Keneally by his friend Iain Finlay.

Ziegler rejected *Ned Kelly and the City of Bees*, a book for children, about a boy who lives for one summer in a beehive with a girl who is 120 years old. She is a colonial who has disappeared from a wagon and dies from exposure. Ever since her death she sleeps in the winter and lives with the bees in the summer. The boy is like a young Keneally, sick with diphtheria, who has strange experiences while in a coma-like state. The story sounds fanciful, and it is. Jonathan Cape in England accepted the book, possibly looking at the bigger picture of becoming Keneally's general publisher. The book is dedicated 'to Jane and Margaret, my daughters, who talked me into writing this story', and was published in 1978.

Jane and Margaret always loved storytelling sessions with their father. Keneally had a set of *Encyclopaedia Britannica*, and its volumes were regarded with awe by the girls, even though they were allowed to look at them whenever they wanted to. Margaret remembers: 'Although access was supervised after I spilt Ribena on one of the volumes, this is part of a theme from throughout my childhood. Whenever we wanted information or showed an interest in a particular topic, Mum and Dad would bend over backwards to feed our curiosity . . . They would never restrict our access to the encyclopaedias or any other source of knowledge.'

Keneally was tempted to write more poetry, especially after attending a conference in Hawaii in 1977. He listened to the poets reading their work, wondering if he could be equally adept at the craft. He had written verse for *Bring Larks and Heroes*, *The Chant of Jimmie Blacksmith* and *Season in Purgatory*, but otherwise the interest went no further than the odd rhyme for a special occasion.

There was another play in production, although Keneally always maintained that a novelist as playwright had the batting average of a fast bowler. The new play was *Bullie's House*, directed by Ken Horler, which opened at the Nimrod Theatre, Sydney, on 6 February 1980. *Bullie's House* is the story of Elcho Island people who allow white men to see their *ranga*, totems which they believe contain the world's secrets. In return, they expect the white men to share the secrets that hold their society together and the mysteries of their technology.

Some people saw the inevitable clash of cultures as a return to *The Chant of Jimmie Blacksmith*, but Keneally denied this. In his introduction to the play, he wrote: '*Bullie's House* was a different sort of story, about cultural dispossession. Anthropologists have noticed a number of cases in which tribal Aboriginals have attempted to achieve *détente* with the white race by offering, as the basis of a treaty, their most sacred and secret objects. The idea has been that such an offering would adjust the fraught balance between the two races. The tragedy of such offers is that we, the whites, have never understood or been impressed by what has been offered.'[14]

The source for Keneally's play was *An Adjustment Movement in Arnhem Land*, a monograph by Ronald Berndt. Keneally's version of the Aborigines' gesture of reconciliation was a source of contention. He seemed to attract difficulties by his close representation of known people. He was unaware that the real-life models for protagonists Bullie and Jimmie were still alive. Nevertheless, Aboriginal people from various tribal backgrounds acted in the play. Although Keneally claimed that he did not intend the play to refer to any living or dead person, he conceded that he would not have written it in later years, when the right of Aboriginal people to their own stories became a more sensitive issue.

Bullie's House was produced again in May 1985, at the Long Wharf Theatre in New Haven, Connecticut. For that production Keneally undertook considerable rewriting, in an effort to universalise the exposition of the *ranga*. He told Lloyd Richards, artistic director of the Yale Repertory Theatre in New Haven, that he wanted to produce a final text which would convince the Elcho Island people that he had not gossiped about them, and this time he would not identify geographical locations too exactly: he would use a story from their past to symbolise the entire history of exchanges between whites and Aborigines.[15] The rewritten script was published by Currency Press in 1981.

'When you enter *Bullie's House* at the Long Wharf Theatre's Stage II,' wrote Ruth Lesser for the local *Journal-Courier*, 'you find a strange and fascinating place. It's the Australian Outback, home of the Aborigines, whose culture is the subject of this interesting American premiere . . .'[16] The production was directed by Kenneth Frankel, Long Wharf's assistant artistic director, who had watched the workshopping of the play at the New Dramatists in New York (1982) with Keneally and his friend Irvin Bauer. Five Aboriginal actors were teamed with three American actors – the first time, Keneally believed, that Aboriginal actors had played in a foreign country alongside foreign actors. Ernie Dingo played the part of Bullie, and Tommy Lewis was Mallie. Some Americans heard the music of the didjeridu for the first time.

The play was also seen on a London stage, Riverside Studios, in April/May 2004 after a tour of various English towns with Border Crossings. This was hailed as 'a history-making collaboration' between Aboriginal and British performers. Natasha Wanganeen, who had made her acting debut in the 2002 film *Rabbit-Proof Fence*, was thrilled to be there: 'I am so proud to be a part of this. I love the story myself, but it's more than that. It's important that people see this.'[17]

The author of *Bullie's House* had a new house of his own at 24 The Serpentine, Bilgola Beach, just south of Avalon, described in *Passenger* as 'a vertical one, three-tiered, affixed to a cliff side'. The purchase, for $90,000, was made on 22 January 1979. The girls attended St Luke's Anglican College for Girls, Dee Why.

It should have been a very satisfying time for the author as he approached the age of forty-five. He had a home in a prestigious location, he was recognised internationally and his family was close around him. The danger he always had to confront was the solitariness of writing, with the attendant introspection and sense of being not much use to the rest of society. The thought of losing whatever talent he had was more worrying than the thought of commercial failure. Was the big breakthrough not coming because of a lack of talent, or might the fault lie with his publishers?

He had his doubts about Collins, although Sayle had received a reassuring letter from Ziegler: 'I hope we convinced you of our enormous enthusiasm for Tom, but also of the very real difficulties which we have in establishing him as a popular best-seller. Personally, I would not have him any different – it would horrify me if he bought popularity at the price of writing less well or on subjects which did not appeal to him – but in literature the price of liberty seems to be eternal penury, or at least to notch up those massive sales achieved by the sausage merchants who churn out a more or less identical product once a year.'[18]

Simon King, in a memo to Ken Wilder of Collins Australia, was ambivalent as he mulled over an author whose work did not fit the standard genre categories: 'Tom bewilders his readers. Thinking about his progress is in one respect a bit like regarding a stationary fly: you know any second it will manoeuvre brilliantly but you haven't the slightest idea what direction it will take. That's Tom.'

King's favourite Keneally was *Blood Red, Sister Rose*, 'a book I enjoyed and admired more than any other novel of anyone's that I ever worked on'. However, he continued gloomily: 'We haven't really succeeded. In fact, we've achieved little with his books ... How to market his paperbacks (find covers, style) that will give readers a sense of consistency so that more than the few faithful buy? ... I do not say he *should* not do what he does: merely that if he wants to see his sales grow he must come to *court* his readers not just, like some splendid peacock, to spread his dazzling feathers ... He should stop toying with his genius and develop some steady vein within it.'[19]

23

One Never Knows with Tom

Philip Ziegler shared Simon King's sentiments and was remarkably tolerant of his will-o'-the-wisp author. Keneally had started a historical novel about Catherine the Great to follow *Confederates*. With his usual method of working on various books at the same time, he was also planning a book about Appalachia. 'This is presumably Tom's next book but one – I am expecting daily a novel set in the United States,' Ziegler explained in a memo to John Hooker at Collins's paperback imprint, Fontana Books. 'However, one never knows with Tom.'[1]

Hooker was not enthusiastic about the Catherine the Great book, which surprised Ziegler. He thought that with such a grand historical background, it would make a good successor to *Confederates*. 'With this following on from *Confederates*,' he suggested, 'we really might at last push Tom out of the "unsaleable literary fiction" slot into which he is now firmly placed by most booksellers.'[2]

Keneally was toying again with the idea of using a pseudonym, which might have helped allay his publishers' concerns that he was churning out books too quickly. He had other reasons in mind, too, as he explained to Ziegler:

> I have two main reasons for wanting to use an alternative name. One is literary and the other persecution a writer is likely to suffer if he or she

> writes an important book which doesn't concern this country. The literary world here is far more snobbish than in Britain – ironic when you think of the image of Oz as a sun-tanned, wenching, boozing oaf . . . These things are laughable as long as you don't live here. The other reason for wanting to use an alternative name is not so easily dealt with. As I told you in June, I saw *Confederates* as the start of a series of historical novels running side by side with my more serious books . . .[3]

Other factors at the time that made a pseudonym desirable concerned the legal bid by Strutton and the threats on Keneally's life. As Keneally researched the Catherine the Great book, he began to envisage two series of books, by 'different' authors, but at that time he went no further with the idea of a pseudonym.

Keneally wanted to know what Ziegler thought about an Australian, rather than an English, publication of a book about a wartime prime minister (based on John Curtin) and the wife of a wronged general caught up in world events beyond their control. Ziegler replied cautiously: 'I cannot believe a novel set in Canberra will be any more difficult to sell here than a novel set in a woman's womb . . . My only preoccupation is that neither here nor in Australia should you appear to be producing more than a book a year – which I'm sure would be damaging to your reputation.'[4]

Ziegler could not make sense of *Love of a Small Kingdom*, the working title of the manuscript that became *The Cut-Rate Kingdom*:

> I must confess that I felt more at sea than I ever have during your excursions into the human foetus or the medieval mind . . . it amazes me that a society which I would have expected to know fairly well should be so alien to me . . . it would be a fearful job to sell here and I think it could only undo all the good which I hope we are going to do by the vigorous promotion of *Confederates*. If we make a real success of this latter, and follow it up 18 months later with an equally popular novel about Catherine the Great, then I think we might really push your sales up and keep them up . . .[5]

Hooker did not like the story and incurred the author's wrath by not making a decision quickly. 'Since you have had the MS of the Mulhall novel for more than a month,' Keneally wrote, 'and I have not had so much as the courtesy of an arrival-of-MS notice, except one which I sought myself through Collins Sydney, I can but presume you have doubts about the MS, and I have therefore forwarded it to other publishers. I would still be interested in a response from you, in view of my continued association with Collins. I might simply remind you that authors *do not* exist for the convenience of publishers.'[6]

Keneally sent the manuscript to Penguin Australia, where Brian Johns made a tentative bid but withdrew it when Keneally asked for more. An $8000 advance was too high, Johns said.[7] Five years later, in the afterglow of *Schindler's Ark*, Penguin did publish *The Cut-Rate Kingdom*. In the early negotiations with publishers, however, Keneally drew blanks and could not understand why. At last he had returned to his own country and found, he believed, a local story that would satisfy a cultural yearning. *The Cut-Rate Kingdom* was his attempt to solve the mystery of being an Australian, in much the same way that Saul Bellow's *Herzog* was dedicated to the mystery of being an East Coast Jew in the United States.

'This is a book about my country in 1942 and an old politician who deals with the coming of the Americans and the Japanese. He has his own ideas of what Australia should be – a paradise in the South Seas – and World War II just doesn't fit in.' That was Keneally's summary given to Ronn Ronk, a *Honolulu Advertiser* journalist who was covering 'The Global Situation: The Writer in the Twentieth Century', a conference sponsored by the East-West Center in Hawaii and the International Cultural Center of Korea. Attending it was a pleasant way for Keneally to begin 1980.

Keneally told Ronk that every Australian who read his new novel would recognise the politician's attitude. He said the belief that Australia could be a utopia, the last chance to get it right, was a strong thread in Australian literature. 'But while the subject matter may touch the heart of Australians, it doesn't mean much to those outside the country. I'm delighted with the novel but it alarms both my overseas publishers and agents.'[8]

Keneally needed money, and the Curtin book was the only finished manuscript he could put on the bargaining table. *Playboy* had accepted a story, 'Going to the Fair', which was published in November 1979. The scene is Cannes: Keneally had attended the film festival and had been fascinated by the lavish events and curious scenes. In the story, Phil Carey is there to see the film *Cut-Rate Kingdom*, starring a black actor, Albie Toombs. The 'filmic pup', based on one of Carey's books, is directed by Carey's friend Andy McNeil. The crowd of Australians at an apartment remind Carey of 'something tribal, Vegemite say, in the window of NSW House in the Strand'.

The story was simple enough, but it also spoke of things that were transparently Keneally's own experience, including the allusions to Schepisi and *The Chant of Jimmie Blacksmith*. The book described in the story had been written before 'the essential date, before 1972, the watershed year when Carey's wife and he had ceased to torment each other and learned to live in union. All pre-1972 Carey novels were dark and savage documents, the work of a tormented young man. All novels since then had been increasingly light and compassionate. Critics disliked the change, but Carey was delighted with it . . .'[9]

'Going to the Fair' brought in $4500. Money from Harper & Row for *Confederates* was expected the following month. In the interim, Georges Borchardt lent $3000 to Keneally in anticipation of the Harper & Row cheque.[10] Borchardt understood the author's need for increased finances while still establishing himself, and his frustrations about not quite making the grade in America, but he believes Keneally and many other artists were unrealistic: 'They feel their talent should be recognised immediately when it usually isn't (Van Gogh I believe only sold one painting in his lifetime – to his brother). Our role as agents is to speed things up, and we are the greedy ones on our authors' behalf.'

At this stage neither Borchardt nor Sayle could resolve the impasse. Keneally entered negotiations with Trevor Kennedy, publisher and editor of *The Bulletin*, to produce *The Cut-Rate Kingdom* in magazine format. It was a daring experiment, proposed by Keneally, and intended to lower expenses for publisher and consumer. The cost would be cut-rate, in keeping with the title of the work. Kennedy and Keneally confidently expected sales of 40,000 to 60,000 copies. With this innovative method, they anticipated putting the book in readers' hands in just a few weeks, instead of a few months.

Andrew Peacock, then Australia's minister for foreign affairs, launched the book in Sydney. He recalled how the introduction of paperbacks by Penguin years earlier had revolutionised the Australian literary scene. 'I have every hope, every reason to believe,' he said, 'that this latest venture will have the same stimulating effect.'[11] The book performed well, despite John Hooker of Fontana Books dismissing it as 'a profound disaster'.[12] Keneally told an Australian Society of Authors gathering that 50,000 copies were sold in the first three weeks.[13] It was published by Wildcat Press in 1980 and marketed as 'first-class, new Australian fiction at a price everyone can afford', which was $2.50 per copy.

It rankled with Keneally that the book, even when published in standard format, received only passing attention. Five years later he wrote a letter, marked 'Private', to Laurie Hergenhan, in response to an article in *Australian Literary Studies* (*ALS*) titled 'War in Post 1960s Fiction: Johnston, Stow, McDonald, Malouf and Les Murray', which made no mention of Keneally:

> Far be it from me to force my work on the attention of critics, but I cannot see your neglect of *The Cut-Rate Kingdom* in your article in the October 1985 ASL [sic] as anything but a mirror of the critical neglect of my work in this country.
>
> *The Cut-Rate Kingdom* has received more critical attention in Britain than any of the other works you mention, but that again is characteristic . . . I can in no way blame you for this exclusion of my work from serious attention in this country. It is matched by the similar neglect of all literary editors. I think it should be a question of curiosity though, to your distinguished self and to your colleagues, why I am taken seriously in Britain and the US and am beneath consideration here . . . I write to you as a leading critic, as a man whom I believe to be large-minded enough to absorb the question, and of course as editor of the *New Literary History*, from which no author would want to be unjustly excluded . . . I am flabbergasted at the age of 50 years at my destiny of being a literary exile in my own nation . . .[14]

This was typical of Keneally's discontent with his critical readership in Australia. The *New Literary History* to which he referred was *The Penguin*

New Literary History of Australia, for which Hergenhan was general editor. Keneally's work was well represented in the book, although *The Cut-Rate Kingdom* was given just a brief mention in the chapter on 'War Literature' by Robin Gerster.

The Cut-Rate Kingdom is set in Second World War Australia. It is narrated in the first person from the recollections of journalist Paperboy Tyson, a close friend of Johnny Mulhall (based on John Curtin). David Rowbotham, reviewing the book for the *Courier-Mail*, thought that Tyson 'turned the screw on all the political, military and domestic intrigue involved in the shaping of Australia's future in epic 1942'.[15] Tyson and Mulhall chew over a wartime situation in which Americans regard Australia as an inferior and unimportant small nation, and anticipate 'buying' it at a bargain price. General Donald McLeod (based on Douglas MacArthur) bounds up the stairs of Parliament House 'like a laird entering his inheritance'. Mulhall, wall-eyed and awkward, greets McLeod's arrival like 'the second coming', much to Tyson's disgust. Similarly, Mulhall is naive and foolish about Mrs Masson, the straying wife of a general. Americans had charm which the Australians 'could mock but never match', and an 'omnivorous politeness we would come to know and mistrust'.

In his author's note, Keneally claimed that 'there was a wartime Prime Minister of Australia, but he was not Mulhall, nor are Mulhall's character, affections and secrets in any way meant to reflect the character, affections and secrets of any Prime Minister of any era . . . Paperboy Tyson and Mrs Masson never existed. This therefore is no *roman-a-clef*, or, if it is, the author hopes the clues refer not to the privacies of any individual but to those that characterise the Australian soul.' This was Keneally on familiar ground, attempting to avert trouble in advance, even when the background details of Mulhall and his associates clearly resembled those of Curtin and his.

At the launch of the book, in a lighthearted response to Peacock's reference to Mulhall/Masson affair as 'the most un-erotic account I have read', Keneally said that he had been accused of being too erotic in the descriptions he gave in two earlier books. 'This time I decided to tone it down a bit.'[16]

Keneally's version of events and personalities is interesting when considered in the context of his own life. He recognised in Curtin some similarity to himself: the workingman's son, a lapsed Catholic, rising with determination above his circumstances. 'It is to me still something of a dream,' Curtin had said in 1944, 'that the small boy who went to school in Creswick and Ballarat in short pants stands before his fellow members today and receives their good wishes on his impending visit to Britain and the USA ...'[17] Likewise, Keneally has often asked himself and others, 'Who, what god, what destiny, ever guaranteed that someone who came from Homebush on the earth's left buttock would grow up to write something people tolerated reading?'[18]

Keneally was intrigued about the wartime years, of which he had some clear memories as a child in Sydney. Books like *The Cut-Rate Kingdom* were written in what was becoming Keneally's trademark style: tales of robust, recognisable characters whose everyday lives, dalliances, predicaments and frailties were already imaginatively there as subtexts in the pages of history books.

Mulhall in *The Cut-Rate Kingdom* is overshadowed by other characters, prefiguring Oskar Schindler, who is seen by many to be secondary in Keneally's book about him, *Schindler's Ark*, which was a kind of documentary novel, more fact than fiction, and over which the author laboured long and hard. This meticulous work challenged Ziegler's opinion that his unpredictable author had a habit of 'dashing off books of really astonishing badness and then relatively cheerfully putting them on one side when his agent and publisher agree that they are non-starters. He has in fact done this twice since *Confederates* ...'[19]

Ziegler contended that *Schindler's Ark* was non-fiction and, contrary to his previous concerns, was anxious about how long the book would be in the making. He had not been happy to learn that Keneally was tackling the subject: 'I will not pretend that I am not somewhat distressed by the news about your new non-fiction venture. Partly this is because the matter has got so far before we have heard anything about it, and it seems that you do not want us even now to have a chance of publishing it, but even more it is because I fear that so long a break between *Confederates* and your next novel can only be damaging to your career. I beseech you not to devote too much time to the Schindler book.'[20]

By 1981 Ziegler and Collins were out of the picture as far as Keneally was concerned. He had been disgruntled by Collins's refusal of his latest efforts. He had been reasonably satisfied with the treatment of *Confederates*, but told Tessa Sayle that he thought another publisher would have done better with a hardback edition.[21] He also suspected that Collins Australia was ready to part company with him because it had not had success with his work. Keneally had what Ziegler described as 'a bad falling out' with Collins Australia. Nor was Fontana interested in him any longer.[22] Hooker decided he'd had enough and wrote to Simon King: 'Tom's work is tremendously up and down . . . In a TV interview he moaned on about the good old days . . . He is a pain in the ass!'[23] In Keneally's recollection, the falling out occurred because he was dissatisfied with Collins Australia's ineffective distribution of his books. Other issues, like an awful cover for *A Victim of the Aurora*, also rankled.

Ziegler hoped to retain Keneally. 'Do you have any news of Tom's progress on the non-fiction book?' he asked Tessa Sayle. 'You will forgive me if in the circumstances I am slightly nervous lest I suddenly wake up and find he has signed for another book with somebody else.'[24] To Keneally he wrote: 'The fact that you are reasonably close to completion does inspire the hope that you will soon be back at work on a novel. I can't tell you how anxious I am to publish a major new Keneally. *Confederates* made a tremendous impression and the scene is set for a breakthrough book . . .'[25]

The breakthrough book had already been promised to another publisher, Hodder & Stoughton, with which there had been preliminary manoeuvres. Keneally had arranged a meeting with the company's head of trade publishing, Michael Attenborough, as early as June 1973, when he was living in London alone. Attenborough had been interested in adding Keneally to his list: 'If ever you feel that Collins are not right for you, then I hope you will come straight to me here or Eddie Coffey in Australia.'[26] (Coffey was the managing director of the company in Australia.)

Tessa Sayle, in one version of events, had been approached by Hodder & Stoughton. 'According to Tessa,' Keneally explained in *Searching for Schindler*, 'with this new book [*Schindler's Ark*], so different to anything else I had written, I had a chance to move to a new British publisher, and the appalling cover designs alone of some of my more recently published books were a provocation to do so . . .'[27]

Ion Trewin, senior non-fiction editor at Hodder & Stoughton in London, recalled having lunch with Sayle early in 1980 and being handed some chapters of a novel set in California that involved drug dealing. Trewin thought that Keneally was at his best when using history as a starting point for his fiction. 'This Californian drugs novel was something different, more likely, I thought, to be written out of his imagination,' he recorded in 2014. 'I was not impressed. I returned it to Tessa with regrets, but said that I would be interested if Keneally had something else in mind. A few months later she telephoned. Tom had not gone ahead with the Californian drugs novel, but had an exciting new project, an intriguing biography – would I like to see his proposal?'[28]

That was the start of Keneally's next new relationship with a publisher. As David Carter observed in his 2013 review of Keneally's international career, there existed 'a complex, sometimes tortuous history of shifting relations between writer, publishers, editors and agents across three continents, three markets and three copyright territories.'[29] The negotiations for *Schindler's Ark* were certainly evidence of that.

The last professional words from Ziegler to Keneally were: 'We are greatly saddened by the news that you want to leave Collins, though I understand the factors that brought you to that conclusion. I honestly feel that we have done as well with your books as any other publisher would have done and that if you wrote another book with the popular appeal of *Confederates*, we would be better able than most to exploit it to the full, but it is contrary to all our instincts to try to hold a reluctant author . . .'[30]

Ziegler said, years after the break, that he was sad when Keneally left Collins. 'I both liked and admired him. I still don't really understand why Tom did go, though I know that authors tend to get a restless feeling and to feel that they are being taken for granted.'

24

A Great Story of Humanity, Man to Man

Keneally's family was at Sydney airport to meet him as he returned home from Los Angeles. He was carrying a new, black pigskin briefcase, not the Globite one they had given him. 'See this briefcase?' he asked. 'I'm sorry, I had to leave the one you girls gave me behind, but I left it in a flash suite at the Beverly Wilshire Hotel.' Keneally urged them to have coffee before they left the airport. He had something special to tell them.

The story, well-known now from repeated telling – it is related in detail by Keneally in *Searching for Schindler* – had started earlier that month. It was October 1980, and Keneally had attended an international film festival in Sorrento, Italy, dedicated to Australian films. He had a marvellous time, mixing festively with actors and directors who were making names for themselves in the industry. The Italians had handed out copious documents, which Keneally had stuffed into his briefcase – and it finally broke under the strain.

He decided to buy a new case in Los Angeles, where he was on the last leg of a tour to promote *Confederates*, an obligation that had been tacked on to the Sorrento trip. On the proceeds of *Confederates* (which Harper & Row had also sold to Berkeley Books for $50,000), Keneally was staying in style for a couple of days on a publisher's account at the Beverly Wilshire, a landmark hotel in Beverly Hills frequented by the likes of

Elvis Presley and John Lennon. He set out one hot Saturday morning along Wilshire Boulevard, deciding against the exclusive shops of Rodeo Drive on his left and instead turning right into South Beverly Drive.

The Beverly Hills Handbag Studio at 149 South Beverly Drive advertised 'Handbags, Luggage and Accessories. Expert Handbag and Luggage Repairing'. It was also promoting its fall sale, and the proprietor, Leopold Pfefferberg, invited Keneally in to look at his range of briefcases. Pfefferberg, whose original home was in Kraków, Poland, had the name Leopold or Paul Page in the United States, where he had lived since 1947. He had been called Poldek, however, since birth. He pronounced his new friend's name as 'Tow-mass'.

'I know a wonderful story,' Poldek told Tow-mass. 'It is not a story for Jews but for everyone. A great story of humanity, man to man. I tell all the writers I get through here ... It's a story for you, I swear.' Keneally had heard such a line many times before, but he had never before been approached by such an engaging, ebullient man as Poldek. 'I was saved, and my wife was saved, by a Nazi,' Poldek explained. 'I was a Jew imprisoned with many other Jews.'

Keneally, with his animated face and keen conversation, engaged easily with the persuasive Pole. The story of Oskar Schindler, an unlikely hero in the Second World War, was put before Keneally for the first time, and soon Poldek was leading him to two filing cabinets at the back of his storeroom. These contained extensive documents concerning the man who had prevented the deaths of 1300 Jews in the Holocaust by employing them in his factories.

'From these documents concerning Herr Oskar Schindler,' Keneally wrote later, 'I gathered he was a ruined Catholic hedonist. As a former seminarian, and a struggling Catholic myself, I had some time for fellows like Oskar ... Some people have always been troubled by Oskar's ambiguity. To me it was from the start the whole point of the tale. Paradox is beloved of novelists. The despised saviour, the humane whore, the selfish man suddenly munificent, the wise fool and the cowardly hero ...'[1]

Poldek had compiled the files in the 1960s, after he had convinced the MGM producer Martin Gosch that Schindler's story would make a great movie. Gosch and screenwriter Howard Koch had begun interviewing Schindler survivors in the Los Angeles area, and they also arranged a meeting with Schindler, who was still alive at the time and living in Frankfurt, Germany. They travelled to Tel Aviv and Jerusalem with Poldek and Schindler in 1963 to interview other survivors. MGM bought the rights to Schindler's story for $50,000, of which $20,000 was given to Schindler's estranged wife, Emilie, then living in Buenos Aires. The film was never made, but Poldek lived in daily hope that a writer would come into his shop and become intrigued by the story.

Keneally took the bait, and soon was carrying a pile of photocopied documents – in his new briefcase – back to his room at the Beverly Wilshire Hotel. He was engrossed by the material and arranged to engage in more discussion with Poldek that evening over dinner at a French restaurant in Brentwood. Poldek's wife, Ludmila Page, and Schindler's lawyer, Irving Glovin, and his wife, Jeanne, were also there.[2] (In another recollection of the book's origins, Keneally said that he read the documents overnight, and that Poldek and Glovin went to the Beverly Wilshire the next morning to discuss the project with him.[3])

Glovin shared Poldek's quest to find another buyer for the Schindler archive and had himself invested considerable time meeting writers, directors and producers, but to no avail. Glovin had a great respect for Schindler, whom he had represented in the negotiations with MGM, which still owned the overall rights to the story.

The lawyer knew Schindler in the post-war era and was not indebted to him for his life. Consequently, his perception of the story and his motivation in promoting Schindler were different. He wanted to have the story told to as wide an audience as possible, but he also planned to establish and develop a humanitarian foundation. In 1980, prior to Keneally's appearance in Poldek's shop, Glovin had purchased an option on the Schindler story from MGM. He represented no one and was obligated to no one. The contract involved an option on book, film and other rights. About May 1980, after Glovin had completed the negotiations, Poldek asked if he could participate, to which Glovin agreed.[4]

Glovin, for whom Schindler's altruism was the core of the story, regarded Keneally with some scepticism. He did not like the idea that the writer was already ambivalent about his hero and would make too much of Schindler as a moral puzzle. Glovin and Keneally from the outset steered around each other cautiously. Years later, searching for the best description, Keneally said that Glovin was honourable but rather bombastic.

The euphoria that always came with the promise of a good story was replaced by doubts. Keneally could list various objections to writing this particular book, among them his ignorance about the Jews and what they had suffered. This book should be written by a Jew, he reasoned, in the same way that an Aboriginal author should have written *The Chant of Jimmie Blacksmith*. The research for the task would be formidable. Would Schindler – a carouser, black marketeer and Nazi collaborator, and a sexually voracious man – dominate the story at the expense of those who had suffered so much, despite his intervention? In other words, whose story was it: his or theirs?

Fifteen years later, after the book had sold millions of copies and the memorable movie had been made, Keneally was still fielding questions about Schindler. 'If I were presented with the Schindler story now,' he admitted to one journalist, 'I would be asking: "What do I know about Jews? What do I know about Europe?"'[5] He often had to defend the book against those who doubted its veracity or his right to it. 'The history of literature,' Salman Rushdie has said, 'is one in which writers have defended their work and I was not going to be the one who didn't.'[6] Nor was Keneally, but the lives of both writers were dogged by the books that brought them the most fame: Rushdie's *The Satanic Verses* and Keneally's *Schindler's Ark*.

Poldek was not put off easily, unlike others whose persuasiveness Keneally had overcome when he really did not want to write a book. The one exception had been when Sir William Collins had charmed him into writing the book *Moses the Law-Giver*, to go with the mini-series of that name. Keneally had done the job reluctantly, without enjoyment or apparent interest in the outcome.

By the time Keneally was ready to leave Los Angeles, he had agreed to contact the Schindler survivors living in Australia and to make a start on a proposal about how he would treat the material. He flew out that evening with Poldek's words at the departure gate ringing in his ears: 'Tow-mass, who will do it if not you? You think I have them queued up?' As the plane crossed the Pacific Ocean, Keneally's head was spinning with plans for the new project.

He was bursting with the excitement of it all by the time he saw the family waiting to greet him. They were shown the contents of the new briefcase and were suitably impressed by the story, which he declared was 'a bloody gift'. His daughters, Margaret, fourteen, and Jane, thirteen, accepted that their unpredictable father was not quite like most dads. Life with him was never dull.

Keneally could be as capricious as the weather. At beautiful Bilgola, when the sun shone and the waves were good, the surfers would be out there making the most of it. On other days, when the sea was dull and flat or the waves were matching the wind for ferocity, there were few board riders to be seen. Keneally's mood often matched that of the sea, but there were always good times, too, when he was on the crest of a wave. His office was dominated by a snooker table, which he had bought from some surfers living next door. He often wrote standing at it, sifting through his papers. The table was ideal for spreading out the Schindler material, which was soon stacking up at an alarming rate.

Keneally made contact with Jews in Sydney and Melbourne whose names appeared on Schindler's list of factory workers, and who had therefore survived the Nazi death camps. Each story was a book in itself, but small details were impressed on the author's mind, like the women who still carried crusts of bread in their handbags, in fear that hunger may strike them once again. Leosia Korn, whom Keneally interviewed in Sydney, was the first of the survivors to talk about crusts of bread.

On 30 November 1980 he returned to California. Poldek was eager to introduce Keneally to more people who had known Schindler, and to hand over more files for his briefcase. An agreement was reached about how the project would proceed; a contract was drawn up and a presentation prepared for potential publishers. The family flew to Hawaii to have Christmas there with Keneally, who was on his way back from Los Angeles. They were camping in the little town of Volcano on Christmas Day, opening presents as heavy rain fell and sulphur fumes pervaded the campervan they had hired. There was something rather symbolic about this volcanic place: soon Schindler's story would be heard throughout the world, and controversy would erupt in places far beyond the great volcano at Kilauea.

The genesis of *Schindler's Ark* is among Nan Talese's favourite memories of Keneally: 'I remember most keenly his writing a hand-written letter about going into a luggage shop and meeting a man who was a survivor of the Holocaust and knew many others. Tom said he was always interested in people migrating and he would like to write a story about these survivors – would I be interested. I wrote and said, "Yes, can you tell me a little more about it?" So then he wrote me a proper proposal. I read it and said I would do it.'

Talese worked with authors, she said, who had three things in common: they wrote well, they were good storytellers and they had a passion for their subjects, whether fiction or non-fiction. She was not in the business of publishing 'commercial' novels. She referred to Keneally's commercial novels as his 'clinkers', but she believed, on the basis of his best work – in her estimate, *Gossip from the Forest* and *Blood Red, Sister Rose* – that he would eventually find a wider audience. She thought, correctly, that Keneally's breakthrough would come with *Schindler's Ark* because he was a good writer and he had in his grasp a big and important subject.

Nevertheless, she had to break down resistance at Simon & Schuster: 'It was a lawyer who was handling the book, not an agent, and he wanted more than half of the advance. Our President said, "No, I don't want to deal with amateurs." I was just convinced I wanted to do this book, and I think I wore Dick [Richard Snyder, chairman of Simon & Schuster] down. We paid $60,000 for world rights to *Schindler's List*! I asked Tom why did you have to have $20,000 on signing and he said it was a lawyer and MGM owned the rights [to Schindler's life story] and he wanted to pay them and get those rights back.'

Keneally's promising start on the book was delayed in the early weeks of 1981 because he and his daughters were ill with what was known as the 'hundred days' disease' in the Third World countries in which it had originated. The symptoms were similar to whooping cough and just as distressing.

From February 1981 Keneally conducted about fifty *Schindlerjuden* interviews around the world. Many took place in the United States, particularly in New York, where it was very cold in early March. For the first time Keneally met *Schindlerkinder*, children who had an association with the deliverer in war-torn Europe. The children, it seemed to Keneally, were often the most deeply scarred and haunted by the war. Some had been teenagers in the camps and were reluctant to talk about their experiences there.

The interviewers moved from New York to Europe, where Keneally and Poldek visited survivors in Frankfurt, and also sites of interest in the Germany of the 1940s. Keneally also saw the apartment in which Schindler had lived during the last years of his life. Then came Munich, followed by Warsaw, where an uprising of the Jews in the ghetto had occurred, and Lodz and Kraków, because Keneally was keen to see first-hand where Schindler had operated.

Gradually, Poldek's own story emerged. He was unusually sober when he showed Keneally the camp at Plaszów, on Kraków's rural edge, where the hill fort was the place of countless executions. Poldek had been among the unfortunate prisoners who'd had to dig up graves as the liberating Russians approached. The remains had been burnt; Poldek said that the dead had seemed to sit up and gesticulate in the flames. He had wept under his rag mask, which had not prevented the smell from filtering through. Keneally was amazed at Poldek's ability to be 'a solemn tourist to his own past misery'.[7]

Poldek and Keneally then went to Vienna, hoping to trace the family of Amon Goeth, the evil Nazi who had dominated the dreams of those who survived his brutal regime, and who inevitably dominated the Keneally book and the film that followed. Goeth's family was not traced in the short time the two men had in Vienna before they proceeded to Israel. It was there, in the Jews' Promised Land, that Keneally had to confront a major concern about the book he was about to write: 'I knew that trying to tell a story, which because of its human scale, made it possible for readers to *imagine* the Holocaust, could be seen by some as an encouragement to Israeli hardliners . . . I believe it is still true that if there are going to be areas of history which are off-bounds, then in principle we are reduced to fudging, to cosmetic narrative. Thus, though worried, I was defiant in my intention to write this book.'[8]

Tel Aviv to Jerusalem: this had been the route that Schindler had taken every year for a decade to meet his Jerusalem survivors, and also the road along which his corpse had been taken for burial in Jerusalem's

Latin Cemetery in 1974. Keneally's father, too, had visited Tel Aviv and Jerusalem during the war.

When a writer returns home with a mass of research material, buoyed by meetings with many people in many places, the task ahead looks easy. How could it fail with so many primary resources? Keneally regarded the time spent researching for his novels as the best and 'most blithe'. When he trawled newspapers (his favourite research) and other sources of information, there were 'many moments of unexpected epiphany which seem to promise you that the writing of the book is going to be easy this time round'.[9]

He had also read a lot of books about the Holocaust. Nora Levin's general history, *The Holocaust*, enabled him to compare the experiences he had heard about in numerous interviews with Levin's facts. Martin Gilbert's book *Auschwitz and the Allies* helped answer the question about how much the Allies had known of the Nazis' destruction process, the so-called 'Final Solution'. Gilbert had also compiled *Atlas of the Holocaust*, which stunned Keneally with its graphic documentation of the work and destruction camps, and *Final Journey*, a chilling account of the precision with which the Jews had been moved around Europe. Gilbert gave Keneally copies of these books when *Schindler's Ark* was being edited. Keneally's copy of *The Destruction of the European Jews*, by Raul Hilberg, became dog-eared from constant use.

Organising all the resources, choosing the narrative approach, resisting the urge to put it all aside for a while and gather some more: those were the factors that made the beginning of a book, let alone its completion, so hard. This was Keneally's problem with the Schindler story: despite all his experience, he had never tackled anything so large before. He was also deeply affected by what he had seen and heard and read, which replayed itself in disturbing dreams and troubling thoughts.

Author Di Morrissey, Keneally's friend and neighbour at Bilgola, learnt what discipline was as she observed him working on the book. She was his sounding board. 'Tom would wander into my kitchen and tell me where he was at, where he was stuck and where to move on from here, and I would listen, say nothing, and twenty minutes later Tom would nod. "You've been a great help," and go back to his den where his desk did not face the ocean view.'[10]

He experienced two weeks of despair in the middle of the writing stage, compounded by the criticism of some who could never get beyond their belief that the Jews had been too passive. One friend claimed over dinner that 'they sold each other out'. Keneally, tired and depleted and overwhelmed by the testimony of too many Jews who could refute that accusation, threw a credit card at his friend and left the restaurant in anger and frustration. Yes, there had been traitors among the Jews, but what about the millions of others?

In doubt about it all, despite his certainty that the friend was wrong, Keneally took comfort from a bottle of whisky and slept beside a heater in the office. His material lay unattended on the snooker table the next day. After that crash, he was able to return to the pile and start again. He had endured such disabling interludes before with other books, and there would be more in the future. There was always the fear, too, that his ability to write would disappear; that would be the end.

Sometimes, it seemed to Keneally that he was the sulky temperamental teenager in the house. He could become morose, sharp or just plain moody. He sometimes drove the girls to school, annoyed that they had missed the bus again but quite enjoying the time away from the office; he always humoured their request to be dropped off some distance from the school's entrance.[11] The winter of 1981 passed, with another diversion provided by the local rugby league team, Manly-Warringah, which Keneally supported fervently.

Back in the office, Keneally was well advanced with the book. He still wrote by hand and then dictated the draft, complete with punctuation marks, onto tape. Barbara Armstrong at Mailbox Services in Avalon then transcribed the tapes. By Christmas 1981 she had completed much of the first draft. At that point Keneally began to rewrite, by hand, reworking or rejecting passages, cutting and pasting. The finished scroll, part typescript, part longhand scrawl, then went to Barbara to be typed up. After final editing and some rewriting, it was ready for a publisher's seal of approval – or a rejection stamp.

Keneally did not write the first draft quickly; completing it was the hardest part of the process. He did not postpone potential problems or a character's motivation or similar crucial questions. He resisted any rewriting until the first draft was done. He has said that he wrote in a strata form: the first layer was the first draft; the second layer was the second draft, which might be a complete rewrite; the third draft and the third layer, the scroll, was untidy and bulky; then came the emerging book, the final draft.[12] On 15 October 1981, about a year after he had first met Poldek, Keneally submitted the Schindler manuscript, complete except for a brief epilogue he intended adding. He was under some pressure to reach that deadline because he had agreed, some time before, to leave for China on 16 October.

Keneally was uncertain how to categorise the Schindler story. He wrote to Nan Talese at Simon & Schuster: 'You know, I'm not sure this is non-fiction. There are so many characters – too many for a novel.' Talese wrote back: 'Just forget about that – just write what you want to write!'

Keneally wanted Talese to edit this book, but she informed him that she was leaving Simon & Schuster for a position as executive editor at Houghton Mifflin:

> This is a most difficult letter to write because it is one that breaks our newly formed but so long sought after author/editor relationship ... It is always painful to leave authors behind but in your case it's particularly painful because we had made so many attempts to work together ... the thing to do is to just move ahead on the Oskar Schindler book. You seemed in such a determined and enthusiastic frame of mind about the project when you were here, so don't let my leaving break that flow of energy ...[13]

Keneally wondered if Patricia Soliman, the editor who inherited *Schindler's Ark*, would have the same interest and belief in the book, but he need not have had any concerns.[14] She was committed to the Schindler book. 'By now you know what a fan I am of the book,' she wrote to Keneally. 'The scenes of life in Krakow in Plashow at the Emalia works and later in Brinnlitz are incredibly moving and bring us a whole new perspective on this dark chapter. So many of the characters will live on in our memory.'[15]

Emilie Schindler, Oskar's widow, provided detailed answers to the questions Keneally sent her, but through her friend and adviser, Juan Caro. 'I hope that the intentions of Mr Thomas Keneally will lead to a good book,' her letter read, 'and I hope also that I will see some support of it, which you may send also to Mr Caro.'[16] Keneally understood that 'some support of it' meant money. Emilie Schindler was not out of the picture yet, even though Poldek had ensured she received a generous share of the MGM money.

Keneally responded promptly to that first communication with 'a return for Mrs Schindler's trouble with those questions'. The 'return' was a bank draft for US$150. That would be just the start of the demands from Emilie, made through Caro, who reminded Keneally after receiving the cheque: 'You shall know that Oskar Schindler never could help so many people without her [Emilie's] help . . . the most financial help after the war was paid to Oskar . . .' Caro left no doubt in Keneally's mind that Emilie expected more money: 'I hope that your book will be a success and that it will be also a financial success for you and Emilie Schindler.'[17]

Glovin, uncertain about the way his hero was being portrayed in the book, telephoned the publishers about his concerns. In addition, Poldek pestered them about their plans for publication – when would that be, and what would the print run be? Glovin also wrote privately to Keneally, expressing his displeasure about some of the author's jovial comments to the media:

> Paul [Poldek] has given me copies of some of the interviews you have given. You're getting the word out which is great. I'd like to comment, if I may, on some things that occur in these articles and, I hope, you will take them in the spirit in which they are being offered. I don't mean to be dramatic but there are some concepts or phrases or words which trigger reactions. I understand how they were intended but they read out different.
>
> For example, in the Quantas [sic] article you refer to Paul on page 36 as 'the Polish bagman'. In the Morning Herald, March 13, 1982 article, you were quoted as saying you have found another 'obsession: Jews'. Further, you are quoted as saying 'It is a book likely to appeal in America because all their grandmothers [are] from Cracow,' said an ebullient Keneally. 'It is a B'nai B'rith special'. That last phrase is repeated under your picture. These remarks will, unwittingly, raise hackels [sic] and make light and denigrate a very serious work of which you should be very proud.[18]

Soliman was unhappy about the book's proposed title, *Schindler's Ark*, writing that she was 'not at all wedded to the notion of having the word Ark in the title. The subtle suggestion that it was the *animals* that went on two by two seems to me to leave a very unfortunate aftertaste.' Her preference was for *Schindler's Jews*, both because they were referred to as *Schindlerjuden* and because of Schindler's growing obsession with 'his Jews' and the obligation to save a thousand out of uncounted millions. She also observed the fatherly stance he took with them.[19]

Tom Wallace, another senior editor at Simon & Schuster, agreed with Soliman, but Keneally stood his ground. 'Why not?' he asked. 'I've discussed it with Ion Trewin [at Hodder & Stoughton]. He has accepted *Schindler's Ark* and I prefer it too.' In fact, Trewin had said he was convinced that the word 'Ark' was crucial: 'I like *Schindler's Ark* and don't share Tom Wallace's objection. Everyone here I've mentioned it to thinks you [should] stick with it.'[20]

Soliman and Wallace's argument for calling the book *Schindler's List*, which won the day for the Simon & Schuster edition, was that one of the underlying themes of the book was the looming of the lists: who would be on the list for annihilation; who would be on the list for at least temporary safety. American Jewry was also very sensitive about the accusation that the Holocaust victims had been too passive in the face of destruction. The word 'Ark' suggested passivity, the prisoners entering two by two.

'What about the Ark of the Covenant?' argued Keneally. 'The idea that there had been a covenant between Schindler and his people?'

'Readers would not get it,' Wallace said.

25

Keneally Opens a Door

Usually, after a manuscript was posted, Keneally packed the research papers in boxes and put them on his shelves. However, in May 1982 the office at Bilgola Beach was still awash with Schindler files. Keneally was in the habit of finishing a book in a year, but this one engaged him in more months of editing than any of his previous titles.

Ion Trewin thought that Keneally had achieved 'a moving, horrendous, astonishing story'.[1] He needed the final proofs, as perfectly complete as possible, to meet the deadline set for submission to the Booker McConnell Prize judges. He believed he had a winner in *Schindler's Ark*. When Eric Major, managing director of Hodder & Stoughton's hardback division, read the typescript he sent a memorandum to Trewin that said, in effect: 'If this book doesn't win the Booker Prize there's no justice.'[2]

Yet classification remained an issue and Trewin was unsure. 'I wondered for a time, whether it might not be better considered wholly as a novel, however closely based on fact,' he told Keneally after his first reading. 'But perhaps it is best considered like Truman Capote's *In Cold Blood* as a work that transcends categorisation, although we shall call it non-fiction for bookshop, best-seller and library purposes.'[3]

Trewin changed his mind on that: 'Eventually Tom asked me if we would agree to his turning it into a novel. He wouldn't falsify the facts, but it would be written as fiction, the only form he felt he understood. I agreed . . .'[4] To be eligible for the Booker, the title had to be fiction, and that decided the issue in the publisher's mind. Simon & Schuster, however, categorised the book as non-fiction.

Collins had been in touch with Tessa Sayle. If *Schindler's Ark* was now a novel, surely it had some rights in the matter, having an option on Keneally's fiction dating back to his last novel? When Trewin had read the proposal for *Schindler's Ark*, Sayle told him that she would also be submitting it to Collins, but as it was non-fiction it would not be their option. Once Trewin's colleagues read the proposal and approved it, Eric Major authorised an offer of £20,000. He had come to the decision quickly, and Sayle moved equally fast, contacting Collins to tell them she had an offer and giving them an hour to respond. There was no answer from Collins by the time an hour was up, so Sayle telephoned Keneally to tell him about the offer from Hodder & Stoughton. 'Accept it!' he said promptly. Legally, Collins had no further claim.[5]

Ziegler contemplated making a bid for the next title, if it were legally possible, promising a large advance, without knowing at that stage just how successful *Schindler's Ark* would be, but certainly knowing from past experience that he risked another 'dud'.[6]

Keneally himself, after finally sending off the typescript, was exhausted and ill. Trewin wrote to Major: 'Tom is suffering what sounds like the author's version of post-natal depression. He needs cheering up and surely the best person to do this would be Eddie Coffey . . . get in touch and have him call Tom and tell him it's a great book . . .'[7]

Trewin wrote to tell Keneally that he had just had a letter from Graham Greene, to whom he had sent the proofs of *Schindler's Ark*. Greene said that the book was 'an extraordinary achievement of research which it must have been as painful to make as it is to read'.[8] Then Trewin learnt that *Schindler's Ark* had been shortlisted for the Booker Prize. Keneally's books had already been shortlisted three times before so he did not get his hopes up too high, especially as there was the 'genre uncertainty'. He received his invitation to the award dinner from Michael Caine, chairman of the Booker McConnell Committee. It was to take place at Stationer's Hall, London, on 19 October.

An Ice-Cream War by William Boyd was firming as the favourite among the punters, with *Schindler's Ark* second at 7–2 at Ladbrokes, the famous London betting agency. Keneally put £50 on Boyd's book. He dressed at the Basil Street Hotel in Knightsbridge, his formal dinner suit provided by Moss Brothers, the traditional London outfitters. At the pre-dinner reception, one of the judges winked at Trewin. Did that mean Keneally's book had won? Nothing was said to Keneally, who was sitting with Trewin and Tessa Sayle, toying with the meal in front of him.

John Carey, chairman of the judging panel, stepped up to the podium and, after discussing the shortlist, paused dramatically and announced that the winner was *Schindler's Ark* by Thomas Keneally. A little the worse for wear, having just consumed two glasses of calvados, Keneally walked forward to accept the prize, $18,000. He commended the judges for their reckless choice and thanked Poldek as the architect of the book.

Then Carey delivered his speech. Apparently, on the day of the big event, the judges had met to decide the winner. Carey had raised the question of *Schindler's Ark*'s dubious classification as fiction. The prize's administrator, Martyn Goff, told him that the judges had made the decision to classify it as fiction when including it on the shortlist. If they changed their minds now, with the award dinner just a few hours away, Goff said, he would have no alternative but to declare that year's prize null and void. The judges were split between *An Ice-Cream War* and *Schindler's Ark*. Then one of them, Paul Bailey, changed his mind, saying that the novel that would remain in his mind was *Schindler's Ark*.

At the dinner, Carey said:

> About Thomas Keneally's *Schindler's Ark* there's been some public debate: is it really fiction? We're used by now, though, to novels that build themselves out of facts. It's a logical conclusion of realism, and also a natural self-protecting strategy for the novel in an age overloaded with newsprint, newsfilm and documentation. We're used, too, to the realisation that history is, anyway, always a kind of fiction – at best a version of and selection from a totality that can never be known.
>
> Keneally shuns make-believe, and that seems the only honourable course, given the magnitude of the tragedy he has to relate. But he still has to order and mould his material as any novelist must. He still has to take a multitude of imaginative decisions about viewpoint,

> emphasis, the interior and exterior of characters. It seems to us that Keneally opens a door. He makes certain possibilities imaginable, which we have too easily said are unimaginable. His book has behind it a powerful organising and speculative mind, exercising great tact and restraint in the presentation of its terrible story. The central character, Schindler, is left in the middle distance, only half-known, as human beings are, yet dramatically present.[9]

At the press conference that followed, Keneally, excitedly outspoken, said that he hoped his winning the prize – a first for an Australian – was the beginning of the end of the Australian cultural cringe, and of England's cultural contempt for its former colony. The actor Bryan Brown, with whom Keneally had struck up a friendship at the Sorrento Film Festival pre-Schindler, phoned him the next morning. 'Isn't it great,' he exulted, 'when two boys from the western suburbs really rip it up the Poms?'[10] Brown had gone on to a successful acting career, including a role in *The Chant of Jimmie Blacksmith.*

'Is the book really a novel?' The question continued to come from all sides. Keneally had his answer ready: 'The judges thought so, and who am I to argue with them?' The controversy worked in his favour, sparking curiosity and boosting sales. As soon as *Schindler's Ark* was declared the winner, the sales director and production editor at Hodder & Stoughton's headquarters were immediately busy taking orders from booksellers.

The publisher celebrated with a cocktail party two days later in the back garden of its office in Bedford Square, London. Behind the lively celebrations, though, as Keneally acknowledged, there was the reality that his success had been achieved by salvaging a story from a multitude of deaths. He was still having nightmares; there was one in particular in which Amon Goeth selected him from a line of prisoners for an unspecified death.

Yet he had to appear jubilant in public, as Hodder & Stoughton had devised a punishing round of appearances and interviews. One was with Maeve Binchy for the *Irish Times.* When they were seated in the lounge room of the Basil Street Hotel, Binchy endeared herself to Keneally by asking, 'Do you think we could have whisky in our tea?' Keneally also had a photographic session for *Vogue* – another first.

He had engagements in the United States, too. 'I think it's enough to write the damned thing without having to sell it as well,' he complained good-humouredly at one point.[11] Back in Sydney, his family was waiting at the airport, brandishing banners and wearing T-shirts designed by their friend and neighbour Iain Finlay, who was there with his wife, Trish Clark, as well as Di Morrissey. The front of the T-shirt was emblazoned: 'Tom's A Winner!' Finlay and Clark had earlier sent a telegram to Keneally at the Basil Street Hotel: 'Fabulous Tom. Just shows what a new briefcase does.'[12] Tom and Elsie had sent a message too. 'Dadda went as far as buying a bottle of Great Western to toast you tonight . . . Ziggy [Tom senior] added: "Congrats. We were all very happy about the result . . ."'[13]

Keneally, after the welcome-home party, was still entertaining uneasy thoughts that it was all happening because of the testimonies of people who had suffered terribly. Nevertheless, given all the accumulated ups and downs of life at home and at his desk and in publishers' offices, he was happy. There had been undisguised joy in the homecoming.

The controversy about the classification of *Schindler's Ark* went on. The general opinion of the 'experts' who participated in a BBC *Critics' Forum* was that the book should not have won the Booker Prize, but that it was an exceptional book. The chairman of the forum, Richard Mayne, asked Alexander Walker if he found the book a successful attempt at fiction, or 'faction.' 'No, I didn't,' Walker replied. 'I don't think it's a book that should have been entered in the Booker competition and I don't think it's a book that should have been rewarded by that . . . I don't think Thomas Keneally does very well in this, that is to say, the imaginative level, but the book succeeds, and succeeds massively by the sheer factual, and harrowing nature of the terrible wrongs and tortures committed against and on the Jews.'

Bryan Robertson agreed that the book succeeded 'frightfully well' for him as a chronicle, but there was 'an unresolved conflict' in this book between the nature of the material and the claims for it to be a novel. Sometimes, he conceded, Keneally associated himself imaginatively with his characters as a good 'non-fiction novelist' would; however, the rest was 'the well organised material of the documentary biography.'[14]

Simon King, Keneally's editor at Collins, wrote lightheartedly to his author: 'Perhaps now they'll let you into the Stafford Hotel restaurant without a tie!' When King had first taken Keneally to lunch at that very smart hotel, the maître d'hôtel had remonstrated with Keneally because he wasn't wearing a tie. He would be permitted to dine, however, if he sat facing the wall of the restaurant so no one could see that he was tieless.

King added, 'From the Collins/Fontana viewpoint I'm naturally very jealous of Hodder & Stoughton. I think the key issue is that we never learned how to turn your writing programme into a successful publishing programme.'[15] Philip Ziegler said, 'Given Tom's original position on the fiction/nonfiction issue, I was amused (and also decidedly irritated) when it [*Schindler's Ark*] won the Booker Prize.'

The media in Australia made much of Keneally, and he particularly appreciated editorials in the *Australian* and the *Sydney Morning Herald*. 'Thomas Keneally's success in the Booker Prize for fiction will be a matter of considerable satisfaction for Australians – not only for the literary-minded, but for all those who admire a craftsman,' wrote the editor of the *Australian*. 'Mr Keneally is essentially a craftsman … He put his years of effort and his delight at winning into words when replying to the announcement of his success: "This is the greatest night of a lonely career." He was referring to the loneliness of the writer, whose world is filled only with creations of the imagination, not to a life of loneliness … he has done Australia and Australian letters great credit.'[16]

'With *Schindler's Ark*,' the *Herald*'s editor wrote, 'Keneally is taking up the techniques developed by the American writers, particularly Truman Capote and Norman Mailer, and investing it [sic] with his own power and authority as a writer …'[17] The thoughtful editorial contrasted sharply with an article written by Susan Molloy for the same newspaper several months previously about 'a little round man [who] scurries around his writer's study like a hyperactive wombat tunnelling for ideas'.

That was the article to which Irving Glovin had objected, when Keneally had referred to the book as 'a B'nai B'rith special'. In truth, Keneally may have set himself up for Molloy's ridicule by complaining yet again about Australian reviewers: 'Perhaps the KGB knows what it wants out of Australian culture and if they do not get it they will put the boot in. We are still very uncool about our status in the world. If we have any success with movies or books we want to beat the rest of the world over the head with it. There is a tendency to bitterly savage writers or film-makers who are seen not to be creating the cultural flags the KGB would like to wave.'[18]

Morris Lurie, reviewing *Schindler's Ark*, did not savage Keneally, but wondered if the author had held 'his considerable novel-writing skills in abeyance'. Lurie contended that 'there is no atmosphere, no mood. You can't see people, smell the weather. There are no sounds . . . One wonders if this book were written to commission, with the chief stipulation being that every fact be recorded, every incident, every name . . .' Lurie conceded that 'the facts parade before you bearing their full historical and emotional weight, and finally they do their work. You are bowed down. You are moved . . .'[19]

Years after the public outcry about *Schindler's Ark* had died down, Keneally reckoned that he had written it with 'a living on the edge of the world and looking in' approach.[20] He had never resolved to his own satisfaction how to classify the book, which read like a factual account of a shameful era in world history. In interviews long after the book was published, he made statements such as, 'It was so little a novel that the characters actually corrected the book after it was finished . . .'[21]

There was also the question of Oskar Schindler's own stature in the book: 'the absentee hero' according to the *Critics' Forum*. Editor Patricia Soliman had not been satisfied that the shadowy figure of Schindler was fully developed:

> The single overarching problem that remains when the manuscript is finished is the enormous question mark that lingers about your own attitude toward Schindler, about his motivation and his meaning. What lifts this book above so many of the accounts of the Holocaust is Schindler himself. The individual stories of ghetto and camp – and you have handled these with great vividness and power – are still not new. What's new is *Schindler* the maverick German who was his own man throughout. He must always remain something of an enigma, but with the script as we have it now the reader finishes in a state of frustration about so many aspects of this complex and paradoxical man . . .[22]

Poldek was volubly thrilled with Keneally's triumph:

> You have to be prepared that this book of yours will be read by many thousands of people and anything you put in the book will have tremendous impact and importance to understand the depth of the tragedy that struck the Jewish people and which could be avoided if more people of Oskar Schindler's stature and strength will understand that in a situation like this, you cannot put your head in the sand and say this is not my problem. The inhumanity of man to man is everybody's problem and you and I know the Holocaust can happen again, and I pray to God that your book can be instrumental to educate the future generations and in this way to prevent a future Holocaust.[23]

The last word comes from Keneally's friend and mentor Brother McGlade from St Patrick's College, Strathfield:

> While you romped fields and lanes and I taught Shakespeare and rolled wickets, such life and death events went on over the other side of the world. It is a fine catharsis to be reminded from time to time of the depravity to which man can sink and the heroism to which he can rise. Both sides of the coin were reflected in your extraordinary story . . .
>
> Fiction does not require the creation of character and events; historical fiction nicely combines reality with some imaginative treatment. The Gospels are good examples of reality conveyed through imaginative writers . . . The style was more restrained than in your previous novels. The very grimness of the story excluded the imaginative flashes that have distinguished much of your writing in the past and which I have considered its finest feature. Here you got hold of a story that was so real and gripping, so full to overflowing of human interest, tragedy and courage that it swept along without time to dally with the flowers and the fancies.[24]

26

An Unattractive Deal

'Tom has gotten involved with some business consultant on the west coast of America . . .'[1] That was the description John Hooker gave to Simon King of a person whose name does not appear either in *Searching for Schindler*, Keneally's account of the book which has been the focus of the last two chapters, or in any other explanation he has given of the book's origins. According to Robert Raymond, the unnamed Australian business consultant, there is another version of how the story evolved.

Raymond claims that none of the big events surrounding Schindler's story would have occurred if it had not been for *his* criticism of Keneally's worn briefcase. Raymond, according to his version, had booked the author into the Beverly Wilshire Hotel when he went to Los Angeles to do the rounds of movie agents with Raymond. He had met Keneally in Sydney and offered to help him in the United States, initially with a publicity tour for *Confederates*.

Raymond described himself as a 'talent manager'. 'Tom admitted he had no idea what a "talent manager" does or could do for his career,' Raymond explained in 2015. 'Especially knowing as I did that after reading all the glowing reviews for *Confederates* there was a small window of opportunity to make a much larger deal with a paperback release for this book if I was given the chance. After listening to my plea Tom allowed me to call Tessa [Sayle] and discuss an idea I had to help make Tom a significant literary name over time in the burgeoning US market, where he was virtually unknown despite having written one of the most brilliant novels set against the Civil War. I had read all of Tom's books and as I was living in the US felt I could make a considerable contribution towards lifting his name and commercial success in such a large market significantly with both publishers and Hollywood producers, to whom I could sell screen rights to his novels.'

When they met in Los Angeles, Keneally was carrying an old Samsonite briefcase, Raymond says. 'It was shabby, had faded labels on it and one of the catches didn't seem to close properly. It contained all his important papers. I said, "Tom, I've got to tell you, I really think you should do something about that briefcase. It looks tatty, makes you appear to be down to your last dime." Tom just laughed.'

He did, however, follow Raymond's advice, and in Raymond's telling the story of Keneally going to Poldek's shop proceeds much as it did in Keneally's memory. Raymond continues: 'I was living off Mulholland Drive at the time, and I went that evening to the hotel to pick Tom up to have dinner with us. I noticed he had this shiny new briefcase. He got out of the car and said, "Listen. I've got to tell you about this extraordinary man I met. He has all these papers in Hebrew and German, an incredible story about a German who saved hundreds of Jews from concentration camps." Tom recounted the whole story and I was fascinated.'

Papers verify that Raymond was involved in the lengthy and tricky negotiations that ensued. In a letter dated 19 November 1980 Irving Glovin outlined the arrangements 'Re Mr Thomas Keneally – Oskar Schindler Story'. The second clause read: 'You [Raymond] will negotiate with the book publishers for our mutual benefit and in consultation with me prior to closing any deal ...'[2]

Tessa Sayle, who became involved in the ensuing dispute, said in 1982 that this clause 'really appalled me and made my blood boil – it is still boiling ... In my first meeting with Robert Raymond on 10 December, and prior to that on the telephone, he *assured* me that he was not a literary agent and that should Tom decide to sack Borchardt it would be up to me to sell the US book rights. This point was not made just once but over and over again during our lunch.'[3]

Raymond had signed the agreement with Glovin on 25 November 1980, 'individually and for Thomas Keneally'. In the early 1990s Raymond recalled that Keneally had delivered to him an enlarged treatment of the story, and that Raymond had then set up a bidding war between publishers. He was to get 10 per cent of future book profits in his role as Keneally's manager/agent. 'I didn't wait for the phone to ring,' he said. 'I went out and hunted and fished.'[4]

Keneally did not notify his regular American agent, Georges Borchardt, until 12 January 1981:

> Dear Georges,
>
> I am writing to tell you of some developments which will put a strain on our business, though I hope not on our personal relationship. A Los Angeles business manager and registered agent named Bob Raymond approached me some time ago with the idea of arranging some projects – movie scripts and so forth – for me on the West Coast . . .
>
> He has now set up a deal, initially through the Western office of Simon and Schuster, for a faction book, the idea for which came from various parties in Los Angeles. The deal is, as you will probably hear, so favourable that I cannot under any circumstances turn it down, and I am of course in the dilemma involved in his natural and just expectation of collecting the agency fee and my long term association with you . . .
>
> I know that this means a termination of our arrangement. I remember with a great deal of gratitude your success in placing *Gossip* and the ill-starred *Season*. But for some time now I've been trying to find a way upwards from the plateau represented by the payments made on those books, and I believe this new book will provide the way.
>
> Please accept my thanks for all your efforts on my behalf and my best wishes for your continuing success, a gauge of which is the high repute you enjoy with all the publishers.[5]

Borchardt knew about Raymond and was concerned about his role. He wrote to Keneally:

> I had written Tessa as far back as October 17th [1980] ('Could you also enlighten me about the role of Robert Raymond who got in touch

> with us to say that he is now Tom's manager. What exactly will he be doing?'); she did not answer. And you may remember I asked you about him when we drove you back to your hotel after the Harper & Row dinner when you were in New York, and you told me he would just do 'PR work' and would not interfere with *our* activities.
>
> As long as an agent represents an author, it is proper for all inquiries concerning the author's work to be referred to the agent. And certainly (until at least January 12th!) we were representing you here; you know this; Tessa knows it; and presumably Robert Raymond knows it. If his role was not clearly defined initially, as it should have been, then surely after we inquired about it, it must have been made clear to him. So *someone* has been acting in bad faith ...
>
> I would feel very sad, both personally (this cannot be the Tom Keneally I know) and professionally (we have done more than place for you the marvellous *Gossip* and the ill-starred *Season*) ... We have stood by you loyally through bad and good times; and done many things you probably are not aware of, such as finally getting a revision of rights on *Jimmy* [sic] *Blacksmith* ...[6]

There is little doubt that Borchardt thought Keneally was the one acting in bad faith. The exchange of letters came at the time when Keneally was ill with the 'hundred days' disease' and he appealed to Sayle for help. She advised writing a letter to Borchardt, explaining that the delay in telling him of a decision had occurred because of the Christmas hiatus and the severe illness.[7] In fact, she said as much herself in a letter to Borchardt.[8]

Sayle was not impressed with Raymond, writing to him in a chilly tone to point out shortcomings in the Simon & Schuster contract, and also to remind him that she would receive 10 per cent on all foreign earnings of the book. She was also indignant that Raymond had told Nan Talese that Keneally was no longer represented by Borchardt without informing Keneally or her.[9]

Raymond objected to Sayle's questioning the terms of the contract, and further said that as *Confederates* was Keneally's 'most widely acclaimed and with the broadest appeal of his books thus far', he and Keneally felt that Sayle should have had some success with foreign sales of the title by then.

Sayle retorted: 'Tom has been kept informed regarding my efforts in selling translation rights. It is a great personal disappointment to me that two years of repeated submissions all over the world, many personal meetings in London and abroad and at two successive Frankfurt Bookfairs have not borne any fruit ... They all love Tom's work but say that *Confederates* is too long and therefore too expensive to translate to make it economically viable as a "literary" book and there isn't enough sex and violence for it to be classed as a commercial novel.'

Raymond told Sayle that 'it became obvious to Thom [sic] and myself that his [Borchardt's] services were redundant although there was not any particular date that Thom decided this. We had agreed that he would not be involved with the Schindler book from the beginning and as I think you already know Thom was never happy with George's [sic] performance. You and I with Thom's consent had agreed on this also, i.e. not to use George any longer. Nan Talese never even knew George was involved with Thom ...'

Sayle could not let that pass: 'Several of Tom's earlier novels, including *Confederates*, were submitted to her by Georges. Talese therefore asked you when you first approached her in November or December 1980 in what capacity you were acting for Tom because she understood Georges Borchardt to be Tom's agent and you replied that Georges was no longer representing Tom ... by not telling Tom about this conversation you have put him in a very awkward situation vis a vis Georges.'[10]

Borchardt told Keneally that he was upset:

> On a personal level I liked you, I liked your wife ... On a professional level, I doubt you have a greater admirer of your work in this country; nor did you have a more devoted one ... what I find 'sickening' is not that you should have decided to leave our agency ... What I object to is for negotiations to have been carried out while we were representing you. Had you said to me when you were in New York last fall that you wanted to leave us, and had you *then* asked Raymond to negotiate for you, I would have no right to object ...
>
> What is at stake is not simply our commission on a contract which indeed we did not negotiate but which should have been referred to us for negotiation; what is at stake also – and here you

> have, albeit unwillingly, done us very serious harm – is our position in relationship to Simon & Schuster, not to speak of the position of all agents in their dealings with publishers on behalf of the authors they represent.[11]

Given Borchardt's own firsthand experience of the Second World War – as a youth, he hid in Paris while his mother and other family members perished in concentration camps – he would no doubt have been attentive to the Schindler story and active in making the best possible deal with a publisher.

There are holes in the story that Raymond told publicly about his involvement with Keneally, starting with his claim that Keneally's fateful visit to Los Angeles followed the Atlanta Book Fair. In fact, this event – which hosted the American Booksellers Association (ABA) convention – was held in May 1981, several months *after* Keneally met Poldek. Raymond was certainly there at the book fair with Keneally, and he was proud of his promotion of *Confederates*. He hired two Confederate army uniforms: his was that of an officer, while Keneally was decked out as a foot soldier.

'Mine looked great,' Raymond said, 'but Tom's didn't fit ... his uniform needed some adjustment ... His trousers hung rather awkwardly over the boots.' The pair were subject to many strange looks until, Raymond said, 'when the time came to announce Tom and his book they freaked out! We were noticed all right. We were a sensation! *Confederates* went on and sold half a million copies.'[12]

Berkeley Books did things in style. The company had paid for Keneally's airfare to Atlanta, which provided the opportunity for him to return home via Los Angeles, where he could do more work on the Schindler book. Berkeley organised the ball at the Anthony Plantation House, which Keneally said was the best party he'd been to. He thanked Victor Temkin, Berkeley's president, for his efforts. He was delighted, he said, that Temkin was attempting, by every trick of his trade, to save *Confederates* from the oblivion that they both knew it did not deserve. 'I hope that all the careful cultivation of distributors will bring you an excellent return on your faith in the book.'[13]

In June 1981 Keneally wrote to Sayle:

> The Atlanta event went superbly and was extremely useful, since it put us in contact with some of the largest distributors in the United States ... More importantly, and I almost forgot to say it, I had what the Americans call a 'full and frank' discussion with Bob [Raymond] about your rights in the matter of foreign editions. I want to assure you that your rights in this matter will be fully protected ... I found the week in Los Angeles this time was a valuable means of getting to know him, and I must say that I was impressed by his standards of professional behaviour, as well as by his effectiveness. I think that from now on there is likely to be a better understanding between the three of us, even though continents and oceans stand between.[14]

Meanwhile, Borchardt had more to say. If Raymond knew he was not Keneally's agent, then he also knew that he was not entitled to Borchardt's 10 per cent on the Schindler story. Keneally should instruct Simon & Schuster to send copies of all statements to Borchardt's agency, along with 10 per cent of earnings for the new book. 'This will, I think, repair much of the damage that has been done,' Borchardt wrote.[15] But the deal with Raymond had already been signed, so Keneally could not do that. Borchardt then subtracted $6000, approximately half of Keneally's *Confederates* royalties, in lieu of the commission he would have received from Simon & Schuster for *Schindler's Ark*.

An unpleasant slanging match followed between agent and author, each arguing on the grounds of professional principle. Sayle counselled Keneally against legal action. New York law, she told him, was more protective of agents' rights than elsewhere; an agent was considered in law to be entitled to a share of earnings from new contracts for a given period after the client/agent relationship terminated; there were statements in writing that would count against Keneally, etc. She urged him to reach a settlement with Borchardt, while at the same time she warned Borchardt that, by taking the law into his own hands and withholding monies, he was exacerbating an already difficult situation.

It was a sad conclusion to a good relationship. Borchardt had sent Keneally what he considered was a 'conciliatory' letter in May, but it included criticism about the contract Keneally had signed with Simon & Schuster – which gave the company British, translation, movie and other rights that would normally be reserved by the author. 'I was recently asked by an editor who had just returned from London why you should have made such an "unattractive" (his adjective) deal. This I concede is none of my business.'[16]

By September Borchardt wanted an end to the nastiness: 'I never heard from you in reply to my conciliatory letter of May 29th. Have you had a chance to discuss it with Tessa? Let us make peace.'[17] Borchardt does not recall receiving a reply, nor does he remember meeting Keneally again. Keneally is not sure either, although he thinks they met again at a couple of National Book Club dinners and had affable exchanges.

Keneally admits that he was so determined to make a living out of writing that he often did things impulsively. In recounting the Raymond debacle, he says that these were the substantial facts: 'I was impatient, very impatient, when things stood in the way. I was worried about representation in New York. Georges was, I felt – and I expressed this to him – too passive. So when this man [Raymond] approached me ... who had represented big companies and whose father Bob was a highly respected documentary maker, I signed on with him. I knew this book, *Schindler's Ark*, was a special book ... [Regarding Borchardt] I think ours was a good faith mistake; it was settled promptly. I never negotiated with him over the Schindler book but he felt he was still representing me. There was no malice on my part. Agents are letter of the law people, and these days you sign an agency agreement. In those days it was an informal agreement and it was possible to make mistakes in good faith.'

Borchardt thinks he and Keneally 'were definitely moving upwards ... I don't remember Keneally being particularly greedy or unrealistic. I just remember him as not being loyal ... my main disappointment is that I believed in Keneally the man, not just Keneally the writer.' Borchardt has never read *Schindler's List*.

Keneally engaged a lawyer, Melvin Simensky, and by the end of 1981 a settlement was reached: Borchardt retained $4000, and Keneally was reimbursed $2000.[18] As far as Keneally was concerned, that was 'fair enough'. At the same time all this was happening, he was also parting company with his publisher in London, Collins. The disputes did not reflect favourably on him. Sayle remained supportive, but after all the accusing correspondence and the painful parting with Borchardt, Keneally's relationship with Raymond also soured.

It was not to do with dedication, but the bookkeeping of Robert Raymond Management left much to be desired. Keneally questioned the figures when he had worked out his own numbers not long after the Booker event: 'I am, therefore, astounded that there happens to be less than $5000 in my account, and that a number of large payments are not covered by any statement . . .'[19] Sayle, who assisted Keneally to draft that letter, had contacted Simon & Schuster on his behalf to obtain a breakdown of payments made by them to Raymond. She spoke to Keneally when he was in New York on the *Schindler's List* promotional tour, and he assured her that all was going well with the publisher, but he was dreading the confrontations he would have to have in Los Angeles.[20]

Matters with Raymond came to a head in 1983, as a movie deal for *Schindler's List* was negotiated with Universal Studios. Glovin was thoroughly disenchanted with Raymond. He told Raymond that, as he had not responded within the specified time to a proposed compromise of release and settlement to do with the Universal negotiations, the offer was withdrawn. 'I have no obligation to you of any kind,' Glovin wrote. 'On the contrary, you are indebted to me in the amount of $1787.50, representing monies received by you for my account which were never delivered. Also, please be advised that I will do all things necessary to protect my rights and the property from the damages you may have caused by your prior actions.'[21]

Glovin sent a copy of his letter to Keneally, saying that he found Raymond 'an unacceptable and unresolved issue'. Keneally had already told Glovin that the project with Universal could be in serious jeopardy if Raymond was involved. Glovin agreed: 'I have done nothing but spend long years trying to move this project forward and Robert, in a very short time, almost scuttled it totally. So much for him.'[22]

Keneally was in a bad situation: 'I recommended Raymond to Glovin, who never forgave me. So we all got caught in this. When Raymond went to represent us in the Schindler negotiations with Universal, he told them that we would not sign a contract unless he was assistant producer. When we found out from [Sidney] Sheinberg, the head at Universal, what Raymond had done, we were shocked. We broke off with Raymond . . .'

Yet Keneally still felt some sense of obligation to Raymond. 'He has written to me,' he explained to Glovin, 'saying that matters are very hard for him at the moment . . . one cannot help feel for him.'[23] Poldek urged payment: 'One thing that bothers me, that I consider unfinished business is a situation with Robert Raymond and I would be very happy to give him the money which I consider is due to him, contrary to Irving's opinion. This man did his job and I personally think that he is entitled to his commission, even though his approach and his actions were not up to the dignity of an agent.'[24]

Keneally agreed, and wrote to Raymond saying that his commission from the book was also assured. The legal department at Simon & Schuster would insist on that anyway. In March 1983 Jeffrey Goldstein, Simon & Schuster's Associate General Counsel, advised Keneally to terminate his agency relationship with Raymond.[25] Keneally signed a letter entitling Raymond to his 10 per cent from the publisher as his agency commission. That money went directly to Raymond; all remaining royalties would be handled by Sayle, who resumed negotiations on Keneally's behalf in the United States.

Borchardt, who would have managed it all well, was no longer an option, although he always hoped that Keneally would return to his agency: 'He seemed perfect for our list and we should have been perfect for him.'

27

We Can Never Be the Same

The euphoria that followed the success of *Schindler's Ark/List* was replaced by exhaustion. In the months following the book's publication, Keneally faced a mass of correspondence, which included compelling letters such as one from the daughter of Amon Goeth, the German commandant who had terrorised and murdered many Jews and whose evil presence dominated *Schindler's Ark*. Goeth's daughter had not known her father was involved in the Schindler story.[1]

Not everyone wrote with congratulations. Some who had been on the famous Schindler's list were upset because they had not been contacted or included. As Irving Glovin wrote to Moshe Bejski, one of the Schindler survivors, 'it was incomprehensible, but true, that some survivors refused to participate or have their names associated with the book. Parenthetically, they now regret it and protest their exclusion.'[2]

The proposed film was a particularly exciting development. Keneally and Poldek met Sid Sheinberg, the head of Universal Studios, and the director Steven Spielberg at Sheinberg's mansion in Bel Air towards the end of 1982. Keneally was impressed that Spielberg was interested in the ambiguity of Schindler, the balance in his character between opportunism and compassion – 'the fact that no one could tell where one ended and the other began'. Keneally also appreciated that Spielberg understood 'the fact that Schindler, the unselfreflective hero, had been unable to tell anyone either . . . Spielberg proved [to be] an accurate reader of the import of the book.'[3] The fact that Spielberg had actually read the book was pleasing; when two screenwriters had taken *Confederates* to an executive to read, he had said, 'Kinda thick, isn't it?'

The meeting at Sheinberg's place ended without any commitment. Poldek insisted, 'I tell you, Steven, you make this film of humanity man to man, it will win you an Academy Award! Guaranteed! You'll get an Oscar for Oskar!'

Keneally received a telephone call from Spielberg's office in the summer of 1983. Could he come to Los Angeles that night to sign a contract with Universal? Keneally went. 'I was on my way to what every writer sometimes secretly dreams of: payday.'[4] Universal agreed to pay $500,000 for the film rights, of which $100,000 would go to MGM, and the balance (after expenses were paid) divided equally between Glovin, Keneally and Poldek. Each signed a contract: Glovin as associate producer, Poldek as technical adviser and Keneally as writer of the screenplay.

Back home, where the proceeds of the Booker Prize had financed renovations, Keneally began work on the screenplay. If he were writing the book again, he would make more of Schindler's pride at being German and his outrage at what was going on in his country. The screenplay did not come readily to him, and he feared that Spielberg might think it too much like the hagiographic *Chariots of Fire*.

In fact, Spielberg was not satisfied by the first draft and recommended that Keneally should try again. The second attempt was rejected too. Glovin was surprised and disappointed. 'I don't understand what happened,' he wrote to Keneally. 'Your work stands on its own and is justly acknowledged and acclaimed. "List" has set in motion a wholly new dialogue which, undoubtedly, will affect our social processes. Schindler reached me as he must have reached you. We can never be the same.'[5]

'I appreciate your concern over the Spielberg matter,' Keneally replied, 'but I understand Spielberg's attitude and, I assure you, am not aggrieved by it, so please don't be upset on my account. Spielberg seems basically to have believed that my closeness to the story made it very difficult for me to telescope events and characters and that my distance from LA created problems of communication. Spielberg seemed to indicate I would still be involved on a consultancy basis, perhaps with the second writer.'[6]

Spielberg then approached Kurt Luedtke, who had won an Academy Award for the screenplay of *Out of Africa*. Luedtke's attempt at the Schindler story also failed, however, and Spielberg moved on to other movies. Poldek continued to harry Spielberg's office but there was no progress for several years. Depleted and depressed, Keneally went to have what he termed a rest cure in Europe. It took the better part of a year for his life to return to near normal – after Schindler, he would not be the same again, as Glovin had predicted.

When Patrick White won the Nobel Prize for Literature, he responded graciously to a letter from Keneally: 'Thanks for your congratulations of months ago. My correspondence has got out of control – my life too, for that matter, but I hope it may be returning to normal. The Nobel Prize for Literature is one more destructive thing that can happen to any writer. So, be warned! Yrs, Patrick White.'[7] White was more reclusive and private than Keneally, who was hardly likely to regard a Nobel Prize, one of his boyhood dreams, as destructive.

In 1983 Keneally was appointed to the Order of Australia. He had been offered a similar honour in 1977 but had turned it down and held a small refusal-of-CBE party at his Avalon home. He explained the situation at the time to Georges Borchardt:

> Here I have got involved in politics – you can be exempted from such activity in someone else's land – been accused of stealing *Season in Purgatory* from another writer – the accusations come from the extreme elitist right, who are very powerful in this country. I have been offered the post of Commander of the British Empire by the Queen and had to refuse it because of my unfortunate Irish origins, my politics, the fact that there's no goddam British Empire left to be Commander of . . . Politics are close to the bone here and for such activities you can be glared at or applauded on the street.[8]

After *Schindler's Ark*, however, it was mostly applause. Keneally wrote to Ion Trewin: 'Thank you for your letter and congratulations about the Order of Oz. It probably means little to a Brit, but to an old Australian nationalist like me it is indeed a great thing to get something with Australia's name attached to it.'[9] Poldek also sent congratulations 'on the

High Recognition which you received from Queen Elizabeth on her Birthday (I am only sorry that I do not know what they call this recognition)'.[10] In notes of thanks to others, Keneally often referred to writing as 'a lonely and benighted business ... we are susceptible to baubles. This is something more than a bauble, having Australia's name attached to it ... Now that I've become a member of the establishment I will have to behave with better grace ... I am wiser now and older.'[11]

In November 1983 Keneally went to California for the presentation of the Los Angeles Times Book Prizes, at which he received the prize for fiction. The judges' comment was perceptive: 'Thomas Keneally's achievement is to portray movingly, stirringly, convincingly, a deeply flawed and miraculously virtuous man. We know what we can know about Schindler, and yet his mystery is left intact. The writer raided history, came back with historical booty, yet found a balance between shame and pride in the possibilities of a human being.'

The overwhelming aftermath of the Schindler story for Keneally was aggravated by a nagging disquiet as the calm of daily writing was denied him, but by February 1984 he was feeling better and back at his desk. As he told his various wellwishers, he had taken their letters out of his memorabilia file on days of depression or in hours of despondency as a defence against the blues. He needed to be writing again.

Outback had been published in 1983. It was an anecdotal book written in a journalistic style, vividly illustrated, for which Keneally had made three visits to the Australian outback. The change of scenery after the hard months of working on the Schindler book was welcome, but the period was marred by the death of Garry Hansen, the cinematographer and photographer who was working with Keneally. Hansen was killed in a helicopter crash in August 1982.

In *Outback*, Aboriginal belief, sacred sites and practices are examined with awe. A link is drawn in the book between the oppression and extermination of the Aborigines in Australia's 'dead heart' and the persecution of the Jews, which had dominated Keneally's thinking for so long.

In 1979 he had been a signatory to an advertisement in the *National Times*, arranged by an Aboriginal Treaty Committee, which stated: 'We Call for a Treaty Within Australia, Between Australians.' Those who signed claimed there was a need for the status and rights of Aboriginal Australians and Torres Strait Islanders to be established. Australia was the only former British colony that did not recognise native title to land.[12] In 1983 Bob Hawke's Labor government promised – but did not deliver – national, uniform land rights legislation. A treaty was not under discussion until several years later.

Keneally's interest in Indigenous Australians continued after *Outback*, as he began a novel about the establishment of an American tracking station on an Aboriginal sacred site; the plot saw an Aboriginal dancer wound the American president and 'sing his blood'. That was abandoned in favour of a book about Captain Arthur Phillip, the man who had led the First Fleet to Australia. It was a story that had never been properly told, Keneally thought, yet the expedition had been an extraordinary social experiment. Phillip was like Schindler, if not as colourful.

It was going to be difficult to find another character as intriguing as Schindler.[13] Keneally now had the label 'winner of the Booker Prize', which would be attached to nearly every future introduction. The label sometimes chafed, seeming to limit his achievement to one title and one preoccupation. He needed an Australian title to affirm his place in Australian letters. He still believed that he was, in biblical terms, a prophet without honour in his own country. He sometimes wondered if his reputation as a novelist had ever fully recovered from the plagiarism accusations after the publication of *Season in Purgatory*.

Other Australian writers, too, had experienced this sense of rejection. Randolph Stow, a Keneally contemporary, confided to a correspondent that the positive response to his work in England was affirming, given the lukewarm or even hostile response he often received in Australia. English publishers and critics, he wrote, 'certainly show up the Australians'.[14] After the harsh criticism of his novel *Tourmaline* (1963), Stow returned to Australia from his home in England only once.

Keneally wanted to write about early Australia in a way that had never been done before, and in 1984 he signed a contract with Simon & Schuster to create a novel about those first young criminals sent to Australia. He found that there was too much material about the period, and the book was unfocused and incoherent. By June 1985 he had written 120,000 words, yet the draft was an 'architectural folly' that needed rewriting. He had already spent the advance paid by Simon & Schuster, but toyed with paying back the money.

Keneally's writing process had undoubtedly been affected by the many media and speaking appearances he was now being invited to make. At the same time, he was becoming increasingly active in organisations that required his attendance at meetings and more paperwork. Too much of the business of writing, which he had been operating for twenty years, was now being conducted away from his desk at Bilgola Beach.

28

Your Robust and Generous Nature

Keneally was now in demand to represent various advocates in the public sphere. He was a popular spokesman with his friendly face, genuine interest and articulate presence. Some organisations had engaged him before the Schindler era, and he continued representing them. One of these was the Australia-China Council (ACC). It had been constituted in May 1978, in the wake of Australia's diplomatic recognition of China in December 1972, and its aim was to develop cultural relations between the two countries, as well as to promote in each a greater awareness of the other. Keneally accepted an invitation from Foreign Minister Andrew Peacock to join the council as a representative of Australian literature. The inaugural meeting took place under the chairmanship of Geoffrey Blainey.

Keneally's role included assessing applications from exchange students, literary groups or individuals wanting to visit China. An Australian writers' delegation went to China in May 1981 for a few weeks. Keneally had been scheduled to go, but could not because of illness and other commitments. Nicholas Hasluck went in his place. Christopher Koch, in his report to the Literature Board of the Australia Council, which he represented on the trip, claimed it was the first official visit to China by a group of Australian writers.[1]

Keneally did go to China with a delegation of the ACC some months later, in October. The visit began in Shanghai and then went on to Beijing, where Keneally and Blainey spoke to 500 staff and students at the Foreign Languages Institute. Keneally also spoke to the Writers' Association there; later, in Xian, he gave a lecture on Australian literature at the Foreign Languages Institute. The group also visited Chengdu and Guangzhou, before ending the visit in Hong Kong.

Contributing to an ACC review booklet in 1985, Keneally wrote: 'In initiating and promoting projects and exchanges in journalism, the arts, scholarship, sport, agriculture, commerce and science, the ACC has fulfilled the wide mandate given it by the Australian Government. It has achieved more in maintaining a genial, generous and valuable relationship between China and Australia than most Australians know. I hope in the future that its projects become better known to the Australian community at large.'[2]

The projects of the Australian Society of Authors (ASA) were gradually becoming better known. Keneally had joined the ASA soon after it was formed in 1963, and endorsed it in 1993 with these words: 'The ASA was one of the best things to occur in Australian writing – it gave writers community and common cause, it let Australia know that its literary community was established and active, and it held out hope of literary equities later realised to an extent by improved contracts, public lending right, photocopying licensing and so on.'[3] He believed in the ASA's commitment to protect and promote writers.

Keneally was on the society's committee of management a couple of times, and was its chairman between 1987 and 1989. The ASA needed established writers who could give it prestige and credibility, but Keneally was a reluctant committeeman. Michael Parer, a member of the committee of management when Keneally was asked to be the chairman, said that the ASA was keen to capitalise on his well-recognised name as the nation's bicentenary approached. Keneally protested, 'I've never run a meeting in my life!' He agreed to help out, with Barbara Jefferis, an ASA stalwart, 'holding his hand'. He was an effective spokesman and determined fighter – even a provocateur at times, according to Parer. In his book *Our Republic*, Keneally described his active years in the role of ASA chairman as 'three turbulent and not very contented years'. He went on to recall the conflicts that bothered him and said he was 'ecstatic' when his three years were completed.

Keneally has been a grateful and well-paid beneficiary of the Public Lending Right and Educational Lending Right schemes, and of the Copyright Agency Limited. He has continued to support the ASA, and became a member of its council in 1981. During the years in which Keneally spent increased time overseas and had many other commitments, he rarely attended functions, but he had a great admiration for the 'workhorses', including Barbara Jefferis and Colin Simpson, who dedicated their energies to the ASA. Keneally's own contribution to the ASA has been acknowledged by Gail Cork, one of the society's executive officers, who has referred to his 'robust and generous nature'.[4]

Keneally was also president of the National Book Council (NBC) from 1985 to 1989. 'I'm a rotten committee person,' he told Candida Baker, 'but somebody feeds me the lines and I say them.'[5] The Literature Board of the Australia Council also enlisted Keneally as a member in 1986. Its aims at the time included facilitating direct support for individual writers, encouraging the promotion of Australian literature and fostering international interest in it – all policies that Keneally had espoused over many years. He joined the Writers' Fellowships Committee of the council, which was responsible for assessing grant applications.

Ed Campion also served on the Literature Board in the 1980s. Campion said that his colleagues spoke highly of Keneally's sympathy for new directions in writing and his knowledge of the world literary scene.[6] Campion was then working on a book, and worried that interruptions would make it difficult to finish. 'Tom, how many words do you write in a day?' he asked Keneally. He got his answer one day after a meeting of the board. The group agreed to meet again for dinner; Keneally rubbed his hands together and said that he would go home and come back later. On his return, he greeted Campion cheerily: 'Hey, Eddie, I wrote 600 words this afternoon!'

Keneally often had to squeeze his writing in around other commitments. As always, he was willing enough to take part, but he was often overcommitted and frequently absent. Thomas Shapcott, director of the board, was asked by the chairman of the Australia Council to contact Keneally at one stage in connection with his absence from three consecutive meetings. 'The Board is delighted to have you as a member,' Shapcott wrote, 'but in view of the constant scrutiny the Australia Council and its Boards are subject to, a strong membership list remains essential ...'[7]

Keneally pleaded overseas work and the business of another body that was taking up a lot of his time: the Constitutional Commission. This, along with its advisory committees, was established by the Australian government in 1985 under Prime Minister Bob Hawke to review the Constitution, which has been in operation since the nation was federated on 1 January 1901. Keneally accepted an invitation from the then federal attorney-general and deputy prime minister, Lionel Bowen, to become involved.

Bowen's telegram to Keneally read: 'I am very gratified to receive your telegram advising as to your willingness to serve on the proposed commission for the reform of the Australian Constitution. I have always remembered your strong value and support for a new constitution for Aust. and I have taken the liberty of mentioning your name in the course of public debate ...'[8] Keneally was involved with the Individual and Democratic Rights Advisory Committee, and his first job was to write an issues paper reiterating the commission's mandate of consultation with the Australian public regarding a review of the Constitution.[9]

To commemorate the events of 1 January 1901, a re-enactment was held on 29 June 1986 in Centennial Park, Sydney, at the site where the Constitution was first proclaimed. 'We're looking for new ideas to adjust the Constitution, not to overthrow it,' Keneally said at the event. 'There are threats to our basic rights like freedom of speech, religion, association and property which are not guaranteed in tough times under the Constitution here as they are in the United States or France.'

Musician Peter Garrett, another committee member, called on the public to be open-minded and involved in the project before it was turned over to politicians, whom he described as 'the paid mouths who think of their own skins. The reason I'm here is to get people excited. The first person to say something negative will be a politician. I'm here to say something positive.'[10] (In 2004 Garrett himself entered federal politics, being elected as a Labor member in the House of Representatives.)

The public responded with many suggestions for reform, including a republic, a cause that Keneally would take up in the years ahead. The commission hoped for changes to be made in a referendum in 1988, the bicentenary of white settlement in Australia; however, all proposed alterations to the Constitution of the Commonwealth put forward were defeated at a referendum held on 25 July that year. Even though most referendums in Australia have failed, this one saw the lowest 'Yes' vote ever recorded.

Keneally acknowledged the landmark year of 1988 with a book, *The Playmaker*. He also wrote the words for a tribute put to music by composer Peter Sculthorpe. Keneally's 'possible Australia Day Anthem, based on traditional themes and metres, dedicated to Henry Lawson' was accepted for the main event and sung by soprano Yvonne Kenny. It began:

So where is the face of Australia
Today – with two centuries done
The shame and the pride
No longer denied
Nor hid from this generous sun?[11]

Patrick White and Judith Wright refused to participate in bicentennial events because of the government's treatment of Aboriginal Australians. Keneally took the view that 'you can't deny a child its birthday cake'. He was in favour of a compact with the nation's Indigenous people: 'We'll be crucified if we don't do something. Hawke has got the message.'[12] Prime Minister Hawke proposed a 'compact of understanding' with Aborigines for the bicentenary, in the face of growing tensions between whites and blacks over demands for a treaty, and threatened protest action during the 1988 celebrations.

Keneally wrote a preamble to a proposed new Australian constitution, which acknowledged Aboriginal peoples' traditional ownership of the land and denied the common law assumption that Australia in 1788 was *terra nullius*. 'We acknowledge that Australia is an ancient land previously owned and occupied by Aboriginal peoples who never ceded ownership,' it read.[13] Later, when the Mabo judgements of the High Court in 1992 inserted the legal doctrine of native title into Australian law, Keneally revised that statement. With Aboriginal land rights now enshrined in law, he wished to be more positive. He now wanted to embrace the spirit of the Mabo decision: Aboriginal ownership was 'recognised according to Australian principles of fairness by Australians of all backgrounds'.[14]

In 1988 Keneally was dividing his time between Australia and the United States. Oakley Hall and Donald Heiney, founders of a creative writing program at the University of California, Irvine (UCI), had invited him to teach there. He began work there in 1985 and in 1991 became a permanent faculty member, as Distinguished Professor of English and Comparative Literature, teaching in the university's prestigious graduate writing program.

Keneally took up residence in an attractive home along Ocean Front, Laguna Beach. Opposite his wood-shingled house was the former home of actress Bette Davis. The locality was similar to Bilgola Beach, with steps leading down to Wood's Cove Beach, over which houses perched precariously on the steep cliffs. Surfers dotted the waves, and pods of dolphins regularly appeared. Keneally swam there or at the adjacent Lovers' Cove.

Eucalyptus, bottlebrush and pepperina trees grew in the area, just like home. The drive from Laguna Beach to the university campus, which was situated among old orange groves, went inland towards hazy hills, through Laguna Woods and Laguna Hills, the place of origin for *A Victim of the Aurora*. Earthquakes were experienced there; Keneally's orientation pack at Irvine included an 'earthquake emergency kit' for car or desk. Forest fires regularly threatened the hills, as they did in Australia.

At UCI, Keneally was observing structured interaction among a small group of people who passionately wanted to write. 'There's an intensity here you don't get in the rest of the English speaking world,' he told a journalist in 1985. 'For a teacher the responsibility is considerable because you have all these people who are obsessed and hoping for some sublime amalgam between instructor and student. In Australia writing classes tend to be summer classes for the dilettantish ... writing is considered a fine amateur endeavour rather than a full-time professional discipline.'[15]

It would be interesting to see in a hundred years, Keneally reflected, which method worked better: the American method of nurturing writers (through programs and academic positions) or the Australian method of assisting through grants and prizes for solitary endeavour – 'sending them to their rooms in Carlton or Balmain to write the bloody thing'. America, in his opinion, was the land of the 'how to', and organised writing programs fitted the national psyche. The program was intended to teach students to be novelists of great competence, if not of great genius. The students received degrees not only for studying the 'greats' but also for their own writing, under the tutelage of mostly older American novelists. 'Such famous American writers as Saul Bellow, the Nobel Prize winner, and Joseph Heller, author of *Catch-22*, taught creative writing programmes,' Keneally marvelled.

Twelve graduate writers chosen from all over the country engaged in peer evaluation workshops, from which those who were good enough would progress to publication. The visiting writers in residence gave lectures on their own writing, and submitted written critiques alongside those of the students assessing the classmate under review. Keneally, who feared he was a soft touch because of his inexperience, then had to give an overall evaluation. He was reluctant to give false hope, wary of encouraging his students to expose themselves to the recurrent pattern, so familiar to him, of obsession, depression and disappointment.

Life in California regularly provided Keneally with a topic for a weekly column he started writing for the *Sydney Morning Herald* in January 1985. In one column he wrote about his class:

> I have been 'teaching' a 28-year-old reformed drug addict and former US serviceman who has written a brilliant and publishable novel called *If Dreams Were Tuna Fish We'd All Eat Cheap*. The Master of Fine Arts writing class at the University of California is a small one. Nevertheless, there are conflicts. The tough-guy, Hemingway-style novelist doesn't like the fellow from Laguna Beach who is trying to write the Great American Gay Novel. The woman who writes gentle *New Yorker* style short stories sticks up for the gay – with the result that the Hemingway tough guy accuses her of writing material which has no plot ... My small group at Irvine includes a young novelist called James Brown, a proud son of working-class people from San Jose, with two published books to his credit ...[16]

Keneally has always believed that some things about writing can be taught in a classroom, but also that writers are born, not made. Even then, it is those who are hungriest, writing from the edge, who will be published.

UCI evaluated applicants for the program on the strength of their submitted manuscripts. Gillian Johnson was one of the students who impressed Keneally. On her evaluation sheet he described her as 'very accomplished, and a sure and novel narrator writing about real things'.[17] She was accepted into the program and became friendly with the Keneallys: 'Tom lived in a house up the hill behind the university and he often invited students up for wine, usually chardonnay, and Trader Joe snacks. We were all awkward and self-consciously literary and the wine was helpful ...'

The 'house up the hill behind the university' was an ordinary suburban brick home at 4 Whistler Court, University Hills. The house at Laguna Beach had become an extravagance when lived in for only part of the year, since the Keneally family returned to Sydney in the American summer. The Keneallys were known to be very hospitable people who easily adopted a lifestyle similar to what they had in Australia. Keneally also relished meeting people at the Hotel Laguna, a place made famous by such patrons as Errol Flynn and Humphrey Bogart.

In another of his *Sydney Morning Herald* columns Keneally recalled *The Loved One*, the story by Evelyn Waugh that had charmed him as a teenager:

> As in Waugh's day, messiahs – legal and other – abound in southern California ... But perhaps for me southern California outdoes itself in the matter of surreal excess in the case of the University of California. The University of California occupies a vast acreage of the state. It is spread over many campuses, each with its own substantial bureaucracy and its own law and security forces. It is involved in real estate, in commercial investments in technology, and its budget rivals that of small Scandinavian states – Norway say, or Finland ... To enter the University of California is to enter a state within a state, and not always a very liberal state at that ...[18]

Keneally was intrigued by Los Angeles, where the margin between the outrageously rich inhabitants and the poverty-stricken immigrants was massive: the suburbs each class lived in could have been on different planets. LA was a place of cities within a vast sprawling city. Keneally had been there during August 1984 to report on the summer Olympic

Games for the *Sydney Morning Herald*. He had stayed at the home of Annette Hutchinson, an aunt of his friend Di Morrissey, who had been reporting for the Channel Ten television station.

Keneally sat in the stands during events staged in searing heat, using a laptop computer for the first time. The man who had written *Schindler's Ark* on lined foolscap paper with a cheap biro had begun using a word processor, although he still did much of his rough work in longhand or with a dictation machine. With characteristic humour, he wrote about the heroes of the games – 'Inside every Australian male writer there is a Robert de Castella fighting to get out (elbowing past the Great Lover, the Great Philosopher and the Great Politician)' – and about the new technology he was using: 'A manuscript was so intimate. You can see the poor devil's whole life right there on the page, even when they've had a cold or a hangover, so I just don't think it will be the same queuing to see Patrick White's floppies in a case in a museum, one day.'[19]

Keneally has always been one of Australia's most public sports enthusiasts. For him, sport had everything: drama, politics, love, hate, tragedy, triumph. He has managed to include a rugby player in many of his books, starting with Detective Constable Trevor Raddles, an international footballer, in *The Place at Whitton*. In a way, Keneally claimed, he owed his very existence to rugby league, since Elsie had first been impressed by a perky five-eighth. Tom senior, by now in his eighties, still burnt a candle in church to ensure the defeat of a team whose coach he disliked. He had been known to put a couple of dollars in the 'poor box' at church in gratitude to Saint Anthony for assisting his betting on a match, especially when St George lost or Wests won.

A good game of rugby league, according to the Keneally clan at large, was the highlight of the week, and 'the aptness and the raw poetry of the barracking' was a delight. Keneally defected from his support of Wests when he moved to the Northern Beaches of Sydney: Manly-Warringah became his club. Until 1972 he had been a 'fibro', meaning a supporter or player from Sydney's western suburbs, before making the move beachside, 'as every fibro wants to.'[20]

After he began writing occasional newspaper pieces about matches, Keneally accepted invitations to games and even into the post-match dressing room. To his mind, this honour was one of the next best things to actually playing. He became a 'tipster' for the *Sydney Morning Herald* in the 1980s. In 1989, against the odds, he argued that Canberra would beat Balmain in the Grand Final. Canberra won, and afterwards, in the dressing room, Keneally spoke to Chicka Ferguson, the Canberra team's winger: 'I know you, mate,' Chicka said. 'You f . . . ing tipped us to win. Good on yer.' Keneally wrote those words down. 'It's my intention,' he declared, 'that they appear on my gravestone.'[21]

There was a 'Chicka Hays' in Keneally's next book, *A Family Madness*, who plays in a team made up of players from the western Sydney working-class suburb of Penrith. Also in the team is five-eighth Terry Delaney, who courts his wife, Gina Terracetti, in much the same way that Tom senior once courted Elsie.

'A sport could be to people like Delaney not merely a sect but a cosmology, a perfect model of an imperfect world,' Keneally suggests in the book. 'Rugby League ... was to Delaney the supreme code, a cellular structure composed of thirteen players which mimicked life and art and war so exactly that it *became* them.'

Keneally acknowledged, via Delaney, that everyone was pleased when the Manly team was beaten: 'they have this reputation for being wealthy aristocrats of league and they live on the beaches and so on'. They were dubbed the 'Silvertails', an elitist tag to which Keneally had aspired when he lived on the wrong side of the railway track at Homebush.

Delaney keeps a match diary, noting his occasional run with the reserve team. One supporter yells, 'Why don't you give this young bloke a run in firsts. At least he bloody tackles.' It had been a boyhood dream for Keneally to be given a run in the firsts at St Patrick's College, Strathfield.

The football fraternity is frequently given bad press for its drunken brawls and excessive behaviour. Keneally in 1987 whimsically compared footballers and writers: 'I went to the Premier's literary lunch in Sydney where everybody got as pissed as a football team on its way to Hawaii. Next night I was at the Rugby League's (best and fairest) medal night where everybody stayed sober! Players have too much to lose these days by getting as drunk as the literary mob.'[22]

As the 1980s progressed, Keneally wondered what life would be like if he were no longer part of the 'literary mob'. Life on the home front was changing. His daughters finished school and started studies at university: Margaret, or Meg as she is often called, at the University of Sydney studying law (she later switched to arts); and Jane at the University of New South Wales, undertaking a degree in commerce. On an ideal day, he would work from nine till one, before a long lunch. Then it was time for the beach – after his absences in England, Keneally was keen to get rid of his 'Pommie pallor' – or a walk to Avalon village, where he would yarn to people for whom his writing meant nothing before returning to his desk for a few more hours. He kept a fridge full of cans of beer in his office, and the old pool table got a lot of use.

He bought a pied-à-terre apartment in Wylde Street, in harbour-side Potts Point, which would enable his daughters to travel more readily to university. Bilgola Beach was a long way out of town. The new residence had large, elegant rooms, high ceilings and another enviable ocean view. Keneally often heard a magnificent voice descending through the ceiling: the celebrated opera singer Dame Joan Sutherland was one of his neighbours.

The prospect of downsizing his life and living permanently at Potts Point was tempting. Keneally may have had a generous nature but he did not have a robust constitution – at least, not one sufficiently robust to cope with the heavy demands on his time. As 1986 was swept away in much the same way as the previous few years, and with the years ahead looking equally challenging, he admitted to feeling very tired. For the first time he had the urge to toss it all in.

29

A Queue of Books

This time of ennui was not the first Keneally had experienced, nor would it be the last. The novelist had to decide, yet again, the direction his future career would take. Keneally had been part of the writer's uncertain world long enough to know that if he persevered, his writing would come in and out of fashion. And during the post-Booker era, his writing was 'in'. Even *The Cut-Rate Kingdom*, about which editors and agents had been doubtful, managed to achieve a place on a number of British bestseller lists.

'I was intrigued by another of your ideas: the notion of a fictionalised account of researching and writing the Schindler story,' Ion Trewin wrote. 'I look forward to you writing it one day, but I think just now is too soon . . .'[1] Keneally compiled a list of alternative suggestions for his publishers, titled 'The Question of a Novel Suitable for Publication in Late 1985', in a bid to find a subject worthy to succeed the Schindler book. The first would be based on his experiences while researching the Schindler story:

> It would concern above all the phenomenon of the fidelity of a Hyman Kaplanesque, Californian businessman to the memory of the Nazi who saved his life. The hero in question, now deceased, would have been an Abwehr agent who for whatever motive provided central European

> Jews with false papers and cover stories. He was also involved in a mass rescue of dwarfs from Auschwitz. Three and a half decades later a Gentile writer and the Californian undertake a journey to look into the hero or anti-hero's wartime career. For the Gentile writer the experience is akin to that of the assistant bank manager in *Travels with My Aunt* [by Graham Greene]. He [the writer] is accompanied not only by the Californian Pole, but by one of the dwarf survivors.
>
> Their journey involves them with Solidarity, with the Polish secret police, [and] with Mossad, the Israeli secret service. Over them hangs the question of the Nazi's heroism ... It is a story which would be like Schindler a celebration of pragmatic if ambiguous goodness and of the honouring of dead heroes ...

The outline was not enlarged to a complete book, but what he wrote had the title 'The Man Who Knew Walesa', described by Keneally as 'a segment from a novel I have never finished, a novel about an Australian Candide travelling in Poland during Solidarity's last summer, before the brutality of martial law descended'. The story was included in *Prize Writing: An Original Collection of Writings by Past Winners to Celebrate 21 Years of the Booker Prize*, published by Hodder & Stoughton in 1989.[2]

Keneally dedicated the story to Salman Rushdie, whose book *Midnight's Children* had won the Booker the year before *Schindler's Ark*. 'The small chapter here presented – with its intimations of threat – reminds me of Rushdie, and how he was in the days before threat, on Booker night 1982, this dinner-suited literary champion who sat at ease in Stationer's Hall, already a winner,' Keneally wrote in the introduction to 'The Man Who Knew Walesa'. 'Recently, at a New York rally in honour of his life and right of free expression, I was handed the poster I was to carry. It said, "Long live Rushdie". The one I would rather have got was the one given to the person next to me. "I am Rushdie", it read. We all are, not in talent, but in solidarity (that good Polish word).' The New York rally in 1989 was held to protest Ayatollah Khomeini's declaration of a death sentence for Rushdie following the publication of *The Satanic Verses*.

Keneally also contemplated a story which would attempt to honour the George Orwell classic *Nineteen Eighty-Four*. 'The world of 1984 is nothing like the world of Orwell's novel,' he wrote, 'yet in its way is equally fantastical. Therefore there is room for a futuristic novel based on the way the world really is in 1984. It has been done often before but usually badly.' He wrote a version of this story in a two-part serial published in the *Sydney Morning Herald* in August 1984, with the title 'The Year 2020'.[3]

For another proposed book Keneally had the details of life in bomber command from his brother-in-law, Max Martin, an RAAF pilot officer who had flown many missions. It would be 'a novel about a brother and sister and the way in which World War II educates them to the size of the earth and the nature of the twentieth century. The brother is a tail gunner in a bomber squadron operating from Yorkshire. The sister is a nun in a nursing order of Irish nuns domiciled in Australia. They are both painfully young, the brother still eighteen at the time of his first mission, the sister only eleven months older.'[4]

This outline became *Act of Grace*, published in 1988. Keneally used the pseudonym William Coyle, and the publisher was Chatto & Windus, London. The book, with the title *Firestorm*, was also published by William Morrow in the United States. In the blurb William Coyle is described as 'the pseudonym of an experienced novelist who divides his time between London, Australia and New York'.

The main interest of this book for Keneally readers is the familiarity with which he describes the life of Reardon and his sister Perpetua. Keneally had access to Martin's logbooks (from which he also obtained a lot of information for his third volume of *Australians*, published in 2014). The close fraternity of Reardon's crew differs markedly from that experienced by his sister in the community of nuns. Those familiar with Keneally's books will recognise the northern town of 'Rossclare', the idyllic beaches nearby at 'Polly Heads' and many other small details.

There are also glimpses of the priest Keneally might have been in the humane Father Murphy and the unfortunate Father Proud. Father Proud declares that the most beautiful line in the English language is 'Thou mastering me, God', from Gerard Manley Hopkins's poem 'The Wreck of the Deutschland'. That line 'fits in superbly with Christ's description of himself as the servant of the servants of God'. The following lines of Hopkins's poem read:

Giver of breath and bread;
World's strand, sway of the sea;
Lord of living and dead . . .

Keneally loves these words, claiming 'there's not as consummate a summation of the deity, even in the psalms, as that one'.[5]

Proud becomes fixated by a painting of St Justin that hangs in the entry hall of the hospital (in the same way that Father Con Keogh had stared at the painting of St Jerome at the Springwood seminary). Ultimately, Proud leaves the priesthood after endangering his life in a brutal act of self-harm.

The last suggestion on the 'suitable novel' list became *A Family Madness*. In his initial outline Keneally wrote:

> Recently, in a western suburb of Sydney, an area of Australia little exploited in literature . . . a family committed mass suicide on the Jonestown model. They were under threat of eviction and chose to die without regret while the police and an estate agent waited downstairs for them to gather their belongings. The family was led by a German immigrant father and were bound by some fierce and proud vision of destiny and, strangely, of a future world in which they would play significant roles . . .[6]

He had read an article by John Larkin, a Sydney journalist, about the mass suicide of five family members in July 1984, and had been to see the police sergeant who investigated the case. Keneally had also spoken to the neighbours. 'What is remarkable is that under the impact of the family delusion these people willingly subjected themselves to the suicide. Certain events which arose in World War II gave rise to some people having a sense of being "chosen".'[7]

In *A Family Madness*, a Western Russian family, the Kabbels, have delusions that stem from the extreme terrors they suffered during the war. Terry Delaney, who works for the father, Rudi, and his two sons, Warwick and Scott, is an Australian innocent who believes he can persuade the daughter, Danielle, with whom he is having an affair, to leave the family. Delaney's marriage is destroyed in the process. '*A Family*

Madness is set in the western suburbs,' Keneally said, 'which I like writing about because it is part of my background ... *Madness* is also about Eastern Europe which is another of my current obsessions dating from my Schindler research. It's also a tract on the limitations of nationalism. The Belorussians were a race of roughly the same population as Australia. They were nationalistic as only Slavs can be. They had their own language, but since the Middle Ages they'd had only six weeks of independence ...[8]

From the first page of *A Family Madness* Keneally comments on Australia in the 1980s: the shops on Main Street, Penrith, that once sold 'real things' have closed down to make way for 'bloody juju medicine stalls'; the government agencies operate as havens for the needy, 'the bureaucrats of small bounties'. The opinions of Tom Keneally senior can perhaps be heard here. The Catholic Church comes under scrutiny in the person of Father Doig, 'a bloody parson, not a priest – so Delaney's father spoke of Doig'. Doig attends what Delaney senior calls 'poofter-and-dunce barbers'. The modern priest does not hear confessions in the old-style confessional boxes but sits at a table by the side altar. He invites penitents to call him by his first name and to seek absolution from the people they have wronged rather than from him. This is called 'the rite of reconciliation'. Delaney does not 'quite feel the lightness that followed old-style confession, but Doig wasn't a bad fellow and was compassionate, even if a little of a smart alec. He understood the real world at least ...'

There is a lot of familiar Keneally in the book, a pastiche of known material, including his rugby league obsession and the books that Danielle reads as part of an English course: novels by Graham Greene, Günter Grass and J. D. Salinger. Delaney and Gina picnic at Palm Beach and walk to the lighthouse – a route that Keneally took often.

Sexuality dominates this book, with adultery, clandestine meetings, group sex, public sex, homosexuality, brothels and incest all in the mix. It sounds sordid but may be read as a metaphor for the experience of Belarus, a country repeatedly pillaged and raped and deceived. Delaney wants to believe in a saying that Brother Aubin once introduced to the classroom: *Ti mon seul desir*: 'You my only desired one.' Keneally had seen this inscription on an old Norman tapestry in Belgium. Aubin, aware of the stresses on modern marriages and the statistics of separations and divorces among 'old boys' of his school, tells his class that *Ti mon seul desir* should be said at the altar and in all the years ahead. It is 'the banner he [Delaney] wanted his manhood to sail under. That was his nature.' Doig reminds Delaney about the way that Catholic schools of Aubin's era taught their students that sex could destroy a person, and that sexual passions were 'runaway monsters'. Sex, according to Doig, is 'a matter of rational negotiation'. He views the 1980s as an age of rational thinking and practical living.

Keneally's 'sex scenes' were occasionally parodied in the press. At a July 1987 conference of the Association for the Study of Australian Literature, held in Launceston, Susan McKernan mocked some of the phrases in the opening pages of *The Playmaker*, the novel that followed *A Family Madness*. When reviewing the book for *The Bulletin* a couple of months later, she pointed out that intimate scenes later in the book were even more deserving of parody.[9]

As well as the criticism that his descriptions of sexual scenes were embarrassingly boyish or theatrical, Keneally was accused of writing in an unsympathetic or sexist way about women and not giving them sufficiently heroic status – with the exception of *Blood Red, Sister Rose*. Jill Neville, interviewing Keneally about *Passenger* for an ABC television program, took pleasure in pointing out similarities between the heroine in that story and a character in *Three Cheers for the Paraclete*: both are drunk, both vomit and both feel subsequent shame. The scene, said Neville, was described similarly in each book. 'The point I was then focused on,' she wrote afterwards, 'was the woman's reaction. Most of us would feel embarrassed or apologetic in such circumstances, not ashamed. I suggested that perhaps this revealed something flawed about his perception of women, or perhaps it was the hangover of an ineradicable Catholic sensibility.'

Neville was astonished to learn that Keneally, stung by the allegation, had telephoned the producer of the program and asked him to cut out the section about women vomiting 'because it might upset my daughters'. Similarly, he had complained about critics who dwelt on his so-called sexual obsessions or preoccupation with violence because their attacks might upset his wife and daughters. Neville could not understand Keneally's attitude.[10]

These issues may appear insignificant, and possibly were not much more than a couple of female reporters enjoying scoring some points off Keneally, but all his heroes when he was younger had been male and he was part of a generation that had to come to terms with the women's liberation movement. Having two self-assured daughters growing up in the 1970s and 80s helped. He wanted to eradicate the perception that his novels' women either wore halos or were weak characters duped in one way or another. He liked writing about women, but he did believe that they were often deceived, and often wrongly supportive of their men. He had a great deal of feeling for Danielle and for Gina, Delaney's wife, in *A Family Madness*. Gina is such an honest woman – but honesty, he suggests, is often not enough in a relationship.

Once he was back in his stride, Keneally told anyone who asked that he had 'a queue of books' that he'd like to write. Any anxiety he had as the 1980s progressed about his passion and boldness was dispelled with *The Playmaker*, a book that came out of his deliberations about the First Fleet. He had included some of his research in a contribution to the non-fiction book of a BBC television series called *Australia Beyond the Dreamtime*.

'As a schoolchild in Australia,' Keneally wrote, 'I studied [Oliver] Goldsmith's poem "The Deserted Village", though it was not pointed out to me that some of the people from "The Deserted Village" were probably in Phillip's convict transports.'[11] He was fascinated by the unlikely convicts who arrived with the First Fleet – Jewish Cockney convicts who wanted to celebrate Jewish High Holidays in Australia in 1788, and 'Black Caesar', a man from Madagascar.

He read *The Recruiting Officer*, a play written by George Farquhar and staged in 1789 to celebrate the fifty-first birthday of the 'mad' English king, George III. The play was a racy comedy performed by convicts and directed by a marine, Lieutenant Ralph Clark. From the balcony of his Potts Point apartment, Keneally could see the island named for Clark, soldier and journal writer, who had grown vegetables there. Notoriously, when the Second Fleet hove into sight off Sydney Heads in 1790, bringing 200 more women, Clark was reported as saying: 'My God! Not more of those damned whores! Never have I known worse women.' Much of Clark's story had already been told in *The Fatal Shore* by Robert Hughes, a non-fiction account published in 1987, which Keneally had reviewed for the *New York Times Book Review*.[12]

Keneally's version of Clark's contribution to the first settlement, *The Playmaker*, was launched in Sydney by David Williamson. The acting high commissioner for Australia, David Evans, and the directors of Hodder & Stoughton also held a reception to celebrate the book's publication in the Downer Room of Australia House, London.

Keneally's book is less about Clark and more about the convict society from which modern Australia has developed. He puts forward his theory of a history that is not taught in schools – at least, not when he was sitting in the classroom of Brother English, his history teacher at St Patrick's, Strathfield. The school textbook then was *History of Modern Europe* by Stephen H. Roberts (1933), key sections of which the boys learnt by rote.

'The reason we are such yobbos and such unbuttoned, boozing hoons is that we're Georgian,' contended Keneally. 'The eighteenth century Englishmen were like this. They were great topers and they gambled on everything. Italians used to go to London and say the English were too emotional! There was an accessibility of politicians and royalty, like the mad king himself, which operates with Australian cabinet ministers and politicians. Anybody can go up and say, "Gidday, Bob [Hawke], how-ya-going?" I'm sure it's where the Australian reputations, for wildness and anarchy on the one hand and conservatism on the other, come from. The passion for gambling and the exaltation of booze . . . We inherited all that from the Brits, and then, because we are so remote from England our development was quite different from either Europe's or America's.'[13]

Keneally warmed to his subject at various gatherings. 'American society began with godly people who were fleeing religious persecution . . . "justification" written all over their foreheads,' he suggested at an *Age* literary lunch in Melbourne. 'Our Adam and Eve had "crime" written all over their foreheads. The effects on the native populations were about equivalent, yet we have produced this remarkable society from all this.'[14]

According to Keneally's theory, the minor criminals who comprised much of the convict population became in Australia people who they would never have become anywhere else. He was intrigued by the fact that although the British government probably expected them to be annihilated or extinguished, the opposite had occurred. This was cause for celebration in Australia's bicentenary year, Keneally reckoned. 'We may have been slightly warty children in some ways, but there are remarkable things done that are worth celebrating.'

Keneally gives an honourable mention in *The Playmaker* to Arabanoo, an Aboriginal man captured by the intruders, a 'pet' of Captain Phillip, who watches the performance of the first play. The book is dedicated 'to Arabanoo and his brethren still dispossessed' – a gesture towards the celebrations of 1988, which Keneally said should acknowledge the country's original inhabitants. He was incomparable on the subject of confrontations between the white newcomer and the black Aboriginal, according to critic Howard Jacobson: 'No one is better on the clash of theologies, the intransigence of belief systems, the havoc wreaked by proselytising moralities. If someone – some white writer, at least – is to tackle the state of play between Europeans and Aborigines in Australia today, it ought to be Keneally.'

Jacobson regarded *The Playmaker* as a bicentenary story – and one revealing Keneally's shrewd sense of the marketplace. In a long article, 'The Small Fiction of a Great Country', Jacobson wrote:

> But that he [Keneally] should have been ready with the ideal Bicentenary novel will come as no surprise to anybody. If the schedule had not been so exacting, even for him, one might have hazarded that he'd made a fiction out of the opening chapters of *The Fatal Shore*, so promptly does *The Playmaker* appear to respond to the challenge implicit in that book that there, among the much maligned and endlessly resourceful first convicts, is material for a novelist of courage ...[15]

Kirkus Reviews claimed that *The Playmaker* was a brilliant fictional corollary to *The Fatal Shore*, and predicted: 'The Nobel committee, given its laggardness, ought to start looking at Keneally now, though he's relatively young. At this rate he'll be edging toward the top of the list soon enough.'[16]

Other pundits thought that Keneally's next book, *Towards Asmara*, might win him a Nobel Prize. When *Our Country's Good*, a stage adaptation of *The Playmaker*, was performed at the Royal Court Theatre, London (alongside a production of Farquhar's *The Recruiting Officer*), Keneally was there to address the cast.[17] He had just made a hazardous journey from Port Sudan, he told them, after leaving Eritrea.

30

Was It God or Politics?

'I have just visited the most remarkable society on earth,' Keneally said in April 1987, after his first visit to Eritrea. His innate restlessness, and recklessness, which always responded enthusiastically to a chance to travel to an unusual destination, had been challenged by a month living in the African nation. For a well-travelled man accustomed to first-class seats and reliable timetables, the journey had been nightmarish.

Keneally entered Eritrea from the north, by way of Khartoum, in Sudan. The first leg of his journey, he thought, could have come straight from a Graham Greene book. After breakfast at the Hotel Acropole, Keneally was informed that his flight to Port Sudan had been cancelled, possibly due to the massacre of a thousand tribespeople in a southern city, or perhaps due to rumours of an army coup. In his diary he wrote:

> Go out to Sudan Air – there are better dairy shelters in New South Wales than the Sudan Air terminal ... barring revolution and riots there will be a flight the next day – all great news to a hearty Oz coward ... the airline office opens. It's like Rugby League, fighting with Dervishes, Dinkas and others to get to counter. Return to hotel ... Booze is not available. Oh Mother Whisky, when I need it, where's your wondrous teat?

Sudan Air was nicknamed Sudden Death Air and Keneally noted that 'my plane nightmares will ever more feature Sudan Air'. The service was usually overbooked, but when a flight was at last available, he was on it. Before take-off, the flight engineer collected all the nomads' swords for safekeeping, while the second officer and some of the Sudanese passengers struggled to force the forward hatch closed.[1]

From Port Sudan Keneally travelled on the back of a truck to the crumbling Sudanese port of Suakin, where the brilliant blue of the Red Sea dazzled the eye, and latrines hanging over the water offended it. There was another wait for a supply truck that would take him down the Red Sea coast and across the border into Eritrea. This part of the journey was shared with a paraplegic soldier of the Eritrean People's Liberation Front (EPLF).

Keneally was hot and uncomfortable in the cramped cabin of the truck. The patient in the back made no complaint, although he was vomiting from the violent motion of the vehicle on the harsh road. Keneally was to learn that the maimed had great honour among the Eritreans. If there was any peril for himself, it came from the crazy roads. For much of the way there was no discernible road, only sandy tracks shared by green aid trucks. Dust swirled and Keneally covered his mouth and nose with a bandana. A nomad was seen occasionally in the distance, resplendent in a brightly coloured jacket and holding his sheathed sword. Inland, towards the hills, camels carried nomad women to tents erected along the wadies.

Keneally's venture had begun when he met Fessehaie Abraham, a leader of the Eritrean Relief Association (ERA) in Australia. Abraham, who in 1993 would become Eritrea's first ambassador to Australia, already had the support of Fred Hollows for the Eritrean cause. Hollows, an ophthalmologist, had helped the EPLF set up and run eye treatment programs; he died in 1993, but a year later an intraocular lens laboratory in his name opened in Asmara, the capital of Eritrea.

Impressed by Hollows and urged on by Abraham, Keneally wanted to go to Eritrea to see for himself what was being done by the ERA and the EPLF. He wrote to Ghebre Haile of the Eritrean Relief Committee in Sydney: 'I have been commissioned by my publishers to write a book concerning the politics of famine in the world. My idea is to examine the way that politics, both international and local, impinge on the welfare of particular peoples, and I know that nowhere is this impact more visible than in Eritrea. I would be very grateful to your Relief Committee if they could make it possible for me to visit Eritrea at my own expense . . .'

Haile replied: 'We have informed our head office, the ERA in Khartoum in the Sudan, to consider your offer. We believe your experience and unique skills of writing will contribute to inform the international community.'[2]

Keneally's application was approved and travel arrangements made. In Eritrea, Abraham insisted, the author would see how famine was not so much an act of God as a political creation. For twenty-five years the Eritreans had been fighting for independence from Ethiopia. In 1952 Eritrea was federated with Ethiopia against the wishes of the people; thousands had died in the long war that followed, with the plight of the people aggravated by famine and drought. The Russians had interfered in the dispute and supported the Ethiopian government.

'When it comes to famine in the Horn of Africa, is the hot breath of conflict more crucial than the hot breath of the Sahara?' Keneally asked in a 1987 article. 'In Eritrea, journalists and aid workers advised me, one sees all the factors at work – tortuous regional politics, the interference of a superpower, a long-fought war.'[3]

Having arrived in the troubled country, Keneally hid in bunkers by day and drove by night. He relied on a guide, Fessaha, a veteran of the conflict. He ate goat meat, *injera* bread and ground-up chickpeas called *shiru*, and drank sweet tea. He watched Muslims take out their prayer mats and bow towards Mecca at dusk. He had adrenaline injections and cortisone to ward off his asthma, and he took anti-malaria tablets, but for his first few days in the country he was ill with a gastric 'bug'. The strangest sensation for Keneally was the lack of communication with the outside world: 'It was like being out of the world because you couldn't send any messages out. There were no faxes, no telephones, and no certainty of transportation.'

One afternoon in the bombed-out town of Nakfa, an artillery barrage began from the Ethiopian side of the lines. Keneally and his companions took refuge in a deep bunker. There were many stories told of people 'going through the lines', but this was the closest he got on the first trip. From a slit in his sandbagged trench he observed the Ethiopians' movements. He then met Isaias Afwerki, the leader of the EPLF, in a remote bunker.

Afwerki told his visitor:

> Here drought is chronic. Every ten to thirteen years there will be a disastrous drought in the Horn of Africa. But you can't blame nature forever. People and governments have to face that and deal with it through basic development programmes. A democratic and efficient regime could deal with drought if only the bombing would stop and the foreign army would go home. The future of the Horn will be conditioned by global, African and Ethiopian politics. The trouble is convincing everyone else, from the Organisation of African Unity – which has in the past declared that Eritrean independence would bring on a rash of 'balkanisation' in Africa – to the superpowers.[4]

Afwerki became the first president of the State of Eritrea in 1993, a position he held well into the twenty-first century. Keneally returned to Australia to mull over what he had seen and heard. He often told others about the people of that distant land who were happy if they had three limbs, if they got one meal a day and if they drank clean water. Margaret and Jane, who had become accustomed to lectures on their 'humble origins' whenever their father was taking them through the western suburbs of Sydney, now heard a more developed version of 'how lucky we are'.

The best way to follow Keneally's Eritrean journey is to read his novel *Towards Asmara*. Henry the aid worker, Darcy the journalist, Christine the girl looking for her filmmaker father, and Julia, an elderly Englishwoman from the Anti-Slave Society, are the characters who put forward all the reader needs to know about Eritrea, as Keneally had observed it.

In the novel's first draft he put in too much, making the book a documentary rather than an absorbing work of fiction; he wrote several more drafts before he was satisfied that the characters had taken over. The process was assisted when Keneally saw the musician Bob Geldof on television, reduced to tears by the destruction of trucks in a food relief convoy heading to Asmara in November 1987. The EPLF claimed responsibility for the bombing, but it claimed that the vehicles were really part of a military convoy, and that they contained armaments for the enemy as well as food. In this case the rebels were wrong – for once, the convoy was carrying nothing but food.

Keneally revised his book to begin with a chapter titled 'The Rock-singer'. That character's 'Worldbeat' concert has raised money for starving Africans. In the novel, Darcy the journalist travels to Eritrea to investigate the attack on the aid convoy. A veteran from the conflict has told Darcy that the rebels responsible had made an error of judgement, but also that the rock singer just does not understand the complexity of the big picture – the politics of food.

'So you will write about the war or the hunger?' the girl Christine asks Darcy.

'About everything I find,' Darcy replies.

That sums up the book. Darcy's experiences mirror those of Keneally, who did not address the question of drought versus politics completely to his or the reader's satisfaction. He now concedes that the book was too didactic, but says it was authentic. *Towards Asmara* immerses the reader in the remarkable society that Keneally had enthused about. Particular people are picked out from among the stoical, ever-courteous Eritreans 'in the daily traffic of the hunger zone': 'an exquisite girl swathed in diaphanous green cloth'; Moka, the skeletal minder; the barefoot cave doctors; the tranquil Amna, tortured by her Ethiopian captors; the soldiers, many of them too young to be bearing arms.

In underground hideouts the activity is endless. Darcy is 'disarmed by the cunning, by the competence, by all the crafts socketed away in these mountains of shale, in these secret and kindly caves which the MiGs and the Antonovs couldn't find'. Lady Julia, the Englishwoman, has the impression that 'these people have taken flight! I mean, *flight*. They are jumping a gulf which no other race has jumped, Darcy.' It is a remarkable society.

Keneally returned to Eritrea in May 1989, accompanied by Judy and a film crew. The filming was arranged by Melvyn Bragg, presenter of the popular British television program *The South Bank Show*. Bragg believed Keneally was a writer with 'a nose for stories', a man who had the knack of 'bringing you the news in a novel'. Bragg was attracted by the unusual scenario of a writer going into a battle zone, seen in a different light to the novelist at his desk. Audiences of *The South Bank Show* warmed to Keneally, whose kind face, sensitivity and intelligent commentary animate the film.[5]

Keneally had vowed that he would not go back to Eritrea, partly because he could not face the difficult journey through Sudan, but he changed his mind for the film venture. 'I am going back because a lot of changes have occurred,' he said on camera. 'I want to re-verify what I found out on that first trip.'[6] Some scenes were indelibly distressing, like the many corpses of Ethiopian conscripts lying along the trenches, their family photographs blowing about in the wind.

He was there in the final stages of the war with Ethiopia. One of his most vivid memories was collapsing with heatstroke in a stone bunker near the city of Keren. The bunker was full of young Eritrean soldiers who were all students. When Keneally regained consciousness, a medic said to him, 'Now you are feeling better, Mr Thomas, could you tell us about the Australian electoral system?'[7]

There was a delay in Port Sudan on the journey home owing to another revolutionary situation, but Keneally went to the airport each day, standing in the glare and heat, and eventually made his escape on a flight to London. The subject of Eritrea continued to resonate and, like the Schindler story, would remain part of his life. Some scenes – such as a nomad girl, just fifteen years old, brought into a hospital on the side of a camel in a sling, having trodden on a mine – would always be with him, and ever since he has been committed to mine clearing.

Keneally wrote an article for *Vogue* in 1989 titled 'Ceremonies of Style on Savage Ground'. One of the things that had impressed him most in Eritrea was the natural grace of the women, who had tribal cuts on their faces and pierced noses. Gliding elegantly in the hazy, dusty squalor, 'these women can make the poorest length of fabric look superb'.

In November 1992, back at Irvine, Keneally took part in a forum titled 'Famine in the Horn of Africa: God or Politics?'. His presentation was one of a series included in the subject 'Global Peace and Conflict Studies', offered at UCI's Centre for Global Peace and Conflict Studies. He was also patron of the Eritrean Students' Club at UCI and one of the subjects he taught was 'Imagining War and Peace'.[8]

Keneally was invited by Amare Tekle, commissioner of the Referendum Commission of Eritrea, to observe the nation's historic referendum process: 'The Commission is aware that you have been a keen and sympathetic observer of recent developments in Eritrea and the region. It also recognises your devotion to the cause of peace and justice based on the respect of essential human rights as well to the creation and preservation of democratic institutions in the Horn of Africa . . .'[9] Keneally attended in April 1993 and was assigned various polling booths to make his observations.

Fred Hollows, who had first visited Eritrea just before Keneally, died a couple of months before the referendum. Keneally became involved in the Fred Hollows Foundation, and in 2003 became the first recipient of the Fred Hollows Award, commissioned by the Eritrean Development Foundation. The award acknowledged his 'exemplary artistic and humanitarian contributions to Eritrea's development'.[10] Hollows's widow, Gabi, holds Keneally in high regard as 'a fantastic humanitarian, committed to social justice'. In Fessehaie Abraham's opinion, Hollows and Keneally really understood the issues and confronted them. He admired their courage, too. 'They went into a war zone and put their lives on the line.'

Keneally returned to Eritrea in 2000, anxious to know if Hollows's Intraocular Lens Factory had survived another invasion by Ethiopia. He was angered about the damage done to a cotton mill in western Eritrea by the Ethiopian army, because this mill had represented progress. The Ethiopians had boasted about its destruction, leaving a hate message to Afwerki on the bombed wall. Keneally dreaded the possibility that Hollows's factory had suffered the same fate, and hoped that if the Ethiopians had captured Asmara, he would have the courage to speak out against the destruction of something in which many Australians had invested time and expertise. He saw many thousands of people on the roads, displaced from their southern farmlands and towns. 'Barely a word in the world's media!' he noted. 'Not a word except from that heroic Irish woman, Moy Robinson [a reporter].'[11] The factory was intact; in more recent times, with ownership transferred to the Eritreans, it has continued to manufacture and export lenses.

Before the 1980s ended, another Keneally book was published, this time about a boy not much younger than most child soldiers in Eritrea. Like them, this boy held a grenade, but it was one that wreaked havoc on a family in suburban Sydney. The boy is Daniel Jordan and the story had already been told in *The Fear*, Keneally's second book. In 1987

Keneally met Craig Munro and D'Arcy Randall, editors at the University of Queensland Press (UQP), who hoped to publish a revised edition of *The Fear*. Keneally was keen to proceed. He had been very dissatisfied with the 1967 Sun Books paperback edition, which had been so poorly produced that it had fallen apart.

Randall has explained the origins of the project: 'During the mid to late 1980s UQP was building a quality paperback list, so we editors were actively seeking works of Australian literature that had gone out of print. I discovered that *The Fear* was out of print and was surprised. Should not all of Keneally's works be available to his readers?' Randall thought it was a 'flawed novel' and 'shambling', the same word Keneally had used when he described it to her. 'Still, the novel contains some very strong episodes ... Despite its numerous problems in style, structure etc. I think this novel should be in print, as much for its high points and insights as for the perspective it gives on one of Australia's most celebrated writers.'[12]

Initially UQP planned a straight reissue, but then Randall put forward another proposal: 'The first section (Chapters 1–17) is marvellously evocative of Australia's home front during World War II ... Reading *The Fear* from an 80s perspective, the first section seemed to have the structural integrity of a short novel ... How would ... Tom feel about our publishing the first 17 chapters as a separate work, titled *The Comrade* ... this could really give the book a new life, we think.'[13]

Keneally by that stage had taken up an appointment at New York University. He had also made a start on a book about Ireland. He explained to Randall: 'Listen, I've just got a problem writing this book on the famine and it consumes all the available oxygen. I agree with you – for sweet Jesus's sake let's not publish the entire solecism! Talk on my return ...'[14] Keneally said he was 'nervous of the title' and suggested *By the Line*. 'I think the title is a little obscure,' Randall told Laurie Muller, UQP's general manager, 'but it's very hard to communicate with Tom these days.'[15] The cover design used detail from the painting *Near the Docks*, a 1949 work by Sali Herman.

In his imagination, Keneally was near the docks at Cobh. The first book he wrote about Ireland and its people was *Now and in Time to Be: Ireland and the Irish*, and the second was *The Great Shame: And the Triumph of the Irish in the English-Speaking World*. The second would be a corollary to the Eritrean story: Was it God or politics?

31

Seanchai: Gifted Storyteller

Publisher David Ryan in London wanted a writer with an Irish background from the furthest rim of the Irish diaspora to write about Ireland, and to test the mythologies learnt from grandparents.[1] Keneally was an obvious choice: a man who wore his Irish origins as comfortably and as publicly as his allegiance to rugby league and an Australian republic.

Now and in Time to Be: Ireland and the Irish is, as the blurb puts it, 'a proud confirmation of the ancient suspicions the Irish retain of their national glory'. Keneally apologetically uses the phrase 'without being too sentimental' throughout the book; nevertheless, it is a sentimental journey, a charming, colourful book full of the characters, prejudices, memorials and anecdotes commonly associated with the country. He could never travel to Ireland without being conscious of its melancholy: 'the vacancies, the absences, the ghosts'.

Few have expressed pilgrim feelings as well as Keneally. He is ever-present in the book, with phrases like 'I thought you might need to know too about . . .' inviting the reader to share the experience. He also has 'the gift of the gab', often attributed to his Irish ancestry, and talked to many people as he drove around the country. Zane Berzins, a friend of the Keneally family in New York, once travelled with them in Ireland. She was astonished when someone recognised Keneally 'in the middle of nowhere' and approached him.

Keneally also had the ready facility to include in his journey the Irish greats – among them William Butler Yeats, Seamus Heaney and James Joyce – and to quote from their work. Keneally particularly admired Heaney – 'the famous Seamus', as he was known. The two writers had met on occasion and enjoyed 'a jar' together. 'Heaney is a Christian Brothers boy like me,' Keneally said in 2007. 'It is his humanity and his sense of the holiness of the past: that what people went through in the past and go through now, are connected by a sacrament of inevitable pain, which we can't avoid.'[2]

Keneally did not have a good relationship with David Ryan and was angry that he sent out 'mere notes to an Irish critic at a stage when they are not even ready for publication, were merely unrehearsed reflections ... This may suit your idea of passing on ideas you don't have the guts to transmit yourself. But it also suits my idea of termination. I won't write under these artificial conditions and constraints ...'[3] Ryan pacified the author, but there was an ongoing dispute about advances and royalties.

At the launch for *Now and in Time to Be*, a reception held at the Irish Embassy in London and hosted by Joseph Small, the Irish ambassador to the United Kingdom, Keneally said mischievously that he offered the book as 'a cultural reparation to Ireland for the Australian export of *Neighbours*' (a long-running television soap opera).[4]

There was limited space in *Now and in Time to Be* to fully explore the bigger picture of Irish politics. Keneally had heard about one relative, John Kenealy, who was among the convicts aboard the *Hougoumont* in 1867. This Kenealy was 'previously respectable', according to the register of the *Hougoumont*, but associated with the Fenian Brotherhood and sentenced to ten years of penal servitude. Then there was the 'bottled-in-bond Irish tragic story' of various Irish forebears: Hugh Larkin, who arrived in Australia aboard the *Parmelia*, and Mary Shields on the convict ship *Whitby*.

The story of Mary Shields would also be told in a musical, *Transport*, for which Keneally wrote the words.[5] He made some notes for a musical play by that name soon after he began the research for the two books about Ireland, but the setting for those notes was Cork Harbour and the ship was the *Respite*.[6] The action of *Transport* takes place on *The Whisper* at sea, but Keneally retains the names of the four female convicts: Bride Riordan, Polly Cantwell, Maggie Carroll and Kate O'Hare.

Keneally had many well-known names for the bigger book, including Meagher of the Sword, one of the leaders of Young Ireland. In *Now and in Time to Be*, Keneally wrote: 'A Christian Brother who taught me, an Australian named Jimmy McGlade, aesthete, classic batsman and fine Rugby League coach, writes to me at least once a year asking whether I am ready yet to produce a great work on Meagher of the Sword . . .' In 1952, Keneally's final year at school, McGlade had expressed an interest in a particular group of Irish political prisoners, and particularly Thomas Francis Meagher, and had set Keneally a research task on Meagher. Many years later, McGlade replied to a fax message that Keneally sent for his eightieth birthday celebrations in 1994. 'At last you have started your homework,' McGlade wrote. Keneally replied that he hoped to get an A when he presented the finished work.[7]

Nan Talese encouraged the venture. At dinner one evening, Keneally said to her: 'People come up to me all the time to talk about *Schindler's List*. It really is a shame that I've never written about my own people. Everyone thinks it was the Famine that caused the great Irish migration. In fact it was the politics of the British.' Keneally sent Talese a detailed proposal for the book, suggesting the titles *The Great Shame* or *The Halving of Ireland*. 'The great shame of the title was the near-halving of the Irish population between 1840 and 1880,' he wrote. 'Concentrating on individuals, and using the same documentary viewpoint as operates in *Schindler's List*, I would like to tell this story in a way which gives the reader a new and invigorating view of this enormous European tragedy . . . Of course, there will not be a central Schindler figure in this dramatic tale, but I hope to give the work narrative unity by dealing with perhaps twenty recurrent figures, some of whom died during the historic framework of the proposed book . . .'

Keneally wanted his readers to see that 'only in the new world does sun shine on the faces of Ireland's children . . . I intend that this tale will be one involving many vigorous and splendid figures, and much tragic fallibility and malice. As in *Schindler*, I will not create events or dialogue but depend on the testimonies of those who suffered through this ruinous half century.'[8]

Above: The Keneally General Store in Kempsey, New South Wales, in 1911.

Right: Tom Keneally's uncle Johnnie Keneally, who fought at Flanders, Amiens and the Somme.

Below: Hilda and Mick Coyle holding Keneally's younger brother, Johnny.

Below right: Kate Keneally with Edmund Thomas.

Above left: Elsie Keneally holding her first son, Thomas Michael Keneally, in 1935.

Above: Tom Keneally, aged around twenty months.

Left: Elsie with Tom, aged six.

Left: Tom Keneally with his father, Tom senior, in the early summer of 1945.

Above: Tom and his younger brother, John Patrick Keneally.

Below left: The Rafferty family, in Homebush, New South Wales. *[Courtesy of Mary Rafferty]*

Above: Tom Keneally as a student at St Patrick's Christian Brothers College, Strathfield, in 1952.

Right: Tom (centre) with his friend Paddy Downie (left) and brother Johnny (right).

Top: Keneally (sixth from left) at St Patrick's Seminary, Manly, after his ordination to subdeacon, 1958. *[Courtesy of Paul Crittenden, who is standing behind Keneally's right shoulder]*

Above left: St Columba's College, Springwood. *[Courtesy of St Columba's Catholic College]*

Above right: St Patrick's College Manly. *[Courtesy of Paul Crittenden]*

Right: Keneally with the Waverley College 12A rugby union side.

Keneally in his early thirties at the State Library of New South Wales.

Top left: Keneally with his daughters, Margaret and Jane, on the verandah at Avalon in around 1972.

Middle left: Father and daughters in about 1976.

Below: Desmond O'Grady of *The Bulletin*, the first editor to publish Keneally.

Bottom: At left, Keneally's US agent Georges Borchardt with his wife, Anne; at right, his editor at Collins in London, Philip Ziegler.

Keneally with Tom E. Lewis, who played the title role in Fred Schepisi's *The Chant of Jimmie Blacksmith*.

Above: Tom and Judy Keneally in 1983. *[Photo by John Constable]*

Left: Holocaust survivor Leopold 'Poldek' Pfefferberg with Simon & Schuster editor Nan Talese (seated), Marcela Berger, director of foreign rights (left), and Julia Knickerbocker, director of publicity (right).

Keneally on the night he was awarded the Booker Prize for his novel *Schindler's Ark*, 19 October 1982.

Opposite: Keneally with film director Steven Spielberg in Kraków.

Above: Keneally in Eritrea with Michele, a member of the Eritrean People's Liberation Front and Keneally's driver during the Eritrean referendum of 1993.

Left: Keneally skiing in the Martini Cross-Country Classic at Perisher, New South Wales, in 1994.

Below: With ophthalmologist Fred Hollows.

Right: Keneally with ABC Managing Director David Hill, a fellow supporter of the Australian Republican Movement, circa 1995.

Below left: With playwright and friend David Williamson.

Below right: In New York at a First Friday lunch gathering, with Edward Burns (left), Frank McCourt and Terry Moran (right). *[Courtesy of Terry Moran]*

Opposite top: Keneally with his daughters Jane (left) and Margaret (right) on the set of *This Is Your Life*, 1998.

Opposite below: Keneally with his brother, Johnny.

Above: Keneally with Brother McGlade. *[Courtesy of the Archives of St Patrick's College, Strathfield]*

Right: Father Patrick Connor. *[Courtesy of Society of the Divine Word Chicago Province Archives]*

Left: With Margaret and grandchildren Rory and Alexandra, early 2000s.

Below: Tom Keneally in the Tom Keneally Centre at the Sydney Mechanics' School of Arts, 2012. *[Photograph © Helen White, from the collection of the Sydney Mechanics' School of Arts, reproduced with permission]*

Keneally had various opportunities in Ireland to conduct research. In 1995 he was the 'star' of a documentary film called *Tom Keneally's Ireland*. In 1996 his name appeared on an official program for a commemorative ceremony held in Dublin on the eightieth anniversary of the 1916 Easter uprising, at which he read out a historical document with the title 'The Provisional Government of the Irish Republic to the People of Ireland'.

The book engaged Keneally in many years of research. 'I sometimes upbraid myself in rare moments of fiscal probity that I have squandered more money on libraries – getting to them, sitting in them – than most habitual gamblers squander on horses,' he wrote in 2005. 'I wanted to tell the story of nineteenth century political convicts sent from Ireland to Australia and found I could not just stop at Australian libraries. In the first place, I had to follow the people from the Irish record into the Australian one, and then, in some cases, back to Ireland or else to America.'[9]

The large, impressive book, and Keneally's breezy comments when it was published, could not possibly tell the bigger story of all the difficulties that had beset its writing. At the beginning Talese declared that she was 'hopelessly at sea' in *Ireland Transported*, the working title of the book that became *The Great Shame*. It was:

> . . . a compilation of your prodigious research but you have not yet begun to write it, transform what you know with your marvellous prose, into a world that comes alive. You do not want to write a history paper or a commentary do you? Ireland is of such great interest now and you have within you the power to make readers understand the roots of its tragedy and triumph.
>
> With the great success of Frank McCourt's *Angela's Ashes* and Tom Cahill's *How the Irish Saved Civilisation* ... the audience is absolutely primed for you ... I trust that now you have put the research on paper, you will return to shape and craft it into the classic it can be. After all, the Irish above all others deserve your storytelling at its powerful best.[10]

Keneally was impatient and frustrated. He wanted to get on with his fiction writing. He referred to the Irish book as 'the monster' and wondered if he would ever be free of its grasp. The schedule of the Serpentine

Publishing Company (the name of his writing business) was already tight. 'The monster' threatened to disrupt the schedule and a personal assistant was employed.

Talese delayed publication until she was fully satisfied.[11] She told Keneally that his comments to her two years before – that he had never told the story of his own people, and that he was amazed that there were only two more citizens of Ireland than there were 150 years ago – had been lost in his story. 'The tremendous research you have taken on and the great expanse of time and territory have made the "event" overwhelm the Irish and the poignancy of your statement . . . the facts gallop over the reader and crush him.'[12]

Keneally confided in his agent, Amanda Urban (who had represented him in the US since 1992):

> I am extremely concerned that we are at cross purposes, that she [Talese] wants a book I cannot deliver without violating my intentions. I am engaged in a large re-write, but I fear at the end it will be contrary to her desires . . . By three weeks ago it was suggested I concentrate on Meagher, and now as you see on O'Reilly. The imputation is that Australian convicts be dropped, but Australian convicts were always part of the agreed-upon formula. This shifting of the ground beneath the book makes my situation impossible. I feel I must buy my way out of this contract . . . unless the problem is a) the mass of material; b) the way the research clogs the narrative; c) the remote tone of the book . . .[13]

Urban advised him to finish cutting and rewriting, and to give the revised manuscript to Talese as it was. Urban was accustomed to Keneally's outbursts and his sudden changes of direction. In the midst of the difficulties with 'the monster', he asked her: 'Do you think Nan would like a novel on the present Irish situation, a brutal-eve-of-peace-in-the-North novel, an end piece to the big Irish book?' Urban replied: 'With Nan up to her ears in one Ireland book, I'm not sure about the wisdom of asking her to consider another. In general, books on modern conflict in Northern Ireland have not sold well (along with books on Vietnam!).'[14]

Keneally's testy comments to Talese continued:

> I have lived with this book 18 hours a day for 3 years, I have thought of it continually, and I must say this: *I know what I want it to be.* I have spent many times my advance in research ... It will be a book rather different from any I have written to this point. It will be – in intent – a pacey and insightful historical narrative full of robust characters and huge tragedies. Anything else would be rightly pilloried by scholars in Ireland and America ... If this plan for my book is unacceptable, it's best to clear that up now, for both our sakes. I can see no sense in your being forced to publish a book you lack enthusiasm for ... [15]

The book was not published in the United States until 1999. 'On balance, I am aware of Nan's virtues,' Keneally wrote to Urban, 'but the impact of Nan's revisions, many of which I could not see the point of anyhow, was to delay publication and put my entire programme, economic and creative, out of whack ...' Nine drafts had been written, a trial which Talese said indicated her sincere dedication to the final work. She consoled Keneally: 'Just to underscore my sympathy and deep caring about this book, what follows is the manifest of the Ship "Niagara", sailing from Cork 29 August 1851 [to Port of New York]. Passenger #243 is Thomas Ahern [sic], age 30, Labourer – my great-grandfather.'[16]

Talese was delighted with the final book. 'It is indeed the voice of Thomas Keneally, storyteller, with all that exhaustive research informing the text through your own mind, but no longer before us at length,' she wrote to him in 1998.[17] Years later, she remained certain that her determination to get it right was vindicated: 'Tom devoted a lot of time to it – look at the size of it! Its success in terms of American sales was astonishing: in hardback 47,186 copies and in paperback 36,867. I suspect that we did well as there was a great number of Irish who came here during the Famine.'

There were many publicity opportunities in the United States, where Keneally's estimated royalties by October 2000 amounted to $32,000. Copies were inscribed for President Bill Clinton, Hillary Clinton, Richard Holbrooke (US ambassador to the United Nations) and Senator Edward Kennedy. The Australian edition was launched in Canberra by Richard O'Brien, ambassador for Ireland, at an event which the Keneallys considered 'the best book launch by far in thirty-odd years of publishing for us' – a compliment that was forwarded to Mary McAleese, president of the Republic of Ireland, who had sent a message to be read at the function.[18]

Keneally often worked every day of the week at home. It wasn't unusual to see him talking into a tape recorder at the beach or an airport. As the 1990s advanced, the demands on his time were affecting everyone, making it hard for him to stay in control. Petitioners were repeatedly told that the author was 'just so swamped at the moment'; in his letters he said things like, 'January and February are mortgaged. I'm sure this fact is a temporary one, but I find myself in the horrifying position where nearly every date between now and March is earmarked.'[19]

He was overcommitted, yet many good things were attached to fame, such as the inclusion of his name on the Writers' Walk at Circular Quay, Sydney, a cultural project undertaken for the Ministry for the Arts in December 1991. Thousands of tourists see these plaques every week and many stop to read them. An exhibition titled 'Uncommon Australians – Towards an Australian Portrait Gallery' opened at the Art Gallery of New South Wales on 22 October 1992. Bernd Heinrich painted Keneally in his favourite working outfit – track pants, T-shirt and joggers – with part of the script of *Schindler's List* painted in behind him. He approved of the finished work. 'I like the way the right foot goes over the edge of the painting which is typical of me,' Keneally commented. 'Fundamental timidity combined with stepping over the edge.'[20]

Between 1988 and 1992 Keneally was the first Berg Visiting Professor at New York University (NYU). The Creative Writing Graduate Program had enjoyed a remarkable group of creative leaders, including the poets Galway Kinnell and Sharon Olds and the historical novelist E. L. Doctorow. Their role was not so much to be teaching as to be leading by example, showing what could be done through their own work. Keneally 'taught' Patrick White's *Voss* to students in a graduate seminar. White's savage judgements on his country have baffled Australian readers, and it was no different in New York. 'What's eating this guy?' asked one girl. 'I've been to Sydney and it's heaven on a stick!'[21]

The lecturers at NYU did not have big classes, but Keneally was impressed by the calibre of the students' work. He has singled out A. M. Homes, a recipient of many literary awards. 'I read with her in England last year [in 2012, at the Shoreditch Reading Series]. Someone came up to me and said, "You're brave calling the eminent A. M. Holmes Amy!" But she had been in my class. She was a very average writer by my standards – there were a lot of writers who were flashier – she was by no means the best writer but she was writing from the edge. She claimed, "I write the things we don't want to say out loud."'

Keneally has said repeatedly that it is the writers who are hungriest for publication, and not necessarily the best, who will see their books in print. Writers must have that lust for the published work. As a teacher, he could offer direction, confidence and contacts, but he had little to teach a naturally gifted writer. 'The great problem with writers of talent is commitment ... the writers, both at NYU and at UCI, who've been published are often the most motivated and the bravest ... It's amazing to me that the ultimate factor in the success of these young writers is temperament.'[22] He warned the students against envy of other writers, telling them that it was the worst disease for writers. 'It will make you a savage person and it will demean your own writing ... don't think that any one writer's glory in any way diminishes your own ... there can be umpteen splendid novels ...'[23]

Keneally loved New York. At first he lived in an apartment in Washington Square Village, close to the campus. Later he bought an apartment in the Silk Building, on the corner of Broadway and East 4th Street, the scene of many good parties. Zane Berzins, who became a surrogate 'big sister' to Keneally's daughter Margaret when she was in New York, remembered that, after one party, Keneally walked down Broadway with Berzins and her companion, seeing them safely to transport, wearing socks but no shoes.

Berzins worked at NYU in the public affairs office and originally had an image of writers as boring people who wrote about dysfunctional families. She was not interested in *Schindler's List*, handed to her by one of her colleagues, but after she read it she wanted to meet the author. She heard Keneally talk about Asmara and went to one of his readings – which happened to be from *A Family Madness*, which was all about a very dysfunctional family. She warmed to Keneally, regarding his empathy as the strength of his writing and liking his ability to talk easily to people. 'He would have made a good Father Confessor! I suggested to Tom that he drop by some time to the Lions Head pub in Sheridan

Square, Greenwich Village. That was a hub for musicians and writers.' Word got around that Keneally was in town. It was not long before he was invited to go along to a gathering called First Friday.

Over the years, from its beginnings in the 1960s, First Friday attracted actors, Irish ambassadors and consuls, speechwriters and public relations specialists, as well as writers such as James T. Farrell, William Kennedy and Frank McCourt. According to an NYU academic, Terry Moran:

> Given the group's oral tradition and the lack of written records, there is no hard evidence to support my remembrance that it was Malachy [McCourt] who proposed that we should further regularise our lives by meeting for lunch on the First Friday of each month, citing the Holy Roman Catholic and Apostolic Church's precedent of promising the faithful that if they would attend mass and receive communion for nine consecutive first Fridays they would be granted 'the grace of a happy death' . . . At first, Malachy promised that all who attended nine consecutive First Fridays would be rewarded with the presence of a bartender at our deaths, thus assuring us of the grace of a final parting glass. For those who found this promise to be too distant, Malachy soon provided a new covenant: 'Do nine First Friday lunches in a row and you get to do nine more.'[24]

'When you meet a famous writer, you don't know how to react – you don't know how he is – you want him to be as wonderful as his writing is,' Moran admits. 'Tom fitted in very readily and *Schindler's List* is the key to that. It was tremendously important to Americans – the book was very successful. New York is a town that is Irish and Jewish. They had very powerful connections and his [Keneally's] was the perfect combination . . . All the writers were there to have a good time, not to be worshipped, but to be part of a company of equals. We were all easy with each other.'

When Keneally arrived on the scene, First Friday was meeting at Eamonn Doran's Bar on 2nd Avenue, just south of 53rd Street. He was soon attracting company because he was known to be what the Irish called a *seanchaí*, a gifted storyteller. He also had a natural ability to initiate the *craic*, a special kind of conversation usually occurring in bars and pubs, where the main purpose of the speaker was to entertain himself and his companions. Obviously, the *craic* was accompanied by what Keneally called 'the jar', a pint of beer.

It became a matter of concern to him that he had taken to the *craic* and the jar in New York. The bars were unusual: there was one where cops from a downtown precinct gathered and where the barman inquired, before he served his customer, 'Is Belfast free yet?' Keneally liked garrulous drinking and arguing sessions, and alcohol could temporarily provide a way to lighten the mood, to forget a problem or soften a disappointment. Writing was the means by which he had escaped the fate of some ex-seminarians: homelessness, alcoholism or mental disease. But the weakness was there – the temptation to resort to 'the booze'.

'Just as I've had a lifelong argument with the church and with my writing, similarly with alcohol,' Keneally says. 'I have had the regrettable capacity to take the stuff and convince myself that I was functioning . . . I have attended a few meetings of Alcoholics Anonymous and was as willing as any of them to get up and say, "My name is Tom . . ." But my life was never taken over totally like some of the people there. The quantities they talked about imbibing made me look like a very average social drinker.'

Tom senior liked his whisky, and his son took pleasure in gifting him the best examples from around the world. Tom senior had the ability to drink a lot without ill effect, until he was getting older, but Keneally became melancholy if he drank 'ill-advisedly'. Like McCloud, the main character in the book *Flying Hero Class*, Keneally had during his writing career flirted with excessive drinking: 'A certain risk to the brain *and* reins, it had seemed justified then by the scope of the work he believed he was writing.'

The narrator in the 1993 book *Jacko* describes New York as 'a fatal city' for the man with a propensity to drink:

> Everywhere the atmospheric bar – from the authentic squalid to the squalid chic to the period-varnished-and-mirrored to the unutterably chi-chi and the unconscionable – and never the responsibility afterwards of driving home . . . I knew I had to stop these boyish sessions soon, because they were endangering my chemistry . . . I knew that I would not reach a *modus vivendi* with all that until I gave up at least

spirits and possibly wine. And doing so seemed as remote and unlikely as the chastity and penance of Egyptian saints of the sixth century.'

While his tenure at NYU was coming to an end, Keneally continued his teaching commitments at UCI. The reality there had turned out to be more complicated than he had been told initially. The graduate fiction writers were demoralised after a visiting novelist from New York, Lynn Sharon Schwartz, wrote an article attacking UCI as having a cold, corporate feel; she described the graduate writers as mediocre and accused them of being more concerned with selling film options than with producing good fiction. Yet Keneally knew from his earlier experience at UCI that the program attracted highly talented students; one was Whitney Otto, author of *How to Make an American Quilt*. Keneally developed friendships with several budding novelists, including Jim Brown and Michelle Latiolais.[25]

Sometimes the demands of his other life took over, meaning that Judith Grossman, the other director of the graduate writing program, shouldered much of the load. Grossman said that she had no complaints: 'I'm pointing out to the students constantly that Tom is an excellent role model. As a fiction writer, he tends to business: he writes the books, which is crucial. Whatever else they're doing, they've got to write their books. Tom does that; he comes through . . . He's also a presence in the world, and we're happy that he does good work of the kind that he does for the public good. That's a gift. I think you'll find the students are very proud of him.'[26]

Keneally took unpaid leave from UCI in 1993, telling the dean, Spencer Olin, that he was finding it 'impossible to adequately honour my diverse responsibilities'.[27] A year later he wrote to Professor Michael Clark, chair of the English and Comparative Literature Department, to inform him that he intended to resign. 'The reason is not to do with any discontent with UCI or my colleagues there, but with the fact that I am torn to the point of exhaustion in two directions. I have been unable to extricate myself from Australia adequately to fulfil my duties to UCI, and particularly to those brilliant young writers who participate in the programme . . .'[28]

Keneally promised to honour his teaching commitments in the winter and spring of 1994. 'I will miss the students,' he told one interviewer, 'and also the exchange of ideas that goes on here.' When asked what advice he had to give the students, Keneally replied, 'Keep writing, you little sods! That's the message!'[29] On Sunday 9 April 1994 he held a farewell party at 4 Whistler Court. He was awarded the UCI Medal for Work in Literature in 1995.

During his years at UCI, Keneally occasionally met Poldek, and sometimes they were asked to tell their joint story at a function. Poldek had continued to pester Steven Spielberg about the proposed movie of *Schindler's List*. 'Don't let me die before you make this film!' he told the director. 'Just make Thomas's story, Steven, and you will have an Oscar for Oskar!'

In mid-1991 Poldek phoned Keneally, jubilantly informing him that at last Spielberg was going to make the film. When Keneally met the director again in early 1992, Spielberg reminded him that he had once said, 'Just film the bloody book, Steven!' Keneally could not remember saying it; he still did not quite believe that the director really intended to proceed.

32

Some Rich Grazing Amongst Other Humans and Events

On the first day of filming in Kraków, Steven Spielberg took a wreath to lay at Auschwitz. 'What I felt was anger,' he said. 'I no longer feel grief. Just anger. This has affected me more deeply than any other film. Every day in Poland I was aware that as a Jew I couldn't have been in Europe 50 years ago.' Spielberg was as haunted, in the making of *Schindler's List*, as Keneally had been in writing the book. Spielberg had considered filming in Spain, Hungary or Britain, but Poldek was insistent: 'You have to film in the streets where the blood, the Jewish blood, was spilled.'[1]

Spielberg admitted that he had been frightened of undertaking the film. Members of his family had died in the Holocaust, and some surviving relatives had sought refuge after the war in the United States. His first concept of numbers came from an Auschwitz survivor who would roll up his sleeve and show a tattoo: 'This is a 4, this is a 7, this is a 2,' and so on. In a sixth-grade classroom the boy Spielberg watched a documentary, *The Twisted Cross*, which included images of the Holocaust that left a deep impression on him. His grandmother taught English to Holocaust survivors, whose stories he heard.

The book *Schindler's List* was given to Spielberg by his early mentor, Sidney Sheinberg, president of Universal/Music Corporation of America (MCA). The director has recalled:

> What appealed to me about the book was that it was so factual, so detached. It was the detached look at the Holocaust that didn't try to eke out an emotional cry from me ... It was a dry, dry book. I thought if I could take the approach with a motion picture, I could present it almost like a series of events and facts and dates. And the emotionality would be much stronger.
>
> I came to realise, the reason I came to make the movie, is that I have never in my life told the truth in a movie. My effort as a moviemaker has been to create something that couldn't possibly happen. So people could leave their lives and have an adventure and then come back to earth and drive home. That was one of the things I thought: if I'm going to tell the truth for the first time, it should be about this subject. Not about divorce or parents and children, but about this.[2]

Spielberg's copy of Keneally's book was annotated and underlined, just like Fred Schepisi's copy of *The Chant of Jimmie Blacksmith*. In the same way that he had pursued that book, so Schepisi repeatedly asked Keneally for *Schindler's List*, but Keneally did not budge. Schepisi has recalled that he arrived at Sean Connery's sixtieth birthday party, in August 1990, 'a little happy'. Spielberg was there, and Schepisi pinned him against the wall, saying, 'You shall not make *Schindler's List*! You are not the right person to do it!' Spielberg responded, 'Oh, really? Who is?' The immediate reply from Schepisi was, 'I am! I am the right person to do it and if you don't let me do it I'll come and I'll haunt you every day!'

Spielberg wanted to know why he was not the right person for the job. Schepisi told him: 'You'll crane shots, you'll emphasise everything. Something like this needs to be ground level; it needs to have things happen to people to whom you least expect it to happen and when you least expect it. Violence isn't structured – it just happens.'

Spielberg asked around to find out about the upstart Schepisi. He then invited the Australian director to meet him and talk about his proposed casting choices. Schepisi took up where he had left off at the party: 'You've got to be kidding! You shouldn't be doing it!' According to Schepisi, when Spielberg was setting up some shots in the film, he was heard to say on the set, 'I'd like to use a cherry picker here, but Fred Schepisi didn't like it!'[3]

'In all honesty,' Schepisi admitted, 'it had to be someone with Spielberg's reputation and contacts. He was a star. You knew he could raise the money. It was never going to happen for me! *Schindler's List* is a really good film.'

After attending the referendum in Eritrea in April 1993, Keneally visited the film set in Poland and left feeling positive. Nan Talese recalled: 'Even when Tom was still in Poland and watching the film being made [and watching the 'dailies', the edited takes shot the previous day], he told me, "Young Steven has really made quite a good film!"'

The film had endorsement from the start when President Bill Clinton and his wife, Hillary, attended its premiere in Washington. Keneally was there, having left his mother's eightieth birthday party early to make it just in time. Elsie and Tom senior had moved to a unit at 29 Lagoon Street, Narrabeen, a northern Sydney suburb closer to their older son's home at Bilgola Beach; their younger son, Johnny, lived at Gladesville, an inner north-western suburb.

Johnny and his wife, Jane, were rearing their family of five children – Ben, Tim, Kate, Josie and Patrick – while Johnny was advancing in his medical career, ultimately heading the Anaesthetics Department at the Children's Hospital, Westmead. Johnny, among diverse interests, was an expert in the serial numbers of locomotives. Spielberg once said to Keneally: 'Tell your brother that all the engines used in this film are correct and of the period.'[4]

It was a special time in Keneally's life when he escorted his parents to the Sydney premiere of *Schindler's List*. Many times he felt he had failed them, but now he could take pride in sharing one of the highlights of his career with them, and enjoy the opportunities he had to ease their lives with holidays and invitations that would have been unthinkable 'back in the day' at Homebush.

The film was voted Best Film of 1993 by the New York Film Critics' Circle and the Los Angeles Film Critics' Association. It won Golden Globe awards for Best Dramatic Picture and Best Director. Then came the 66th Academy Awards, in Los Angeles. Keneally was not sure if he could stand the stress of watching the presentation on 21 March 1994, but he and Poldek both attended. Before the big event, Keneally sipped champagne at the Four Seasons Hotel in Beverly Hills, smartly dressed in a new tuxedo with gold UCI cufflinks at the wrists, and his Order of

Australia gold pin on the lapel. His daughter Jane nodded her approval. 'I think people are really going to find it difficult to tell the difference between Dad and Paul Newman tonight!'[5]

Schindler's List had been nominated for twelve Academy Awards and it won seven, including Best Director for Spielberg and Best Adapted Screenplay for Steven Zaillian. Poldek's belief in his 'great story of humanity, man to man' had now been doubly vindicated with the success of both book and film. After the ceremony he grabbed one of the Oscars that Spielberg was holding. 'What did I tell you?' he demanded. 'What *did* I tell you? An Oscar for Oskar!'

Just as the book had caused controversy in the months after the Booker Prize, so too did the movie in the hype surrounding the Academy Awards. In an article published in the *Los Angeles Times*, headlined 'For Gentiles, Too, the Holocaust is Never to be Forgotten', Keneally used a local incident to make the point that over every question of race or group hate lay the shadow of the Holocaust: 'Often, particularly in America, race hate or group hate seems rootless, as in the now famous case of the two young men who attacked a Vietnamese stroller in Laguna Beach because they thought he was gay. It did not seem that the young men had any measurable reason, any damage they could point to or quantify, to explain why they wanted to beat the hell out of either Asians or gays.'

Keneally told his readers that, 'for the moment', the Holocaust questions were associated with Spielberg's film of his book. 'As a Gentile, an Australian of Irish Catholic background, I have no hesitation in saying that the Holocaust should be talked about again and again and should not be forgotten. The reason is that the Holocaust is the most extreme version of rootless race hate in European history ...' Keneally declared that he had been amazed and appalled at Hitler's 'final solution', but at the time he was writing the article he was amazed and appalled that Jews such as Spielberg were being blamed for remembering, 'for reviving the memory that is not only Jewish but human'.[6]

After the film was screened at the Norris Theatre, University of Southern California, the campus newspaper, the *Daily Trojan*, reported that Keneally had spoken to a crowd of 1000 people. There were angry responses from a few people who had read the article in the *Los Angeles Times*, among them the criticism, 'You're out of your depth ...'[7]

Keneally had many opportunities to front an audience through a lecture tour organised by Carol Bruckner, an agent with the International Creative Management Agency. Often it was a double act with Poldek, which both men enjoyed. It was also lucrative; for example, the Atlanta Jewish Community Center was prepared to pay a fee of $12,500 plus first-class domestic air travel and accommodation.[8]

In 1994 Keneally celebrated the thirtieth anniversary of his writing career – which had started with *The Place at Whitton* – at the *Northern Herald* Bookoccino Literary Luncheon at La Palma Restaurant, Palm Beach. In April 1998 he was honoured when Channel Nine featured him on *This Is Your Life*. The program included a tribute from Senator Edward Kennedy, whom Keneally first met in 1987 when he was seeking support for the Eritrean cause. Kennedy had also expressed an interest in *The Great Shame* and acknowledged the copy sent: 'I'm delighted to have a copy and I look forward very much to reading about the Larkins, the Kenealys, the Meaghers, and the other giants of those extraordinary times. You've certainly whetted my appetite well!'[9]

Keneally was now moving in high places, including the White House, to which he was invited for dinner. He stayed at the Willard Hotel in Washington, described in *Searching for Schindler* as 'the most resonatingly famous of all Washington hotels where Thomas Francis Meagher, one of the Australian convicts I was researching, had always stayed'. He had packed what he thought was his new Armani dinner suit, but discovered that, due to his colour blindness, he had packed a navy blue one instead. The staff of the Willard – 'so associated with presidents, generals, writers and other riffraff' – quickly arranged a hired suit.

President Clinton, according to his Australian guest, had 'a campaigner's capacity to fix you with his eye and to engage you . . . as if you were somehow the focus of the room. He possessed a capacity, that is, to convince you of the special relationship he had with you. I had seen this in other men before. Bob Hawke, Australian prime minister, had the same talent.'

At the height of this era of recognition and acclaim, Keneally commented: 'I do lead an extremely active life, politically, socially and personally. I have some rich grazing amongst other humans and events.'[10]

His family was enjoying the opportunities too. Margaret was an enthusiastic fellow traveller for part of her father's research trip to Ireland for *Now and in Time to Be*. She also helped with the research for *The Great Shame* and *Flying Hero Class*. Margaret had decided against law and, with an inclination to being a novelist herself one day, pursued a career as a journalist. She worked as a junior public affairs officer for the Australian Consulate-General at the Rockefeller Center in New York, before moving to Dublin, where she became a journalist for the *Irish Times*. Then she returned to Sydney, working for the *Daily Telegraph* and later as a producer for Radio 2UE.

Margaret married Craig Coverdale in 1998 at St Francis of Assisi Catholic Church, Paddington, with a reception afterwards at Pruniers in Woollahra. Keneally found it impossible to restrict his speech to the five-minute limit. Margaret and Craig have two children, Rory Thomas and Alexandra Judith.

Jane, who assisted her father with his correspondence at times in the hectic 1990s, also joined him for trips and celebrity events. Keneally dedicated a travel book, *The Place Where Souls Are Born: A Journey to the Southwest*, to her: 'To my daughter Jane, natural traveller and buoyant companion.' She completed a Master of Arts (Film and Television) degree at the Australian Film, Television and Radio School in Sydney. She married Eddie Cockrell, a US film critic, in Central Park, New York, in 2005. The ceremony was conducted by Keneally's friend Father Pat Connor, whom he had once described as 'the best priest we ever had'. Jane and Eddie have established careers with the Big Picture Film Festival, a social justice–themed film event, for which Keneally is an ambassador. They have two children, Clementine Ann and Augustus Kramer.

For the Keneally family, time together at the Bilgola home (where Sparkplug the cat and other resident felines such as Aurora and Whisky Bylines also lived over the years) was becoming harder to arrange. Keneally had VIP cards for various sporting events and had taken up cross-country skiing. He was invited to be a guest on the ship *Queen Elizabeth 2*, once for a World Cruise in 1998 and again for the Millennium World Cruise in 2000, in return for which he had speaking engagements on board. He had an arrangement with United Airlines in the United States for international upgrade certificates in exchange for short travel articles.

In an annual report for UCI, Keneally detailed his various accomplishments in 1994, a typical year: teaching, completing and revising *A River Town* and a memoir provisionally called *A Year in the Antipodes*, writing articles for various newspapers and researching *The Great Shame*. Under 'public service' he listed many speaking engagements, including a speech at the US Embassy in Vienna in honour of Spielberg. He delivered thirty-nine lectures throughout the United States, and a variety of television and radio interviews there and in Great Britain and Australia.

His list of honours was impressive: Fellow, American Academy of Arts and Sciences, October 1993; Doctorate *Honoris Causa*, University College Dublin, April 1994; Doctorate *Honoris Causa*, Fairleigh Dickinson University, New Jersey, June 1994; Humanitarian Award, Democratic Party of Orange County, April 1994; Scripter Award, University of Southern California, February 1994; Micah Award, Jewish Community Center, Orange County, 1994; and the New York Public Library Literary Lion Medal, November 1994.[11]

Keneally also included on the list his directorship of the Australian Republican Movement, and a dinner speech for the Republican Movement in Adelaide in July 1994. In an article published in *New University*, a UCI bulletin, Keneally was reported as leaving his university post to contribute full-time to what he then called 'an ad hoc political movement' in Australia.

33

Have I Lost the Plot?

When Keneally was a child, his maternal grandfather, Mick Coyle, had embarrassed him by not standing in the Vogue Picture Palace at Homebush for the national anthem, 'God Save the King' – the usual prelude to a film screening. George VI was the reigning monarch; his successor, Elizabeth II, for whom Keneally wanted the anthem played at his production of *Julius Caesar* at Springwood, was also subject to Old Mick's scorn.

On Christmas Day at the Keneally home in Homebush, Old Mick refused to listen to the Queen's Christmas message on the wireless and fought with Keneally's Aunt Annie, Tom senior's sister, over her wish to listen. While Aunt Annie listened loyally, Old Mick did his best to disrupt the broadcast with references to 'the Saxon yoke', 'German interlopers', 'the potato famine' and 'the Curse of Cromwell'. Old Mick Coyle believed that all things English were bad, and all things Irish good.

While Keneally was ready to stand up for the Queen at Homebush and at Springwood, his ideas about a republic started to change when he was at Manly. One of his lecturers, Patrick Ford, had been writing a book on the development of the Labor Party, and he had engaged a group of students, including Keneally, to search copies of the *Freemans' Journal* of the 1890s for references to Cardinal Moran's connection with the maritime strike of 1890 and the Labor Leagues, and to the response of the Catholic community.[1]

'I suppose this was the new beginning of my very secular fascination with politics and Republicanism,' Keneally wrote in *Our Republic*, published in 1993. 'I was politically and nationalistically stimulated by the traces I found in the old newsprint of this extraordinary workers' initiative. I was excited too by the idea that Cardinal Moran had supported the strikers in 1890. His cardinal's biretta and stole were encased in a glass fronted cavity by the chapel. The relics struck me as heroic, champion-of-the-people stuff. In many ways Moran was that. In some ways he was the usual closed-minded sectarian of his day. But I liked his bravery in 1890.'

Keneally emulated Old Mick's stance when he served for a time in the Commonwealth Military Forces artillery unit. 'I appalled the Regimental Sergeant Major by asking if I could take an oath to Australia instead of the Queen. He told me to shut up and not be such a silly bastard.'

In Australia, conflicting loyalties to the Pope and to the King or Queen were accepted. Protestants were the main players in society, while Catholics, by and large, were regarded with suspicion, if not outright hate. By the time Keneally wrote *Our Republic*, the influence of the papacy had declined and most Protestants were reconciled with their Catholic neighbours, and vice versa. The British monarchy, though, still claimed the allegiance of most Australians.

Keneally might be accused of taking up the cause of republicanism because of the lasting influences of Old Mick and his Catholic upbringing. A sectarian childhood could not be denied, but he had long since abandoned his allegiance to the Catholic 'tribe'. Although devoted to his Irish inheritance, he also rejected claims that his republican beliefs were linked to that. He questioned whether the Irish background of any Australians influenced their attitude towards a republic. He argued that in the first 150 years or so of Australian history, when Australians of Irish background were the underclass of Australia, it was up to them to prove that they were Australians and the equal of any man or woman of English background. War veterans like Uncle Johnnie, Tom senior's brother, and Max Martin, his brother-in-law, had gone into battle with that belief.

As the republican debate intensified in the last years of the twentieth century, even Prime Minister Paul Keating, whose republican preference was never in doubt, was derided for his Irish background in some British newspapers. The *Sunday Times* on 1 March 1992 wrote of Keating: 'Like many of Irish-Australian descent, he may have ancestral hang-ups about the British nothing can remove ...' Keneally was similarly denigrated, 'as if the very fact of Irish derivation made us unfit – as against Anglo-Australians – to make up our minds on, and be players in Australia's destiny'.[2]

Keneally pointed to the membership of the Australian Republican Movement (ARM), for which he was the first chairman, to prove his point: most of its members had no Irish affiliation. They included Donald Horne (whose 1964 book *The Lucky Country* put the case for republicanism to its many readers), fashion designer Jenny Kee, lawyer (and now politician) Malcolm Turnbull and writer Faith Bandler. 'Of all the committee of the Australian Republican Movement, only [broadcaster] Geraldine Doogue and myself have any connection by descent with Ireland,' Keneally said in a debate on the topic, 'and we envisage an Australian republic, a mature entity, and we have no interest in settling perceived historic scores.'[3]

ARM held its first meeting in December 1990 in Sydney. Its existence had begun the previous year, when Keneally went to lunch at the home of Neville Wran, a former premier of New South Wales, and his wife, Jill Hickson. Wran broached the subject of republicanism and proposed a small committee of visible and dedicated people who would work towards the establishment of a republic by 2001, the centenary year of Australia's federation as a nation. The committee needed prominent republican citizens who could not be dismissed as 'fringe ratbags' by the public they wanted to reach.

Keneally was the committee's reluctant chairman. He had not enjoyed the role at the Australian Society of Authors, and earlier in 1990 had refused an offer to be chairman of the Australia Council. Apart from anything else, he doubted his ability to lead a group that included seasoned campaigners such as Wran and Horne. 'My only organisational capacity,' he told Wran, 'is that of being a spokesman.' Wran replied, 'That's exactly what we want.'

The first task was the recruiting of foundation members. Keneally enlisted actor Bryan Brown, writer Peter Carey and his then wife, Alison Summers, film director Fred Schepisi and playwright David Williamson.

Some of those approached were republicans but did not join, including the singer Peter Garrett, whose primary cause was the environment. Others were worried that aligning themselves publicly with republicanism might adversely affect their social or commercial interests.

Keneally himself was anxious about the possible effect on his book sales, and also on a business venture in which he was involved with friends Iain Finlay and Trish Clark and others. They had invested in a guesthouse, Echoes, at Katoomba in the Blue Mountains. Echoes opened on St Patrick's Day 1991, and it was slow work building up a clientele. The other concern for the supporters of the republican movement was the possibility of physical violence against themselves or their families, although ARM hoped to achieve its aims by friendly discourse and referendum.

After the launch of ARM, Keneally was uncertain how much friendly discourse he might expect when he next went to Brookvale Oval to watch his rugby league team, Manly-Warringah. Rugby league was a proletarian game, but Brookvale was located in a conservative region. None of his 'crowd' voiced antagonism. In fact, one said, 'You reckon you want to say goodbye to them [the Royal Family] with a kiss. I don't agree with that. I think they're a pack of bludgers. Tell 'em to go to buggery.' The wife of one of the club's committee members had a softer response: 'I'm so pleased you said that we'd leave with a kiss. I think that's the right way.'

Keneally had joined the Narrabeen branch of the Australian Labor Party in 1972. Australia had been under conservative government since 1949, and Labor's Gough Whitlam had boldly declared that change was needed. When Whitlam stood up on 13 November 1972 to deliver his famous 'It's Time' speech, Keneally was in the front row. Whitlam had a decisive win in the federal election held on 2 December 1972.

Keneally's participation in the Labor Party was limited – as ever, he was busy with multiple projects – but he established friendships with many prominent Labor politicians, including Whitlam and his wife, Margaret. On one occasion, during a party held at Bungan Beach on Sydney's North Shore, where the surf was rough, Whitlam announced that he was going to have a swim. Margaret said, 'No you are not, Gough! We've already lost one prime minister that way!' She was referring to Harold Holt, Australia's seventeenth prime minister, who had disappeared in the surf, and was presumed drowned, in 1967.[4]

Keneally delivered the McKell Lecture in Sydney in December 1984. William McKell had been premier of New South Wales in the 1940s and later governor-general, working closely with two wartime prime ministers, John Curtin and Ben Chifley. McKell was close to Jack Lang, a favoured politician in the Keneally household. Tom senior and Elsie attended their son's lecture, at which Keneally told his audience that McKell was one of 'the Labor demi-gods of childhood'.[5]

Keneally was for a while also a member of an organisation called Citizens For Democracy, where he shared the platform with Donald Horne and Lionel Bowen, a former Labor attorney-general and deputy prime minister. The group organised 'Republic Day: Towards a New Constitution' on 11 November 1979 at the Sydney Town Hall, an event at which historian Manning Clark and Gough Whitlam spoke. The date 11 November 1975 had particular significance for the latter, being the day that Governor-General John Kerr had, as the Queen's representative in Australia, dismissed Whitlam's government.

Keneally corresponded with Labor Prime Minister Paul Keating, who took the republican cause into parliament, a risky political manoeuvre. Keating set up a Republic Advisory Committee in 1993, with Malcolm Turnbull as chairman. In 1995 Keating wrote to Keneally. He referred to the writer as a rugby league 'silvertail', but was glad of his participation 'in the struggle against the Grey Dwarf (this is such an apt name that I hope you don't mind if I use it myself some time) . . . Having a doughty warrior like yourself in the lists as well will do a great deal for the fighting spirit and capability of Labor.'[6]

The Grey Dwarf was John Howard, then leader of the Liberal Party, whom Keneally confronted on the republican issue in a BBC broadcast, and also in 'The Great Debate: Should Australia Become a Republic and Does the Fact that We Are Irish Influence Our Thinking on This Matter?', organised by the Tipperary-Australian Association and held at the University of Sydney. Howard's main argument was that the monarchy had given Australia decades of stability; Keneally echoed Turnbull's belief that the country's political stability was due in large measure to the political creativeness of Australian people.

Keneally described Howard as 'under-gifted' in a letter to Senator Edward Kennedy, whose help he sought when he wanted an invitation to a dinner in honour of President Clinton and his wife, Hillary, to be hosted by Howard in 1996. He told Kennedy that the Clintons' visit was significant for both countries and that he would love to see them on his own turf. 'Our crowd – Labor – are out of power at the moment,' Keneally explained to Kennedy. 'Though the present Prime Minister has no particular malice towards me, we *have* debated face to face on Australia becoming a republic and I'm not an obvious choice to bid to the table where the President will be honoured, and most interesting of all, the First Lady will speak.'

Keneally did attend the luncheon in honour of the Clintons, held on 20 November 1996. Clinton, having accepted a toast to himself as head of state of the United States, then proposed a toast to the Queen, the head of state of Australia. 'Though he and the State Department were on absolutely secure constitutional grounds in so doing,' Keneally wrote to Kennedy, 'they served to point up the absurdity of our present constitutional arrangement. I was but one of many who withheld the fine Australian chardonnay from our lips for ten seconds before drinking perceptibly but without impropriety simply to the community of the Australian people.'[7]

In his speech at the opening of ARM, Keneally argued that a republic was not a denial of Australian identity but a confirmation of it. A basic model of the proposed republic would be made and ultimately finalised by public debate. Meanwhile, Keneally said, it was time 'we did ourselves the honour of finding from within our own resources and from amongst ourselves a Head of State whose identity is entirely Australian and does not depend for its legitimacy on anyone other than us and anything other than our institutions'.

Keneally was not personally antagonistic to Queen Elizabeth II, and had taken pleasure in accepting an offer from the *National Times* to travel with the press corps that followed a royal visit to Australia in 1977. 'Travelling With Two Aging Icons' was a lighthearted article in which Keneally related his anxiety, as he waited in a reception line at Government House, that the Queen may not have liked what she had read of his work. 'What was soon obvious was that the Queen had not read any of my books. It had caused me much sweat in the hallway to imagine the crowned head frowning over a copy of *A Dutiful Daughter* ...' Keneally liked the lively, companionable Prince Philip, Duke of Edinburgh, and appreciated the Queen's wry humour. He rather pitied her for the unreality of the demands put upon her, and in the end declared that the highlight of the assignment for him was 'the fine and amusing company of the girls and boys on the press bus'.[8]

In London during 1992 to promote one of his books, Keneally was invited by Melvyn Bragg to talk on his Radio 3 program, *Start of the Week*. The subject of Australia's republican debate came up and Keneally was surprised at the level of sympathy or indifference to the prospect of an Australian republic. He told listeners that the 'goodbye to Great Britain' would be said with 'the ambiguous nudge of affection which characterises the relationship between the two nations'.

The final form of an Australian republic was constantly debated. Would there be a president of Australia? A snap poll was conducted at ARM's second anniversary dinner, at Parliament House on 16 October 1992, asking who its preferred president would be. Trevor Kennedy suggested Gough Whitlam, Bryan Brown put forward David Hill (managing director of the Australian Broadcasting Commission), Keneally favoured Faith Bandler or Jenny Kee, and Malcolm Turnbull was not sure but thought it should be Tom Keneally.[9]

ARM was well represented at a Constitutional Convention in January 1998, but Keneally missed it because he was ill. By the time of the convention he had handed over the chairmanship of the organisation to Turnbull. He was optimistic about the future: 'It looks as if we'll have a Republic by the Olympics in 2000 or by 2001,' he wrote to Nan Talese. 'I would like to see Australia as a republic hosting the Olympic Games.'[10] Many Australians, including his brother-in-law Max Martin, had long decorated their homes with a Eureka flag or a similar Australian republican flag, and plans were now made to unfurl ARM's banner on the top of Mount Kosciuszko, Australia's highest peak, in August 1999.

'I got a call from Tom's daughter a few months before the referendum,' Keneally's friend Bryan Brown said. 'She told me that her dad was going to Thredbo to hang the Australian flag on Kosciuszko. Would I like to join them? I jumped on board ... Tom had us all charged up ... unfortunately it was a day of extreme wind and cold and snow. After about two hours of not being able to see our hands in front of our faces, the guide suggested that we give up – it was too dangerous. Not a chance. Tom was our leader. Some of us continued to within 250 metres of the top and we had to stop. It was very disappointing.'[11] The attempt was not repeated.

The opinion polls looked promising, but on 6 November 1999, when Australians were asked to vote on the establishment of a republic, with the Queen and governor-general being replaced as head of state by a president, who would be appointed by a two-thirds majority of the members of the Commonwealth parliament, the majority said no. It was not a crushing defeat for ARM: 45.13 per cent of the voters had said yes.

Voters were more adamant about the second question on the referendum paper, which suggested the insertion of a preamble into the nation's constitution: 60.66 per cent voted against the proposal. Prime Minister Howard had released his preferred draft preamble on 23 March 1999, while Keneally and others also put forward versions. Howard had said that he would not support a new preamble that went beyond simple recognition of prior occupation by Indigenous people. His draft preamble included the statement: 'Since time immemorial our land has been inhabited by Aborigines and Torres Strait Islanders, who are honoured for their ancient and continuing cultures.'[12]

Since the failed referendum, Keneally has not had any active involvement with ARM, but he has been 'wheeled out occasionally as a kind of venerable elder.'[13] He established a $10,000 Republic Prize to recognise a work of fiction, poetry, history or biography which best exemplified the good intentions of the ARM. It was awarded annually from 1996, with Paul Kelly's book *1975* being the first winner. Keneally devoted his PLR payments – $16,000 in 1996 – to fund the prize and its administration. He pledged his PLR till 1999, after which he would take it back 'for his old age.'[14]

When Prince Charles and his wife, Camilla, Duchess of Cornwall, visited Sydney in November 2012, Keneally admitted that ARM had treated the couple acrimoniously in the heat of the republican campaign. The Royal Family was under siege in the 1990s, and ARM had used this against the monarchists, arguing that Australia would not tolerate Charles as king and Camilla as queen consort. 'We tended to look upon monarchists as anachronisms,' Keneally admitted, 'and you can't do that to your fellow citizens. And I was as guilty as anyone . . . in the remains of my youth, I used to love to rile people up.'

In 2012 Keneally met the Duchess at a reception at St James Palace, London. The meeting occurred, he claimed, 'out of pure villainy by my publisher', who had asked him if he would like to meet Camilla. 'I do reassure all good republicans that I was hiding in a corner ... but even a republican yobbo can't very well, being in their own house, having gone there, say no.' The Duchess was interested in Keneally's writing and congratulated him on the reviews of *The Daughters of Mars*. He found Camilla charming, and said he had 'a weak spot' for Charles, heir to the throne. 'First of all Charles said it [a republic] was always up to Australians, which was constitutionally true. He never seemed to be appalled by the idea, and he is a trier.' In what might be interpreted as a volte-face, Keneally also said: 'I think monarchists are to be respected, not mocked. I mean, you get these wisdoms once you get into the 70s.'[15]

In May 2013 the ABC television program *Lateline* raised the republican question with speakers including Turnbull and Keneally. Turnbull stated firmly that 'we will win this battle, we will become a republic, when we have succeeded in engaging all of the Australian people'. Keneally said that the desire to make Australia a republic was symbolic and constitutional. 'I also believe it will give us finally the sense of identity and that it will institute a period of creativity, confidence and trust from our neighbours as well.'[16]

Twenty years had elapsed between that statement and the publication of *Our Republic*, Keneally's book about ARM, but its author still had not decided to his own satisfaction the form a republic should take. The book's blurb referred to it as 'a blueprint for Australia's future', yet its readers were left in doubt as to how a republic in Australia would work – the blueprint was incomplete. This omission was immediately taken up by reviewers, including Tony Abbott, a future Liberal prime minister. In his review, Abbott wrote: 'The republican case boils down to the proposition that we would be a more cohesive, dynamic nation under a president. By what mental gymnastics a process which bitterly divides the Australian community can produce a more united society is never made clear ...'

Abbott's review was published under the scornful heading 'Uncle Tom's Republic', and was published in the *Adelaide Review*, edited by the pro-monarchy Christopher Pearson, who was decidedly anti-Keneally.

On Adelaide radio Pearson had derided Keneally as 'a burnt-out' novelist who was pursuing the republican cause as a means of rediscovering 'a role for himself as a man of public affairs'. Keneally had refuted that charge, telling Pearson that his opinion of Keneally's writing was not shared by the *New York Times Book Review*, and that Pearson's accusation was typical of the 'normal small town literary malice which journals like yours exhibit'.[17]

Some of Abbott's comments are harder to refute:

> At his best, Keneally can penetrate close to the heart of human experience. His *Three Cheers for the Paraclete*, for instance, has helped keep two generations of seminarians more-or-less sane. Tom's personal story has some charm and insight. But this work [*Our Republic*] is constantly jumping genre, from autobiography to Constitutional history to political polemic and never really succeeds at any level . . . it is an extraordinarily self-absorbed story . . . On we go, voyeurs to one man's emotional and political meanderings, eavesdroppers to his numerous meetings with national and international glitterati, via extensive detours . . .[18]

Conservative academic Imre Salusinszky went further in a review titled 'Mad Detour on Republican Pilgrimage', taking Keneally and his publisher, Heinemann, to task for shoddy writing and editing: the book was 'littered with eccentricities of style, diction and grammar'. Salusinszky proceeded to give various examples of the overuse of adjectives, long and confusing sentences and poor punctuation.[19]

Salusinszky continued his attack in an article titled 'Thomas Keneally: My Part in His Downfall' and published in *Quadrant*, the journal that had gone to great lengths to damage Keneally over *Season in Purgatory*. Salusinszky's provocative piece included comments about an article written by Keneally and published in the *Weekend Australian*. Its title, 'Critical Correctness', had this lead: 'Tom Keneally feels that criticism of his work has been coloured by the belief in literary circles that he has "lost the plot". Here he attempts to set the record straight.'

Keneally's decision to hit back at his critics was prompted by a review of his book *Jacko*, written by Michael Sharkey for the *Weekend Australian*.

'Keneally is trying too hard,' Sharkey had suggested, 'to convince us he has what one back-cover commentator assures us is "one of the finest moral imaginations in literature". No one doubts the calibre of Keneally's moral perceptions. But one can criticise his technique. I doubt whether the novel would be lapped up by a publisher if it bore anyone else's name on the title page.'[20]

Sharkey's review was thoughtful and thorough, although Keneally understandably took exception to its opening gambit: that 'many of Thomas Keneally's regular readers appear to think that, somewhere between *Bring Larks and Heroes* and *Women of the Inner Sea*, he has lost the plot'. A 1991 *Australian* review by Salusinszky of *Flying Hero Class* would have hurt Keneally more. There, Salusinszky had spoken of the author's 'deathly treatment' of moral dilemmas, and the book's 'priceless dialogue', absence of excitement and 'sheer wordiness'.[21]

At the time Keneally was lashing out, he had just been inducted as a fellow of the American Academy of Arts and Sciences in Boston and he would attend the premiere of *Schindler's List* in New York a couple of weeks after his article was published. Perhaps it was the knowledge that he was being feted in the United States that prompted his indignant outburst against Australians who did not extend him the same admiration.

'In that supposed period of plot-loss,' he wrote, 'my work has been seriously published by a string of foreign publishers, including British and American as well as Australian and has been seriously sold and criticised overseas. This, I have to say on basic professional grounds, doesn't happen to people who have lost the plot.' Keneally then listed his awards and honours, and asked, 'Are the Americans and British right in their general critical support, or have I lost the plot?'[22]

It was a pity that Salusinszky's article had such a misleading title, but perhaps that was the work of the *Quadrant* editor. The article was a fair critique, if unnecessarily derogatory in places. Salusinszky was right in saying that Keneally seemed to be forgetting the mass of positive criticism that he had enjoyed in Australia, and that he ran the risk of implying that British and American critics had superior taste to their Australian counterparts.[23]

Barry Oakley, literary editor for the *Australian*, replied to Keneally's complaint:

> Tom Keneally is quite wrong to place Michael Sharkey's review of *Jacko*, his last novel, within a context of provincial envy and resentment. I wouldn't assign a book to a reviewer if I believed he or she would respond in so constricted and spiritless a way. I have enough faith in Michael Sharkey – and in Imre Salusinszky, who unfavourably reviewed Tom Keneally's previous book – to know that their responses, as well as being considered, are also honestly felt and unmalicious. That's why I send books to them: I like their openness and directness.[24]

Today, Keneally still disagrees with Oakley's assessment of his writers. He was not suggesting that Australian critics were inferior, only that biased reviewers were frequently chosen. Keneally was living a favoured life, admittedly, after working extremely hard for it. In America in the 1990s he could command a figure of $8500 for giving a university lecture or speaking at a dinner or reception, with accommodation and travel costs provided. His Australian agent, Jill Hickson, was negotiating high fees for his contributions in writing and personal appearances. In 2000 he received $5000 to give an after-dinner presentation on '*The Great Shame*: The Irish Myth' on St Patrick's Day, 17 March, to the Sydney chapter of the Young Presidents' Organisation.[25] This is not to say that he did not also speak and give freely at fundraising and special-purpose events. He has always been generous with his time, his money and his name.

In the public life he generally relished, Keneally was constantly under scrutiny; like many other prominent people, he had to live with censure as well as commendation. To walk freely was an unrealistic expectation, and as he got older he took the critics less seriously. 'I ignore them now,' he says. 'I once wanted them all to like me, which was a vanity.'

Peter Pierce gave a more balanced view of Keneally in *Australian Melodramas: Thomas Keneally's Fiction* (1995). This book was launched at an Association for the Study of Australian Literature (ASAL) conference in Adelaide by Shirley Walker, then a senior lecturer in Australian literature at the University of New England, and president of ASAL. Walker thought she had a good relationship with Keneally and in her speech told a story about a previous ASAL conference they'd attended:

'A very long time ago I had written an article on Tom's fiction, something about the special agonies of being a woman, but he didn't hold it against me and, forgiven and forgiving, we proceeded to the dance floor.'[26] Walker's summary of Pierce's book was brisk but appreciative. It was 'a totally satisfying book, passionate and convincing as all good criticism is, yet scholarly and analytic at the same time'. She sat beside Keneally quite affably at the post-launch dinner.

A few days after the launch, Keneally wrote to Walker, telling her that he found her speech:

> . . . excruciatingly embarrassing as any sensitive human would. What in God's name other than unadulterated malice and a taste for bullying caused you to read out aloud [Patrick] White's insults and slanders as if I would enjoy them, or as if the audience could get anything from it all but a belly laugh? . . . And why should every participant in the process – editors, publishers, critics – go praised and unmocked except the subject himself? Again, would you have presumed to speak as you did that night against other Australian writers? Would you have been so belittling of David Malouf, Peter Carey or whomsoever?
>
> . . . What I found was someone who reiterated the same dreary furphies and low jokes as ever, and then after giving her half-hearted improvement award, retired from the podium delighted with her effort. I tell you without any ambiguity that I found it the most depressing night of my Australian literary existence. What I sniffed in the air was not your concern and interest but your determined contempt . . .[27]

To Walker it seemed, in the light of what she had said in her speech, that Keneally was railing at her about a completely different address and person. The only thing to which he could rightfully have taken exception was her reading out of White's cruel comments, but White was notoriously nasty to people, even those who regarded him as a friend. Walker, in her reply to Keneally, said she was 'totally bowled over, astonished, by its contents'. She told him that her intention had been to give an overwhelming endorsement of Pierce's book. The response that she'd had from others to her speech was positive, including that from Pierce.

'I was especially outraged by White's personal comments,' she told Keneally. 'These indicate not only his spiteful bitchiness but also the way in which we, the Irish and the descendants of the Irish, are denigrated not only in religious and racial terms, but also in class terms. I made this quite clear.' She apologised to Keneally for quoting White's remarks directly, but added that it was the only aspect of the speech that she regretted.[28]

Walker invited Keneally to write to her again after he had read a transcript of her speech, but he did not do so. They were on the same panel at the Byron Bay Writers' Festival in 2012, and Walker said to Keneally, 'Look, Tom, I'm sorry I upset you years ago.' He replied, 'Yes, I was a prick, wasn't I?' Walker did not argue with that, but she was quite touched by his moment of self-revelation. Recalling the exchange in 2015, Keneally says: 'I do regret not answering Shirley's letter.'

Keneally was impulsive and sometimes gave way to pique hastily, without due cause or consideration for the consequences. Like his father, he was quick to 'call someone on'. The outbursts could only harm his professional standing. Some of his friends, knowing a cheerful, even-tempered man, were surprised when they occasionally saw anger get the better of him. Terry Moran, Keneally's friend at NYU, recalled a reception at the Australian Consulate: 'The Consul-General said, when introduced to Tom, "I hope you notice that in your honour I am wearing the proper colours." He was wearing black and tan and Tom went ballistic. He said "That's like telling a Jew that you're wearing storm trooper colours. Do you know how offensive that is?" And he was just so angry.' Keneally made peace with the Consul-General some years later.

There was another occasion in a restaurant when Moran and his wife, Elise, saw Keneally go red in the face with anger. One of the Morans' friends, an Englishwoman, had a very superior attitude towards the Irish. 'She riled Tom up ... he was so angry that he got up and left the restaurant,' Moran said. 'Tom was talking about his wife's great-grandmother who had been transported – Val gave the impression that she thought such people were Irish trash. Tom called me the next day from a plane heading for California to apologise.'

Anyone with a cause can get angry when it is mocked or maligned. In the same way, when work is undervalued or misjudged, anger is the usual reaction. Fred Schepisi remembers that someone asked Keneally,

'What do you do?' Keneally answered, 'I'm a writer.' The inquirer was not satisfied and thought Keneally had misunderstood. 'What do you really do?' Keneally, Schepisi says, was irascible. 'After that Tom always referred to that man as "Camel's Puke".'

Keneally said when talking about Charles and Camilla, 'I used to love to rile people up.' Perhaps people like Salusinszky liked to rile him up, too. Keneally had a quick temper, but his anger dissipated just as quickly. The trick, for him, was not to dash off hasty letters or make sharp replies. His only real defence, as he already knew, was to keep writing, and probably to decide, as some other notable writers have done, never to read the reviews.

34

The Nether Regions of the West Wing

Many Keneally books were plotted during the long walks he took along the beaches and around the headlands of Sydney's Pittwater and Palm Beach peninsula. Sometimes he was observed talking into a dictaphone. At other times he would plunge into the surf, refreshing body and brain and preparing for another mind-to-manuscript marathon.

'I've often thought I'd like to make a film of the labour and birth of a Tom Keneally book,' Di Morrissey wrote in 1987.

> Others can make the movies of the novels. I wish I could capture the mysterious magical process from a friend and neighbour gnawing over subject matter until the day the physical embodiment is slapped in front of me.
>
> You generally know when conception has taken place. The solitary trudging on the beach stops as Tom disappears into the nether regions of the west wing and over a coffee break is distracted as if listening to conversations we can't hear. Occasionally he will wander in and talk about a bit he's writing like an actor rehearsing his lines, then disappear back to his desk and you feel as if you really needn't have been there.[1]

Not all books were written at the desk in the west wing. Although a nervous passenger, Keneally worked a lot on planes as he flitted about between Australia, England, Ireland and the United States. *Flying Hero Class* (1991) is about the hijacking of a plane by a group of terrorists and is noteworthy for the way its author attempts to delve into the thinking and behaviour of both the hijackers and the hijacked. The task was complicated by the need for Keneally to authentically represent the various nationalities on board the plane, especially the Palestinian terrorists and the Indigenous Australians who are on a world tour – the Barramatjura Dance Troupe.

Keneally was having trouble satisfying James Frost, his editor at Warner Books, which was publishing the book in the United States: 'Firstly, the book is intended to be a journey by a hapless everyman,' the author wrote. 'It is therefore intended to be universal . . . I want to retain a certain shadiness and mystery in the book – unknown destinations and arrivals, obscure motivations which nonetheless work . . . a few of your suggestions seem to urge me in the direction of another book, not mine.'[2] Ion Trewin was working on the UK edition of *Flying Hero Class* for Hodder & Stoughton. 'Warners are being funny about more revisions,' Keneally told him. 'I think they're berserk, but I am re-working and fine-tuning the book one more time.'

The general opinion was that the psychology of *Flying Hero Class* is absorbing, but the book lacks the suspense and drama associated with such a theme. The story, as one critic observed, becomes an 'airborne seminar on Third World politics'.[3] Keneally told interviewers: 'A hijacked aircraft is like a ghetto in the sky. There is some resistance but most people want to co-operate.' *Flying Hero Class* was launched by the Australian actress Diane Cilento, who likened Keneally to a Provençal truffle-hound: 'Let's face it, his nose for a good story is quite extraordinary.'[4]

While *Flying Hero Class* didn't become a general favourite among Keneally's readers, his next novel, *Woman of the Inner Sea*, certainly did. This time the main character is a woman, and understanding her mindset and behaviour came more readily to him. 'I never found myself in a position,' Keneally reflected about the writing of *Woman of the Inner Sea*, 'where I said to myself, "Tom, how do you reckon a woman would feel in this situation?" I believe, rightly or wrongly, that I knew . . . I didn't have to grope for what I would have considered maternal or feminine responses.'[5]

Keneally had heard an extraordinary story from a publicist in New Orleans during a book tour. 'An American woman told me a story about losing her children and then leaving everything and going into places she had never been to before, trying to change herself into the woman who had not lost her children. Then she found out certain things about the responsibility for the deaths of the children and went back, confronting the whole damn mess on the grounds where it occurred. And, of course, redeeming herself in the process.'[6] Keneally asked the woman if she would mind if he transposed her story to an Australian setting. She agreed, on the condition that her name was not revealed.

The book tells the tale of a wealthy young Sydney woman, Kate Gaffney-Kozinski, whose two children die; a tragedy that prompts her to undertake a redemptive journey to the Australian inland. Keneally lived for a while in Nyngan, in western New South Wales, researching the way that remote country pubs operate. He learnt how to pour and serve beer as Kate does when she works as a barmaid.

Woman of the Inner Sea began a pattern that would be repeated in future titles, in which Keneally made identifiable reference to people and events in Australia. It was as if he was consciously making an effort to connect in a more contemporary way with his home country. Prime Minister Bob Hawke is recognisable with 'his craggy face and avian eyes'. He has a crooked grin, 'which was worth a fortune electorally'. Keneally mentions events and places from his own experience: the abandoned soldier-settler homes in western New South Wales, still standing with old newspapers beneath the linoleum and iron bedsteads in the rooms, were familiar to him from his time working in the west as a builder's labourer.

Nan Talese thought that *Woman of the Inner Sea* was a beautiful book. 'Nan will write one of her famous letters to her list of key independent bookstores (about 100 or more stores) positioning this novel alongside of *Schindler's List*,' Amanda Urban informed Keneally. 'She seems utterly committed to revitalising your career in the US and believes that your television novel [*Jacko*] could be a winner as well . . .'[7]

A copy was sent to Hillary Clinton, who complimented the author at the premiere of *Schindler's List* in Washington. When Keneally visited the White House, he had what he later described to Edward Kennedy as 'a sort of literary-daydream experience – the First Lady discussed one of my novels she had read at some earlier stage'.[8]

Paul Taylor, reviewing *Woman of the Inner Sea*, linked it with another Keneally book that had recently been published, *The Place Where Souls Are Born*, observing that 'the novelist does his best travel-writing in fiction'.[9] *Woman of the Inner Sea* is indeed as much about the panorama of the Australian outback as it is about the woman exploring that 'inner sea'.

The British travel writer and historian Jan Morris had invited Keneally to write a book about the Four Corners, the US region where the borders of four states meet: Colorado, New Mexico, Utah and Arizona. Morris wrote in the introduction to *The Place Where Souls Are Born* that Keneally illuminated the region from a different perspective: 'He is a New Man in the southwest, bringing to its mountains, deserts and pueblos comparisons born out of the Outback and the aboriginal encampment.' The distance between the new man in America's remote places and the new woman in Australia's arid inland is not great, which makes reading the novels back-to-back an interesting experience.

Keneally first visited the south-western states of the United States in 1975–76, when he and the family camped in Colorado. His fascination with the region went back even further, to the 1940s, to Saturday afternoons at the Vogue Picture Palace in Homebush, where he watched Westerns. He was intrigued by the mesas and canyons and the ponderosa pines, and captivated by the Native American inhabitants.

The book was dismissed in a lacerating review in the *New York Review* by Robert Adams:

> Keneally is an Australian writer whose experience of the American West dates to a movie house in a suburb of Sydney where he grew up ... It's not clear that he wouldn't have done better to stay in Sydney and read a better collection of books than the potboilers and flash-in-the-pans that make up his present reading list ... With disarming frankness, Keneally describes how he picked up his information on the fly, as he drove his rented car around ... Not surprisingly, there's a good deal of the Southwest that he doesn't know about, or even suspect of existing ... Keneally's book is a shallow and careless work of journalism.[10]

Perhaps Keneally did not know enough about the Southwest of the United Sates to write about it to the satisfaction of some American critics, but he did know a lot about rugby league. If there was a spectator activity that the young Keneally enjoyed more than the Western movies, it was rugby league. From the age of three, when his father introduced him to an Eastern Suburbs player named Dave Brown, he followed the fortunes of such men slavishly. He had admired a player called Des Hasler for about ten years before meeting him. In 1992 Hasler asked if Keneally would consider writing his biography.

The man known variously as 'Dessie', 'Hasler the Dazzler' and 'Sorry' was a reticent man, but he went to Keneally's home most Wednesday winter nights for a session of questions and answers over a cup of tea. The book that Keneally wrote honours Hasler as one of Australia's best-known utility players, meaning that he could play in a range of positions. Even for someone with no interest in rugby league, *The Utility Player: The Des Hasler Story* has charm and appeal: it is an endearing picture of a player who does not big-note himself.

Keneally turned to the world of television in his next book, *Jacko*, a novel. The narrator is an author, visiting a cattle station and observing simiiar scenery to what Keneally had seen on his research trips for *Outback*. The narrator travels with a photographer, Barry Larson, who, like Garry Hansen, is killed in a helicopter accident.

The lines between real life and invention are not so much blurred in *Jacko* as constantly crossing. The author is 'allowed' to teach at New York University. The novelist and 'teacher-manqué' and his tolerant, generous wife, Maureen, live in an apartment in 'the narrow Cotton Building on the corner of East Fourth and Broadway'. The author and Maureen return to Sydney every year for at least five months, where Maureen is his protector and mediator with the world. The author in *Jacko* loves his work, lives in two enviable locations, creates fiction and should be a very contented man, but he is 'unhappy somehow with my own writing, with my publisher, and with my purely literary prospects'. This was Keneally's known world, lived between two countries and between creative and destructive impulses.

The author in the book begins to watch morning television, once anathema to him because he believes that, 'like liquor, the flippancy of the medium could only be decently resorted to after sunset, and could only be justified even then by a day of keen endeavours'. The attraction on a morning program is Jacko, whose antics as a 'video trespasser' – 'acting the goat' – are attracting an audience. Keneally based Jacko on an expatriate identity, Gordon Elliott in New York, who told him some tales about experiences on his WNYW television show, *Good Day New York*. As a feature reporter, Elliott used to talk his way into people's homes like a larrikin Norman Gunston. In the novel, Jacko's 'live' intrusion into New York homes for his show, *Live Wire*, is vulgar reality television.

Keneally settled some scores in *Jacko*. Some internationally known Australian writers, according to the novel, have 'broken the rules by writing about subjects other than the *Australian* subjects approved by the Aussie culture police, the critics whose purpose in life was to convince themselves there *was* indeed an Australian literature – as indeed there was, independent of their huffing and puffing and however indifferent the large world might be to it ...' The author in the novel has enjoyed 'occasional commercial success' and is placed 'on the cusp between a certain international renown and the perceived duty to write continuously about Australia and enrich the national cultural well-springs'.

Keneally is also on the trail of Patrick White: 'Michael Bickham' is an aged novelist who wins the Nobel Prize, 'culturally validating the nation in the mid-1970s. When I was young I'd been compared to him, but I had disappointed those who had first nominated me to be his heir.' Bickham despises the herd and has nothing to do with the Sydney 'literary mafia'. The author in *Jacko* contrives a meeting in Centennial Park with Bickham, during which Bickham has a severe asthma attack. Helping Bickham into his house, where he is revived with oxygen, means that for the first time the author pushes open a door that previously refused him entry. According to Jacko's mother, Chloe, the author is 'really a kind old bugger' compared to Bickham. As for Bickham, she asks, 'Do you have to be an utter prick to be a genius?'

White died in 1990 so never knew about his place in *Jacko*. A decade or so later, Keneally summed up his opinion of the Nobel Prize–winner: 'Although he wasn't a "nice" man and indeed was, perhaps rightly, scathingly dismissive of my and other Australian writers' works and origins unless they were his friends, he was a genius.'[11]

The considerable attention devoted to Bickham in *Jacko* raises the question of why Keneally went to such lengths. He appears to be humanising Bickham, pulling him down to the ranks of everyday life, where an asthma attack, a social occasion away from his own home and an amiable friendship with a reader are normal. At the party, held at a Sydney Northern Beaches home, Bickham is in the company of equals, including Dick Evans (who resembles David Williamson) and Norris and Marie Chambers (Gough and Margaret Whitlam). Williamson has recalled that, in *Jacko*, Keneally exactly reproduced a real party that he had attended, except that White was not present.[12]

Bickham is reduced to a realistic literary level where the author himself has a position of some importance and can show that he mixes with the best socially, even though he has not been born with the same advantages as Bickham, nor is he feted as a 'Nobelist'. From his outburst to Shirley Walker, it may be assumed that Keneally was sensitive to White's aversion to him. In creating Bickham, Keneally is perhaps reinventing White on terms more acceptable to himself.

Nan Talese at Doubleday rejected the manuscript of *Jacko*. 'Jocko [sic] contains what seems an uncontrollable flow of words, and yet when I put down the MS I realise that the action has barely progressed, nor has my understanding of the characters increased ... I am worried. I had hoped *Woman of the Inner Sea* would set you back on a course that would bring you the readers you deserve – those who to this day still talk about *The Chant of Jimmie Blacksmith*, *Confederates*, *Gossip from the Forest*, *Schindler's List* etc. I feel Jocko is going to be a backwards step.'[13] It may be that the authorial presence in *Jacko* takes over, in the same way that Keneally's personal story takes over *Our Republic*. The first-person commentary might work if it were not so obviously the author's own real story, rather than Jacko's.

Reading Keneally's books consecutively, the reader cannot help but notice how much he observes and comments on marriage. In *Jacko*, marital situations abound. Jack Emptor and his wife, Chloe, present, on their homestead verandah, what the author regards as a picture that says 'everything about the casual power, the lasting hostilities, the persistence of marriage'. Mark Torlucci – whose long friendship with the author in *Jacko* sounds remarkably like Keneally's with Fred Schepisi –

is 'calmly devoted to Rachel in a way that hadn't prevailed in his earlier loves'. Keneally may well have reflected, over nearly fifty years of marriage, as his character Hope Mockridge does in *The People's Train*, that 'marriage has a power beyond the sum of its two members and it holds people in place even when they dream of being free'. Keneally and Judy, too, shared a long history of experiences and memories.

Likewise, in *Chief of Staff* (1991), for which Keneally again used the pseudonym William Coyle, marriage and fidelity are as much under examination as the performance of Galton Sandforth, chief of staff to Drummond Wraith. Sandforth has an affair with Dim Lewis, wife of an Australian army officer. The story is loosely based on the affair that Douglas MacArthur's chief of staff, Richard K. Sutherland, had with Elaine Bessemer Clarke, a British army officer. There are shrewd comments about the effect on the younger woman, who is not merely a 'good-time girl' for the older man: 'She thought, this is why the Bible forbids adultery. It diminishes people. It brings on a squalid kind of stress ... old-fashioned sexual shame ...' Lewis is unhappy with her 'marginal and secretive life', poor compensation for the loyalties of a marriage of 'secret pleasures and griefs'. Keneally's preoccupation with marriage suggests that he was frequently re-examining his own and observing the partnerships of others. He seems to be saying that the woman generally bears most of the emotional stress; a man like Sandforth is more concerned for his standing in the work and social environment.

The book is a mix of a war won and a romance lost: a good read, with evidence of Keneally's usual impeccable research for historical fact against which to bring the semi-fictional romance to life. He told Peter Pierce that *Act of Grace* and *Chief of Staff* were 'raunchy straightforward novels of the kind where one is not inhibited by one's reputation ... I wrote these for recreational purposes to be liberated from the duty of writing seriously'.[14] In fact, neither book is raunchy; if anything, the scenes of intimacy are far more believable than most sex scenes in other Keneally books.

The books are also a curiosity because of Keneally's use of his pseudonym. Carmen Callil, who edited both books for Chatto & Windus in London, said in one note that she had a lovely time publishing *Act of Grace* and 'couldn't care less about pseudonyms and so on'.[15] However, she was keen to dispense with the pseudonym for *Chief of Staff*:

> You know I did an enormous amount of promotion and spent a great deal of money on promotion material to promote *Act of Grace*. We got a lot of copies out both here and in Australia: our returns were dire. Pan have also done very badly with the book . . . Let's put it to you like this, on the advance of £25,000 for *Act of Grace* we have an unearned amount of £18,369.45. Of course I want to avoid this with *Chief of Staff*; but it's more than that. I want to publish the book properly and make it sell this time. I also think that William Coyle is part of your writing persona and I cannot see the harm in people knowing who you are . . .[16]

Callil was also puzzled as to why she could not speak to Ion Trewin about Keneally's worry that there would be a clash with Hodder & Stoughton's publishing program for Keneally books. 'I have no wish to hurt Hodder in any way,' Callil assured Keneally, 'but there seems to be some extra problem relating to them that is not clear to me. You see I publish a lot of authors whose regular publisher is not Chatto. I've never had the same anxiety expressed in these circumstances . . . Ion is an old friend of mine.'[17]

Callil suggested Keneally approach Hodder to publish his Coyle books. 'But please do not worry about this Tom: you and I have known each other long enough to know that we can sort it out. What it will come down to, in the final analysis, is what you want/what you feel you can do.' To which Keneally replied, addressing Callil as 'Carms':

> The first matter, disclosure. Given Chatto's enthusiasm for the book, Tessa [Sayle] and I are agreed that there should be disclosure . . . either on the flap or in a form on the cover such as by Tom Keneally writing as William Coyle.
>
> About contact with Ion . . . Hodder have a novel of mine to bring out in March and probably another the following April [*Flying Hero Class* and *Woman of the Inner Sea*] . . . so it seems unlikely I can do personal promotion of *Chief of Staff*.[18]

Callil contacted Trewin, who told her that she could not use Keneally's name on the front cover, the back cover or the spine, but she could identify him on the inside front and back flaps. Callil was optimistic about her chances with *Chief of Staff*. To cover the lack of interviews and similar promotions, she decided that she would come up with a good answer: 'These are your Graham Greene-like "entertainments" and they stand or fall on that level . . .'[19]

A River Town is another 1990s book by Keneally that fits the 'entertainments' category. A story about his paternal grandparents migrating to Kempsey sounds bland after the variety of Keneally's previous subjects, but he could be relied on to provide enough unexpected scenery to make the journey interesting. In this book's startling beginning, a description of a glass jar containing the severed head of a young woman, which is displayed around town, sets the scene for the twists and turns that follow.

Keneally had always wanted to write a fictional book about his forebears and hoped that *A River Town* would be the first part of a trilogy. 'I'm retreating to that discredited writing class dictum that you should write what you know,' he said in 1995. 'Of course, any good writer writes precisely about what he *doesn't* know – the writing is an act of discovery in itself. As you get older, you get more interested in ancestor worship and mythologising. Doing things on the behalf of ancestors is a profound human impulse, and I guess this book is about that. And that's what I'll be doing for a while.'[20]

A River Town was published by Nan Talese, whose editorial input Keneally cautiously accepted. He had an uneasy relationship with Talese, evidenced in the editing process for *The Great Shame*. He was fond of her but described her as a type of 'Mother Superior'. In one interview he said that Talese would make 'a gushing response' to a new manuscript, but then her enthusiasm would tail off. 'It was a case of "unless you do what I say" you were in trouble,' he recalls. After he had written the book three or four times on his own, he'd had enough of it. 'I've lost all my distance from it and can't discriminate. This is a common experience with writers: your own fiction is like an unhappy marriage; everyone else can work out what's wrong except for the participants.'[21]

Talese was disappointed with *A River Town*'s overall sales, although she believed in the book. 'It very much gives you a sense of Australia. It feels so real. The thing is we must publish titles that interest Americans. It was just too far away. It was a terrific book.' Each Keneally book was different, but as he pointed out, each one had to make it on its own merits. 'Believe me, if I could find another Schindler to write about, I would!'

Schindler's advocate, Poldek, died suddenly on 9 March 2001 at the age of eighty-seven. He was Keneally's special friend, who liked to tell anyone prepared to listen how he had given Keneally a tremendous discount on a briefcase just to keep him listening to his story that day years ago in the Beverly Hills leather goods shop. According to Bob and Vivian Folkenflik, Keneally's friends and colleagues at UCI, 'Poldy was a kind, funny man and energetic, enthusiastic, eager to engage. He and Tom were made for each other as storytellers and listeners.'[22]

Some years earlier Keneally had been unprepared for the death of Tessa Sayle, on 27 May 1993. He always reproached himself for not attending her memorial service, held the following September at St James's Church, Piccadilly. He sent a tribute, which was read at the service:

> We came to you warts and all, wanting a voice in British publishing, and found in you a resonating generosity of soul and a broad professional skill. No one fought for a client as you did, even if that client was 12,000 miles away. No one spoke better sense to publishers and writers . . . I will always retain a picture of you, on visits to Sydney, exclaiming about the size of the fruit, and standing like the Hapsburg you were on a tarred apron of road in a Sydney heat wave crying, 'This is marvellous!' Now we say it of your work and memory. 'This is marvellous!'[23]

Tom senior was in poor health as the 1990s progressed. Known affectionately as 'Tom Pa' or 'Ziggy', he had darkly humorous names for hospitals such as 'the murder factory' for the Mona Vale Hospital. 'He never emerged from the hospital,' Keneally said. 'He took a couple of months to die. If I had my way again I would have been tempted to give him a big merciful injection a couple of days after he entered hospital.' Tom died on 18 August 2000 at the age of ninety-two.

At the Holy Name of Mary Church, Hunters Hill, where the funeral was held, a large crowd filled the church and the parish hall beside it. After a Mass of thanks for his life was offered, Tom was buried at Macquarie Park Cemetery, North Ryde. Keneally, paying tribute to his father's legacy, acknowledged his gift for storytelling, 'but as soon as you asked him to talk about all this in a formal way, as soon as you wanted to tape him so that an ordinary man's experience could be set down in a more permanent way, he went funny and reticent. "Why would you want to record what a boofhead like me has done? Man's not a bloody show pony."'[24]

Keneally recalled seeing his father, then an old man, enraged that someone was parking a car illegally outside the Narrabeen unit where he and Elsie lived. 'I'll call you on!' he shouted, shaking his walking stick. Tom senior's sister Annie had often said he would 'fight a tiger with a twig'. At his funeral, a man from the Returned and Services League described Tom as 'the good sergeant'. Keneally wept for his father, a man he had only partially succeeded in knowing. They had not dared, he said, to fully understand each other.

For the rest of the year after his father's death, Keneally felt that he was finished, physically and mentally: 'I was struck both by an acute depression, the unuttered disease of my parents' generation. I think my father suffered from it a great deal . . . I was very ill. I got into respiratory trouble and I got into a disabling depression.' Keneally was also being treated for a disease he had contracted in Eritrea, probably from water that had not been properly boiled. The beginning of the new millennium was not auspicious.

35

This Year's Feather Duster

A young Eritrean woman runs away from the stream, pulling her little boy along with her. She does not want him to excrete in the water. Whenever Keneally thought of his visit to Eritrea in 2000, during a bitter and hateful war, this image came to mind. The Eritreans had a good sense of hygiene and did their best to maintain it, even under the hard conditions on the road along which refugees like this mother and child moved.

'A million and a half people were on the road,' Keneally told his friends Bob and Vivian Folkenflik, 'driven by invasion from the populous towns of Southern Eritrea, and much infection and much horror were abroad. No shelter, no running water, no sanitation. In fact, there were scenes which reminded me very forcefully of the famous London Illustrated News engravings of famine scenes in Ireland in the Great Famine.'[1]

Keneally traced his latest illness to the water supply: 'The women wanted to treat you to coffee . . . coffee is richly, culturally important and an assertion of dignity. All these women had their coffee pots – it's a symbol of womanhood almost. The water would not always be properly boiled . . .' His old enemy asthma also returned in a severe attack. 'I was taking too many antibiotics and being prescribed too much cortisone. A doctor sent me to get immune system treatment – to an immunologist. He said your immune system is compromised because of whatever it was you caught and by other infections. He put me in hospital to have a monthly infusion of an immune product called Intragan, which is a blood product, and that has contributed greatly to my health and sanity.'

The man who had been named one of Australia's Living Treasures in 1997 seriously feared that he might soon be a dead and buried one. He had sometimes joked, 'They say this year's rooster is next year's feather duster ... I'll be back as a feather duster in no time.'[2] Having pushed himself beyond the limits of his endurance, Keneally certainly did not feel like strutting the world stage in the last months of 2000. He had been driven by the urgent need to earn more because he had a big monetary worry in the 1990s.

The Blue Mountains guesthouse, Echoes, was in financial trouble. Five couples had put in $100,000 each to demolish a dilapidated building on the property and build a new guesthouse. One of the group, Peter Doreen, was an architect, and another, Tony Menna, was a master builder. It had seemed like a good plan at the time, but they had borrowed money when interest rates were high. The project ended disastrously, with bankruptcy for some and an expensive lawsuit for others. Keneally, Iain Finlay and Menna were left with big debts. However, on one memorable day, thanks to money coming for both Keneally (from the film of *Schindler's List*) and Finlay (from the television program *Beyond 2000*, of which he was a founder), they were able to pay out the money owing.

With that worry behind him, and his health issues taken care of, the way ahead into a new decade for Keneally was cleared. He attended some events at the 2000 Olympic Games, held at Olympic Park in Homebush Bay, close to his old home. He provided a farewell piece, 'The Flame Above Us', for the Games' closing ceremony booklet.[3] Not long before, Keneally, the would-be athlete and enthusiastic skier, had also written the script for *Olympic Glory*, the first official IMAX film of the Winter Olympics, which covered the 1998 Winter Olympic Games in Nagano, Japan.

Yet everyone, it seemed, was asking him the same question: 'Are you writing anything now?' Of course he was! Keneally no longer needed his writing to survive financially, but he needed it to survive emotionally. His life was characterised by a restlessness that drove him on: to the next title, the next intense writing phase and the next book tour.

He kept his literary agents on their toes, admitting that he was 'a serial bigamist' when it came to them. Amanda Urban, whom Keneally called Binky, represented him for thirteen titles in the United States between 1992 and 2013. The list did not include *Bettany's Book*, published in 2000 and dedicated to 'Rory Coverdale, fresh to Australia and the world'. Rory was Margaret's son and Keneally's first grandchild; the proud grandfather described the baby to friends as the 'wunderkind of the antipodes'.[4]

It was a pleasure for Keneally to publish *Roos in Shoes* (2003), a book in verse for children, written while on a cruise on board the *Queen Elizabeth 2* in February 2002. The attractive book was illustrated by Gillian Johnson, his student at UCI who had gone on to a successful career as a writer and illustrator of children's books. 'It took about five months to complete the illustrations,' she remembers. 'I loved the project. When I finished I wanted to start all over again . . . The book never earned back its advance. It is a lovely book but too much of a polemic for many kids.'

Keneally's friends noticed a change in him with the advent of grandchildren. He was not so keen to be on the run to other places and was more contented. After the illness of 2000 he had rearranged how he worked. 'I shamelessly use my grandchildren for therapy,' he told guests at a testimonial dinner in 2014, during which a couple of those children frolicked happily on the stage.

The courtyard beside the kitchen of the Bilgola Beach home was converted into a glass-walled playroom for the grandchildren and stocked with toys and books. The grandchildren all call him Tommy. 'I think this is because they view him as a playmate,' Keneally's daughter Margaret says, 'as he is so patient and so good at being in the moment with them. When each grandchild was around three, we would ask them how old Tommy was, and they would say he was three also.'

When asked in 1995, 'What or who is the greatest love of your life?' Keneally replied, 'I have to be honest: my daughters.'[5] Ten years later he would have answered, 'My grandchildren.' He was also asked what single thing would improve his quality of life, and replied that he wanted the ability to act his age and relax. He did indeed seem to be taking a more relaxed attitude to the critics, whose opinions had once kept him awake at night. By 2014 he believed he had learnt to ignore their carping.

No author wanted to see what Clive James called 'a carefully constructed, beautiful book in the hands of someone whose own prose reveals he has no sense of rhythm at all'. James also said that he's had everything hurled at him, especially in Australia. 'Australia is where the tough journalists are.' James, himself a veteran critic, finished by saying: 'But the older I get, I become more convinced the thing a critic should do is point toward the things he or she admires, for the benefit of the next generation ... Only be hostile in defence of a value.'[6] Those were statements that resonated with Keneally.

Bettany's Book is to be admired for the complex crafting of a story that is really two stories: about happenings in Sudan and happenings in Australia. Keneally explores the better life that some Irish had made for themselves here despite their convict past; at the same time this is the book he had wanted to write about the situation in Sudan, which the international community did not know about or chose to ignore; and he contemplates his life among the favoured in Sydney. The book is concerned with these three matters: ancestral beginnings, third-world realities and the privilege of a harbourside home. Like Keneally, Dimp lives in the world of writers, who are 'easily enthused if you tell them a tale'. The historian Benedetto, gesturing at the luxurious house and the harbour, observes of Prim: 'She's a storyteller, you see. She hasn't stopped being one, just because of all this ...'

Keneally does not agonise so much about marriage and the vagaries of love in this book as in his previous ones. He had reached that stage in his life where, like one of couples in *Bettany's Book*, he and his wife 'should not be apart now. After so much. With old age coming on. With all mistakes acknowledged and set aside!'

The Bettany story has much to say about Australia's attitude to its Indigenous inhabitants. Keneally held strong views about the wrongs inflicted on Aboriginal people:

> Every ethnic group has a different map of the world, and therefore, it is a bit like living on parallel planets ... The great human secret is that there's a lot of richness in having your map of the planet but not to deny the legitimacy of other maps. Racism is as human as love. We all need a sense of community identity and even a sense of tribe and clan,

> and obviously that's precious to us. Nonetheless, there is a sort of backside to identity. The ugly baboon backside to identity is to say 'This is the only acceptable identity. There's no room for any other identity . . .' and it takes the oxygen out of all other identities . . . You see that happening all the time.
>
> A lot of people didn't just say there is not a legal basis for Aboriginal land rights. They said, 'The Aboriginal Culture, what is it, after all? They're Palaeolithic. They didn't invent the 747. They didn't build any Sheratons.' There were bitter attacks on the Aboriginal culture itself. If I'd been an Aborigine, I'd be very offended by how the yokels crapped all over that identity and denied it had a valid existence.[7]

Bettany, the early-nineteenth-century landholder, is cautiously accommodating of the 'sables' or 'Moth people' (Aborigines), but inevitably the book includes mistreatments and massacres of those people and their ineffectual retaliation. There are some familiar Keneally scenarios: the background of the Irishman Long resembles that of Hugh Larkin, family ancestor; Frank Varduzzi, the filmmaker, whose career is made with a film selected for showing in Directors' Week at Cannes, recalls Fred Schepisi; and there is a sprinkling of clergymen and nuns.

A clergyman, Father Frank Darragh, is the central figure in Keneally's next work of fiction, *An Angel in Australia* (2002). Attention has already been drawn to the autobiographical content of this book, which reveals much about Keneally's wartime childhood and his dream of becoming a priest. Father Darragh, naive and compassionate, is the exemplar of Father Michael Keneally, the priest who never was.

Darragh at one point stands 'constructing a history and a soul' for Mrs Heggarty, the young Sydney mother whose husband has been captured and interned by the Germans. In *An Angel in Australia* Keneally also constructs a history and a soul for the sort of priest he might have been. He returns to the Manly seminary with Darragh, traversing 'the long driveway with its deep-green sentries of Norfolk pine' and approaching 'the iron gates with their wrought deigns of harps, mitres and Celtic crosses . . .'

Keneally describes affectionately and knowledgeably all the ceremonial mysteries, vestments and ritual movements that go with the priestly duties – the sacramental apparel that would always be attractive to him. He recalls memories of himself and other boyish seminarians at Springwood, traipsing down into the deep gullies of the Blue Mountains to cut the native palms that are pushed fresh and moist into sacks and sent to parishes around the state for use on Palm Sunday. 'Palms clipped by virgin youths were piled on the truck-bed . . .'

Such details, more than forty years later, are useful in considering the person Keneally might have been. He once described himself as a post-colonial innocent when starting life as a writer, and he would have started out in a similarly ingenuous way as a Catholic priest. Like Darragh, he would likely have believed that the salvation of the world was his task: 'a terrible, scruple-ridden tendency'.

Andrew Riemer, who had followed Keneally's career and applauded his earlier books, was disappointed that, in his judgement, *An Angel in Australia* did not measure up as a novel. 'It seems to me clear, however, that Keneally has turned away by now from those ambitions that made many of us sit up and take notice of him almost 40 years ago,' Riemer wrote. 'One day, perhaps, he will write something as challenging, discomforting and memorable as *Bring Larks and Heroes*, *The Chant of Jimmie Blacksmith* or, indeed, the splendid *A Dutiful Daughter*. In the meantime, *An Angel in Australia* is unlikely to displease those who admire his facility, his ability to tell a good yarn and his gift for turning out a professional book on almost any subject.'[8]

Riemer's tastes were for less-conventional and harder-to-digest stories. He admitted that his opinion might be regarded as 'the high-culture obsessions of an old fogy', but he had correctly gauged that Keneally was now in the 'brave new market-driven millennium' and had to compete in a broader, different hard-sell environment. Keneally quickly embraced the new technologies that multiplied in the years beyond 2000: he uses his smartphone constantly, he has a Kindle to read ebooks and he tweets regularly about footy, politics and books.

Barry Oakley, reviewing *An Angel in Australia* for *The Bulletin*, asked if it was possible to keep up with Keneally. 'Here he comes again in his all-terrain vehicle,' Oakley wrote, 'into home territory this time. With *An Angel in Australia*, he's back where he began, all those innumerable books ago, with novels such as *Three Cheers for the Paraclete* . . .'[9] Oliver

Herford, writing for the *Times Literary Supplement*, criticised the book for having too much plot, a familiar refrain about Keneally's tendency to write three books in one.[10]

Keneally dedicated *An Angel in Australia* to his father, for whom he was still grieving: 'To the memory of Sergeant Tom Keneally, 3rd Australian Squadron, RAAF, North Africa, WWII.' He had often wondered about the life his mother had known in her husband's wartime absence, but there are only fragmentary glimpses of an Elsie-like figure in *An Angel in Australia*.

Keneally had not finished with that era, however, especially after he made a trip to Cowra, where Japanese prisoners of war had once been confined in a camp. On the night of 5 August 1944 about 1000 of these men attempted to escape, expecting to be killed but preferring death to the shame of capture. The Australian guards were unprepared and 350 prisoners escaped into the bush. 'I felt very close and very fascinated by the enemy,' Keneally said in 2013. 'The Cowra breakout was a big event of my childhood. I had an aunt who lived near Cowra and she was very scared of it. She was a very sturdy woman and she slept with an axe, but the proposition behind that was they were coming to get us.'[11]

Keneally's novel *Shame and the Captives*, his thirtieth, is a book about the mutual cultural incomprehension of white Australia and Asia. 'The novel is not really as much about war as about cultural and political frontiers in collision with each other,' he claimed. 'Such conflicts have been a preoccupation, certainly since *The Chant of Jimmie Blacksmith*.'[12]

Nan Talese expressed an interest in *Shame and the Captives*, but it was promised as part of a two-book contract, one of the strategies of the 'brave new market-driven millennium'. The other half of the deal was *The Daughters of Mars*, which was not a novel at all in Talese's opinion, and she did not think there would be an audience for it in the United States. The two books were eventually published by Random House in Australia and by Atria Books in the United States.

Atria Books is a division of Simon & Schuster in New York. Judith Curr, its Australian founder and publisher, made a statement when Keneally signed the two-book deal: 'Over a career spanning five decades, Thomas Keneally has proven himself one of the world's great storytellers. In *The Daughters of Mars* he sets a cast of extraordinary female characters against the backdrop of a world gone mad, and the result is a novel that is vast in scope and yet extraordinarily intimate. We are delighted to welcome him to Atria Books.'[13]

The Daughters of Mars is another war novel, this time about the Great War. Keneally had always enjoyed his father's Anzac Day yarns, told after Tom senior had marched and visited the local RSL club. After Anzac Day 1982, he told his son, 'It was just like Gallipoli all over again at the RSL. Turks on the top tables – all the high vantage points were held by the Turks!'

Through the experiences of two sisters, Sally and Naomi Durance, both nurses, readers are diverted from the familiar scenes of the trenches to the makeshift hospitals where desperate action of a different kind goes on day and night. Keneally read war diaries at the Australian War Memorial in Canberra and various other primary sources about 'the medical war' for all the historical details he required. The ABC television drama *ANZAC Girls* – screened in 2014 as Australians prepared for the 100th anniversary of the first Anzac Day in 2015 – was similar in content to *The Daughters of Mars*. Keneally has always disputed the widely held notion that Australia was born at Gallipoli. 'Australia was born in 1901 and there needs to be a certain amount of de-mythologising. Let's hope the historians win out over the politicians, who strike me as fairly jingoistic.'[14]

Keneally has admitted to an obsession with war. 'And I'm in a conundrum: I write about war but I don't approve of it. Novelists disapprove of social injustice and manic tribalism and ethnic hysteria and discrimination and marginalisation of people, but that's where all their work comes from! So we disapprove of the bad habits of mankind but if we're all nice to each other there would be no novels! It took me a long time to admit because I'm a child of the Vietnam War era that I'm fascinated with war. I don't know why.'

Andrew Riemer judged that *The Daughters of Mars* was a powerful work: 'There are, as in most self-respecting traditional novels, many stories here – stories of heroism and cowardice, of candour and duplicity, stories of how some men and women break under the strain of extreme hardships and how some transcend the seemingly intolerable.'[15]

These war books were taking Keneally in a different direction, but readers were following and he was gaining in popularity. Some who had once complained that they found him too difficult or demanding to read were drawn to the notion of an 'easy read'. Keneally was also enjoying better reviews. The *Weekend Australian* devoted three columns to *The Daughters of Mars* and Ashley Hay's review was dazzling by anyone's standards: 'The translation into fiction of all that he uncovered is one of this novel's finest achievements.' The pegging out of all the intricate details, Hay continued, resembled the plans of a battle strategist.[16] Keneally was particularly pleased by a generous review in the *New York Times*. Alan Riding thought Keneally's description of the chaos when a ship was torpedoed was masterly.[17]

There was one more book in the cluster of Keneally war titles of this era: *The Widow and Her Hero* (2007), a smartly told story of heroism, a subject of interest to Keneally since his youthful admiration of heroic Irish Catholic priests. *The Widow and Her Hero* is a clever reconstruction of the commando raids by men in small boats against the Japanese-controlled Singapore Harbour. Keneally chose to tell the story of the clandestine warfare in the first person, mainly from the point of view of Grace Waterhouse, the widow of one of the leaders of the mission. Andrew Riemer rated *The Widow and Her Hero* as the best of Keneally's novels for many years: 'an accomplished and highly readable book' that provided some memorable portraits.[18]

Keneally liked the novelty of speaking in a woman's voice. He was fond of *The Daughters of Mars*, he said, because of the nurses: 'I love those two girls.' For that book and *Shame and the Captives*, he continued on his quest to 'understand women – a late-blooming endeavour of mine'.[19]

If the growing list of titles Keneally had published since the unfortunate experiences of 2000 was anything to go by, he was in no danger of becoming a feather duster just yet. Perhaps the image of a new broom would be more appropriate.

36

All the Best Books Are Ahead

On his seventy-eighth birthday, Keneally tweeted: 'Scribo, ergo sum. I write, therefore I am. No writing, no am.' In his latest bout of writing he insisted that he was not a historian, but 'a novelist who nicks stories from history – and contemporary stories'.[1] He also said that he was not particularly pleased with the books he'd written, although at the time of writing each one he had the conviction that 'the world needed this book'.[2] He was never inclined to reread any. The best book was always ahead of him.

Of all his many books, Keneally was fondest of *A River Town*, for which he read countless microfilmed copies of the local newspapers the *Macleay Argus* and the *Macleay Chronicle*. Keneally had travelled the world but he made a regular pilgrimage 'home' to Kempsey, usually accompanied by Elsie, who celebrated her ninetieth birthday on 24 November 2003. She still enjoyed family parties, conversing brightly and accepting a glass of wine, explaining that it was only her high heels that were making her unsteady after drinking just a bit too much. She did fall and fracture her pelvis after having minor surgery for skin cancers. She died on 22 April 2008, and was buried beside Tom senior at Macquarie Park after a Mass of thanksgiving for her life at the Holy Name of Mary Church, Hunters Hill.

Together, Elsie and Tom senior had always been a striking couple: a nattily dressed larrikin and a stylishly dressed lady. Tom senior loved to rile Elsie, and she would protest, 'You can't say that, Tom!' All their grandchildren enjoyed close relationships with them, and Elsie became a favoured confidante. After she died, her two daughters-in-law cleared out the Narrabeen unit where she had hoarded many things. 'One whole room had been out of bounds to us during her latter years,' Jane remembers, 'as it was full of "things I need to sort through".' Jane kept some of the items treasured by Elsie and worked them into seven family quilts, one for each grandchild.

Keneally had always been very close to Elsie. In his contribution for *My Mother, My Father: On Losing a Parent*, he wrote:

> A mother is a goddess, even if her name is Elsie, the name my mother never forgave her engine-driving father for giving her. Elsie or Denise or Judy, the mother is the person who above all gives unity to our childhoods. And since in her presence we never cease to be her child, she never ceases to seem more eternal and fixed than the stars. She never ceases to be a given of the universe we inhabit. They'll never make a bullet to get her, any more than they could make a bullet to get Aphrodite or Minerva. That's why her death is so astounding. She has been our chief praiser and indeed, our chief appraiser.[3]

Keneally's piece about his parents was a sentimental tribute, but his indebtedness to Elsie for her unfailing belief in him in the bad times was heartfelt. He had tried for most of his life to make up for all his perceived failures as a younger man. When he came to sit at her bedside towards the end, she said, 'I know you have friends in another room. I can hear them talking. Go and join them.' Watching her slip into morphine-induced unconsciousness was one of the hardest experiences of his life.

Elsie had plenty of opinions, and maintained her well-honed sense of social justice until her death. She telephoned her older son regularly to tell him about particular articles in the *Sydney Morning Herald* concerning asylum seekers. She was appalled at the treatment they received: the controversy about the arrival of 'boat people' in Australian waters was a big subject in the last years of Elsie's life.

Keneally picked up the subject in *The Tyrant's Novel*, which Elsie read. Keneally confidently predicted that it would be a winner. In a personal covering note issued to reviewers, he wrote: 'This book will always be my favourite and I believe it's my best.'[4] In New York, Amanda Urban said she was thrilled with the book and she would consult with Nan Talese,[5] who praised its 'fierce moral tone that is the hallmark of Keneally fiction. Not preaching or in any way instructive, but your underlying compassion and seeing the just cause.'[6] Deborah Rogers, Keneally's London agent, was also in favour, describing it as 'something very extraordinary'.[7]

The novel was prompted by the author's visit with journalist Caroline Baum to the Villawood Detention Centre in western Sydney – where he had delivered soft drinks many years previously. They went to see Aamer Sultan, a doctor and political refugee from Baghdad, who had seen the film of *Schindler's List*. Sultan was delighted when Keneally gave him a signed copy of *Schindler's Ark*, calling out to his friends to come and meet the author. They sat in a respectful circle, listening to the author tell stories about Eritrea and Ireland.

Baum hoped that Keneally would speak out 'against the injustices and indignities of detention and perhaps be inspired to write something. I knew there were stories in there he would find irresistible.' Keneally said that the place was 'a sink of desolation, inertia and bureaucracy that left me bewildered and outraged, along with many other Australians, that it is being done in our name'. Having profited from the writing of *Schindler's Ark*, about camps in Europe, he decided he had to react in some way to a camp in Sydney suburbia.

In the novel Keneally introduces Alice the journalist. She was like Baum, who had written about visiting Sultan in an article titled 'Someone to See You'.[8] Sultan was furious at the reference Baum made to his flirtatious behaviour, claiming that it brought him dishonour and disgrace and might cost him his bid for freedom from Villawood. He never wanted to see Baum again, but Keneally continued to visit him regularly. In his book, Keneally included a description of the misunderstanding that had ended Baum's contact with Sultan, with only the names changed.

When Baum challenged Keneally about Alice, he looked bewildered. She told him that she was writing an article about authors who used the stories of real people insensitively and asked why he had not given Alice a different identity. He replied with astonishment: 'Gee, that never occurred to me, but now that you mention it, I wish I had. To me, the moment she became Alice she was no longer you.' Keneally told Baum that in earlier years he had borrowed from reality with conscious disregard for the feelings of his real-life characters. 'They recognised themselves,' he said, referring to the monsignors in *Three Cheers for the Paraclete*. 'It was a case of institutional vengeance on my part.'

Baum was unhappy about the way that Keneally, and others whom she knew about, sometimes wrote too close to life. He told her that he thought 'writers do this so lightly because the world of the novel seems more important'. Unlike journalism or non-fiction, there was no code of ethics for fiction, no protocol or etiquette, 'as if we just assume imagination and integrity automatically go together'.[9] According to Baum, Keneally had offered her the chance to read early proofs of the book, assuring her that she would not recognise herself and nor would anyone else. Keneally was mortified and apologetic about how his portrayal of Baum had hurt her.

Malcolm Knox, literary editor for the *Sydney Morning Herald*, described the liberties that authors could and did take as 'a moral morass'.[10] Keneally and others were venturing into a hazardous zone by including real people in their stories – it was a zone in which Keneally had been harmed with *Season in Purgatory*, causing damage which still came back to haunt him from time to time. The use of sources in fiction is a minefield, as Keneally understood from writing *Schindler's Ark*. He knew he had a good story, one that excited him with its potential, but he hesitated to tell it.

In writing about Holocaust victims, asylum seekers and the like, had he the right to profit from their suffering or to be rewarded for publicising their pain? Yet without his books, and the willingness of authors like him to go to the frontline, how would the wider world know about these people's troubles? Once Keneally was on the side of the Jews, Eritreans or asylum seekers, he followed up in practical ways.

Keneally expected some abuse over *The Tyrant's Novel*. He had written it hastily, in response to an existing impassioned debate that was polarising Australians: should the nation permit asylum seekers to enter, let alone stay in, the country, and if it did, what should be the conditions? Prime Minister John Howard's hard line – 'We will decide who comes to this country and the circumstances in which they come' – appeased the conservative voters, who were not necessarily racist or insensitive, but who supported an orderly system and due legal process in the handling of refugee applications.

Writer Rosie Scott, representing Australians for a Fair Australia, arranged for a statement headlined 'Australia and the Refugee Crisis' to be published on 6–7 October 2001 in the *Weekend Australian*. The organisers had the support of many people, whose names followed the statement: 'We are outraged and ashamed at this country's contemptible treatment of men, women and children seeking asylum in Australia, a country which has given a new home and new life to countless thousands of immigrants . . .' In 2002 Keneally and Scott organised a demonstration in front of the Department of Immigration and Multicultural Affairs building in Sydney. With only ten days' notice, 500 people turned up on a weekday. They taped their mouths shut in a gesture of solidarity with the detainees in the camps, some of whom had resorted to extreme actions – such as hunger strikes and sewing their lips together – to protest their treatment.

Scott was the chair of the Sydney PEN Writers in Detention Committee, created in 2001. She invited Keneally to join, which he did, and together they edited *Another Country: Writers in Detention* (2004) on behalf of PEN. 'We believed that this book would humanise these "faceless people" and also affirm them,' Scott says. 'It took a harrowing year to get these pieces because detention centres were so closed to the public . . . Tom and I and many other members of PEN wrote letters of support for the contributors. Eventually all were released.'

Sultan, by then on a temporary protection visa, contributed an essay titled 'The Curse'. It detailed the difficulties he'd faced in starting a new life after being released from Villawood, tormented by his witnessing of 'the stripped-of-hope' inhabitants of 'the cave', the detention centre. In 2004 Keneally and Scott were nominated for the Human Rights Medal. That year they were back outside the Department of Immigration and Multicultural Affairs in Sydney for an all-night vigil supporting Sydney PEN member Sarath Amarasinghe, who was on a hunger strike in the Baxter Detention Centre, in South Australia. Their action received international media attention. 'Fear not,' Keneally wrote to Bob and Vivian Folkenflik, 'as much as I might need it, I am not on hunger strike myself and indeed am trying to stop it behind the scenes.'[11] Amarasinghe and the other Sri Lankans involved were all later released.

Keneally and Scott co-edited a collection of stories, poems and essays, *A Country Too Far* (2013), which aimed to emphasise the humanity of asylum seekers. The book was a critical and commercial success, enabling the editors to donate thousands of dollars in royalties to various asylum-seeker advocacy and support groups. 'Let's use mandatory detention only for health, identity and security checks that do not take years, but weeks,' Keneally suggested. 'Let's have accommodation centres – not prisons. And for God's own sweet sake, let's release all children from mandatory detention . . .'[12]

Another unnecessary evil that weighed upon Keneally was famine. He'd witnessed its impact in Eritrea, and written about it in his books about Ireland. His 2010 non-fiction book *Three Famines* was 'a narrative essay on the nature of famine'. He studied three of the worst cases of mass starvation in history: the Irish potato famine of the 1840s, the Bengal famine of the 1940s and the Ethiopian famine of the 1970s and 1980s. Keneally was influenced by the work of Amartya Sen, winner of the 1998 Nobel Prize in Economics. Sen wrote in his book *Development as Freedom*: 'No famine has taken place in the history of the world in a functioning democracy.' *Three Famines* makes a humane and thoughtful contribution to the considerable bibliography on a subject that deserves constant revisiting.

37

Dig and Dig and Disappear

Keneally was a well-known visitor at the Mitchell Library in Sydney. 'I've always had a sense from my research at the Library that you could just dig and dig and disappear into the collections,' he wrote in 2009. 'When they're old enough, I want to take my grandchildren into the Mitchell Library and show them copies of 18th century court papers from the Old Bailey. Most got a trial of five to ten minutes and on that basis they were sent to the end of the Earth.'[1]

The Commonwealth of Thieves: The Sydney Experiment (2005) follows those who travelled on the First Fleet, mostly rejects of Britain, to Botany Bay, and observes their improbable beginnings in another world. Names from Australian history books take on new life, particularly Captain Arthur Phillip. Carmen Callil wrote: 'Using contemporary documents, Keneally makes us feel the lash on the back of convict and soldier alike, but it is in his placement of the Aborigines as equally at the centre of the story that gives his tale much of its interest ... Keneally acknowledges that, like Palestine, the white settlement of Australia was, and is still, a catastrophe for its indigenous people ... Keneally has always had a grand talent for the telling of a tale. His rattling account of the genesis of his native city is one of his best.'[2]

In *The Commonwealth of Thieves*, and in his later multi-volume project *Australians*, Keneally is able to portray real people 'close to life' in a way that got him into trouble in fiction. In the first volume of *Australians*, titled *Origins to Eureka* (2009), the author's intention is made clear: the books would be about individual Australians in a historical context, rather than a history in which those individuals rated occasional mention. At the start of the second volume, *Eureka to the Diggers* (2011), Keneally wrote: 'So what I am trying to present in these pages is the narrative of men and women struggling with the histories in which they are stuck, histories in which some perish, histories through which others endure, histories through which some dance ... The purpose of the book is to attempt to place the reader inside the very flesh and breath and passion of Australian life in the past.'

The idea for the books came from an editorial meeting chaired by Patrick Gallagher at Allen & Unwin in 2005. Gallagher's colleague, Paul Donovan, said that it must be time for a big new history of Australia. 'The guiding principle was that this would be a "People's History", telling the stories of the well- and the not-so-well-known figures who have made our history,' Gallagher explains. 'Our working title of *A People's History* I think says it all ... Tom's prowess as a novelist makes him uniquely qualified to bring the past and the people to life.'

Keneally was not rewriting history in *Australians*, nor was he interpreting it. His work, which continued with a third volume, *Flappers to Vietnam* (2014), is a big, easily accessible biography: the story of many people over many years. (A fourth volume is due in 2016.) In *Australians*, readers will notice many names, familial and famous, that have featured in Keneally's own life: Edmund Campion, Mick and Elsie Coyle, John Curtin, George Johnston, Douglas MacArthur, Max Martin, Gough Whitlam.

Keneally had written two biographies previously, both about American men. A signed copy of the first, *Lincoln* (2003), was presented as an official gift to President Barack Obama by Prime Minister Kevin Rudd in March 2009, when the two leaders first met. Keneally deals with Lincoln in a similar way to the dramatis personae in *Australians*: he concentrates more on the man and less on the historic events associated with his name. Lincoln's dogged life is matched by Keneally's matter-of-fact style. The author describes Lincoln and his wife, Mary, as 'complicated and fretful souls. Lincoln seems to have been a sometimes acute depressive, whereas Mary exhibits a bipolar volatility.' Lincoln called his recurrent and severe melancholia 'the hypo', which became an abiding companion. 'But, depressed or not, he was unrelenting. Perhaps the depression and the steadfastness were two faces of the one being, and one entailed the other. He had learned from his youth how to endure debilitating self-doubt.' (That description sounds very much like Lincoln's biographer.)

Lincoln also features in an earlier Keneally biography, *American Scoundrel* (2002), which follows the controversial life of Dan Sickles, friend of Thomas Francis Meagher. Sickles, a lawyer, politician and libertine, murdered his wife's lover. He was the first man in the United States to be found not guilty of murder on the grounds of temporary insanity. A friend of Lincoln, Sickles redeemed himself in the Civil War.

The original title was *The Sickles*. Nan Talese told the author that she had enjoyed reading the first draft, but as usual she wanted him to take more time with it:

> I don't want to discourage you and I feel you are easily discouraged ... This is not the story of a husband and wife as the title implies. It is really the life of a cad – an intelligent, brave, ambitious selfish womaniser – the research is there, ordered and cohesive, but no narrative, no tension, no story to keep the reader interested ... now you need to bring to life Dan Sickles' life and all the attendant characters ... I know you can do it – I have full confidence in that and when you look at it in this light I think you will realise that much of the writing is here. In repositioning it, it will come to life. But I also know how you usually want to rush on to the next book. As you think this over, think of what a difference that extra time meant to *The Great Shame*: 50,000 copies at $35 in h/c. We would never have gotten near that if you had not returned to write more drafts.[3]

Keneally did delve into another story while reworking the manuscript. 'I'm just doing initial research on a novel on Chas. Dickens' youngest son, Edward Bulwer Lytton Dickens, cut adrift at the age of 17 in the Australian bush,' he told his London agent, Deborah Rogers. 'Both projects have me well and truly gripped.'[4] The Dickens story was not written as a historical novel but he touches upon it in *Australians*.

One edition of *American Scoundrel* is subtitled 'Love, War and Politics in Civil War America' and another 'The Life of Notorious Civil War General Dan Sickles'. *American Scoundrel*, as one reviewer put it, is 'a rollicking good read'.[5] It was included on the *New York Times Book Review*'s list of Notable Books for 2002.

It was the first book for which Fiona Inglis acted as literary agent for Keneally. Inglis was one of the team at Curtis Brown, which bought Jill Hickson's agency in 1999 and inherited Hickson's contracts. Inglis – whom Keneally regards as an important friend and adviser – has been responsible for negotiating all his Australian deals since then, while Amanda Urban continues to represent his interests in the United States. In London he had engaged Deborah Rogers, who established the Rogers, Coleridge & White Literary Agency, but she died suddenly on 30 April 2014. Ion Trewin, who wrote her obituary for *The Guardian*, said that she was widely considered to be 'one of the most influential literary agents of her generation'. Jennifer Hewson, at the same firm, took over as Keneally's agent in London.

One of the fictional books that Keneally submitted to his agents was *The People's Train* (2009), whose main character, Artem Samsurov, is based on an escaped Russian prisoner named Artem Sergeiv, who lives in Brisbane with other Russian escapees and exiles. 'I encountered his story, by accident,' Keneally wrote in his author's note, 'in an article by Tom Poole and Eric Fried: "Artem: A Bolshevik in Brisbane" from the *Australian Journal of Politics and History*. Like Samsurov, Sergeiv is in regular trouble with the Queensland police and spends time in Boggo Road jail.' Marxism was a subject that had always interested Keneally: its belief system was almost theological. He had been to Russia and Siberia and was perplexed by the culture. Yet he recreated aspects of it with the assured voice of firsthand knowledge and convincing detail in *The People's Train*, which was longlisted for the Miles Franklin Award in 2010.

This book is Keneally at his best: revolutionary figures cleverly drawn against a huge historical backdrop, creating a fascinating picture of early 1900s Brisbane in the first part of the narrative and revolutionary Russia in the second. Reviewers generally agreed. 'Keneally builds terrific momentum by drawing on extraordinary events: The Russian Revolution and the onset of World War I,' wrote Patrick Allington in *Australian*

Book Review. 'If the scaffolding of this novel is now and again exposed, that is something historical fiction can never fully overcome.'[6]

Thomas Poole, in whose article Keneally had found the story of Sergeiv, saw various faults in the 2009 edition of *The People's Train*, particularly in the transliteration of Russian words into English and the misprint of well-known Russian names. 'There were at least 75 such errors in the 2009 version of the novel,' Poole wrote, 'which seemed never-ending to this reader. However, to the credit of Vintage, a corrected copy of Keneally's novel was brought out in 2010, only a few months after the original version appeared in bookstores … a modest suggestion offered by this reviewer is that the author work more closely next time with an exacting editor and with a specialist in early Soviet history.'[7]

Ensuring the accuracy of names had been a big factor in *Schindler's Ark*, but there are so many factors that combined to make that book pre-eminent in the author's list of works. In Keneally's opinion, the story is exceptional because 'through this very flawed Nazi, using him as a lens, one could see every stage of the Holocaust – from confiscation of property, to ghettoisation, to slave labour, to internment camps, to destruction camps. I felt that it brought a great catastrophe, a great human catastrophe, to an imaginable scale … six million were killed in the Holocaust – three million non-Jewish Poles as well – these are meaningless figures. They defeat the capacity of the imagination to latch onto them, but [in *Schindler's Ark*] you could see it happening to people you could identify with.'[8]

Critics' Forum, the BBC Radio program, had come down heavily on *Schindler's Ark* after it won the Booker Prize, but one of the critics who took part in the debate, Claire Tomalin, qualified her comments with a suggestion: 'I should like to know very much more about the background of this book. I hope Keneally will publish something about how it was researched and how all the material came to him. There could be a dossier on *Schindler's Ark*, which might be even more interesting than the book as it stands.'

'The quest for Schindler, in fact,' suggested chair Richard Mayne.[9]

Tomalin had in mind a reference companion to the novel – a return to the factual sources of *Schindler's Ark*. Plenty of textual records are stored at the State Library of New South Wales and the National Library of Australia, including sound recordings of the many interviews conducted with 'Schindler's Jews'. Keneally did return to the Schindler research files to write *Either Or*, a Holocaust play about Kurt Gerstein, a German Lutheran engineer and an SS officer. He was responsible for the introduction of Zyklon B, used in the gas chambers, and witnessed one of the early mass killings of Jews. Gerstein is not as large a character as Schindler, but his moral struggle to choose between absolute evil and absolute good fascinated Keneally. *Either Or* was produced at Theatre J, at the Jewish Community Center, Washington DC, and was directed by Daniel De Raey. It opened in May 2007.

That same year, Keneally's memoir *Searching for Schindler* was published. The book is largely Poldek's story, told blithely and affectionately by a genial companion, Keneally, on the journey they take together to find out all they can about the man who saved Poldek's life. Some critics of the book regarded Keneally's effusive style dubiously, and some dismissed it as slapdash, ridden with clichés.[10] The book enlarged the popular Schindler myth – a myth that took shape in *Schindler's Ark* and grew with the movie.

As with Keneally's previous autobiographical books – *Homebush Boy* and *Our Republic* – the author keeps the tone lighthearted, glossing over or leaving out the less palatable material. In *Schindler's Ark* he told the unvarnished facts about Schindler and his Jews. That book defied classification but arguably belongs in his impressive list of non-fiction work.

Ion Trewin, the editor at Hodder & Stoughton who had guided *Schindler's Ark* to publication and had to decide on its classification, died on 8 April 2015 at the age of seventy-one. In an obituary written for the *Guardian*, Alastair Niven claimed that 'Trewin's influence on the gestation of one of the most gripping and morally enthralling tales of the 20th century cannot be exaggerated'.[11]

Schindler's Ark cast a long shadow over the author, from which he has perhaps never fully emerged. Keneally has long seemed to be on some sort of mission to find the topic and write the book that would match *Schindler's Ark*. As he said in 2004, 'It gives us authors something to do in our old age to try and unseat that book, to get another work on our epitaph.'[12]

Epilogue

Interestingly Enough...

Searching for Tom Keneally has been rather like going on a long expedition such as travellers take to further their knowledge of particular subjects. The Keneally Tour begins in unremarkable homes in New South Wales, which are still standing, if a little older and shabbier. Elsie would be dismayed to see how the upstairs flat at Loftus Crescent, Homebush, has deteriorated, although she might be glad to know that in 2013 it was shared by a group of overseas students. The back yard where Tom senior once grew vegetables is now bare.

The bedroom Keneally shared with his brother, Johnny, is as cluttered with textbooks and personal belongings as it was 'back in the day'. Johnny died in 2012. An obituary written by a colleague, David Baines, described the younger Keneally as 'one of the doyens of Australian paediatric anaesthetic practice'. Baines said that while 'JK' thought of himself as the brother of a famous author, 'We at the Children's Hospital saw him as the famous brother of an Australian author!'[1] The brothers followed each other's career closely and Johnny was called upon from time to time to check medical details in Keneally's books.

One of Johnny's sons, Ben, married Kristina Kerscher, who became a Labor politician and later premier of New South Wales between 2009 and 2011. In a St Patrick's Day speech Kristina Keneally said that bearing a distinctive Irish name has some advantages: 'Admittedly it [the name] is by the good fortune of a great marriage, but it is one of the many reasons I feel very much at home here today. And, by further good fortune, the most widely read authority on Irish-Australian history is a distinguished member of my extended family, Tom Keneally.'[2]

Keneally's interest in Irish-Australian history began with Brother McGlade at St Patrick's Christian Brothers College. Teacher and pupil returned regularly to the college for special functions. They attended the funeral of Paddy Downie in 2010, at St Martha's Catholic Church, Strathfield, with McGlade giving the eulogy. Downie's schoolmates chanted the school war cry as his coffin was carried out of the church. McGlade died in 2013. Gerald Walsh, Keneally's 'Celestial' friend, died in 2014. Pam Davis (Bernadette Curran in *Homebush Boy*) and Mary Rafferty (Rose Frawley) have kept in intermittent contact with the man who once visited their childhood homes in Strathfield.

St Columba's seminary at Springwood is now a Catholic college of secondary education. The big sandstone building was covered by a pall of ash and smoke in October 2013 when bushfires raged through the Blue Mountains, but none of the school buildings was damaged. St Patrick's College at Manly has been converted to an International College of Management, with male and female students offered accommodation in the rooms once occupied by seminarians. James Madden would have been scandalised to see rooms with feminine apparel, bottles of alcohol and DVDs strewn about.

Some ex-seminarians, including Tony Abbott, thought that the Catholic Church had abandoned a sacred site: 'Now that the seminary has gone, my thoughts echo those attributed to Henry II: alive I did wish him dead; dead I do wish him alive. The Church leasing St Patrick's is as significant as the royals leasing Buckingham Palace. It is the ecclesiastical equivalent of the fall of Singapore.'[3]

Keneally felt no such sentiment. In 2008 he left Bilgola Beach and moved to an apartment on St Patrick's Estate, where the seminary's piggery (which features in *The Place at Whitton*) was once located. Ever since Baz Luhrmann filmed the big Gothic building as Jay Gatsby's mansion for the 2013 film *The Great Gatsby*, Keneally has referred to it as St Gatsby's Palace. Keneally says he is not haunted by the place, but his move back there does prompt questions about how well he has confronted his memories of the past. It is a defiant gesture from one who left that precinct with such misery in 1960.

Keneally looked for much more in the Catholic Church than it had to offer. Tony Abbott wrote that he sought 'a spiritual and human excellence to which the Church is no longer sure she aspires,' and Keneally might well agree. 'The same sense of boundless human potential, of man soaring to God's right hand, which led me toward the priesthood led me away in the end,' Abbott concluded.[4] Keneally probably would not care for the comparison with Abbott, who is entrenched on the other side of the political divide, but they were both fervent young men with hubristic yearnings when they entered the seminary. Abbott has maintained his faith, acknowledging that it is important to him, as it is to millions of Australians of various religious persuasions.

'In a way, Australia is like Catholicism,' Keneally said in 2001. 'The company is sometimes questionable and the landscape is grotesque. But you always come back.'[5] His practice of Catholicism has been intermittent. 'I still feel the pull to meditation and prayer,' he allowed, 'inspired by the old symbols – the sanctuary lamp, the tabernacle, the Stations of the Cross. But I have been unable to find my way back to regular observance and obedience, past the strictures, the follies, and the hypocrisies of the official Church ... I cannot return to the generous mystery of my boyhood faith.'

Father Patrick Connor, whom Keneally once claimed to be 'the best priest we had', has also been described as 'one of the most famous priests in America'. He was eulogised as a 'missionary priest, author and champion for social justice'. Connor was the priest Keneally may have been. Keneally was not destined to become a missionary priest, but he is certainly recognised as an author and a champion for social justice. His books do not include such titles as *Whom Not To Marry: Time-Tested Advice from a Higher Authority* (Connor's book published in 2010), but, interestingly enough, Keneally has had a lot to say in his work about marriage.[6]

Keneally's wife, Judy, has been in most of the scenes of his life, although her presence is not obvious in this biography. Keneally reckons he is the show pony, not his wife, who guards her privacy fiercely. Grahame Greene wrote, in *Ways of Escape*, that he respected the 'copyright' held by others who had been part of his life; in the same way, Judy's 'copyright' over her life with Keneally has, at her request, been respected in this book. At a dinner in 2014 Keneally paid her a uniquely Australian compliment: she is 'an absolutely top sheila'.

Opportunities to live in enviable places, meet interesting people and travel the world have been the upside of marriage to a peripatetic and increasingly famous and affluent author. As Tom senior once exclaimed, 'I never thought I'd see that this side of the long box!' His son and daughter-in-law have been privileged to see much of the world, although Sydney has always been home. Keneally values his home city most of all, even though he was tempted at times to live an expatriate life in places where his work was more appreciated; he once contemplated applying for American citizenship. But, as he wrote in *Jacko*, 'Nothing is like Sydney; nothing is like the arms of the Harbour on which our low-grade immigrant forebears stumbled.'[7]

Keneally is mostly just the same at home as in public: he is chatty, humorous and kind. 'Just the same but more so,' Margaret says. 'Very kind, very gregarious, very loud, adores telling lame "Dad" jokes and teasing people. He is endlessly patient with and attentive to his grandchildren.' Margaret accepted full-time employment as her children got older, working in corporate affairs for a major financial services company and part-time as a scuba diving instructor. She has been co-writing a historical crime series with her father. The idea for a series of murder mysteries set in colonial penal stations came to Keneally when researching a gentleman convict, James Tucker. Father and daughter enjoyed daily discussions on plot development.

The Keneallys value strong friendships with people from all walks of life. Di Morrissey cherishes the memory of a skiing expedition with them: 'Tom persuaded me to join him on a cross-country trek as he had become a keen cross-country aficionado. He told me it was a long trudge, a good walk with pretty scenery. However, on the downhill bits his encouraging "Follow me!" shouts as he took off ended in near tears for me. Tom was like those round toys you knock over and they flip straight back up again, something to do with their centre of gravity!'[8] Iain Finlay and Trish Clark also recall trips with the Keneallys, including memorable walks along the South Coast Track in Tasmania and the Ninety Mile Beach in Victoria.

Friends from the literary and entertainment worlds honoured Keneally at a testimonial dinner in June 2014. Playwright David Williamson spoke of a friend who has been part of his imaginative life for a long time. Author Richard Flanagan appreciates Keneally's kindness to many writers, including himself. 'I think Tom has for too long been misunderstood and underestimated in Australia,' Flanagan said. 'So much is missed with Tom ... His immediate virtues of gusto and bravura cloak a deeper and more profound humanity and obscure the substance of a finally inexplicable achievement ... he taught us all this: "We are no less then they".'

Actor Bryan Brown recalled a film festival in Sorrento, Italy, in 1980 (just before Keneally's visit to the bag shop in Beverly Hills). When the Australian group showed up at the party on the final night, the contrast between the beautifully dressed Italians and the motley bunch of badly attired Australians could not have been greater. Keneally, who never cared much about his appearance, was bursting out of a light-coloured suit. One of the host journalists asked, 'Who dresses these Australians?'

Fred Schepisi told the audience that Keneally talks like he writes: 'He has the facility to be so expressive, so articulate.' Schepisi commented lightheartedly that Keneally had a few crushes on young actresses.[9] Keneally was quick to retort that he wasn't the only one.

He loves women, became infatuated with a few of them and yet initially had difficulty writing about them. He has a faithful following of editors who think of him more as a friend than a client, including Carole Welch at Hodder & Stoughton, London; Judith Curr at Atria, New York; Rebecca Kaiser at Allen & Unwin, Sydney; and Meredith Curnow at Random House, Sydney. Nan Talese in New York is very fond of Keneally: 'Even when he was not being published by me, we kept in touch ... My husband Gay said, "I don't understand it. You decide not to publish authors, but you continue to see them!" I do believe in writers – I'm married to one!'

Keneally remains in contact with Carmen Callil. He sent her copies of his books, including *Flying Hero Class*, which was inscribed: 'To Carmen, dear friend and admired publisher. Tom Keneally 1991.' They often participated together on programs, such as one in January 2013 on BBC Radio 4, hosted by Mariella Frostrup, about Australian classics, including *Bring Larks and Heroes*.

Gillian Johnson often thinks about Keneally's claim that 'the truth always comes out in the end'. She says that 'Tom's soul is deep and wide and one feels connected to something bigger in his company. He was an awesome teacher for that reason . . . I think of Tom often and with huge affection.' Caroline Baum, who is still friendly with Keneally despite her distress over the introduction to *The Tyrant's Novel*, commented that he was always genuine in his apologies, and never slow to say, 'I screwed up.' That attitude, Baum says, means that 'you tend to treat him like a child who has done something silly. Because he is so hurt and bewildered, you end up saying, "It's okay, don't worry about it . . ."'

Others who had reason to be angry or disappointed with Keneally say things like, 'I'm really rather fond of the old bugger.' There are similarities with the 'author' in *Jacko*, who is 'really a kind old bugger'. Melvyn Bragg asked, 'Who could not like Tom?' Georges Borchardt is among those who liked Keneally, but more than forty years after the split he is still puzzled about Keneally leaving his agency, one of the most respected in the world. 'I always hoped Tom would come back to us some day and am still wondering what, in his view, we did wrong.'

Keneally, like his father, was once quick to 'come the knuckle', but less so with advancing age. He has the 'half-glass' nature, given to vivacity or melancholy, also like his father and grandfather. In this Keneally resembles another Australian writer, Randolph Stow, who claimed that he had inherited 'the vile Stow melancholy' he had witnessed in his father and grandfather.[10] The dark nights of the soul receded for Keneally, who endeavoured to fill his mind with the voices of the characters of his current book rather than of those accusing him personally. 'I tend to spend a lot of time repressing memories of meannesses and viciousnesses in my past,' he admits. 'They recur in idle hours. The old scruples will rush in as they did in those past days.'

There are not many idle hours in Keneally's life, probably because a full diary keeps the demons at bay – at least until he collapses with exhaustion. He was living at the pace of a man half his age as his eightieth birthday approached in 2015. He has been a spokesman for many organisations, including the Constitution Education Fund Australia (CEFA), created to inform and engage Australians of all ages about the country's democracy and Constitution, and he is involved in promoting 'Educating for Democracy' projects in schools. CEFA is committed to completing the Constitution with full recognition of Aboriginal and Torres Strait Islander peoples.

Keneally contributes readily to the national debate on various issues, including reconciliation and republicanism. He is always in demand as a social commentator and as a public speaker, which is hardly surprising, given how entertaining he is and how readily he charms an audience. 'I didn't want you to stop,' said David Malouf when chairing a session at the Adelaide Writers' Festival in 2010. Keneally has said that only Gough Whitlam could compete with him when it came to being garrulous.

Artem Samsurov, in *The People's Train*, does not 'flee a rostrum', and nor does Keneally. For both, this confidence is bolstered by 'the vanity of believing I have something to tell people'. Keneally delivered the 2014 Ray Mathew Lecture at the National Library of Australia on 4 September 2014, his topic being the future of the physical book: 'Gutenberg Fights On: A Survival Story'. He uses a Kindle occasionally to read books, and many of his titles are available as ebooks, but he considers these as 'electronic siblings' to the printed book form in which his books first appear.

Many technological changes have been absorbed into the business of writing he has built over many years. 'All my writing life,' he told an audience at an Australian Society of Authors function in 2013, 'I've been told that the book is dead. The book is still here – young writers want to be published in that physical form.'[11]

It is hard to imagine a world in which a Keneally book does not regularly appear among the new releases. In 2014 he was working on yet another novel, this time about the Balcombe family, who were neighbours to the exiled Napoleon on the island of St Helena before coming to Australia. Keneally's story, prompted by a Melbourne exhibition of Napoleonic memorabilia, will focus on the relationship between Napoleon and the teenager Betsy Balcombe. *Napoleon's Last Island* is scheduled for publication in November 2015.

He was also writing another story about a Catholic priest. 'I'd like to finish a realistic novel – sexually, socially and theologically – about a good priest who is a whistleblower ... I want to try and find what the good ones believe in. You can be sure it isn't the virgin birth.'[12] It seems rather appropriate that Keneally's last novel should be not simply about a priest but about a triumphantly *good* priest. Now eighty years old, he maintains that the world doesn't need any more Keneally books, but he needs them for his mental well-being.

In 1974, when *Blood Red, Sister Rose* was published, fellow Australian writer Nancy Keesing wrote to him: 'This is a very good book indeed and quite your best so far by a long long way (not excluding Jimmie Blacksmith). I've always expected you to approach greatness but, in the past have thought some of your works far from that – yet. I do think Australian writers are done no service by critics who apply limited and/or local standards to the works of potentially outstanding writers – of whom Australia can only claim a few which is not surprising in view of the population numbers.'[13]

'*Blood Red, Sister Rose* was a book of rare brilliance,' declared Simon King, Keneally's first editor at Collins, forty years after its publication, 'in which page after page sparkles with those rare story-telling gifts that distinguish Tom from so many other writers . . . he is one of the English-speaking world's great writers (and one of the most self-effacing of men).'

Peter Quartermaine, whose monograph titled *Thomas Keneally* was published in 1991, contended that 'Keneally's own geographical and cultural position is so unwaveringly Australian, that it is the scholarly criticism by his fellow-Australians that have best advanced our understanding of his work (however much he may complain – like Patrick White before him – about their lack of appreciation for his talents); and that such talents as he does have – and they are considerable if uneven – are best enjoyed and understood in the context of a wider appreciation of the range and diversity of Australian life.'[14]

The critics have been the bane of Keneally's existence, but they have good reason to respect an author who does approach greatness. He has written so many books, pounced on so many subjects and created so many vivid impressions; each new story is like a painting that has to be looked at a few times before one can fully appreciate its imagery. Just as a work of art may have flaws, so too may a book, and in Keneally's case the experts are particularly quick to spot imperfections.

Keneally has to be restrained near an art gallery because of his impulse to buy yet another painting. At home he paints acrylic abstracts, completes cryptic crosswords and walks around the vast parkland with its panoramic views. He listens to Bach cantatas and Gregorian chants; he has Mozart, Bach, Palestrina, Scarlatti, Handel and Irish folk music on his iPod. He says he has always been 'rock illiterate', although he did once go to a Kiss concert with Margaret when she was an adolescent. He sings folk songs in the shower. Relief from writing also comes from his sporting interests: snorkelling, kayaking, cross-country skiing and parasailing. In the footy season he still follows the fortunes of the Manly-Warringah Sea Eagles, and once proudly held their number-one ticket.

Across many years, Keneally has had the lead role in a long dramatic production with a huge cast and multiple scenes. In places all over the world his work has been rewarded with curtain calls and standing ovations, and sometimes dismissed with boos or walkouts, provoking him to extemporise heatedly. Onstage, he has spoken his lines charismatically and convincingly, an astute witness to life.

What a production it has been: *Homebush Boy Becomes Big Star*. The prelude to the script of his own life would read simply: 'Interestingly enough . . .' Keneally, who is fascinated by the everyday matters that make life interesting, frequently uses this expression. One of his early admirers, George Johnston, noted that Keneally was 'endlessly curious'.

Keneally has won award after award for his performances, including the Cultural Ambassador Award presented by the Council for Cultural Affairs, Taiwan in 2011 in recognition of his contributions to literature and human rights. He won the Colin Roderick Award in 2012 for *The Daughters of Mars* and in 2003 for *The Tyrant's Novel*. Each won on the basis of being the best book on an aspect of Australian life published in the previous year. That was gratifying for an author once accused of thematically deserting his country in favour of foreign subjects.

Keneally was particularly pleased to receive the Australia Council's highest accolade, the Award for Lifetime Achievement in Literature, which he was awarded in March 2015. 'You have to be my age to know how much this means,' he said. 'Writers start out wanting to conquer the world, dreaming of the acclaim of strangers, but as you get older it's the validation of your peers and your community that's most important.'[15]

In a move reminiscent of his returning grant money to the Literature Board in the 1970s, Keneally declined the $50,000 prize money that went with the award. He asked that it be given instead to a mid-career writer. Back in the 1970s he was secretly proud not to be dependent on the Literature Board; in 2015 he expressed his concern at the federal government cutting, by $105 million, the Australia Council's budget in order to fund a government-run arts program. His gift assisted at least one other writer who would otherwise have missed out.[16]

In 2014 Charlie Flanagan, Ireland's minister for foreign affairs and trade, announced that Keneally was among the recipients of that year's Presidential Distinguished Service Award. It recognises the contribution of the Irish abroad to Ireland and its international reputation. The award was presented to Keneally by President Michael Higgins in October 2014.

Keneally is also one of the huge troupe of characters in *Australians*. He warned readers that 'anyone who wears poncy breeches and a wig is in danger of being investigated in this book in terms of what's he's like in his vest and long johns'.[17] This search for Keneally has not exposed him quite so flagrantly, but he has been pinned down in various unexpected places. Versions of him or people known to him are easy to identify in his work. Interestingly enough, he lives daily with the characters of his current book and is quick to replace them when their story has been told.

Keneally is among the few Australian authors who have successfully engineered an international writing career. He has had a controversial relationship at times with editors and agents, which is inevitable when writing is a business conducted over many years. His books are found in distant places. Many have been translated for foreign editions, starting with a Dutch edition of *Three Cheers for the Paraclete* in 1970 and a Norwegian edition of *Bring Larks and Heroes* in 1971.

The most translations of Keneally titles, about thirty, were made of *Schindler's Ark*, the book that will forever be connected with his name. Steven Spielberg, in a pre-recorded film shown at Keneally's testimonial dinner in 2014, said to him: 'You've changed a lot of lives through those five decades of work, but you especially changed my life, and the life of global Jewry, with your amazing book, inspired by Poldek Pfefferberg, *Schindler's Ark*, and I have to tell you that nothing's been the same since. It took me ten years to decide to make *Schindler's List* from your book *Schindler's Ark*, but when it finally came to pass, it changed everything.' Di Morrissey thought that the story of Schindler probably changed Keneally's life too. 'But Tom never changed.'

'Thomas Keneally,' wrote Ludmila Page, Poldek's widow, in 2015, 'is a very fascinating, colourful, interesting human being, and a wonderful subject for a biography. We also consider him to be a very good friend of ours.'

When asked how he would like to be remembered, Keneally replied: 'As someone who genuinely interpreted the world and Australia, to the world and Australia.'[18]

His family has been lightheartedly prepared for Keneally's departure from this world. He says that he cannot get a headache without thinking he has brain cancer or a brain tumour and has everyone prepared for his imminent demise. 'I've always said to them, "If I look as if I am about to drop dead, tell me a joke, rejoice," because that's the way I want to go, smiling rather than gasping like a landed fish.'

His preferred death would be in the midst of a sentence, between a vowel and a consonant, without missing a breath. In the huge collection of his papers and memorabilia at the National Library, there is a small folder with tiny icons and the instruction: 'I am a Catholic. In case of accidents call a priest. Michael Keneally.'[19] Thomas Michael Keneally may well call on a Catholic priest when he is dying. He hopes Ed Campion will be still around to do the honours at his funeral. 'My dear friend Eddie is the only priest in the archdiocese willing to bury me in my time. So stay well, Eddie!'

You stay well too, Tom Keneally. There might yet be another *Schindler's Ark* to put on your epitaph. In any case, to use another of your favourite expressions, there are many other stories already written worthy of permanent inscription.

Acknowledgements

I am indebted to staff at the following institutions for their ready assistance: Australian Defence Force Academy Library, Canberra; Cobh Museum (Ireland); Columbia University Rare Book & Manuscript Library, New York (USA); Dixson Library, University of New England, Armidale; Duhallow Heritage Centre, Newmarket (Ireland); Edmund Rice International Heritage Centre, Waterford (Ireland); Hodder & Stoughton Archives, London; Macleay River Historical Society, Kempsey; National Film and Sound Archive, Canberra; National Library of Australia, Canberra; Queenstown Story Heritage Centre (Cobh, Ireland); State Library of New South Wales, Sydney; Sydney Archdiocesan Archives, Sydney; University of Glasgow Archives (Scotland); University of New England Archives, UNE Heritage Centre, Armidale; Veech Library, Catholic Institute of Sydney, Strathfield; Writers Victoria, Melbourne.

Many people have assisted me with the research and writing of Tom Keneally's life. I acknowledge with gratitude your help and interest: Fessehaie Abraham, John Atchison, Mark Baker, Lesley Banson, Mark Barker, Caroline Baum, Zane Berzins, Rochak Bhatta, Georges Borchardt, Melvyn Bragg, Bryan Brown, Rosie Cady, Carmen Callil, Edmund Campion, Theresa Carson, Trish Clark, David Coffey, Richard Connolly, Paul Corkeron, Beth Crawford, Don Crawford, Paul

Crittenden, Catherine Culloty, Christine Cummings, Meredith Curnow, Rohan Curnow, Tim Curnow, Maree Curry, Helena Custin, Pamela Davis, Paul de Launay, Paul Dellit, Agnes Dening, Judy Dolin, Peter Downie, Anthony Evans, Caroline Evans, Iain Finlay, Richard Flanagan, Nikki Fochesato, Robert Folkenflik, Vivian Folkenflik, John Ford, Charmian Frize, Therese Fuller, Patrick Gallagher, Chris Geraghty, Wendy Gooden, Ed Gregson, Peter Grose, Bill Guest, Peter Harrington, John Hitchen, Moy Hitchen, Gabi Hollows, Leone Huntsman, Michael Johnson, Lisa Jordan, Simona Jovanovic, Geoff Kempster, Gretel Kempster, Jane Keneally (née Hall), Jill Keneally, Kerry Keneally, Margaret Keneally, Nina Keneally, Pat Keneally, Tricia Keneally, Trevor Kennedy, Brian Kiernan, Simon King, Peter Lawler, Catherine Leutenegger, Jacquelin Low, Grahame Marks, Michael Matthews, Malachy McCourt, Athanasius McGlade, Robyn Moore, Elise Moran, Terry Moran, Imelda Moynihan, Celia Munro, Craig Munro, Helen Neill, William Oates, Carole O'Brien, Geoff O'Brien, Desmond O'Grady, Terry O'Neill, Rod Page, Michael Parer, Eleanor Parnham, Greg Parnham, Yvonne Protheroe, Mary Rafferty, D'Arcy Randall, Robert Raymond, Jennie Richardson, Steve Roberton, Jo Robertson, Michael Robson, Della Rowley, John Ryan, Fred Schepisi, Rosie Scott, Robert Sessions, Sandy Shapley, Paul Sharrad, Tony Sillavan, Margaret Smith, Nan Talese, Noel Ticehurst, Mick Tierney, Ion Trewin, Penny Tribe, Warren Turner, Debbie Underwood, Amanda Urban, Monsignor Usher, Shirley Walker, Tony Walton, Carole Welch, Shirley Yates, Philip Ziegler, Desmond Zwar.

I appreciate my agent, Sally Bird, and my publisher, Black Inc., for their belief in this book and their dedication to presenting it in fine form. Three scholars in particular have been very generous in assisting me: Paul Sharrad shared research materials from overseas archives and from his own Keneally project at the National Library; Terry O'Neill contributed a great deal from his expertise in Catholicism, books and authors, and helped with editing; and Paul Crittenden answered innumerable questions about Catholic practices and personnel. I hope this book justifies your investment in time and interest.

Using guidelines from the National Library of Australia, permission has been sought when extensive use has been made of archival material. When a brief reference or extract has been used, I have followed guidelines regarding fair use. Permission was sought from, and kindly granted by, the owners of copyright in various archives to quote from their correspondence: Tom Ascheman (Provincial, SVD Chicago Province for Father Pat Connor), Michael Attenborough, Georges Borchardt, Janet Buick (for Barbara Buick), Rachel Calder (The Sayle Literary Agency, for Tessa Sayle), Carmen Callil (Chatto & Windus correspondence), Peter Cinch (Province Leader, Christian Brothers Oceania Province, for Brother A. McGlade), Curtis Brown London (for Jacqueline Reynolds), Irving Glovin, Peter Grose, HarperCollins Australia (for John Abernethy and Alec Bolton), Houghton Mifflin Harcourt (for Thomas Stewart, Harcourt Brace Jovanovich), Brian Kiernan, Simon King, Paul G. Kirk Jr. (executor for the estate of Edward Kennedy), Chris Meney (Chancellor, for the Trustees of the Roman Catholic Church, Archdiocese of Sydney), Barbara Mobbs (agent for the George Johnston Estate), Ludmila Page (for Leopold Page), Robert Raymond, Robert Sessions, Simon & Schuster (for the letters of Patricia Soliman), Nan Talese, Simon Trewin (for the Estate of I.C.G. Trewin), University of Queensland Press (for D'Arcy Randall correspondence), Viking Press (an imprint of Penguin Publishing Group, a division of Penguin Random House LLC, for Corlies Smith and Alan Williams), Shirley Walker, Michael Wilding, David Williamson, Philip Ziegler.

To Tom Keneally, whose 'interestingly enough' reminiscences add zest to this book, I extend special thanks.

Notes

Archival Sources

Papers of Thomas Keneally, National Library of Australia: NLA MS 6428, NLA MS Acc05.198. Note that Acc05.198 has been extensively archived since much of this biography was researched, and there may now be discrepancies in box numbers. When the revised box number is uncertain it is shown in square brackets.

Papers of Thomas Keneally, State Library of New South Wales: MLMSS 2289, MLMSS 6101.

Papers of Brian Kiernan, National Library of Australia: NLA MS 7017.

Papers of Curtis Brown, National Library of Australia: NLA MS 10063.

Sydney Archdiocesan Archives, St Mary's Cathedral, Sydney (SAA): Individual Seminarian File: T. Keneally, Sydney.

Fryer Library, University of Queensland, The Hanger Collection of Australian Playscripts UQFL H0965 A and B: Thomas Keneally: *An Awful Rose* manuscripts.

Fryer Library, University of Queensland: Papers of John Beston: UQFL 429.

Fryer Library, University of Queensland, The Hanger Collection of Australian Playscripts: UQ HO 967: *Essington* manuscript.

Fryer Library, University of Queensland: UQFL 198: UQP Archive, Box 401, Unnumbered Folder: Keneally, T. *By the Line*.

Fryer Library, University of Queensland: UQFL 372, Shirley Walker Collection, Box 1, Folder 1.

Chapter 1: The Arrival of Thomas Keneally

1. Sydney Archdiocesan Archives, St Mary's Cathedral, Sydney: Individual Seminarian File: T. Keneally, Sydney. Notes and medical certificates addressed to Rev. Father J. Madden from Dr F. J. Kyneur, Blashki House, 61 Hunter Street, Sydney: 13 July, 30 July and 23 September 1959.
2. Sydney Archdiocesan Archives, St Mary's Cathedral, Sydney: Individual Seminarian File: T. Keneally, Sydney. Petition addressed to 'Most Blessed Father' (translated from the Latin original), 31 August 1961.

3. Sydney Archdiocesan Archives, St Mary's Cathedral, Sydney: Individual Seminarian File: T. Keneally, Sydney. Reference for Thomas Michael Keneally, from T. D. Garvey, Principal, St Patrick's College, Strathfield, 28 October 1952.
4. *Manly*, vol. 9, no. 1, 1958, pp. 14–15. Photograph of Keneally at award ceremony. His name was included in the List of Students (*Manly*, October 1959): Rev. T. Keneally S.T.B. He had been accorded the title Reverend when ordained as a deacon. 'S.T.B.' in Latin: *Sacrae Theologiae Baccalaureatis*; that is, Baccalaureate (Bachelor) of Sacred Theology.
5. 'The Unique Colonial', *Manly*, vol. 9, no. 2, 1958, pp. 72–74. Keneally was not acknowledged as the author.
6. Otherwise known as a 'late vocation'. The term 'delayed' was familiar to Manly seminarians. See 'Delayed Vocations', *Manly*, vol. 9, no. 1, 1957, pp. 29–30.
7. Edmund Campion, 'House of Dead Souls: Remembering Manly's Past'. Unpublished address given at the closure of the Manly seminary, September 1995.
8. Examples on pp. 41, 132, 149 and 180 of the Belmont edition of *The Place at Whitton* (New York, 1971).
9. Max Harris, 'The Arrival of Thomas Keneally' (review of *The Place at Whitton*), *Australian Book Review*, vol. 3, no. 9, 1964, p. 168.

Chapter 2: From Cove to Cove

1. In different documents variously spelled as Ann or Anne; McSweeney, McSwiney or McSweeny.
2. See www.census.nationalarchives.ie/reels/nai000534626.
3. Jane Keneally Family Archives: Letter from Aunt Nell, Timothy's sister, to his oldest daughter, Molly, 24 April 1934, addressed from Main Street, Newmarket, Co. Cork, Irish Free State.
4. Jane Keneally Family Archives: Names of children listed on a Keneally genealogical chart. There may have been others or variations in the names given.
5. Letter from John Keneally (Keneally's younger brother) to his parents, Tom and Elsie Keneally, written from Ireland, 11 September 1980. He had visited Newmarket, where he was told about Ellen and Hannah, sisters of Timothy Keneally. See also letter from Aunt Nell, Timothy's sister: endnote 3.
6. There are discrepancies in Timothy Thomas's birth date on various documents; however, Timothy's sister Nell, in her letter to Molly, told her niece that 'a big mistake' had been made in Timothy's year of birth. Nell checked the Newmarket Parish Book, in which Timothy's baptismal date was registered as 10 March 1859. In 2013 Catherine Culloty, a researcher in Newmarket, also checked the baptismal entry: 'Timothy was baptised "Tim" on the 10th of March 1859 to Jeremiah Kenely and Ann McSweeney.'
7. Timothy's name has not been found on lists of passengers, assisted or unassisted, migrating to Sydney. It is possible that he went to another port first and moved to New South Wales; however, this has not been verified. On his death certificate, it is stated that he had been in New South Wales (not Australia) for 49 years. He died in 1933, which means he would have arrived in New South Wales c. 1884, the year his sponsored siblings arrived. Timothy, as 'depositor' or nominator, made the sponsorship application in June 1883, at which time his place of residence was listed as Harwood, Maclean (possibly Macleay).

8. Quoted in Keneally, *Now and in Time to Be*, London, Ryan Publishing, 1991, p. 193. Copy in Thomas Keneally Family Archives and NLA MS Acc05.198, Box 3 (was 124/137), item 5 of 10.
9. State Records Authority of New South Wales, Series 5264, Reel 2675: Immigration Deposit Journals, 1853–1900, database sighted online at www.ancestry.com, 11 September 2013.
10. Nora married John Joseph Cusack and settled in Wallangarra, in southern Queensland. In the letter to Molly, Ellen referred to three families in Australia, which would have been Timothy, Jeremiah (Jerry) and Nora. Presumably Johannah died or returned to Ireland.
11. According to John Keneally's letter (see note 5), at least two of Timothy's siblings returned home from the United States: Hannah and Ellen, both having married there. Ellen Fitzgerald was listed in the 1901 Census of Ireland as living with her parents. Her four children were also there: Edward (incorrectly given as Edmond on the census form), Victor, Nance (Annie on the census form) and Loretta (Lorretto on the census form), all under ten years of age at the time. Ellen's occupation was listed as 'dressmaker'.
12. State Records of NSW: 'Online' Microfilm of Shipping Lists, Reel 2142 [4/4807], p. 125. Kenna is variously given as McKenna or Kennah. On her certificate of marriage it is Kenna.
13. Jane Keneally Family Archives: obituary for Mrs Kate Keneally (no date or publication details).
14. Thomas Keneally Family Archives: a newspaper cutting dated 5 August, c. 1889, described (Timothy) Thomas Kinneally [sic] applying for a licence for the Pelican Island Hotel: 'The applicant stated that he was an unmarried man, but intended shortly to go through that ceremony, as his intended was on board the *Woodburn*.' The *Woodburn* was a coastal steamer owned by the Clarence and Richmond River Steam Navigation Company. It was a passenger vessel used along the New South Wales coastline. Presumably Kate Kenna had been in Sydney or another coastal port before her wedding.
15. Ribbonmen belonged to the Ribbon Society, an agrarian secret society of rural Catholics, active against landlords and agents. Members tied green ribbons in their buttonholes.
16. Keneally, *Now and in Time to Be*, p. 204.

Chapter 3: Pudding Genes and Potato Faces

1. Obituaries for Timothy Keneally, published in the *Macleay Argus* (18 August 1933) and the *Macleay Courier* (16 August 1933), referred to his 'entering the employ of the late Mr. P.C. Hill'. The *Macleay Argus* (27 July 1889: Notice of Kempsey Licensing Court) included mention of transfer of the Pelican Island Hotel to Thomas Kenneally [sic] on 23 July: 'On application by Mr Jones adjourned for 14 days.' The *Macleay Argus* (10 August 1889: Notice of Kempsey Licensing Court) included proceedings at which Keneally's application for the licence of the Pelican Island Hotel was granted on 6 August, a few days before he married Kate Kenna.
2. Keneally, *A River Town*, New York, Doubleday/Nan Talese, 1995, p. 56.
3. See http://trove.nla.gov.au/ndp/del/article/22340313 and http://twgpp.org/information.php?id=1814143. Cusack's grave is in the Bailleul Communal Cemetery.

4. Thomas Keneally Private Archives.
5. Keneally, 'My Father's Australia', *The Bulletin*, 8 August 2000.
6. SLNSW ML MSS 2289, Box 1, Folder 3: typescript of 'In the Day of Anger' by 'Bernard Coyle', n.d.
7. Thomas Keneally Private Archives: letter to Kate Keneally from Johnnie, 14 April 1918.
8. Thomas Keneally Private Archives: letter to Dan Keneally from Johnnie, 6 February 1918.
9. Keneally, *Homebush Boy: A Memoir*, Port Melbourne, Heinemann, 1995, p. 94.
10. Keneally recalls Honner as old and patriarchal – the well-known Sydney doctor of later years – but he would have been thirty-eight at the time of Keneally's birth. See Leila Barlow, 'Honner, Richard St John (Dick) (1897–1962), *Australian Dictionary of Biography*, National Centre of Biography, Australian National University (http://adb.anu.edu.au/biography/honner-richard-st-john-dick-10534/text18701, accessed 27 May 2013).
11. Keneally, 'Waiting for a Hinterland Demagogue', *The National Times*, 28 February–5 March 1977.
12. SLNSW ML MSS 2289, Box 1, Folder 3: typescript of 'Death of An Innocent' by 'Bernard Coyle', n.d.
13. Copy provided by Edmund Campion, a contemporary of Keneally at Manly.

Chapter 4: I Hope the Germans *Do* Shoot You!

1. Tom Keneally Private Archives: Father Tom Keneally's War Diary, purchased 25 August 1943.
2. Jane Keneally: Family Archives.
3. Patrick White, *Happy Valley*, pp. 128–130.
4. David Marr, *Patrick White: A Life*, p. 56.
5. Sydney Archdiocesan Archives, St Mary's Cathedral, Sydney: Individual Seminarian File: T. Keneally, Sydney. Medical certificate under the letterhead of Dr J. G. Buckley and Dr H. P. Tindale, 7 Wentworth Road, Homebush, n.d. (c. November 1952).
6. Keneally, 'Independence Days', in Susan Wyndham (ed.), *My Mother, My Father: On Losing a Parent*, Sydney, Allen & Unwin, 2013, pp. 27–41.
7. Keneally, eulogy at the funeral of his brother, John Patrick Keneally, 30 July 2012.
8. Tom Keneally Private Archives. The second war diary is inscribed 'Thomas Keneally LC 74378 RAAF Staff Base PO Middle East'.
9. Jane Keneally: Family Archives.
10. Rosie Cady (née Keneally): Family Archives.
11. NLA MS 6428, Box 1, Folder 4: 7 June 1957. Letter from Registrar, Department of Labour and National Service, National Service Registration Office, Grace Building, 77 York Street, Sydney, addressed to Mr Thomas M. Keneally, St Patrick's College, Manly.
12. Keneally, interviewed by Robin Hughes, 9 September 2002 (see www.australianbiography.gov.au/subjects/keneally).
13. Keneally, 'Independence Days', pp. 27–41.
14. Keneally, interviewed by Rosanna Greenstreet, *The Guardian*, 12 September 2009 (see www.guardian.co.uk/lifestyle/2009/sep/12/thomas-keneally-interview).

Chapter 5: The GMH Fanatic

1. Keneally, 'Independence Days'.
2. Keneally, 'Memoirs of a Catholic Boyhood', *National Times Magazine*, 3–8 October 1977.
3. Keneally, 'Timelines', *Sydney Morning Herald*, 20 July 2013.
4. Keneally, speaking to Rachael Kohn: Spiritual Classics Series, ABC Radio National, broadcast 13 July 2014 (first broadcast 2007) (see www.abc.net.au/radionational/programs/spiritof things/spiritual-classics2c-poetry-and-exercises/5549964).
5. Keneally, *Homebush Boy*, p. 114.
6. Paul Crittenden, *Changing Orders: Scenes of Clerical and Academic Life*, Blackheath: Brandl & Schlesinger, 2008, p. 12.
7. Keneally, *Homebush Boy*, p. 35.
8. Keneally, *An Angel in Australia*, Sydney, Doubleday, 2002, p. 22.
9. Leone Manning (later Leone Huntsman) attended Marist Sisters' College in Woolwich, Sydney. She is the author of *Sand in our Souls: The Beach in Australian History* (MUP, 2001). Keneally has made mention of the prize-winning essays being published in *The Catholic Weekly*; however, no published account has been located. Manning (Huntsman) said that she was sure her parents would have kept a copy if that were the case. She has no recollection of publication.

Chapter 6: The Goodly Company

1. Bernard Curran, according to Ed Campion, was 'an attractive Dominican friar who also spoke at the Catholic Evidence Guild pitch at Park Street in the city on Sunday evenings'.
2. Street numbers have changed since 1952. The Davis home is now 64 Shortland Avenue.
3. Bernadette Chua, 'Homebush Boy Returns a Hero', *Strathfield Scene*, April 2013.
4. Keneally, 'The Cyclical Supremacy of Australia in World Cricket', in Michael Meye (ed.), *Summer Days: Writers on Cricket*, London, Eyre Methuen, 1981, pp. 115–118.
5. Keneally, 'The Cyclical Supremacy of Australia in World Cricket'.
6. Keneally, 'The Performing Blind Boy', in Brian Buckley & Jim Hamilton (eds), *Festival and Other Stories*, Melbourne, Wren, 1974, pp. 23–28.
7. Crittenden, *Changing Orders*, p. 12.
8. Email to author from Father John Ford, 31 July 2013.
9. Chua, 'Homebush Boy Returns a Hero'.
10. Keneally, *Homebush Boy*, p. 30.
11. Richard Connolly, interviewed by R. J. Stove, 'Visions of Ceremony', *Quadrant*, October 2013, pp. 109–113
12. Keneally, *Homebush Boy*, pp. 41, 89.
13. Crittenden also notes that McGovern was one of the first priests on the scene at the Granville (Sydney) rail crash in 1977 – Australia's worst railway disaster, in which eighty-three people were killed. A tribute was paid to McGovern in *The Catholic Weekly* on 25 January 2012, thirty-five years after the tragedy.
14. Keneally, *Homebush Boy*, p. 41.
15. Keneally, *An Angel in Australia*, p. 22.
16. Keneally, *The Place at Whitton*, London, Cassell, 1964, p. 68.
17. Keneally, *An Angel in Australia*, p. 111.
18. The number of the Downie house has since changed to 19 Shortland Avenue.

Chapter 7: This Closed Society

1. Keneally, *The Place at Whitton*, p. 12.
2. Keneally, 'Thomas Keneally', in Terry Lane (ed.), *As The Twig is Bent: The Childhood Recollections of Sixteen Prominent Australians*, Blackburn, Collins Dove, 1979, p. 121.
3. Sydney Archdiocesan Archives, St Mary's Cathedral, Sydney: Individual Seminarian File: T. Keneally, Sydney: Medical Certificate of Master Michael Keneally, signed by J. G. Buckley, n.d.
4. Sydney Archdiocesan Archives, St Mary's Cathedral, Sydney: Individual Seminarian File: T. Keneally, Sydney: Keneally to 'Most Blessed Father', 31 August 1961.
5. Sydney Archdiocesan Archives, St Mary's Cathedral, Sydney: Individual Seminarian File: T. Keneally, Sydney: [W. J.] Williams to Dunne, 20 November 1952.
6. Sydney Archdiocesan Archives, St Mary's Cathedral, Sydney: Individual Seminarian File: T. Keneally, Sydney: T. B. Garvey to Dunne, 28 October 1952.

Chapter 8: The Place at Manly

1. Keneally, *Three Cheers for the Paraclete*, Melbourne, Penguin, 1969, p. 14.
2. Crittenden, *Changing Orders*, p. 109.
3. Edmund Campion, 'House of Dead Souls: Remembering Manly's Past', September 1995 (unpublished).
4. Keneally commented on *The Boys in the Island* after Koch died in September 2013: 'For me as for many, Chris's first book, *The Boys in the Island*, was a proof that a young Australian could write fiction . . .' Keneally and Koch last met at the Adelaide Writers' Festival in February 2013. (Details from Stephen Romei, 'A Pair of Ragged Claws', *Weekend Australian*, 28–29 September 2013.)
5. Christopher Geraghty, *The Priest Factory: A Manly Vision of Triumph 1958–1962 and Beyond*, Richmond, Spectrum Publications, 2003, p. 143.
6. Edmund Campion, *Rockchoppers: Growing Up Catholic in Australia*, Ringwood, Penguin Books, 1982, p. 14.
7. Dr Rohan Curnow, Academic Registrar at the Catholic Institute of Sydney, compiled Keneally's results for the years at Manly: 1955–1959. Full academic transcript dated 11 November 2013.
8. Sydney Archdiocesan Archives, St Mary's Cathedral, Sydney: Individual Seminarian File: T. Keneally, Sydney: Keneally to Madden 14 September 1956.
9. Ed Campion, 'The Young Keneally', *Report: International Catholic News*, 18 April 1969.
10. Ed Campion Private Archives. The two poems, one dated 1956 and one dated 1957, are annotated: 'Tom Keneally, Early Poem. St Patrick's College Manly Poetry Society.' Campion, in correspondence dated 25 June 2013, wrote that he has not been able to locate anything about the Poetry Society. He thinks it may have been a 'fly-by-night' gathering of 'wannabe' poets.
11. Keneally, 'Cold Sanctuary: How the Church Lost Its Mission', *The New Yorker*, 17–24 June 2002.
12. Keneally, 'Cold Sanctuary'.

Chapter 9: Jesus and His Mates

1. Sydney Archdiocesan Archives, St Mary's Cathedral, Sydney: Individual Seminarian File: T. Keneally, Sydney: Keneally to Gilroy, 18 November 1958. Gilroy was then the primary bishop of Sydney (with a couple of 'auxiliary' bishops) but Sydney is an archdiocese, so the chief bishop was also archbishop. He was also a cardinal, an appointment determined by the pope.
2. Sydney Archdiocesan Archives, St Mary's Cathedral, Sydney: Individual Seminarian File: T. Keneally, Sydney: Thomas Keneally's request to the Vatican, 31 August 1961.
3. Crittenden has recalled that in 1958, four students were not allowed to proceed to subdiaconate or diaconate in the November ceremony. This was an unprecedented disciplinary punishment. They continued their studies with the class of 1959, gained approval after a couple of months, were ordained to the two orders in May and were then ordained as priests with their original class in July 1959.
4. Jo Robertson, office and service manager at the Sydney Archdiocesan Archives, has conducted a comprehensive search of Archbishop Carroll's papers to check for reference to Keneally's mission. No record was located.
5. Campion describes his association with the Movement in a chapter of *Rockchoppers: Growing Up Catholic in Australia.*
6. Sydney Archdiocesan Archives, St Mary's Cathedral, Sydney: Individual Seminarian File: T. Keneally, Sydney: Kyneur to Madden. Variations in titles and names have been transcribed as they appear in the original documents.
7. Keneally, 'Cold Sanctuary', p. 58. *Caritas Christi* means 'the love of Christ'.
8. Sydney Archdiocesan Archives, St Mary's Cathedral, Sydney: Individual Seminarian File: T. Keneally, Sydney: Questionnaire Regarding Mr Thomas Kenneally [sic], Candidate for Sacred Orders. Signed by G. Humphrey, Priest in Charge, Homebush, 17 October 1958.
9. Keneally, interviewed by Robin Hughes, 9 September 2002 (see www.australianbiography.gov.au/subjects/keneally).
10. SLNSW ML MSS 2289/1/1: handwritten story, no title, no date.
11. Sydney Archdiocesan Archives, St Mary's Cathedral, Sydney: Individual Seminarian File: T. Keneally, Sydney: Questionnaire Regarding Mr Thomas Kenneally [sic], Candidate for Sacred Orders. Signed by G. Humphrey, Priest in Charge, Homebush, 17 October 1958.
12. Keneally, 'Cold Sanctuary', p. 60.
13. Keneally, interviewed by Robin Hughes, 9 September 2002 (see www.australianbiography.gov.au/subjects/keneally).
14. Keneally, interviewed by Robin Hughes, 9 September 2002 (see www.australianbiography.gov.au/subjects/keneally).
15. Keneally, 'Cold Sanctuary', p. 60.
16. Details provided by Paul Crittenden, with David Coffey's permission, email dated 25 July 2013.
17. Pope John XXIII, 'Counsels for Seminarians', 28 January 1960. The third and final session of the Roman Synod had taken place the day before this talk to the seminarians.
18. Sydney Archdiocesan Archives, St Mary's Cathedral, Sydney: Individual Seminarian File: T. Keneally, Sydney: Thomas Keneally's request to the Vatican, 31 August 1961 and other papal documents.

Chapter 10: Banal and Glorious Motives

1. Scully later reviewed one of Keneally's books, *Season in Purgatory*, calling it a book 'for those who like their drama played out by real people in a real place' (*The Catholic Weekly*, 30 December 1976).
2. *The Australian*, 30 October 1969.
3. NLA MS Acc05.198, Box 281, n.d.
4. SLNSW ML MSS 2289, Box 1, Folder 4.
5. In 1970, when Lawler was a member of the Leeton Apex Club, one of its charitable fundraising activities was the publication of a satirical newspaper, *Leeton Libel*. Keneally agreed that Lawler could contribute the poem for inclusion. The poem was published as 'Precautionary Tales' by Thomas 'Kenealty'.
6. NLA MS Acc05.198, Box 320, File 2: O'Grady to Keneally, 11 April 1962.
7. Bernad Coyle, 'The Sky Burning Up Above the Man', *The Bulletin*, 23 June 1962. It was also included in *The Bulletin Book: A Selection from the 1960s* (Melbourne, F.W. Cheshire, 1966, pp. 5–9).
8. Keneally, interviewed by Robin Hughes, 9 September 2002 (see www.australianbiography.gov.au/subjects/keneally).
9. Keneally, interviewed by Robin Hughes, 9 September 2002 (see www.australianbiography.gov.au/subjects/keneally).
10. Keneally, 'Blackberries', *10 Short Stories You Must Read*, Australia Council Books Alive: An Australian Government Initiative, 2009, pp. 135–168.
11. SLNSW ML MSS 2289, Box 1, Folder 2. Hand-written application note for copy-writer clerk.
12. MLMSS 2289, Box 1, Folder 3. Keneally, 'What's God Doing This Week?', *The Bulletin*, 1 February 1964.

Chapter 11: A Roman Catholic Writer

1. Gloria J. Moore, 'On Tom Keneally's Catholic Novels', *Quadrant*, vol. 38, no. 4, 1994, pp. 66–68.
2. Ed Campion, 'The Young Keneally'.
3. Keneally, 'The Humanist Priest', *The Australian Humanist*, December 1969, pp. 10–11.
4. NLA MS Acc05.198, Box [42]: Parnham to Keneally, 16 March 1994.
5. Andrew Taylor, 'A Library He Calls His Own', *Sydney Morning Herald*, 24 July 2011.
6. Graham Greene, preface to *Ways of Escape*, London, The Bodley Head, 1980.
7. NLA MS Acc05.198, Box 148: Gilian Clark, Literary Directors' Department, Cassell & Company, to Keneally.
8. NLA MS Acc05.198, Box 148: Eleanor Corey, assistant to Bryen Gentry, director of Cassell & Company, to Keneally.
9. NLA MS 6428, Box 1, Folder 7: Corey to Keneally, 24 September 1963.
10. Max Harris, 'Recent Publishing and the Australian Identity', *Hemisphere*, vol. 10, no. 2, February 1966, pp. 2–6.
11. Max Harris, 'The Arrival of Thomas Keneally', *Australian Book Review*, vol. 3, no. 9, 1964, p. 168.
12. Noel Buckley, 'Black Magic', *The Bulletin*, 28 November 1964.
13. Keneally, 'First Voice: Tom Keneally Looks Back at the Writing of His First Published Book', *The Age*, 13 May 2006.

14. Rosalind in some references. A biography of Norton, *Pan's Daughter: The Magical World of Rosaleen Norton*, was written by Nevill Drury and published in 1988.
15. Graham Greene, introduction to *Brighton Rock*, Harmondsworth, Penguin, 1970.
16. Keneally, interviewed by Robin Hughes, 9 September 2002 (see www.australianbiography.gov.au/subjects/keneally).
17. Quoted by Edmund Campion in *Ted Kennedy: Priest of Redfern*, pp. 171–172.
18. Keneally, *The Place at Whitton*, p. 162.
19. John McLaren in *Overland*, 31 March 1965, pp. 48–49.

Chapter 12: The Fear

1. NLA MS Acc05.198, Box 148: O'Connor's reference, dated 1 May 1964.
2. NLA MS Acc05.198, Box [35], Bag 1: report dated 22 December 1964. The name of the reader was not given, nor was the report initialled; however, Robert Sessions has identified the reader as Nan Hutton, a journalist with *The Age*.
3. NLA MS Acc05.198, Box 148: Flower to Keneally, 22 May 1964.
4. NLA MS Acc05.198, Box 141B (probably old box 95), Envelope B. Nicholas Flower, Cassell and Company London to Keneally, 15 September 1964.
5. Bob Sessions, 'Farewell to the Book Trade', *Books & Publishing*, issue 4, 2013, p. 9. *The Fear* was not published till 1965. The manuscript would have been at the Melbourne office for a couple of months only.
6. NLA MS Acc05.198, Box [170]: Sessions to Keneally, 20 February 1968.
7. Neil Jillett, 'Neill Jillett Talks to Thomas Keneally', *The Age*, 11 November 1967.
8. NLA MS Acc05.198, Box [35]: Hutton's report, 22 December 1964.
9. NLA MS Acc05.198, Box [170]: Sessions to Keneally, 20 February 1968.
10. NLA MS 6428, Box 1, Folder 6: Buick to Keneally, 9 May 1967
11. NLA MS 6428, Box 1, Folder 6: Buick to Keneally, 8 August 1967.
12. Keneally, interviewed by Robin Hughes, 9 September 2002 (see www.australianbiography.gov.au/subjects/keneally).
13. Susan Wyndham, 'Interview with Tom Keneally', *Sydney Morning Herald*, 9–10 November 2013.
14. George Meredith was Spiritual Director at St Columba's, Springwood, and later the parish priest of St Columba's Church in North Leichhardt, which was the parish of the Martin family.
15. The Hospitaller Order of St John of God came to Australia from Ireland in 1947 to care for people experiencing disadvantage.
16. Heather Kennedy, 'The Happiest Family of Them All', *Woman's Day*, 22 February 1968, pp. 4–5. Details of Martin's early life.

Chapter 13: Individuality of Style

1. Gavin Souter, 'Refugee from Good Old Irish Theology: A Profile of the Novelist Thomas Keneally', *Sydney Morning Herald*, 4 November 1967.
2. Patricia Rolfe, 'The Flavor of Life', *The Bulletin*, 4 September 1965.
3. NLA MS 6428, Box 9, Folder 88: Keneally to Moore, 28 June 1966.
4. Gavin Souter, 'Refugee from Good Old Irish Theology'.
5. NLA MS 6428, Box 1, Folder 6: Bolton's Reader's Report, 8 or 6 [indecipherable] February 1967, to John Abernethy.

6. NLA MS 6428, Box 1, Folder 13: Keneally to Moore.
7. Jacqueline Kent, in her biography of Beatrice Davis, *A Certain Style: Beatrice Davis, a literary life* (Ringwood, Viking, 2001), wrote that the novel was called *Larks and Heroes*. 'Anthony Barker, a relatively new member of the editorial staff, suggested the addition of "Bring"' (p. 241). The poem from which the title was taken has the line 'Bring larks and heroes to our hedge'.
8. NLA MS Acc05.198, Box [75]: transcript of ABC, Victorian Branch, Education Department Series, 'For the Senior Student.' Broadcast title, 'The Novelist and the Theatre', 3 March 1970.
9. SLNSW MLMSS 2289, Box 3, Folder 1.
10. Jillett, 'Neil Jillett Talks to Thomas Keneally'.
11. NLA MS 6428 Box 1, Folder 7: Moad to Keneally, 2 February 1967.
12. NLA MS 6428, Box 1, Folder 6: Cassell correspondence with Keneally, December 1966 to December 1967.
13. NLA MS Acc05.198, Box [75].
14. *The Spectator*, 29 February 1968.
15. Quoted in Gary Kinnane, *George Johnston: A Biography*, Melbourne, MUP, p. 268. Johnston made the comment in a paper, 'Aspects of the Novel', presented at an Australian Society of Authors seminar, 9 February 1968.
16. NLA MS Acc05.198, Box [75]: Johnston to Keneally, 12 November 1967.
17. NLA MS Acc05.198 Box [75]: Clift to Keneally, 12 November 1967.
18. NLA MS Acc05.198, Box 245: copy of St Martin's Theatre program for *Halloran's Little Boat*, St Martin's Theatre Company, St Martins Lane, South Yarra, c. February 1968; includes blurb about Keneally by Johnston, p. 15.
19. David Marr (ed.), *Patrick White Letters*, Milsons Point, Random House, 1994, p. 325: White to James Stern, 18 March 1968.
20. Marr (ed.), *Patrick White Letters*, n. 41, p. 325.
21. Kent, *A Certain Style*, p. 241.
22. NLA MS 6428, Box 1, Folder 6: Curtain/Keneally correspondence.
23. NLA MS 6428, Box 1, Folder 7: Sessions to Keneally, 14 July 1967, in reply to Keneally's letter of 6 July 1967.
24. NLA MS 6428, Box 1, Folder 7: Sessions to Keneally, 11 September 1967.
25. NLA MS 6428, Box 1, Folder 6 and MS Acc05.198, Box 281: Moad correspondence with Keneally.
26. NLA MS Acc05.198, Box 281: Sessions to Keneally, 15 December 1967, 20 February 1968.
27. NLA MS Acc05.198, Box [75 or 161]: Johnston to Keneally, 2 May [c. 1968]. Johnston referred in his letter to imminent hospital treatment – he had lung surgery that year. NLA MS Acc05.198, Box [75 or 161]: Hunter to Keneally, 3 January 1969.
28. NLA MS 6428, Box 1, Folder 7: Reynolds to Keneally, 11 August 1964.
29. NLA MS 6428, Box 1, Folder 7: Reynolds to Keneally, 13 February 1967.
30. NLA MS Acc05.198 Box [80]: Reynolds to Keneally.

Chapter 14: I Stand by the Book

1. Greene's praise appears on the dust jacket of the hardback edition of *Three Cheers for the Paraclete*, and the back cover of the paperback.
2. NLA MS Acc05.198 Box 281: Greene to Keneally, 17 July 1970.
3. Edmund Campion, 'Chaplain Championed New Kind of Catholic', *Sydney Morning Herald*, 1 July 2009.
4. NLA MS Acc05.198, Box [161]: Roger Pryke to Keneally, 27 September 1968.
5. Candida Baker, 'Thomas Keneally', in *Yacker 2: Australian Writers Talk About Their Work*, Sydney, Pan, 1987, pp. 116–142.
6. 'Books: Spoiled Priest's Tale', *Time*, 28 March 1969, p. 102.
7. NLA MS Acc05.198, Box [161]: Manning Clark to Keneally, 10 October 1968.
8. Brian Kiernan, 'Great Expectations – Not Quite Realised', *The Australian*, 12 October 1968.
9. Keneally, 'Keneally on Critics: Have a Chocolate-Coated Funnel-Web', *The National Times*, 20 May 1972.
10. NLA MS 7017: Papers of Brian Kiernan, Box 1, Folder 1: Keneally to Kiernan, 14 October 1968.
11. NLA MS Acc05.198, Box 281: Kiernan to Keneally, 18 October 1968.
12. NLA MS 7017: Papers of Brian Kiernan, Box 1, Folder 1: Keneally to Kiernan, 24 October 1968.
13. NLA MS 6428, Box 1, Folder 4: Kiernan to Keneally, 30 October 1968.
14. NLA MS Acc05.198, Box 245: copy of St Martin's Theatre program for *Halloran's Little Boat*, St Martin's Theatre Company, St Martins Lane, South Yarra, c. February 1968; includes blurb about Keneally by Johnston, p. 15.
15. NLA MS Acc05.198, Box [161]: Johnston to Keneally, 30 September [c. 1968].
16. Letter from E. J. Trait, Cheltenham (Victoria), *The Bulletin*, 7 July 1962.
17. 'Two Cheers for Keneally', *Southerly*, vol. 29, no. 2, 1969, pp. 131–138.
18. NLA MS 7017: Papers of Brian Kiernan, Box 1, Folder 1: Wilding to Kiernan, 27 November 1969.
19. Tom Keneally, 'The Novelist's Poison', *The Australian Author*, vol. 1, no. 4, 1969, pp. 3–6.
20. 'Q&A: Thomas Keneally', *The Age*, 2 January 1995.
21. *The Bulletin*, 4 September 1965.
22. NLA MS Acc05.198, Box [161]: Harrington to Keneally, 24 October 1968.
23. NLA MS Acc05.198, Box [67]: Connor to Keneally, 20 October 1968.
24. Campion, 'The Young Keneally'.
25. Keneally, 'Keneally on Critics'.
26. Martin Levin, *New York Times Book Review*, 13 April 1969.
27. NLA MS Acc05.198, Box 232: Williamson to Playwrights, 26 August 1990. The copy in Keneally's papers – possibly a draft – differs slightly to the final version, quoted in full in *David Williamson: A Writer's Career* by Brian Kiernan, pp. 262–263.

Chapter 15: Why Not Write the Great Australian Drama?

1. Keneally, *The Survivor*, Melbourne, Penguin, 1970, p. 7.
2. 'Thomas Keneally', interviewed by Ros Dunn and Alex Stewart, *Neucleus* [UNE student newspaper], 19 September 1969.

3. Keneally, *The Survivor*, p. 19.
4. Geoffrey Hutton, 'Keneally on Stage', *The Age*, 2 March 1968.
5. *Halloran's Little Boat* was published by Penguin Books Australia in 1975, as part of its Drama 2 series. It was bound with Kenneth Cook's play *Stockade: A Musical Play of the Eureka Stockade*.
6. NLA MS 6428, Box 10, unnumbered folder, annotated 'added July 1987': Script of *The Childermas*. Clark's observation in annotations on typescript. 'This copy carries every evidence of the play's development in production. It is heavily annotated, revised and corrected, with carbon-copy inserts and stapled overlays of new text (an acknowledged Keneally method of revision).' A bound copy of *Childermas*, the version first performed at the Old Tote Theatre on 3 February 1968, is kept in the Main Collection at the National Library of Australia.
7. NLA MS Acc05.198: Box 245: Program for *Childermas*, Canberra Repertory Society, Playhouse, Canberra Theatre Centre, 15–18 October 1969.
8. NLA MS 6428, Box 1, Folder 7: Details of CLF lecture tour.
9. Details in file kept at UNE Archives, UNE Heritage Centre, Armidale.
10. Craig McGregor, *In the Making*, Melbourne, Thomas Nelson, 1969, pp. 252–253.
11. NLA MS Acc05.198, Box [145]: telegram dated 2 April 1968, addressed to Keneally at 5 Hibble Street, Ryde.
12. Jillett, 'Neill Jillett talks to Thomas Keneally'.
13. *The Armidale Express*, 4 October 1967.
14. Parer's book was published by Angus & Robertson in 1971 with the title *Dreamer by Day: A Priest Returns to Life*.

Chapter 16: The Survivor

1. Thomas Keneally, 'Origin of a Novel', *Hemisphere*, vol. 13, no. 10, October 1969, pp. 9–13.
2. NLA MS 6428, Box 1, Folder 4: Phillip Law to Keneally, 4 December 1967.
3. *The Canberra Times*, 24 October 1968, p. 3.
4. NLA MS Acc05.198, Box [281]: Zelman Cowan to Keneally, 30 October 1968.
5. Keneally, 'Origin of a Novel'.
6. Robert Barnard, *Death of An Old Goat*, London, Collins, 1974.
7. NLA MS Acc05.198, Box [75]: Keneally/Abernethy correspondence and readers' reports. First reader's report dated 1 December 1968. The second, and Abernethy's first letter, are undated.
8. NLA MS Acc05.195, Box 163: Nigel Watson to Keneally, 19 May 2003.
9. Nancy Keesing, 'The Traps Keneally Does Not Survive', *The Bulletin*, 8 November 1969.
10. NLA MS 7017, Box 1, Folder 1: Michael Wilding to Brian Kiernan, 27 November 1969.
11. Michael Wilding, 'Writer and Reader', *Southerly*, vol. 30, no. 1, 1970, pp. 70–74.
12. Brian Kiernan, 'Middle-brow Keneally', *The Australian*, 1 November 1969.
13. Judah Waten, 'Sin and Guilt According to Keneally', *The Age*, 1 November 1969.
14. *The Age*, Saturday Review, Letters, 8 November 1969.
15. NLA MS Acc05.198, Box [75]: Abernethy to Keneally, 4 February 1969.
16. 'The Survivor', *Kirkus Reviews*, 1 March 1970.

17. NLA MS Acc05.198, Box [75]: William Crook to Keneally, 29 December 1969. Crook later became a member of the Episcopal Church. He and Bill Jnr went to Ethiopia under the auspices of the Episcopal Church and established two orphanages during the 1985 famine. Crook contracted hepatitis B in Ethiopia, which led to his death in 1997.
18. NLA MS Acc05.198, Box [75]: Abernethy to Keneally, 2 August 1971.
19. NLA MS Acc05.198, Box [75]: Abernethy to Keneally, 24 November 1970.
20. John Ryan, 'Thomas Keneally in Armidale', p. 88.
21. McGregor, *In the Making*.
22. NLA MS Acc05.198, Box 263: correspondence between Keneally and the Adelaide Arts Festival Committee, 1968–1969.
23. Copies of the transcript are kept in the Barr Smith Library at the University of Adelaide and at the Flinders University Central Library.
24. NLA MS Acc05.198, Box [316]: Ron Blair to Keneally, 8 December 1969.
25. MS6428, Box 1, Folder 4: Correspondence between Patricia Zeppel, Assistant Representative, British Council, Sydney, and Keneally.
26. NLA MS 6428 Box 1, Folder 4: Kevin Long to Keneally, 8 June 1970.

Chapter 17: A Literary Juggler

1. Lamb's biography of Astley, *Thea Astley: Inventing Her Own Weather*, was published by University of Queensland Press in 2015.
2. Margaret Keneally, 'Astley's Great Escape', *Daily Telegraph Mirror*, 8 May 1993.
3. 'The Little That Helps', *The Bulletin*, 8 June 1968. Compiled by Denis O'Brien. Contributors: Patricia Rolfe and Sandra Hall.
4. Margaret Jones, 'Authors Bent on Joining the Affluent Society', *Sydney Morning Herald*, 25 October 1969.
5. NLA MS Acc05.198, Box [28]: contract signed 10 April 1970 with Commonwealth Film Unit, Department of the Interior.
6. NLA MS Acc05.198, Box [146]: Quoted from a *Sydney Morning Herald* column dated 10 January 1985.
7. Keneally, 'Bore Vidal', *The New Republic*, 2 July 1984.
8. MS 6428, Box 1, Folder 4: Alec Bolton to Keneally, 24 November 1970.
9. Keneally, *A Dutiful Daughter*, Fontana, 1979, p. 79.
10. Quoted by Keneally in articles. Review not located.
11. Angela Carter, 'High Gothic in the Outback', *New York Times Book Review*, 12 September 1971.
12. Garry Wills, 'Catholic Faith and Fiction', *New York Times Book Review*, 16 January 1972.
13. Keneally, 'Keneally on Critics'.
14. Baker, *Yacker 2*, pp. 116–142.
15. Keneally, foreword to *The Last Confession* by Morris West, Sydney, HarperCollins, 2000.
16. David Carter, '*Traduit de l'américain*: Tom Keneally and the Mechanics of an International Career', *Book History*, vol. 16, no. 1, pp. 364–386.
17. Years later, Keneally watched Evans in a Paris court engaged in a case about the explosion of an oil refinery in Kuwait.

18. NLA MS Acc05.198, Box [245]: Abernethy to Keneally, 24 November 1970. *Bulletin* articles listed in List of Works.
19. NLA MS Acc05.198, Box 245: MS of *Four Days of the Life of Jesus: ha Nosri.*
20. NLA MS 6428, Box 1, Folder 4: Abernethy to Keneally, 18 May 1971.
21. NLA MS Acc05.198, Box 281: Smith to Keneally, 26 April 1971. Copyright © 2015 by Penguin Random House, LLC, from LETTERS by Corlies M. Smith.
22. Nigel Kershaw, 'Two Steps to the Top', *POL Magazine*, July–August 1978.
23. Elizabeth Riddell, 'A "Literary Juggler" Comes Home', *The Australian*, 23 October 1971.
24. Keneally, 'Thomas Keneally – The Chant of Jimmie Blacksmith', in Kate Grenville & Sue Woolfe (eds), *Making Stories: How Ten Australian Novels Were Written*, Crows Nest, Allen & Unwin, 2001, pp. 184–205.
25. Keneally, 'Searching with Schepisi', *The National Times*, 2–7 May 1977.
26. Keneally, 'The Blacks' Camp', *Sydney Morning Herald*, 21 December 1974.
27. NLA MS Acc05.198, Box [67]: Smith to Keneally, telegram, 9 August 1971, and letter, 16 August 1971.
28. SLNSW MLMSS 2289/5/3: Abernethy to Keneally, 19 July 1971.
29. Keneally also spoke about including Slessor in Vol. III of *The Australians*: 'I write a lot about Slessor as a lens to the war. I think it is important to get away from the standard histories and look at the war through the poet war correspondent and someone like Damien Parer, a war photographer.'
30. 'Thomas Keneally Wins "Herald" $2,500 Award for Novel', *Sydney Morning Herald*, 21 October 1972.
31. NLA MS 6814, Papers of Jill Hellyer, Box 7, Folder 32.2: Keneally to Jill Hellyer, n.d. (but written from the Avalon address to which Keneally moved on 10 May 1972).
32. The Booker Prize in 1972 was won by John Berger for his novel *G*.
33. NLA MS 6428, Box 1, Folder 4: Abernethy to Keneally, 18 May 1971; NLA MS Acc05.198, Box 281: Smith to Keneally, 26 April 1971.
34. NLA MS Acc05.195, Box [149]: Keneally to Prime Minister Gough Whitlam, 29 December 1972.
35. NLA MS Acc05.198, Box [22]: Whitlam to Keneally, 6 February 1973.
36. *The Australian Author*, vol. 7, no. 2, 1975, pp. 23–27 (published version of Whitlam's speech at the Sydney Opera House on 4 March 1975).
37. NLA MS Acc05.198, Box [22]: Michael Costigan to Keneally, 13 February 1974.
38. Ed Campion, 'Morality Probed by Imagination', *The Times*, 4 September 1987.
39. Margaret Jones, 'The Hero as Victim', *Sydney Morning Herald*, 16 September 1972. (The article was reprinted in the *West Australian* as 'A Steady-Growth Stock on the Literary Market', 16 December 1972.)
40. Andrew Clark, 'Portrait of a Powerful Woman', *The Bulletin*, 24 April 1979.

Chapter 18: Don't Go Back, You Silly Bastard!

1. Jones, 'The Hero as Victim'.
2. Marr (ed.), *Patrick White Letters*, p. 399: White to Elizabeth Harrower, 1 June 1972.
3. Williamson's speech at Keneally testimonial dinner, Sydney, 11 June 2014.
4. NLA MS Acc05.198, Boxes 245, 248, 281: typescripts, notes and fragment of MS.
5. NLA MS Acc05.198 Box [21]: Smith to Keneally, 3 January 1973. Copyright © 2015 by Penguin Random House LLC, from Letters by Corlies M. Smith.

6. NLA MS Acc05.198 Box [21]: Smith to Keneally, 12 March 1973. Copyright © 2015 by Penguin Random House LLC, from Letters by Corlies M. Smith.
7. NLA MS Acc05.198, Box [67]: Simon King to Keneally, 24 November 1972.
8. NLA MS Acc05.198, Box 248: Typescript of *The Story of Little Ben*.
9. NLA MS Acc05.198, Box 245: Reynolds to Keneally, 24 November 1971, and Box 131B, Reynolds to Keneally, 23 December 1971.
10. NLA MS 6428, Box 1, Folder 4: Grose to Keneally, 2 October 1970.
11. Report of Abernethy's death: *Sydney Morning Herald*, 18 December 1972.
12. NLA MS Acc05.198, Box [80]: Grose to Keneally, 29 August 1972.
13. H. G. Kippax, 'Keneally's Year', *Sydney Morning Herald*, 3 June 1972.
14. Derryn Hinch, 'Breaking the US Book Barrier', *The National Times*, 30 October–4 November 1972.
15. Peter Cole-Adams, 'Novelist in Search of the Irreplaceable'. *The Age*, 17 November 1973.
16. NLA MS Acc05.198, Box [248]: Jean Battersby to Keneally, 6 June 1973.
17. NLA MS Acc05.198, Box [248]: Jeffrey Smith, Editorial Services Officer, QANTAS, to Keneally, 15 June 1973.
18. Sabine Durrant, 'How We Met: Carmen Callil and Harriet Spicer', *The Independent*, 23 May 1993. Spicer worked for Callil for many years.
19. NLA MS 6428, Box 1, Folder 4: letter from Carmen Callil to Keneally, n.d. [c. November 1973].
20. NLA MS 6428, Box 10, Folder 93: Tom Keneally. Draft of an article, 'The Genesis of a Novel'.
21. NLA MS 6428, Box 1, Folder 4: King to Keneally, 6 March 1973.
22. Keneally interviewed by Helen Frizzell, 'Saint Joan Exorcised', *Sydney Morning Herald*, 16 November 1974.
23. NLA MS Acc05.198, Box [67]: Simon King, Report on 'Joan of Arc: Thomas Keneally' to Chairman, William Collins Sons & Company Limited, 6 January 1973.
24. UQFL 12, Box 3: King to Keneally, 20 September 1973.
25. UQFL HO967: Television Drama ABC Release Script.
26. NLA MS Acc05.198, Box [20]: article by Jill Neville [*The Australian*, December 1978], but not located in newspaper search.
27. NLA MS Acc05.198, Box [18]: Daughter's note to Keneally, 12 November 1973.
28. NLA MS Acc05.198, Box [18]: Aerogramme, 12 August 1978, from P. H. Hardyment to Keneally.

Chapter 19: The Count and the Accusers

1. Frizell, 'Saint Joan Exorcised'.
2. Frank Moorhouse, 'Moorhouse and Keneally Review Each Other', *The National Times*, 3 February 1975.
3. Rudi Krausmann, 'A Coming to Terms', *Aspect: Art and Literature*, vol. 4, no. 1–2, 1979, pp. 42–44.
4. Granada television adapted *Gossip from the Forest* (see p. 189) and the ABC produced *The Survivor* as a mini-series (see p. 194).
5. NLA MS 6428, Box 10, Folder 94: Tsutomu Oyabu, 'An Interview with Tom Keneally', c. 1977.

6. UQFL 12, Box 2: Ziegler to Keneally, 17 July 1974.
7. Collins Archives, Glasgow: Keneally to Ziegler, n.d. [c. December 1974].
8. NLA MS Acc05.198, Box [61]: letters from K. L. Wright, Manager, Bank of NSW Avalon Beach, 17 October 1974, and from W. R. Parker, Manager, Bank of NSW Ashfield, 2 December 1974.
9. NLA MS Acc05.198, Box [22]: Alan Williams to Keneally, 10 October 1974. Copyright © 2015 by Penguin Random House LLC, from LETTERS by Alan D. Williams.
10. NLA MS Acc05.198, Box [280]: Ziegler to Keneally, 6 February 1975.
11. NLA MS Acc05.198, Box [280]: Peter Kemeny to Keneally, 19 March 1975.
12. NLA MS Acc05.198, Box [280]: Ziegler to Keneally, 6 February 1975.
13. NLA MS 6428, Box 1, Folder 2: Tessa Sayle to Georges Borchardt, 6 March 1976.
14. NLA MS Acc05.198, Box [280]: Kemeny to Keneally, 19 March 1975.
15 Columbia University Borchardt File: SERIES II Box 116: Hope Leresche Sayle 1970–75 File 3, Nan Talese to Borchardt, 21 March 1970.
16. NLA MS Acc05.198, Box 22: Talese to Keneally, 17 April 1975.
17. Borchardt Archives, Columbia University, Series II, Box 116: Hope Leresche Sayle 1970–75, File 3: Borchardt and Keneally correspondence.
18. *New York Times Book Review*; quoted on dust jacket of HBJ edition.
19. George Steiner, 'Petrified Forest', *New Yorker*, 23 August 1976.
20. *New York Times Book Review*, 11 April 1976.
21. D. R. Burns, 'The Ninth Green and the First Hole', *Nation Review*, 5–11 December 1975.
22. Brian Kiernan, 'Thomas Keneally in Top Form', *The Age*, 22 November 1975; Neil Jillett, 'Tom Hits the Heights', *Herald* [Melbourne], 11 December 1975.
23. Morris Lurie, 'Drink, Drugs, Style, Flair . . . but So What?' *National Times*, 1–6 March 1976.
24. *Times Literary Supplement*, 23 January 1976.
25. NLA MS 6428, Box 10, Folder 93: Letter quoted in the draft of article by Keneally, 'The Genesis of a Novel'.
26. NLA MS 6428, Box 1, Folder 3: Ziegler to Keneally, 25 February 1977.
27. NLA MS Acc05.198, Box [67]: Simon King to Keneally, 21 August 1974.
28. *Nation Review* 17–23 March 1977.
29. *Nation Review* 24–30 March 1977.
30. *Quadrant*, vol. 21, no. 5, 1977, pp. 4–11.
31. NLA MS 6428, Box 10, Folder 94: Tsutomu Oyabu, 'An Interview with Tom Keneally', c. 1977.
32. NLA MS Acc05.198, Box [67]: Ziegler to Keneally, 6 February 1975.
33. NLA MS 6428, Box 1, Folder 5: Ziegler to Keneally, 9 May 1977.
34. NLA MS 6428, Box 1, Folder 5: Sayle to Keneally, 22 June 1977.
35. NLA MS Acc05.198, Boxes 144 and 156: Stephen, Jaques and Stephen to Tress, Cocks and Maddox, Sydney, 26 June 1979.
36. NLA MS 6428, Box 10, Folder 93: Draft of article by Keneally, 'The Genesis of a Novel'.

Chapter 20: A Literary Bikie

1. UQFL 429. Papers of John Beston, Box 1, Folder 3: Keneally to Rose Marie Beston, 12 March 1975.
2. Report in the *Sydney Morning Herald*, 19 July 1975.

3. NLA MS Acc05.198, Box 149: details of fellowships.
4. The conference was billed as a 'Salute to the Pacific Honouring Patrick White, Nobel Laureate, MLA Fellow: World Literature Written in English', as part of the 12th Annual Meeting of the MLA, San Francisco, 27 December 1975, at the Continental 5, Hilton. Keneally spoke on 'The Earth's Worse End?: Split Consciousness in Australian Writing from the First Fleet to the Present'.
5. NLA MS 6428, Box 1, Folder 6: McCarthy to Keneally, 7 October 1977.
6. Borchardt Archive, Columbia University, Series II Box 223, File 3: Hope Leresche Sayle 1976: Talese to Keneally, 21 March 1975.
7. NLA MS 6428, Box 1, Folder 5: Sayle to Keneally, 22 June 1977.
8. Keneally, interviewed by Robin Hughes, 9 September 2002 (see www.australianbiography.gov.au/subjects/keneally).
9. NLA MS Acc05.198, Box [61]: 'The Treatment'.
10. Wayne Harrison (ed.), *Gossip from the Forest*, Sydney, New South Wales Building Society and Sydney Theatre Company, 1983.

Chapter 21: Close to the Intention of the Book

1. Fred Schepisi speech at testimonial dinner for Keneally, Sydney, 11 June 2014.
2. NLA MS Acc05.198, Box [161]: Information about a new feature film, *Libido*, dated 2 March 1973.
3. Borchardt Archive, Columbia University: Series 4, Box 223, File 4: Keneally to Borchardt, 5 January 1977.
4. NLA MS Acc05.198, Box [157]: Allan Scott to Richard Odgers, 9 March 1973.
5. NLA MS Acc05.198, Box [157]: Di Morrissey to Keneally, 16 March 1979.
6. Nigel Kershaw, 'Two Steps to the Top', *POL Magazine*, July–August 1978.
7. Kershaw, 'Two Steps to the Top'.
8. Robert Drewe, 'Inside the World of Jimmie Blacksmith', *The Bulletin*, 30 May 1978.
9. Thomas Keneally, 'Going to the Fair', *Playboy*, December 1979.
10. Turkiewicz's documentary film *Once My Mother*, released in 2014, returned in part to the story told in *Silver City*. Her mother was one of the Polish refugees who made a new life in Australia.

Chapter 22: Quite a Job

1. NLA MS 6428, Box 1, Folder 5: Transcript of interview between Peter McCarthy (for 2ARM-FM radio) and Keneally, c. 1977.
2. 'A Conversation with Thomas Keneally', host Martin Bookspan, presented on NBC Radio Network, 13 March 1983. Copy of transcript in NLA MS Acc05.198, Box [320].
3. Borchardt Archive, Columbia University Series 4, Box 223, File 4, Hope Leresche re Keneally 1978–83: Borchardt to Keneally, 5 December 1978.
4. NLA MS 6428, Box 1, Folder 1: Thomas Stewart to Keneally, 13 November 1978.
5. NLA MS Acc05.198, Box [320]: Ziegler to Keneally, 13 February 1979.
6. Stephen Vaughan, 'Boys in Blue', *The Observer*, 21 October 1979.
7. NLA MS Acc05.198, Box 38/7, Stewart to Keneally, 9 April 1979.
8. *Kirkus Review*, 1 July 1980.
9. Otto Scott, 'The Civil War as Seen by a Kangaroo', *Chronicles of Culture*, September–October 1981.

10. NLA MS Acc05.198, Box [320]: Sayle to Keneally, 2 November 1979.
11. NLA MS Acc05.198, Box [320]: Ziegler to Keneally, 19 June 1979.
12. Borchardt Archive, Columbia University, Series 4, Box 223, File 4: Stewart to Borchardt, 7 December 1977.
13. Borchardt Archive, Columbia University, Series 4, Box 223, File 4: Stewart to Borchardt, 27 January 1978. Copy in NLA MS 6428, Box 1, Folder 1.
14. Keneally, introduction to *Bullie's House*, Sydney, Currency Press, 1981.
15. NLA MS Acc05.198, Box [86]: Keneally to Lloyd Richards, 24 March 1982.
16. Ruth Lesser, *Journal-Courier* [New England], 9 May 1985. Copy in NLA MS Acc05.198, Box 87.
17. Damian Pointon, 'Aboriginal Theatre in London', *In the Spotlight*, a free entertainment guide sighted in 'Ephemera (PROMPT)' at the National Library of Australia, which included programs of *Bullie's House* productions.
18. NLA MS Acc05.198, Box [320]: Ziegler to Sayle, 2 April 1979.
19. Collins Archive, Glasgow: King to Ken Wilder, 1 February 1979.

Chapter 23: One Never Knows with Tom

1. Collins Archives, Glasgow: Ziegler to John Hooker, 13 December 1978.
2. Collins Archives, Glasgow: Ziegler to Hooker, 14 September 1979.
3. Collins Archives, Glasgow: Keneally to Ziegler, 20 February 1979.
4. Collins Archives, Glasgow: Ziegler to Keneally, 20 December 1978.
5. NLA MS Acc05.198, Box [76]: Ziegler to Keneally, 23 August 1979.
6. NLA MS Acc05.198, Box [320]: Handwritten note from Keneally to John Hooker, in sealed envelope, unstamped, dated 3 August 1979. Keneally may not have sent it.
7. NLA MS Acc05.198, Box [320]: Brian [Johns] to Keneally, 27 August 1979.
8. Ronn Ronk, 'A Global Perspective in Literature: Who's Got the Roots Down Under?' *Honolulu Advertiser*, 7 January 1980.
9. Keneally, 'Going to the Fair'.
10. Borchardt Archive, Columbia University, Series 5 Box 267, File 4, Hope Leresche File [Tessa Sayle Correspondence]: Borchardt to Keneally, 29 October 1979.
11. Derril Farrar, 'New Book-Style: Biggest Leap Since Paperbacks', *The Bulletin*, 26 August 1980.
12. Collins Archives, Glasgow: Hooker to Simon King, 16 March 1981.
13. NLA MS Acc05.198, Box 94: Keneally speaking at Brisbane General Members' Meeting at QIT, 27 June 1987.
14. NLA MS Acc05.198, Box 173: Keneally to Hergenhan, n.d. Hergenhan's article was published in *ALS*, vol. 12, no. 2, 1985, pp. 248–259. No reply from Hergenhan was located in Keneally's papers or Hergenhan's at Australian Defence Force Academy (ADFA) Library.
15. David Rowbotham, 'The Fight Among the Generals', *Courier-Mail*, 30 August 1980.
16. Farrar, 'New Book-Style'.
17. Quoted by David Day in *John Curtin: A Life*, Sydney, HarperCollins, 1999, p. 31. Day points out that that Curtin had 'invented' his school career, but the fact remains that he rose above humble beginnings.
18. Keneally, *Searching for Schindler*, Sydney, Random House Australia, 2007, p. 36.
19. Collins Archives, Glasgow: Memo from Ziegler to Ian Chapman, 29 April 1982.

20. Collins Archives, Glasgow: Ziegler to Keneally, 21 January 1981.
21. Collins Archives, Glasgow: Mentioned in memo from Ziegler to Ian Chapman, 8 June 1982.
22. Collins Archives, Glasgow: Memo from Ziegler to Peter Henson, 21 July 1982.
23. Collins Archives, Glasgow: Hooker to King, 16 March 1981.
24. Collins Archives, Glasgow: Ziegler to Sayle, 23 June 1981.
25. NLA MS Acc05.198, Box 78: Ziegler to Keneally, 13 August 1981.
26. Hodder Archives, London: Michael Attenborough to Keneally, 27 June 1973.
27. Keneally, *Searching for Schindler*, p. 154.
28. Ion Trewin, 'Recollections of Schindler's Ark', paper written as background information for Morgan Library in New York; provided to the author by Trewin, May 2014.
29. Carter, '*Traduit de l'américain*'.
30. NLA MS Acc05.198, Box 78: Ziegler to Keneally, 16 June 1982.

Chapter 24: A Great Story of Humanity, Man to Man

1. Keneally, *Searching for Schindler*, pp. 21–22.
2. Keneally, *Searching for Schindler*, pp. 33–36.
3. Keneally, 'Genesis of a Story'. *QANTAS Airways*, March–April 1982, pp. 34–36.
4. NLA MS Acc05.198, Box [59]: details of Glovin's involvement in a letter from Glovin to Dr Moshe Bejski, 26 May 1983. Bejski was a judge in the Supreme Court of Israel at the time Keneally interviewed him and Glovin wrote to him. Bejski was Schindler's forger in one of the prison camps.
5. Tim Warren, 'Keneally the Outsider Looking Into His Own Heritage', *The Sun*, 27 April 1995. Copy in NLA MS Acc05.198, Box 3.
6. Stephen Romei, 'Rushdie's Cursed Verse "was worth dying for"'. *Weekend Australian*, 30–31 August 2014.
7. Keneally, *Searching for Schindler*, pp. 109–110.
8. Keneally, *Searching for Schindler*, pp. 124–126.
9. Keneally, 'Archival Footage', 'Song of the Pen', *Australian Author*, vol. 37, no. 3, 2005, pp. 6–7.
10. Di Morrissey, 'My Mate the Laughter-Maker (Tom Keneally)', unpublished, written 28 July 2014.
11. The school has since been incorporated with two other schools and is now a co-educational school, St Luke's Grammar School.
12. Keneally, interviewed for *Making Stories: How Ten Australian Novels Were Written* by Kate Grenville, 1993.
13. NLA MS Acc05.198, Box [78]: Talese to Keneally, 23 April 1981.
14. Keneally misspelled Soliman's name as Solomon in *Searching for Schindler*. It was not possible to interview Soliman for this book, as she died in 2010.
15. NLA MS Acc05.198, Box [78]: Soliman to Keneally, 12 February 1981 [the letter is dated 1981, but it seems strange that it came before Talese's letter informing Keneally of her leaving Simon and Schuster. Perhaps it was a typo: 1981 should read 1982.]
16. NLA MS Acc05.198, Box [78]: Emilie Schindler to Glovin, 1 June 1981.
17. NLA MS Acc05.198, Box [78]: Keneally to Caro, 15 August 1981, and Caro's reply, 19 September 1981.
18. NLA MS Acc05.198, Box [78]: Glovin to Keneally, 26 March 1982.

19. NLA MS Acc05.198, Box [78]: Soliman to Keneally, 12 February 1981.
20. NLA MS Acc05.198, Box [77]: Trewin to Keneally, 5 November 1981.

Chapter 25: Keneally Opens a Door

1. NLA MS Acc05.198, Box 59: Trewin to Keneally, 5 November 1981.
2. Trewin, 'Recollections of Schindler's Ark'.
3. NLA MS Acc05.198, Box 59: Trewin to Keneally, 5 November 1981.
4. Trewin, 'Recollections of Schindler's Ark'.
5. Trewin, 'Recollections of Schindler's Ark'.
6. Collins Archives, Glasgow: Memo from Ziegler to Ian Chapman, 8 June 1982.
7. Hodder Archives, London: Trewin to Eric Major, 23 June 1982.
8. NLA MS Acc05.198, Box 79: Trewin to Keneally, 26 August 1982.
9. John Carey, *The 1982 Booker McConnell Prize Speech*. London, Faber & Faber, 1983.
10. *Searching for Schindler*, Sceptre edition, 2009, p. 199.
11. NLA MS Acc05.198, Box 79: random comments from press reports post-Booker prize.
12. NLA MS Acc05.198, Box 41: Finlay to Keneally.
13. NLA MS Acc05.198, Box 41: Tom and Elsie Keneally to Keneally, n.d.
14. NLA MS Acc05.198, Box 41: transcript of *Critics' Forum*, 6 November 1982.
15. NLA MS Acc05.198, King to Keneally 26 October 1982.
16. Editorial, *The Australian*, 21 October 1982.
17. Editorial, *Sydney Morning Herald*, 23 October 1982.
18. Susan Molloy, 'Thomas Keneally Wrestles with the Cultural KGB', *Sydney Morning Herald*, 13 March 1982.
19. 'Keneally's Good German Schindler', *National Times*, 5–11 December 1982.
20. Tim Warren, 'Keneally the Outsider Looking Into His Heritage', *The Sun*, 27 April 1995.
21. David Young, 'From Holocaust to Outback', *NZ Listener*, 5 May 1984.
22. NLA MS Acc05.198, Box 59: Soliman to Keneally, 12 February 1981.
23. NLA MS Acc05.198, Box 79: Leopold Page to Keneally, 6 May 1981.
24. NLA MS Acc05.198, Box 41: McGlade to Keneally, 17 January 1983.

Chapter 26: An Unattractive Deal

1. Collins Archives, Glasgow: John Hooker to King, 16 March 1981.
2. NLA MS Acc05.198, Box 79: Glovin to Robert Raymond, 19 November 1980.
3. NLA MS Acc05.198, Box 77: Sayle to Judy Keneally, 3 November 1982.
4. For details of Raymond's version of events, see 'The Man Who Uncovered Schindler', Chapter 16 of *The Queen, Rupert and Me* by Desmond Zwar. Raymond told his story to Zwar in Cairns just before the world premiere of the *Schindler's List* movie. The story, with some variations, is also told on several internet sites.
5. NLA MS Acc05.198, Box 77: Keneally to Borchardt, 12 January 1981.
6. NLA MS Acc05.198, Box 77: Borchardt to Keneally, 19 January 1981.
7. NLA MS Acc05.198, Box 19: Sayle telegram to Keneally, 23 April 1981.
8. NLA MS Acc05.198, Box 77: Sayle to Borchardt, 30 April 1981.
9. NLA MS Acc05.198, Box 77: Sayle to Raymond, 27 March 1981.
10. NLA MS Acc05.198, Box 77: Raymond to Sayle, 9 April 1981; Sayle to Raymond, 21 April 1981.
11. NLA MS Acc05.198, Box 77: Borchardt to Keneally, 14 April 1981.

12. Quoted in Desmond Zwar, 'The Man "Behind The Book", *Schindler's Ark* and the Movie, *Schindler's List*'. Version of Raymond's published story in *The Queen, Rupert and Me*, sent to author by Desmond Zwar.
13. NLA MS Acc05.198, Box 77: Keneally to Victor Temkin, 2 June 1981.
14. NLA MS Acc05.198, Box 77: Keneally to Sayle, 2 June 1981.
15. NLA MS Acc05.198, Box 77: Borchardt to Keneally, 14 April 1981.
16. NLA MS Acc05.198, Box 77: Borchardt to Keneally, 29 May 1981.
17. NLA MS Acc05.198, Box 77: Borchardt to Keneally, 2 September 1981.
18. Borchardt Archive, Columbia University, File 5: settlement dated 17 December 1981.
19. NLA MS Acc05.198, Box 77: Keneally to Raymond, 28 October 1982.
20. NLA MS Acc05.198, Box 77: Sayle to Judy Keneally, 3 November 1982.
21. NLA MS Acc05.198, Box 79: Glovin to Raymond, 27 January 1983.
22. NLA MS Acc05.198, Box 79: Glovin to Keneally, 27 January 1983.
23. NLA MS Acc05.198, Box 79: Keneally to Glovin, handwritten, n.d.
24. NLA MS Acc05.198, Box 79: Poldek to Keneally, 16 July 1983.
25. NLA MS Acc05.198, Box 107: Jeffrey Goldstein to Keneally, 25 March 1983.

Chapter 27: We Can Never Be the Same

1. Mentioned by Keneally in 'Ark Angel', interview with Paddy Burt, *Homes and Gardens*, December 1983, pp. 98–100.
2. NLA MS Acc05.198, Box [59]: Glovin to Bejski, 26 May 1983.
3. Keneally, *Searching for Schindler*, pp. 212–213.
4. Keneally, *Searching for Schindler*, p. 215.
5. NLA MS Acc05.198, Box 79: Glovin to Keneally, 16 January 1984.
6. NLA MS Acc05.198, Box 79: Keneally to Glovin, handwritten letter, n.d.
7. NLA MS Acc05.198, Box [67]: White to Keneally, 10 February 1973.
8. Borchardt Archive, Columbia University, Hope Leresche Sayle File 4: Keneally to Borchardt, 10 August 1977.
9. NLA MS Acc05.198, Box [41]: Keneally to Trewin, 19 July 1983.
10. NLA MS Acc05.198, Box [41]: Poldek to Keneally, 16 July 1983.
11. NLA MS Acc05.198, Box 41.
12. *National Times*, 18–25 August 1979.
13. Burt, 'Ark Angel'.
14. Stow, quoted in Gabrielle Carey, *Moving Among Strangers: Randolph Stow and My Family*, Brisbane, UQP, 2013, p. 124.

Chapter 28: Your Robust and Generous Nature

1. NLA MS Acc05.198, Box 38: details of visits to China.
2. NLA MS Acc05.198, Box 38: copy of *ACC Review: ACC 1978–1985*, booklet published by Ron Patten Publicity, St Leonards, [1985].
3. NLA MS Acc05.198, Box 44: fax sent by Keneally for the ASA's 30th birthday dinner on 10 November 1993. Keneally was unable to attend.
4. ASA Archives, NSW Writers' Centre, Rozelle, Box 60: Cork to Keneally, 23 November 1988. More details of Keneally's involvement in the ASA are provided in Stephany Steggall, *Status and Sugar: A History of the Australian Society of Authors 1963–2013*, Sydney, Keesing Press, 2013.

5. Baker, *Yacker 2*, pp. 116–142.
6. Edmund Campion, 'Morality Probed by Imagination', *The Times*, 4 September 1987.
7. NLA MS Acc05.198, Box 94: Shapcott to Keneally, 15 May 1987.
8. NLA MS Acc05.198, Box 90: Bowen to Keneally, 12 August 1985.
9. NLA MS Acc05.198, Box 124: details of the Constitutional Committee.
10. Report on the Centennial Park event by Brad Norington in the *Sydney Morning Herald*, 30 June 1986.
11. NLA MS Acc05.198, Box 96, annotated with notes to Peter [Sculthorpe].
12. Judith White, *Sun-Herald*, 18 October 1987.
13. Available online at www.home.aone.net.au/~byzantium/preambles/tk.html.
14. NLA MS Acc05.198, Box 180: copy of Keneally's statement published in *The Australian*, 10 February 1999.
15. 'Cultural Conflict Intrigues UCI Visiting Writer', *Los Angeles Times*, 2 June 1985.
16. Keneally, column in the *Sydney Morning Herald*, 7 May 1985.
17. NLA MS Acc05.198, Box 175: UCI Files: Keneally's comments on MFA MS Evaluation Sheet, 14 January 1993.
18. Keneally, 'This Excess Success of Southern California', *Sydney Morning Herald*, 4 June 1985.
19. NLA MS Acc05.198, Box 146: copy of article by Keneally published in *Today's Computers*, November 1984, pp. 14–18.
20. Bob Gosford, 'Ten Questions for Tom Keneally – Ubud Writers Festival Diary Day 4', *The Northern Myth*, 11 October 2010.
21. Keneally, 'The Other Code', *Esquire*, November 1991, pp. 72–74.
22. Report in *The Sun*, 17 October 1987.

Chapter 29: A Queue of Books

1. NLA MS Acc05.198, Box 232: Trewin to Keneally, 31 August 1984.
2. Keneally, 'The Man Who Knew Walesa', *Prize Writing*, London, Hodder & Stoughton, 1989, pp. 188–195.
3. Keneally, 'The Year 2020', *Sydney Morning Herald*, 4 August 1984 and 11 August 1984.
4. NLA MS Acc05.198, Box 122: All details from 'The Question of a Novel Suitable for Publication in Late 1985'.
5. Keneally, speaking to Rachael Kohn: Spiritual Classics Series, ABC Radio National, broadcast 13 July 2014 (first broadcast 2007) (see www.abc.net.au/radionational/programs/spiritof things/spiritual-classics2c-poetry-and-exercises/5549964).
6. NLA MS Acc05.198, Box 122: All details from 'The Question of a Novel Suitable for Publication in Late 1985'.
7. Baker, *Yacker 2*.
8. Baker, *Yacker 2*.
9. Susan McKernan, 'Keneally at Work in a Wretched World', *The Bulletin*, 20 October 1987.
10. Jill Neville, 'Tom What-Will-the-Neighbours-Think', *National Times*, 7–14 July 1979.
11. Keneally, 'Here Nature is Reversed', *Australia Beyond the Dreamtime*, Richmond, William Heinemann, 1987, pp. 11–72. (Patsy Adam-Smith and Robyn Davidson also contributed to the book.)

12. Keneally, 'Rogues' Continent', *New York Times Book Review*, 25 January 1987. *The Fatal Shore* was published by Alfred A. Knopf, New York, as well as by Collins Harvill, London and Sydney (both 1987).
13. Baker, *Yacker 2*.
14. Rod Usher, 'Victoria Saved – and So Were We – From Deadly Dull Ernest', *The Age*, 15 October 1987.
15. Howard Jacobson, 'The Small Fiction of a Great Country', *Weekend Australian*, 26–27 December 1987.
16. NLA MS Acc05.198, Box 133: copy of *Kirkus Review*, 1 August 1987.
17. *Our Country's Good* was written by Timberlake Wertenbaker and directed by Max Stafford-Clark. The play premiered at the Royal Court Theatre, London in September 1988. *Our Country's Good* and *The Recruiting Officer* then toured Australia in 1989 and returned to the Royal Court, before transferring to the Garrick Theatre, London, in 1989. It opened at the Hartford Stage, Connecticut, in 1990 and on Broadway in 1991. It was also in the repertoire at the National Theatre, Bucharest. Keneally addressed the cast during the play's second season at the Royal Court Theatre in 1989, after his second visit to Eritrea.

Chapter 30: Was It God or Politics?

1. NLA MS Acc05.198, Box 111: exercise book in which Keneally kept a diary of his first visit to Eritrea.
2. NLA MS Acc05.198, Box 111: Keneally to Haile, 13 January 1987; Haile to Keneally, 6 February 1987.
3. Keneally, 'In Eritrea', *New York Times Magazine*, 27 September 1987, pp. 42–57.
4. Keneally, 'In Eritrea'.
5. 'Tom Keneally', *The South Bank Show*, London, Directors Cut Productions, 80476, 8 October 1989. Produced and directed by Don Featherstone; edited and presented by Melvyn Bragg.
6. Dialogue in film made for *The South Bank Show*.
7. Keneally talking to Mark Corcoran, for *Foreign Correspondent*, ABC Television, broadcast 25 May 2004.
8. NLA MS Acc05.198, Box 13: copy of subject outline.
9. NLA MS Acc05.198, Box 13, received 1 July 1992.
10. NLA MS Acc05.198, Box 29.
11. Keneally, interviewed by Robin Hughes, 9 September 2002 (see www.australianbiography.gov.au/subjects/keneally).
12. UQFL 198, UQP Archive, Box 401, Unnumbered Folder: Keneally, T., *By the Line*, Randall's report, 28 August 1987.
13. UQFL 198, UQP Archive, Box 401, Unnumbered Folder: Randall to J. Keneally, 15 September 1987.
14. UQFL 198, UQP Archive, Box 401, Unnumbered Folder: Keneally to Randall, 4 June 1988.
15. UQFL 198, UQP Archive, Box 401, Unnumbered Folder: Randall to Laurie [Muller], 8 December 1988.

Chapter 31: *Seanchaí*: Gifted Storyteller

1. NLA MS Acc05.198, Box 132: Keneally comment about the origins of the book.
2. Keneally, speaking to Rachael Kohn: Spiritual Classics Series, ABC Radio National, broadcast 13 July 2014 (first broadcast 2007) (see www.abc.net.au/radionational/programs/spiritof things/spiritual-classics2c-poetry-and-exercises/5549964).
3. NLA MS Acc05.198, Box 233: David Ryan Publishing Correspondence: Keneally to Ryan, 12 December 1990.
4. NLA MS Acc05.198, Box 13: Keneally's comment at book launch.
5. Performed by a cast at the Irish Repertory Theatre, New York. Directed by Tony Walton; music and lyrics by Larry Kirwan; opening night 16 February 2014.
6. NLA MS Acc05.198, Box 211: 'Transport: Some Notes for a Musical Play', n.d.
7. NLA MS Acc05.198, Box 44: Keneally/McGlade correspondence 29 August 1994.
8. NLA MS Acc05.198, Box 12: Book Proposal: *The Great Shame* or *The Halving of Ireland*.
9. Keneally, 'Archival Footage'.
10. NLA MS Acc05.198, Box 137: Doubleday – Nan Talese Correspondence: Talese to Keneally, 11 November 1996.
11. The US edition of 1999 is titled *The Great Shame: And the Triumph of the Irish in the English Speaking World*. The UK and Australian editions, published in 1998, are titled *The Great Shame: A Story of the Irish in the Old World and the New*.
12. NLA MS Acc05.198, Box 138: ICM Agency Correspondence: Talese to Keneally, 10 October 1997.
13. NLA MS Acc05.198, Box 138: ICM Agency Correspondence: Keneally to Urban, 11 October 1997.
14. NLA MS Acc05.198, Box 138: ICM Agency Correspondence: Keneally to Urban, 17 July 1997; Urban to Keneally, 18 July 1997.
15. NLA MS Acc05.198, Box 137: Doubleday – Nan Talese Correspondence: Keneally to Talese, 11 November 1997.
16. NLA MS Acc05.198, Box 137: Talese to Keneally, 31 October 1998.
17. NLA MS Acc05.198, Box 11: Talese to Keneally, 26 June 1998.
18. NLA MS Acc05.198, Box 176: J. Keneally to Richard O'Brien, 17 November 1998.
19. NLA MS Acc05.198, Box 176: Keneally to Mark Aarons and John Loftus, 13 December 1993.
20. *Sydney Morning Herald*, 17 October 1992.
21. Keneally, 'Inner Struggles: *Voss* by Patrick White: A Re-Reading', *The Bulletin*, 17 December 2002–14 January 2003.
22. Samuel McCulloch, interview with Thomas Keneally, UCI, 8 April 1994.
23. Keneally, interviewed by Robin Hughes, 9 September 2002 (see www.australianbiography.gov.au/subjects/keneally).
24. Terence Moran, 'First Friday', *The Southampton Review*, vol. 3, no. 2, 2007, pp. 47–53.
25. Details in Keneally, *Our Republic*, Port Melbourne, Heinemann, 1993, pp. 183–184.
26. Dennis McLellan, 'For Keneally, There's No Place Like Oz', *Los Angeles Times*, 15 April 1993.
27. NLA MS Acc05.198, Box 43: Keneally to Spencer Olin, n.d. [c. 10 July 1992].
28. NLA MS Acc05.198, Box 43: Keneally to Michael Clark, 27 July 1993.
29. Millie Escalante, *New University*, vol. 28, no. 4, 1994, p. 1.

Chapter 32: Some Rich Grazing Amongst Other Humans and Events

1. Douglas Martin, *New York Times*, 15 March 2001, reporting on the death of Poldek.
2. NLA MS Acc05.198, Box 211: details of Spielberg and the film *Schindler's List* taken from miscellaneous articles in a folder, 'Movie of the Year' scrapbook, compiled by Walter Palevoda, Miami, Florida.
3. Schepisi speech at Keneally testimonial dinner, Sydney, 11 June 2014.
4. Tom Keneally Family Archives, eulogy for John Patrick Keneally, died 21 July 2012. Funeral held on 30 July 2012.
5. Ann Conway, 'Keneally Has Faith in Schindler, Spielberg . . .', *Los Angeles Times*, 22 March 1994.
6. Keneally, 'For Gentiles, Too, the Holocaust is Never to be Forgotten', *Los Angeles Times*, 31 January 1994.
7. NLA MS Acc05.198, Box 12: report of *Daily Trojan*.
8. NLA MS Acc05.198, Box 138: ICM Agency General Correspondence: Esther Solin to Carol Bruckner, 3 June 1998.
9. NLA MS Acc05.198, Box 176: Edward Kennedy to Keneally, 9 December 1998.
10. NLA MS Acc05.198, Box 211: details of Keneally and the film *Schindler's List* taken from miscellaneous articles in a folder, 'Movie of the Year' scrapbook, compiled by Walter Palevoda, Miami, Florida.
11. NLA MS Acc05.198, Box 12: Keneally's Yearly Report addressed to Clark, n.d. [c. December 1994].

Chapter 33: Have I Lost the Plot?

1. On p. 35 of *Our Republic* Keneally refers to Father John Ford, but the name of the lecturer was Patrick Ford. He published a book titled *Cardinal Moran and the ALP: A Study in the Encounter between Moran and Socialism 1890–1907* (Melbourne University Press, 1966). Paul Crittenden, a contemporary of Keneally at Manly, remembered being involved in the extracurricular research for Ford, called 'Flash Ford' by the students.
2. NLA MS Acc05.198, Box 132: Keneally's address in 'The Great Debate: Should Australia Become a Republic and Does the Fact that We Are Irish Influence Our Thinking on This Matter?' Organised by the Tipperary-Australian Association, n.d.
3. 'The Great Debate: Should Australia Become a Republic and Does the Fact that We Are Irish Influence Our Thinking on This Matter?'
4. Recollection of David Williamson at Keneally's testimonial dinner, Sydney, 11 June 2014.
5. Keneally's address published in *The Radical: Australian Labour Party*, vol. 16, no. 1, March 1985.
6. NLA MS Acc05.198, Box 176: Prime Minister Paul Keating to Keneally, 22 December 1995.
7. NLA MS Acc05.198, Box 176: Keneally to Kennedy re Clintons' visit, 9 November 1996 and 22 November 1996. Box 34: Keneally to Kennedy re Howard, 29 June 1997.
8. Keneally, 'Travelling With Two Aging Icons', *National Times*, 14–19 March 1977.
9. NLA MS Acc05.198, Box 132: ARM ephemera: Republican Movement's second anniversary dinner at Parliament House, on Friday 16 October [from the *Sydney Morning Herald*, 19 October 1992].

10. NLA MS Acc05.198, Box 137: Keneally to Talese, 3 February 1998.
11. Bryan Brown's speech at Keneally testimonial dinner, 11 June 2014.
12. NLA MS Acc05.198, Box 180: copy of article, published in *The Australian*, 10 February 1999.
13. Email from Keneally to Bob and Vivian Folkenflik, 21 March 2001.
14. NLA MS Acc05.198, Box 180: Republican Movement Papers.
15. Jamie Walker, 'Even to Staunch Republicans and First Australians, This Royal is in a League of His Own'. *Weekend Australian*, 10–11 November 2012.
16. Ellesa Throwden, 'Turnbull Re-launches Campaign for Australian Republic', *Lateline*, ABC Television, broadcast 10 May 2013.
17. Pearson/Keneally exchange reported in Peter Pierce, *Australian Melodramas: Thomas Keneally's Fiction*, St. Lucia, University of Queensland Press, 1995, pp. 4–5.
18. Tony Abbott, 'Uncle Tom's Republic', *The Adelaide Review*, October 1993, p. 35.
19. Imre Salusinszky, 'Mad Detour on Republican Pilgrimage', *Weekend Australian*, 29–30 May 1993.
20. Michael Sharkey, 'Tom Tries Too Hard', *Weekend Australian*, 30-31 October 1993.
21. Imre Salusinszky, 'Nothing But Disaster on This Flight', *Weekend Australian*, 23–24 March 1991.
22. Keneally, 'Critical Correctness', *Weekend Australian*, 13–14 November 1993.
23. Imre Salusinszky, 'Thomas Keneally: My Part in His Downfall', *Quadrant*, vol. 39, no. 10, 1995, pp. 23-26.
24. Barry Oakley's reply to Keneally: *Weekend Australian*, 13–14 November 1993.
25. NLA MS 10063, Curtis Brown Papers, Series 1, Box 186, Folder 1189: Hickson & Associates figures. Hickson & Associates also acted as literary agents for Thea Astley.
26. The article that Walker referred to was 'Thomas Keneally and "The Special Agonies of Being A Woman"', in Shirley Walker (ed.), *Who Is She?*, St Lucia, University of Queensland Press, 1983, pp. 150–162.
27. UQFL 372, Shirley Walker Collection, Box 1, Folder 1: Keneally to Walker, 10 July 1995.
28. NLA MS Acc05.198, Box 175: Walker to Keneally, 28 July 1995.

Chapter 34: The Nether Regions of the West Wing

1. Di Morrissey, 'The Literary Hell's Angel', *Daily Telegraph*, 10 October 1987.
2. NLA MS Acc05.198, Box 140: Keneally to James Frost, 4 June 1990.
3. Digby Diehl, 'The Reality and Psychology of Terrorism', *Los Angeles Times*, 7 April 1991.
4. NLA MS Acc05.198, Box 141: comment in the *Sunday Telegraph*, 17 March 1991.
5. McLellan, 'For Keneally, There's No Place Like Oz'.
6. McLellan, 'For Keneally, There's No Place Like Oz'.
7. NLA MS Acc05.198, Box 46: Amanda Urban, International Creative Management, Fax to Keneally, 6 February 1992.
8. NLA MS Acc05.198, Box 176: Keneally to Kennedy, 9 November 1996.
9. Paul Taylor, 'Looking for Nowhere to Be a Nobody: "Woman of the Inner Sea" and "The Place Where Souls Are Born"', *The Independent*, 2 August 1992.
10. Robert M. Adams, 'Frontier Fantasies', *New York Review*, 28 May 1992.
11. Keneally, 'Inner Struggles'.

12. Williamson's speech at Keneally testimonial dinner, Sydney, 11 June 2014.
13. NLA MS Acc05.198, Box 137, Doubleday Nan Talese file: Talese to Keneally, 18 November 1992.
14. Pierce, *Australian Melodramas*, p. 21.
15. NLA MS Acc05.198, Box 233: Chatto & Windus Correspondence: Carmen Callil to Keneally, 7 September 1988.
16. NLA MS Acc05.198, Box 233: Chatto & Windus Correspondence: Callil to Keneally, 3 December 1990.
17. NLA MS Acc05.198, Box 233: Chatto & Windus Correspondence: Callil to Keneally, 3 December 1990.
18. NLA MS Acc05.198, Box 233: Chatto & Windus Correspondence: Keneally to Callil, 17 December 1990.
19. NLA MS Acc05.198, Box 233: Chatto & Windus Correspondence: Callil to Keneally, n.d. [c. December 1990].
20. Warren, 'Keneally the Outsider Looking into His Own Heritage'.
21. Mark Annichiarico, 'The Birth of a Book: Doubleday Delivers *A River Town*', *Library Journal*, 15 February 1995, pp. 122–124.
22. Email from Bob and Vivian Folkenflik to friends, 13 March 2001.
23. NLA MS Acc05.198, Box 227: Tessa Sayle Correspondence: Keneally tribute, n.d.
24. Keneally, *The Utility Player: The Des Hasler Story*, Sydney, Sun, 1993, p. 9.

Chapter 35: This Year's Feather Duster

1. Email from Keneally to Bob and Vivian Folkenflik, 21 March 2001.
2. Keneally to Elinor Brecher, *The Miami Herald*, 6 March 1994.
3. *The Games of the XXVII Olympiad Closing Ceremony*, published by the Sydney Organising Committee for the Olympic Games (SOCOG), 1 October 2000.
4. Email from Keneally to Bob and Vivian Folkenflik, 21 March 2001.
5. 'Q&A: Thomas Keneally', *The Age*, 2 January 1995.
6. Dwight Garner, 'Up Late With Clive James', *The Weekend Australian*, 2–3 March 2013.
7. NLA MS Acc05.198, Box 48: Folder 'Movie of the Year' scrapbook, compiled by Walter Palevoda, Miami, Florida. Keneally quoted in an interview given at the time of the *Schindler's List* film's release.
8. Andrew Riemer, 'An Angel in Australia', *Sydney Morning Herald*, 12–13 October 2002, p. 10.
9. Barry Oakley, 'Triumphant Reincarnation', *The Bulletin*, 20 October 2002, p. 97.
10. Oliver Herford, 'A Woman Taken in Adultery', *TLS*, 22 November 2002, p. 21. Herford was reviewing the Sceptre edition, titled *Office of Innocence*.
11. Susan Wyndham, 'Interview: Tom Keneally', *Sydney Morning Herald*, 9–10 November 2013.
12. Wyndham, 'Interview: Tom Keneally'.
13. 'Atria Books Signs Thomas Keneally to Two Book Deal', *Readers Read*, 30 January 2013, www.readersread.com/atria-books-signs-thomas-keneally-to-two-book-deal-13020131.
14. Kathy Marks, 'Thomas Keneally: "I hope no one says Australia was born at Gallipoli"', *The Guardian*, 18 February 2014.
15. Andrew Riemer, 'Where Angels Fear to Tread', *Sydney Morning Herald*, 2 June 2012.

16. Ashley Hay, 'Sisters Offer a Fresh Focus on a Brutal War', *Weekend Australian*, 16–17 June 2012.
17. Alan Riding, 'Witness to War', *New York Times*, 16 August 2013.
18. Andrew Riemer, 'When the Home Fires Went Out', *Sydney Morning Herald*, 17–18 March 2007.
19. Wyndham, 'Interview: Tom Keneally'.

Chapter 36: All the Best Books Are Ahead

1. Wyndham, 'Interview: Tom Keneally'.
2. Keneally, interviewed by Robin Hughes, 9 September 2002 (see www.australianbiography.gov.au/subjects/keneally).
3. Keneally, 'Independence Days'.
4. Alfred Hickling, 'Also Known as Saddam', *The Guardian*, 31 January 2004.
5. NLA MS Acc05.198, Box 137, Curtis Brown Agency (Fiona Inglis) + Hickson Associates file: email from Urban to Keneally, 16 October 2002.
6. NLA MS Acc05.198, Box 37, Doubleday - Nan Talese file: Talese to Keneally, 21 November 2002.
7. NLA MS Acc05.198, Box 137, Curtis Brown Agency (Fiona Inglis) + Hickson Associates file: Rogers to Keneally, 25 October 2002.
8. Caroline Baum, 'Someone to See You', *Sydney Morning Herald*, 20 April 2002.
9. Caroline Baum, 'Only the Names Have Been Changed: The Writer Who Mistook My Life for a Novel', *Sydney Morning Herald*, 12 July 2003, pp. 4–5. Baum's experience was reported in Malcolm Knox, 'Tale of Morass - Or Writers' Lives', *Sydney Morning Herald*, 12 July 2003.
10. Knox, 'Tale of Morass - Or Writers' Lives'.
11. Email from Keneally to Bob and Vivian Folkenflik, 2 December 2004.
12. Keneally, speech to graduates at Melbourne campus of the Australian Catholic University, 2013. On that occasion Keneally received an honorary doctorate from the ACU.

Chapter 37: Dig and Dig and Disappear

1. 'Tom Keneally's Australians', *SL: State Library of New South Wales Magazine*, August 2009, pp. 12–13.
2. Carmen Callil, 'The Bounders of Botany Bay', *The Times*, 24 June 2006.
3. NLA MS Acc05.198, Box 137, Nan Talese file: Talese to Keneally, 28 November 2000.
4. NLA MS Acc05.198, Box 137, Deborah Rogers file: Keneally fax to Rogers, 27 November 2000.
5. Christopher Bantick, 'Rollicking Good Read', *West Australian*, 4 May 2002.
6. Patrick Allington, 'Keneally's Humid Cauldron', *Australian Book Review*, no. 314, September 2009, pp. 36–37.
7. Thomas Poole, 'Review of *The People's Train*', *The Queensland Journal of Labour History*, no. 12, March 2011, pp. 38–41.
8. Tom Keneally speaking to Jennifer Byrne on *The Book Club*, ABC Television, 16 September 2014.
9. NLA MS Acc05.198, Box 41: Transcript of *Critics' Forum*, 6 November 1982, sent to Keneally by Philip French, producer of the program.

10. Julia Pascal, 'Clichéd Chronicle of the Novelist and His Famous Tale of a Heroic Saviour', *The Independent*, 3 November 2008. See also Dwight Garner, 'A Wartime Tale That Had to Be Told', *New York Times*, 25 December 2008.
11. Alastair Niven, 'Ion Trewin Obituary', *The Guardian*, 9 April 2015.
12. Hickling, 'Also Known as Saddam'.

Epilogue: Interestingly Enough . . .

1. David Baines, 'Obituary: John Patrick Keneally AM', n.d., www.apagbi.org.uk/about-us/membership/obituaries/john-keneally.
2. Speech by New South Wales Premier Kristina Keneally, delivered at the Lansdowne Club Lunch, Sydney, 19 March 2010.
3. Tony Abbott, 'St Patrick's College, Manly, Seminary Becomes a Hotel School!', *AD2000*, vol. 9, no. 1, February 1996, p. 7.
4. Tony Abbott, 'Why I Left the Priesthood', *The Bulletin*, 18 August 1987.
5. 'A Century of Achievement: The 100 Most Influential Australians: An Impact Beyond Celebrity', Part 3, *Sydney Morning Herald*, 24 January 2001.
6. Connor's funeral Mass was held on 18 April 2015. He was well-known for inspiring Pulitzer Prize–winning columnist Maureen Dowd to write 'An Ideal Husband', one of the *New York Times*'s most emailed articles (published 6 July 2008). Following its success, Connor appeared on the *Today Show* and wrote the book *Whom Not to Marry: Time-Tested Advice from a Higher Authority* (Hyperion, New York, 2010).
7. Keneally, *Jacko*, Port Melbourne, William Heinemann Australia, 1993, p. 113.
8. Morrissey, 'My Mate the Laughter Maker: Tom Keneally'.
9. Speeches at Keneally's testimonial dinner, Sydney, 11 June 2014.
10. Stow, quoted in Gabrielle Carey, *Moving Among Strangers*, p. 41.
11. Tom Keneally in conversation with Angelo Loukakis, Sydney, 20 February 2013.
12. Chris Johnston, 'The Good Life: Lunch with Tom Keneally', *The Age*, 20 December 2014.
13. NLA MS Acc05.198, Box 21: Nancy Keesing to Keneally, 21 December 1974.
14. Peter Quartermaine, *Tom Keneally*, London, Edward Arnold, 1991.
15. Stephen Romei, 'Tom Keneally Collects Lifetime Achievement in Literature', *The Australian*, 9 March 2015.
16. Susan Wyndham, 'Thomas Keneally's Generosity Funds Novelist Ashley Hay', *Sydney Morning Herald*, 18 June 2015.
17. Keneally, speech at the launch of Volume I of *Australians*, 27 August 2009.
18. 'Q&A: Thomas Keneally', *The Age*, 2 January 1995.
19. NLA MS Acc005.198, Box 148.

List of Works

Novels (first editions)

The Place at Whitton, London, Cassell, 1964.
The Fear, Melbourne, Cassell, 1965.
Bring Larks and Heroes, Melbourne, Cassell, 1967.
Three Cheers for the Paraclete, Sydney, Angus & Robertson, 1968.
The Survivor, Sydney, Angus & Robertson, 1969.
A Dutiful Daughter, Sydney, Angus & Robertson, 1971.
The Chant of Jimmie Blacksmith, Sydney, Angus & Robertson, 1972.
Blood Red, Sister Rose, London, Collins, 1974.
Gossip from the Forest, London, Collins, 1975.
Moses the Lawgiver, London, Collins, 1975.
Season in Purgatory, London, Collins, 1976.
A Victim of the Aurora, London, Collins, 1977.
Confederates, London, Collins, 1979.
Passenger, London, Collins, 1979.
The Cut-Rate Kingdom, Sydney, Wildcat Press, 1980.
Schindler's Ark, London, Hodder & Stoughton, 1982.
A Family Madness, London, Hodder & Stoughton, 1985.
The Playmaker, London, Hodder & Stoughton, 1987.
Act of Grace, London, Chatto & Windus, 1988.
Towards Asmara, London, Hodder & Stoughton, 1989.
By the Line, St Lucia, University of Queensland, 1989.
Flying Hero Class, London, Hodder & Stoughton, 1991.
Chief of Staff, London, Chatto & Windus, 1991.
Woman of the Inner Sea, London, Hodder & Stoughton, 1992.
Jacko, Port Melbourne, Heinemann, 1993.
A River Town, New York, Doubleday/Nan Talese, 1995.

Bettany's Book, Sydney, Doubleday, 2000.
An Angel in Australia, Sydney, Doubleday, 2002.
The Tyrant's Novel, Sydney, Doubleday, 2003.
The Widow and Her Hero, Sydney, Doubleday, 2007.
The People's Train, Sydney, Random House, 2009.
The Daughters of Mars, Sydney, Random House, 2012.
Shame and the Captives, Sydney, Random House, 2013.

Non-fiction

Outback, Sydney, Hodder & Stoughton, 1983.
Now and in Time to Be: Ireland and the Irish, London, Ryan Publishing, 1991.
The Place Where Souls Are Born: A Journey into the American Southwest, New York, Simon & Schuster, 1992.
Our Republic, Port Melbourne, Heinemann, 1993.
The Utility Player: The Des Hasler Story, Sydney, Sun Books, 1993.
Homebush Boy: A Memoir, Port Melbourne, Heinemann, 1995.
The Great Shame: A Story of the Irish in the Old World and the New, Milsons Point, Random House Australia, 1998.
American Scoundrel: The Life of the Notorious Civil War General Dan Sickles, New York, Doubleday, 2002.
Lincoln, New York, Viking Weidenfeld and Nicolson, 2003.
Searching for Schindler, Sydney, Random House Australia, 2007.
Australians: Origins to Eureka (vol. I), Crows Nest, Allen & Unwin, 2009.
Australians: Eureka to the Diggers (vol. II), Crows Nest, Allen & Unwin, 2011.
Australians: Flappers to Vietnam (vol. III), Crows Nest, Allen & Unwin, 2014.

Drama

Halloran's Little Boat: A Play Based on the Novel 'Bring Larks and Heroes', Ringwood, Penguin Books Australia, 1975. (Part of the Drama 2 series, bound with Kenneth Cook's play, Stockade: A Musical Play of the Eureka Stockade.)
Childermas, Old Tote Theatre, University of New South Wales, 1968.
An Awful Rose (typescript), Hanger Collection of Australian Playscripts, Fryer Library, University of Queensland, 1972.
Bullie's House, Sydney, Currency Press, 1981.
Gossip from the Forest (edited by Wayne Harrison, Sydney Theatre Company Playtext Series), Sydney, NSW Building Society and Sydney Theatre Company, 1983.
Either, Or, produced at Theatre J, Washington DC Jewish Community Centre, Washington, 2007. Directed by Daniel De Raey. (No typescript located.)
Transport, produced at the Irish Repertory Theatre, New York, 2014. Directed by Tony Walton.

Film scripts

'The Priest', segment for *Libido*, Producers' and Directors' Guild, 1973.
Essington (manuscript), Hanger Collection of Australian Playscripts, Fryer Library, University of Queensland. ABC Television film, 1975.
Silver City (with Sophia Turkiewicz), Australia, Limelight Productions, 1984.

Children's books

Ned Kelly and the City of Bees, London, Jonathan Cape, 1978.
Roos in Shoes, Milsons Point, Random House, 2003.

Short stories

'The Sky Burning Up Above the Man', *The Bulletin*, 23 June 1962.
'What's God Doing This Week?' *The Bulletin*, 1 February 1964.
'The Performing Blind Boy', in Brian Buckley & Jim Hamilton (eds), *Festival and Other Stories*, Melbourne, Wren, 1974.
'Going to the Fair', *Playboy*, December 1979.
'The Year 2020', *Sydney Morning Herald*, 4 August 1984 and 11 August 1984.
'The Tormented Brother', *Australian Literary Magazine*, 28–29 September 1985.
'Aunt Cloe', *Antipodes*, vol. 2, no. 1, 1988.
'Sisters Under the Skin', *Outrider: A Journal of Multicultural Literature in Australia*, vol. 5, no. 1/2, 1988.
'The Man Who Knew Walesa', in *Prize Writing: An Original Collection of Writings by Past Winners to Celebrate 21 Years of The Booker Prize*, London, Hodder & Stoughton, 1989.
'Blackberries', in *Ten Short Stories You Must Read This Year*, Strawberry Hills, Australia Council for the Arts, 2009.

Articles, columns, essays, introductions, obituaries and reviews

'A Novelist Looks at Prose Writing', *Opinion*, August 1967, pp. 34–40.
'Thomas Keneally Meets the Press: Subsidies for Authors', *The Canberra Times*, 27 January 1968, p. 12.
'Short Change for the Deaf', *The Australian*, 30 October 1969, p. 9.
'The Novelist's Poison', *The Australian Author*, vol. 1, no. 4, 1969, pp. 3–6.
'Origin of a Novel', *Hemisphere*, vol. 13, no. 10, 1969, pp. 9–13.
'The Humanist Priest', *The Australian Humanist*, December 1969, pp. 10–11.
'Keneally in New York', *The Bulletin*, 24 October 1970, pp. 43–45.
'Keneally in Ireland', *The Bulletin*, 21 November 1970, pp. 47–49.
'Keneally in County Galway', *The Bulletin*, 12 December 1970, pp. 47–49.
'Keneally Meets a Welshman', *The Bulletin*, 2 January 1971, pp. 32–33.
'Keneally and the Girls of Ireland', *The Bulletin*, 20 February 1971, pp. 45–46.
'Keneally on Critics: Have a Chocolate-Coated Funnel-Web', *The National Times*, 20 May 1972, p. 5.
'The Blacks' Camp', *The Sydney Morning Herald*, 21 December 1974, p. 15.
'Waiting for a Bush Demagogue', *The National Times*, 28 February–5 March 1977, pp. 3–8.
'Searching with Schepisi', *The National Times*, 2–7 May 1977, pp. 46–49.
'Travelling With Two Aging Icons', *The National Times*, 14–19 March 1977, pp. 3–10.
'In Reply to D. Jenkyn', *Nation Review*, 24–30 March 1977, p. 532 [microfilm National Library of Australia].
'Memoirs of a Catholic Boyhood', *The National Times Magazine*, 3–8 October 1977, pp. 17–22.
'Thomas Keneally', in Terry Lane (ed.), *As the Twig Is Bent: The Childhood Recollections of Sixteen Prominent Australians*, Blackburn, Collins Dove, 1979.
'The Cyclical Supremacy of Australia in World Cricket', in Michael Meyer (ed.), *Summer Days: Writers on Cricket*, London, Eyre Methuen, 1981, pp. 115–118.

'Genesis of a Story', *QANTAS Airways*, March–April 1982, pp. 34–36.
'Bore Vidal' (review of *Lincoln: A Novel*, by Gore Vidal), *The New Republic*, 2 July 1984, pp. 32–34.
'A GMH Morning, 1952', *Overland*, vol. 96, 1984, pp. 42–46.
McKell Lecture, *The Radical: Australian Labour Party*, 16.1, March 1985.
'In Eritrea', *New York Times Magazine*, 27 September 1987, pp. 42–57.
'Here Nature Is Reversed', *Australia Beyond the Dreamtime*, Richmond, William Heinemann, 1987, pp. 11–72.
'Rogues' Continent' (review of *The Fatal Shore* by Robert Hughes), *The New York Times Book Review*, 25 January 1987, Section 7, p. 1.
'Ceremonies of Style on a Savage Ground', *Vogue Australia*, December 1989, pp. 200–201, 230.
'The Other Code', *Esquire*, November 1991, pp. 72–74.
'My Uncle Johnny', *The Daily Telegraph Mirror*, 28 August 1993, p. 96.
'Critical Correctness', *The Weekend Australian*, 13–14 November 1993, The Weekend Review, p. 4.
'For Gentiles, Too, the Holocaust is Never to be Forgotten', *Los Angeles Times*, 31 January 1994, p. 7.
'My Father's Australia', *The Bulletin*, 8 August 2000, pp. 44–50.
'The Flame Above Us', *The Games of the XXVII Olympiad Closing Ceremony*, 1 October 2000, Sydney, Sydney Organising Committee for the Olympic Games (SOCOG).
Foreword to *The Last Confession* by Morris West, Sydney, HarperCollins Publishers, 2000.
'Cold Sanctuary: How the Church Lost Its Mission', *The New Yorker*, June 17 & 24 2002, pp. 58–66.
Introduction to *Through Other Eyes: The Fred Hollows Foundation Ten Years On*, Sydney, Pan Macmillan Australia, 2002, pp. 1–7.
'Inner Struggles: *Voss* by Patrick White: A Re-Reading', *The Bulletin*, 17 December 2002–14 January 2003, pp. 38–39.
'Archival Footage: Essay by Thomas Keneally', *Australian Author*, vol. 37, no. 3, 2005, pp. 6–7.
'First Voice: Tom Keneally looks back at the writing of his first published book', *The Age*, 13 May 2006, 'Books', p. 27.
'James Athanasius McGlade, MBE, 1914–2013' (obituary), *The Sydney Morning Herald*, 20 July 2013, p. 17.
'Independence Days', in Susan Wyndham (ed.), *My Mother, My Father: On Losing a Parent*, Crows Nest, Allen & Unwin, 2013, pp. 27–41.
Ghandi Oration, 30 January 2014, at University of New South Wales, Sydney.
Other incidental writing of Keneally's is acknowledged in the Notes. For more information, refer to www.austlit.edu.au.

Index